BBC

Bitesize

Bitesize
Pearson Ed
GCSE (9-1)
COMBINED SCIENCE
REVISION GUIDE
HIGHER

Series Consultant:
Harry Smith

Authors:
Karen Bailey
Jen Randall
Mike Smith

Contents

GCSE Science

☑ Tick off each topic as you go.

How to use this book

Use the features in this book to focus your revision, track your progress through the topics and practise your exam skills.

 Features to help you revise

Scan the **QR codes** to visit the BBC Bitesize website. It will link straight through to more revision resources on that subject.

Questions that test **maths skills** are explained in callouts and in the *Exam skills* section at the back of the book.

Topics that are related to **working scientifically** are explained in callouts throughout the book.

Each bite-sized chunk has a **timer** to indicate how long it will take. Use them to plan your revision sessions.

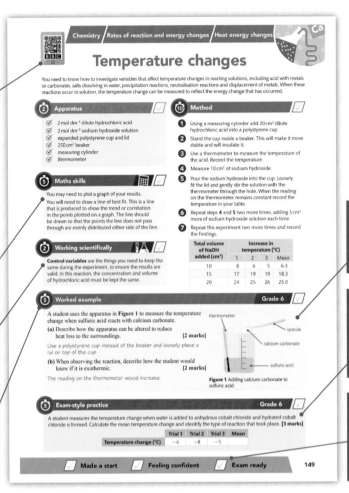

Completed **worked examples** demonstrate how to approach exam-style questions.

Test yourself with **exam-style practice** at the end of each page and check your answers at the back of the book.

Tick boxes allow you to track the sections you've revised. Revisit each page to embed your knowledge.

 Exam focus features

The *About your exam* section at the start of the book gives you all the key information about your exams, as well as as showing you how to identify the different questions.

You will also find green *Exam skills* pages and purple *Practical* pages. These work through an extended exam-style question and provide further opportunities to practise your skills.

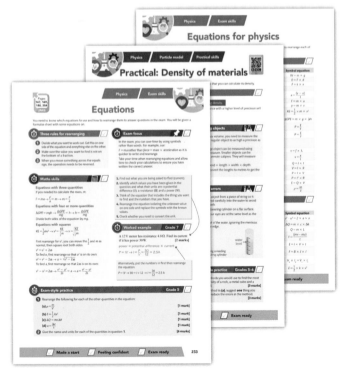

ActiveBook and app

This Revision Guide comes with a **free online edition**. Follow the instructions from inside the front cover to access your ActiveBook.

You can also download the **free BBC Bitesize app** to access revision flashcards and quizzes.

If you do not have a QR code scanner, you can access all the links in this book from your ActiveBook or visit **www.pearsonschools.co.uk/BBCBitesizeLinks**.

Your Science GCSE

This page will tell you everything you need to know about the structure of your upcoming Pearson Edexcel GCSE (9–1) in Combined Science (Higher Tier) exams.

 ## About the exam papers

You will have to take **six** papers as part of your Pearson Edexcel GCSE (9–1) in Combined Science (Higher Tier) qualification: **two biology, two chemistry** and **two physics**. The papers will test your knowledge and understanding of different topic areas and your ability to work scientifically.

Paper 1
Biology 1
1 hour 10 minutes
60 marks in total

Paper 2
Biology 2
1 hour 10 minutes
60 marks in total

Paper 3
Chemistry 1
1 hour 10 minutes
60 marks in total

Paper 4
Chemistry 2
1 hour 10 minutes
60 marks in total

Paper 5
Physics 1
1 hour 10 minutes
60 marks in total

Paper 6
Physics 2
1 hour 10 minutes
60 marks in total

 ## Exam topics

Topics include: key concepts of physics; energy – forces doing work; forces and their effects; electricity and circuits; magnetism and the motor effect; electromagnetic induction; particle model; forces and matter

Topics include: key concepts of physics; motion and forces; conservation of energy; waves; light and the electromagnetic spectrum; radioactivity

Topics include: key concepts in chemistry; groups in the periodic table; rates of reaction and energy changes; fuels and Earth science

Topics include: key concepts in biology; cells and control; genetics; natural selection and genetic modification; health, disease and the development of medicines

Topics include: key concepts in biology; plant structures and their functions; animal coordination, control and homeostasis; exchange and transport in animals; ecosystems and material cycles

Topics include: key concepts in chemistry; states of matter and mixtures; chemical changes; extracting metals and equilibria

Pie chart:
- **Paper 6 Physics 2** 16.7%
- **Paper 1 Biology 1** 16.7%
- **Paper 5 Physics 1** 16.7%
- **Paper 2 Biology 2** 16.7%
- **Paper 4 Chemistry 2** 16.7%
- **Paper 3 Chemistry 1** 16.7%

 ## Maths skills

You will be required to demonstrate the following mathematical skills in your GCSE Science exams:

- rearranging equations
- interpreting data from graphs and tables, including finding a gradient
- converting units
- using standard form
- using ratios, fractions and percentages
- calculating mean, mode and median
- using geometry (volumes, areas, angles, working out sides of triangles).

Working scientifically

There are 21 required practical activities you will carry out during your GCSE Science course.

Practical activities are an opportunity for you to apply your knowledge and understanding, while developing relevant practical skills and techniques.

You need to know how to:

- plan and carry out an investigation
- use apparatus correctly and safely
- take accurate measurements and record data appropriately
- analyse your findings
- evaluate your investigation.

 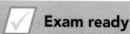

Multiple-choice questions

Multiple-choice questions give you several options to choose from. You must indicate the correct answer by marking your choice clearly.

1 Types of multiple-choice question

- tick box
- linking boxes
- sentence completion

1 Exam focus

Bold words usually give important instructions. Read them carefully.

e.g. Give **one** way in which a second allele for eye colour might be different.

5 Exam explainer

Clearly mark the answer you think is correct with a tick in the box. If you change your mind, draw a line through the incorrect answer and tick the correct answer.

A cricket ball is hit by a bat. The bat and ball exert a force on each other. Which of the following statements about the two forces is true? **[1 mark]**

- ☐ **A** The force on the bat and the force on the ball are in the same direction
- ☐ **B** The bat has a larger mass so it exerts a larger force on the ball
- ☑ **C** The two forces are equal
- ☐ **D** The two forces give the bat and ball equal accelerations

If you are unsure of the answer, use what you know to rule out the incorrect options.

Use a pencil to draw lines, so you can change your answer easily, if necessary.

Draw **one** line from each diagram to the name of the cell. **[3 marks]**

Diagram	**Name of cell**
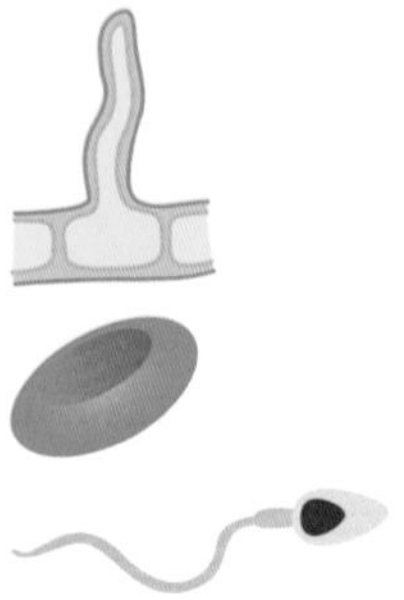	red blood cell
	sperm cell
	root hair cell

Read the question carefully. Here, you are instructed to only use words from the box provided. You would not be awarded marks for using similar words.

The pH scale is a measure of the acidity or alkalinity of a solution.
Use words from the box to complete the sentences. **[3 marks]**

neutral	acidic	alkaline

A solution with a pH value of 5 is ____________.

A solution with a pH value of 7 is ____________.

A solution with a pH value of 13 is ____________.

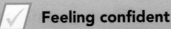

Short-answer questions

Short-answer questions come in a variety of forms and are the most common type of questions.

 Exam explainer

Underline key information, such as numbers and units. Make sure you include the correct units in your answer.

A power station has an efficiency of 0.45. Its energy comes from burning coal, which it uses at a rate of 300 MW.

(a) Calculate the useful output of electrical power. **[2 marks]**

(b) Describe the advantages and disadvantages of this type of power station compared to a wind turbine. **[3 marks]**

It is important to show your working when answering a calculation question. If done correctly, you will get method marks even if the final answer is wrong.

For a sketch question, you only need to draw approximately. You should only use a ruler if it helps you to make your answer clear.

Sketch a reaction profile for an endothermic reaction. **[3 marks]**

A student investigated the rate of reaction between calcium carbonate and hydrochloric acid.

Figure 1 The student's results for one concentration of hydrochloric acid.

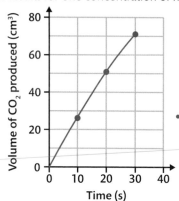

You will need to be able to interpret information from a graph, photo, table or image in any of your exam papers.

The table shows the student's results when the concentration was two times greater than the results shown in **Figure 1**.

Time (s)	Volume of CO_2 (cm³)
0	0
10	41
20	62
30	71

(a) Plot the results shown in the table on the grid in **Figure 1**. Draw a line of best fit. **[3 marks]**

(b) Give **one** conclusion about how the rate of reaction changed when the concentration of hydrochloric acid was changed. **[1 mark]**

Extended-response questions

Some questions require a longer written response or a multi-step calculation. They are typically worth 4, 5 or 6 marks. You will need to give a coherent and sustained line of reasoning in your answer.

2 Command words

- explain – set out purposes or reasons
- evaluate – consider evidence for and against and conclude
- calculate – use numbers provided to work out the answer
- compare – identify similarities and/or differences
- describe – recall some facts, events or processes

2 Structure your answers

1. Make a **point** – for example: *Embryo screening is an expensive procedure.*
2. **Develop** your point – for example: *This means that the procedure is available only to people who can afford it.*
3. **Link** your point back to the question – for example: *This is a socio-economic issue because the procedure is not accessible to everyone.*

5 Exam explainer

4 mark questions have **two** levels:

1. basic
2. clear.

A clear answer interprets, evaluates or analyses scientific information or resources.

Aluminium can be extracted from its ore by electrolysis.
Explain how aluminium is extracted from aluminium oxide by electrolysis. **[4 marks]**

For this question, you are expected to use your knowledge of electrolysis to explain how the process can be used to extract aluminium from aluminium oxide. You need to include reference to ions, electrodes and reduction in your answer.

For this type of question, you should provide specific examples for each of the issues mentioned, interpreting them in an objective way, and finishing with a reasoned conclusion.

Evaluate the use of embryo screening for cystic fibrosis. In your answer discuss the economic, social and ethical issues. **[6 marks]**

6–9 mark questions have **three** levels:

1. basic
2. clear
3. detailed.

A detailed answer shows understanding of scientific topics and knowledge of specific information. It is presented in a clear and balanced way.

When asked to calculate something, always show your working. There are often some marks available for method and it also helps you to check your answer.

Calculate the mass of calcium carbonate needed to produce 56 g of calcium oxide during thermal decomposition. **[5 marks]**

Levels of organisation

You need to understand the principles of organisation within living organisms.

 Organisation

Cells are the fundamental building blocks of all living things. Simple organisms, such as bacteria, consist of just one single cell (**unicellular**). **Multicellular** organisms have various levels of organisation within them, ranging from the individual cell to the entire organism. The levels of organisation range in complexity, from simplest to most complex, and in size, from very small to large.

Cells contain **organelles**, also known as sub-cellular structures, which perform specific functions within the cell. Individual cells can perform specific functions (page 4). Groups of specialised cells which all have a similar structure and function are called **tissues**. Groups of tissues that perform specific jobs are known as **organs**. Groups of organs form **organ systems**.

Cells are very small. You need a microscope to be able to examine them. Go to pages 5 and 6 for more about microscopy.

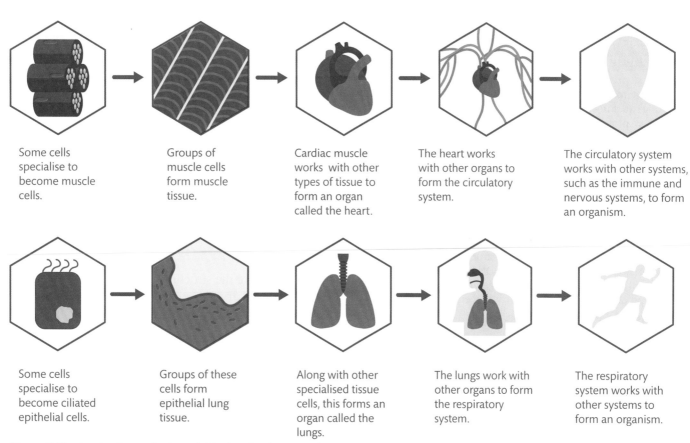

Some cells specialise to become muscle cells.

Groups of muscle cells form muscle tissue.

Cardiac muscle works with other types of tissue to form an organ called the heart.

The heart works with other organs to form the circulatory system.

The circulatory system works with other systems, such as the immune and nervous systems, to form an organism.

Some cells specialise to become ciliated epithelial cells.

Groups of these cells form epithelial lung tissue.

Along with other specialised tissue cells, this forms an organ called the lungs.

The lungs work with other organs to form the respiratory system.

The respiratory system works with other systems to form an organism.

Figure 1 The levels of organisation within the circulatory and respiratory systems

Worked example Grade 4

Go to page 18 for more about the human nervous system.

Describe the levels of organisation within the human nervous system. **[4 marks]**

The nervous system is an organ system made up of several organs, including the brain and spinal cord, working together. The organs consist of different types of nervous tissue, made up of different types of nerve cell (neurones).

Exam-style practice Grade 4

1 Describe what is meant by an organ system. **[2 marks]**

2 Describe the levels of organisation within the human circulatory system. **[4 marks]**

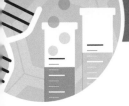

Eukaryotic and prokaryotic cells

You need to know the differences in structure and function of eukaryotic and prokaryotic cells.

10 Eukaryotes and prokaryotes

Cells can be classified as either **eukaryotic cells** (eukaryotes) or **prokaryotic cells** (prokaryotes). Animals and plants consist of eukaryotic cells. Bacteria consist of prokaryotic cells. Eukaryotic cells are larger and more complex than prokaryotic cells. Eukaryotic cells contain membrane-bound **organelles** (sub-cellular structures) which are not found in prokaryotic cells. Animal cells contain the organelles nuclei and mitochondria; plant cells contain these, as well as chloroplasts.

There is more about the different structures of plant and animal cells on page 3.

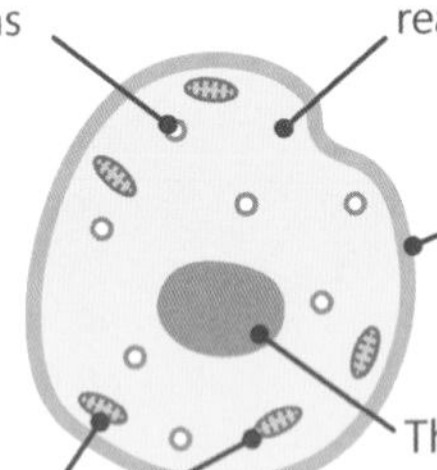
Ribosomes are tiny structures where proteins are made.
Cytoplasm is a jelly-like substance where chemical reactions take place.
The **cell membrane** controls the movement of substances into and out of the cell.
The **nucleus** is a large membrane-bound structure which contains DNA. DNA controls the growth and development of every living thing.
Mitochondria release energy for cell processes. The energy is a product of respiration.

Figure 1 An animal cell – an example of a eukaryotic cell

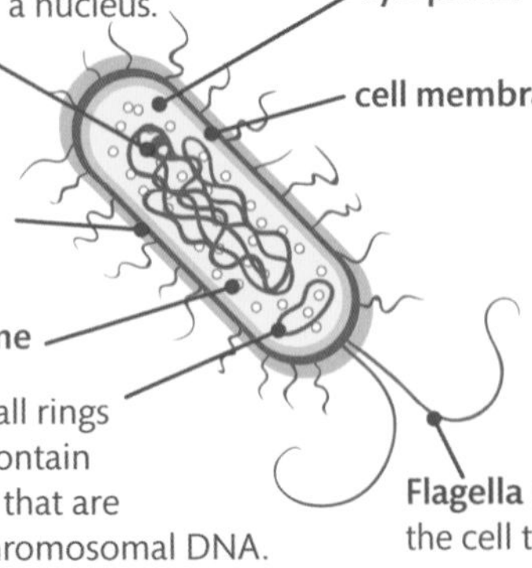
A **single loop of DNA**, called chromosomal DNA, not contained within a nucleus.
cytoplasm
cell membrane
A **cell wall** protects the cell.
ribosome
Plasmids are small rings of DNA, which contain additional genes that are not present in chromosomal DNA.
Flagella enable the cell to move.

Figure 2 A bacterial cell – a prokaryotic cell

2 Working scientifically

Most cells are microscopic. You need to understand the scale and size of cells and use the correct prefixes.

The following are compared to one metre.

centimetre (cm) = one hundredth or 10^{-2}

millimetre (mm) = one thousandth or 10^{-3}

micrometre (μm) = one millionth or 10^{-6}

nanometre (nm) = one billionth or 10^{-9}

picometre (pm) = one trillionth or 10^{-12}

Remember, prokaryotic means 'before nucleus'. Prokaryotic cells do not have a nucleus. They contain a single DNA loop (chromosomal DNA) and small rings of DNA called plasmids.

5 Worked example — Grades 5–6

1 State where DNA is found in prokaryotic cells. **[1 mark]**

Chromosomal DNA and plasmid DNA are found in the cytoplasm. They are not enclosed in a nucleus.

2 Compare the structure of eukaryotic and prokaryotic cells. **[2 marks]**

Eukaryotic cells are larger and have more complex structures than prokaryotic cells. One important difference is that the genetic material in eukaryotes is enclosed in a nucleus.

Eukaryotic cells and prokaryotic cells are similar in that they both have:

- a cell membrane
- cytoplasm
- ribosomes.

Prokaryotic cell structures differ from eukaryotic cells because:

- they do not have a nucleus
- they do not have mitochondria.

5 Exam-style practice — Grades 5–6

1 Compare and contrast eukaryotic and prokaryotic cells. **[3 marks]**

2 Look at **Figure 1**, a diagram of a eukaryotic cell. Give the organelles in size order, starting with the smallest first. **[2 marks]**

Animal and plant cells

You need to be able to describe and explain the differences in structure of animal and plant cells.

[10] Animal and plant cell structures

Although both animal and plant cells are eukaryotic, there are important structural differences between them. Plants stay in the same place and produce their own food. Animals move around in search of an external supply of food. These differences are the main reasons why animal and plant cell structures differ.

Algal cells have a similar structure to plant cells. They also have a cellulose cell wall that strengthens the cell.

Go to page 2 to revise the functions of organelles.

Organelle	Plant cell	Animal cell
nucleus	✓	✓
cytoplasm	✓	✓
cell membrane	✓	✓
cell wall	✓	×
mitochondria	✓	✓
ribosomes	✓	✓
chloroplasts	✓	×
permanent vacuole	✓	×

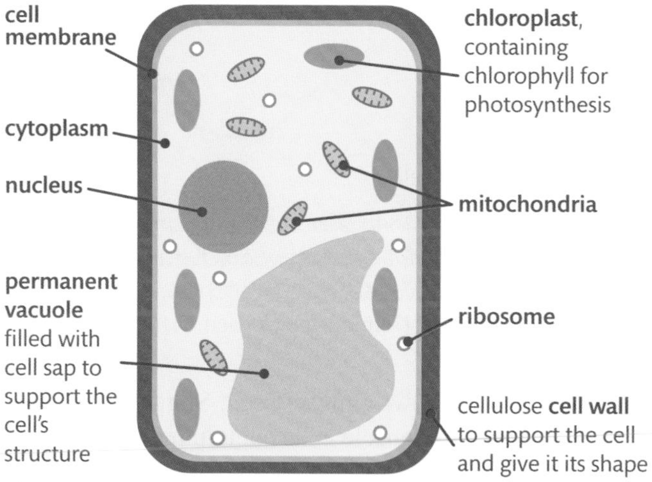

cell membrane
cytoplasm
nucleus
permanent vacuole filled with cell sap to support the cell's structure
chloroplast, containing chlorophyll for photosynthesis
mitochondria
ribosome
cellulose cell wall to support the cell and give it its shape

Figure 1 A plant cell

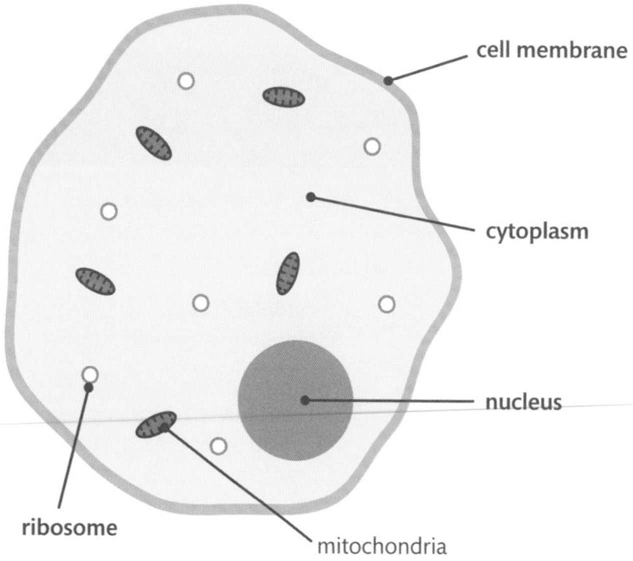

cell membrane
cytoplasm
nucleus
ribosome
mitochondria

Figure 2 An animal cell

Structure is often related to function. Think of how animals and plants function differently from one another.

[5] Worked example — Grade 5

Explain how the structures of plant cells are adapted to carry out their function. **[4 marks]**

Plants must produce their own food as they cannot move. Plant cells contain chloroplasts, which use sunlight to convert water and carbon dioxide into glucose and oxygen (photosynthesis).

Unlike many animals, plants do not have a skeleton, so they need another form of support and protection. Each cell has a cellulose cell wall and a sap-filled vacuole which makes the cell much firmer and helps support the plant.

'Estimate' means you don't have to make exact measurements or calculations. Only an approximation is required.

[5] Exam-style practice — Grades 5–6

1. Look at **Figure 3**.

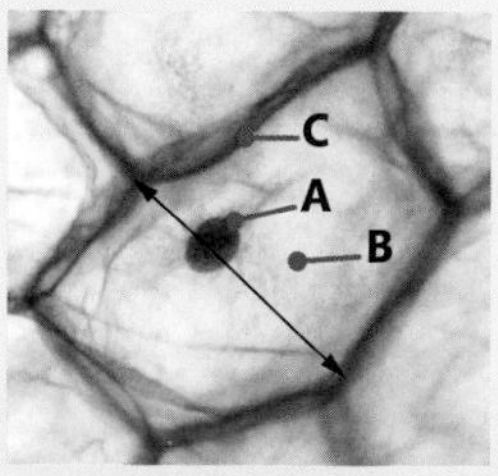

C
A
B

Figure 3 A plant cell as seen under a light microscope

(a) Identify which letter shows the nucleus. **[1 mark]**

(b) Estimate how many times wider the cell is than its nucleus. **[1 mark]**

2. Describe **three** differences between animal and plant cell structures. **[3 marks]**

Specialised animal cells

Multicellular organisms are large organisms, like animals, made up of more than one type of cell. You need to know about the structural adaptations of specialised cells that enable them to perform specific functions. Go to page 47 to read about specialised plant cells.

(5) Specialised animal cells

You need to know how the following animal cells are specialised to carry out a particular function.

Sperm cells swim and fertilise egg cells.

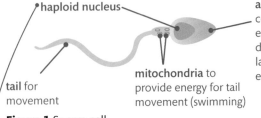

haploid nucleus

acrosome containing enzymes that digest outer layers of an egg cell

mitochondria to provide energy for tail movement (swimming)

tail for movement

Figure 1 Sperm cell

A haploid nucleus contains half the normal number of chromosomes found in body cells. See page 19 for more about haploid cells.

Egg cells are fertilised by single sperm cells and then develop into an embryo.

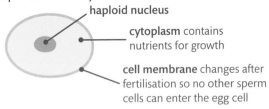

haploid nucleus

cytoplasm contains nutrients for growth

cell membrane changes after fertilisation so no other sperm cells can enter the egg cell

Figure 2 Egg cell

Ciliated epithelial cells, such as those in the trachea, move substances in a particular direction.

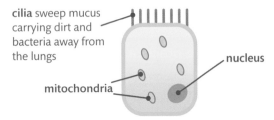

cilia sweep mucus carrying dirt and bacteria away from the lungs

nucleus

mitochondria

Figure 3 Ciliated epithelial cell

Red blood cells and white blood cells are other types of specialised cell.

Go to page 59 for more about the functions and adaptations of red blood cells and white blood cells.

(5) Worked example | Grade 5

1 **Figure 4** shows a nerve cell (neurone). Describe **two** ways nerve cells are adapted for their function. **[2 marks]**

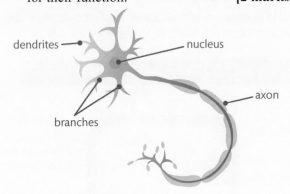

dendrites

nucleus

axon

branches

Figure 4 A nerve cell

Nerve cells have long axons so they are able to transmit nerve impulses between distant parts of the body. They also have branched endings called dendrites that connect with other nerve cells.

2 **Figure 5** shows a muscle cell. Suggest a reason why muscle cells contain many mitochondria. **[1 mark]**

nucleus

mitochondria

Figure 5 A muscle cell

Mitochondria are where respiration happens, so they release the energy needed for muscles to contract.

(10) Exam-style practice | Grade 5

Describe **two** ways that each of the following are specialised to perform their functions:

(a) egg cells

(b) sperm cells

(c) ciliated epithelial cells. **[6 marks]**

Microscopy

You need to know how microscopes have developed, allowing scientists to examine increasingly smaller cellular structures.

 Types of microscope ✓

Microscopes are used to study cells. Over time, different kinds of microscope have been developed. The first light microscope, which could be used to observe simple cell structures, was invented about 350 years ago. This was gradually improved upon and refined to give the compound light microscopes that we use today. Very small cell structures can be studied with electron microscopes which were first developed in the 1930s.

Tiny cell organelles can be observed with an electron microscope. Ribosomes can be seen with an electron microscope but they are too small to be seen with a light microscope. The nucleus and mitochondria can be seen with a light microscope. The nucleus is larger so can be seen more clearly.

 Worked example | **Grade 5** ✓

Figure 2 shows a scale drawing of a cell.

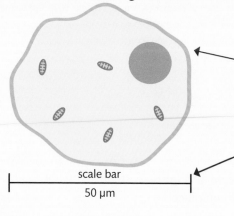

scale bar
50 μm

Figure 2

Calculate the magnification of the image in **Figure 2**. **[3 marks]**

size of image = 5 cm

5 cm = 50 000 μm

size of real object = 50 μm ← from scale bar

$$\text{magnification} = \frac{50\,000}{50} = \times 1000$$

  Magnification and resolution ✓

Magnification is the measure of how many times bigger the image is than the object.

If a microscope has an eyepiece lens of ×10 and an objective lens of ×50, the image looks 10 × 50 times bigger, that is, 500 times bigger.

Light microscopes use light to see an image. They can only magnify up to about ×1200, due to problems with resolution.

Resolution is the measure of how well a microscope can distinguish between two very close objects.

Above ×1200, light microscopes cannot distinguish between two close objects. This is due to the wavelength of light.

Electron microscopes use electrons rather than light. Electrons have a much shorter wavelength than light. This means they can resolve two very close objects at a much higher magnification, some even reaching up to ×10 000 000.

Maths skills

You need to know how to work out magnification using the equation:

$$\text{magnification} = \frac{\text{size of image}}{\text{size of real object}}$$

Use a ruler to measure the size of the image.

 Maths skills ✓

When calculating the size of microscopic cells, you may need to use standard form. Standard form is an efficient way of writing very big or very small numbers. For example:

35 000 000 can be written as:

3.5 × 10 × 10 × 10 × 10 × 10 × 10 × 10

or 3.5×10^7 in standard form.

 Exam-style practice | **Grades 5–6** ✓

1 A cell has a width of 100 μm. A scale drawing of the same cell has a width of 20 cm. Calculate the magnification of the drawing. Write your answer in standard form. **[2 marks]**

2 A microscope has an eyepiece lens of ×15 and an objective lens of ×50. Calculate how many times bigger the image is than the object. **[2 marks]**

 Made a start | **Feeling confident** | **Exam ready** | 5

Practical: Using microscopes

You need to know how to set up and use a microscope to look at cells. You also need to be able to draw and label cell images from a microscope.

 Using a microscope

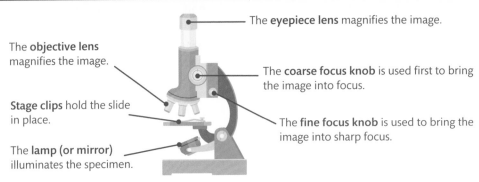

The **eyepiece lens** magnifies the image.

The **objective lens** magnifies the image.

The **coarse focus knob** is used first to bring the image into focus.

Stage clips hold the slide in place.

The **fine focus knob** is used to bring the image into sharp focus.

The **lamp (or mirror)** illuminates the specimen.

Figure 1 A light microscope

 Worked example **Grade 5**

1 Explain how you would prepare a slide of onion epidermal tissue. You may use a diagram to help you answer. **[3 marks]**

Peel off a one-cell-thick layer of cells and place it on a glass slide. Add one drop of stain, such as iodine, to the tissue. Use a mounted needle to lower the cover slip slowly and carefully to avoid trapping any air bubbles.

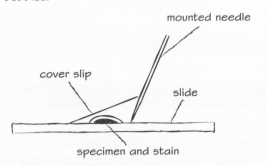

mounted needle

cover slip

slide

specimen and stain

Tissue samples are stained to add contrast because most cells are colourless. Samples should be one cell thick so that cells can be seen clearly.

- You should only draw the things that you can see.
- Do not use shading.
- Keep the labels simple and clearly identified.
- Remember to include a scale bar on your drawing.

2 Explain how you would view the slide under a microscope. **[4 marks]**

Place the prepared slide under the stage clips of the microscope. Use the coarse focus knob to lower the low power objective lens to just above the slide. Look through the eyepiece lens and raise the lens until the image is nearly in focus. Use the fine focus knob to get a clear sharp image. To see parts of the specimen in more detail, move the slide so the parts you are interested in are in the middle of your field of view. Then use a higher power objective lens, and focus as before.

(c) Look at **Figure 2**. Draw and label an onion cell. **[2 marks]**

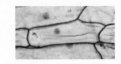

Figure 2 An onion cell

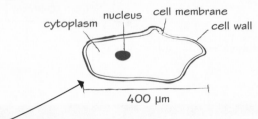

cytoplasm   nucleus   cell membrane   cell wall

400 μm

 Exam-style practice **Grade 5**

1 Explain why tissue samples must be very thin to be viewed with a microscope. **[2 marks]**

2 Explain why scientists often stain tissue samples before viewing them with a microscope. **[1 mark]**

Enzyme action

You need to know how enzymes work and the factors that affect their activity.

Enzymes

Enzymes are biological **catalysts**. This means they speed up reactions without themselves being changed. Most chemical reactions that occur in living organisms involve enzymes, because otherwise processes such as respiration or photosynthesis would happen far too slowly for organisms to survive.

> The enzymes you will be most familiar with are those involved in digestion. See pages 8 and 9.

Enzyme molecules are **specific**, with each enzyme having a 3D shape that corresponds to the shape of the molecule (**substrate**) it works with. The part of the enzyme that binds to the substrate molecule is the **active site**.

High temperatures or extremes of pH affect an enzyme's molecular structure, irreversibly changing the shape of the active site. This means that the active site will not fit the substrate and the enzyme will no longer work. It has become **denatured**.

Lock and key model

1 Substrate collides with active site of enzyme and becomes attached.

2 Enzyme catalyses breakdown of substrate.

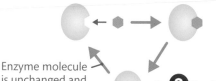

Enzyme molecule is unchanged and can be reused.

3 Products released from active site.

Figure 1 The lock and key model helps explain how enzymes work. Each type of enzyme has a differently shaped active site so can only work with a specific shape of molecule.

> As substrate concentration increases, the rate of reaction increases due to more collisions between enzyme and substrate molecules. Eventually the rate of reaction levels off as each enzyme active site is fully occupied.

Worked example — Grade 6

If you increase substrate concentration, eventually the rate of an enzyme-catalysed reaction becomes constant. Explain **one** way you could increase the rate further. **[2 marks]**

Increase the temperature so that the particles move and collide more quickly.

Factors affecting enzymes

The rate of an enzyme-catalysed reaction is affected by pH, temperature and substrate concentration.

Temperature

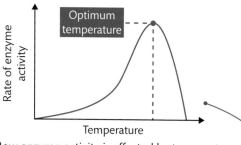

Figure 2 How enzyme activity is affected by temperature

> As temperature increases, particles move and collide more quickly increasing the rate of reaction up to a maximum (its **optimum temperature**). Above this temperature, the enzyme molecules become denatured reducing the rate of reaction.

pH

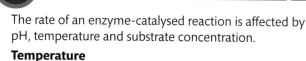

Figure 3 How enzyme activity is affected by pH

> Each enzyme has its own **optimum pH**. Above or below this, the enzyme becomes denatured so the rate of reaction decreases.

Substrate concentration

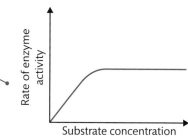

Figure 4 How enzyme activity is affected by substrate concentration

Exam-style practice — Grade 5

Explain the mechanism of enzyme action. **[4 marks]**

Made a start | Feeling confident | Exam ready

Practical: Enzymes

You need to know how to investigate the effect of pH on the rate of reaction of an enzyme. Most enzymes will only work efficiently within a narrow pH range.

② Apparatus

- ☑ three beakers containing the same amount of water
- ☑ three test tubes containing starch solution
- ☑ three test tubes containing amylase solution in a buffer solution
- ☑ water bath
- ☑ spotting tile with iodine solution
- ☑ thermometer
- ☑ pipettes

Working scientifically

You must control temperature during this investigation, as it affects the behaviour of enzymes.

Working scientifically

Interpreting these results is tricky. Iodine solution turns from yellow to black in the presence of starch. When the spots on the tile no longer turn black or brown, but remain yellow, all the starch has been broken down into maltose by the amylase.

You need to make a sensible judgement of when all the starch has been broken down.

⑩ Method

1 Add one drop of iodine solution to each well in the spotting tile.

2 Make up three beakers of water, each containing a test tube of starch solution and a test tube of amylase solution in a buffer solution. (Buffer solutions maintain constant pHs.) Each buffer solution should be at a different pH, for example: pH 7, pH 8 and pH 9.

3 Using a water bath, heat the three beakers to 25 °C.

4 Pour the test tube of amylase solution into the test tube of starch solution.

5 Starting at 0 seconds, take a drop from each test tube every 30 seconds and add it to the iodine using a pipette.

② Maths skills

You need to know how to calculate the rate of a reaction. The rate of a reaction is inversely proportional to the time taken for it to complete.

$$\text{rate} \propto \frac{1}{\text{time}}$$

⑩ Worked example — Grades 5–6

1 Look at **Figure 1**. At which pH does the enzyme amylase break down starch the quickest? Justify your answer. **[2 marks]**

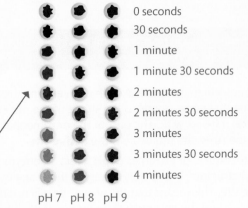

			0 seconds
			30 seconds
			1 minute
			1 minute 30 seconds
			2 minutes
			2 minutes 30 seconds
			3 minutes
			3 minutes 30 seconds
			4 minutes

pH 7   pH 8   pH 9

Figure 1 Results

pH 7 – at pH 7 the drops go from black to yellow the quickest, showing that the starch breaks down the quickest at pH 7.

2 Explain why it is difficult to decide how long it takes for amylase to break down the starch at pH 8. **[2 marks]**

The drops change from black to brown gradually over a period of 2–4 minutes, and at the end of the experiment not all the starch has been broken down as the iodine still does not remain yellow.

3 A student investigated the time taken for amylase to break down starch at different pH values. Calculate the rate of reaction for each pH value. Give your answers to two significant figures. **[3 marks]**

pH	Time taken for starch to disappear (s)	Rate of reaction (per second)
4	480	0.0021
6	120	0.0083
8	270	0.0037

⑤ Exam-style practice — Grade 6

1 Explain why temperature must be controlled during this experiment. **[3 marks]**

2 Describe **one** way the experiment could be improved. **[1 mark]**

☑ **Made a start**   ☑ **Feeling confident**   ☑ **Exam ready**

Digestion and enzymes

You will have already studied the digestive system in Key Stage 3 Science. For the GCSE exam, you need to know how the digestive enzymes, carbohydrase, protease and lipase, act.

 Digestion and enzymes

Digestion is the process of enzymes breaking down large insoluble food molecules into small soluble molecules that can be absorbed into the bloodstream. Enzymes catalyse and speed up chemical reactions. They work best at specific temperatures and pH levels.

Protease enzymes

- Proteases, such as pepsin, break down proteins into amino acids in the stomach and small intestine.
- They are produced in the stomach, small intestine and pancreas.
- Protease enzymes in the stomach need acidic conditions to work.

Carbohydrase enzymes

- Carbohydrases, such as amylase and maltase, break down carbohydrates into simple sugars.
- Amylase is produced in the salivary glands, small intestine and pancreas. Maltase is produced in the small intestine. Amylase and maltase work together to break down starch into glucose, starting in the mouth and finishing in the small intestine.

Lipase enzymes

- Lipases break down lipids (fats and oils) into fatty acids and glycerol in the small intestine.
- They are produced in the pancreas and the small intestine.
- They need alkaline conditions.

The products of digestion are used by the body in many ways, for example, some of the glucose produced is used for respiration and the release of energy. Other products of digestion are used to build up new proteins, carbohydrates and lipids in our body.

Protein molecule

Starch molecule

Maltose molecule

Fat or lipid molecule

Figure 1 Enzymes in digestion

 Worked example **Grade 5**

Figure 2 shows the effect of pH on two different protease enzymes, **A** and **B**, found in the human digestive system.

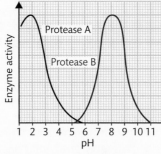

Figure 2 The effect of pH on protease enzymes

(a) Give the optimum pH of both protease **A** and protease **B**. **[2 marks]**

The optimum pH of protease **A** is pH 2 and the optimum pH of protease **B** is pH 8.

(b) The pH in the stomach is normally in the range of 1.5 to 3.5. Explain whether the two protease enzymes could be active in the stomach. **[2 marks]**

Protease **A** would be active because its optimum pH is in the pH range found in the stomach. Protease **B** would not be active in the stomach because it is completely denatured at the pH range found there.

 Exam-style practice **Grade 7**

Explain why acid from the stomach must be neutralised before it enters the small intestine. **[2 marks]**

Diffusion

You need to know how some substances move in and out of cells by diffusion and how multicellular organisms have adaptations to enable the effective exchange of substances.

(5) Rate of diffusion

Diffusion is the **net movement** of particles of gas or in solution, down a **concentration gradient**, from an area of higher concentration to an area of lower concentration. Diffusion is an important process that occurs in both plants and animals. Useful substances such as oxygen and glucose diffuse into cells. Waste products diffuse out of cells. Carbon dioxide is a waste product of respiration, given out during gas exchange in fish gills, leaf cells and the lungs. Urea is a waste product made by the liver, which diffuses into the blood plasma and is then excreted in the kidney.

Certain factors affect the rate of diffusion:

- **difference in concentrations** – the greater the concentration gradient, the greater the rate of diffusion
- **temperature** – the higher the temperature, the higher the rate of diffusion because molecules have more kinetic energy so move faster
- **surface area** – the greater the surface area, the greater the rate of diffusion.

> The surface area:volume ratio is even more important. Go to page 57 to read more about this.

Figure 1 Diffusion occurs due to the random movement of particles. Particles move into and out of cells by diffusion until they are evenly distributed in space.

(5) Exchange surfaces

Substances diffuse in and out of small unicellular organisms by passing through their cell membrane. Multicellular organisms have evolved to have specialised exchange surfaces and organ systems that maximise diffusion by having:

- a large surface area
- a thin membrane for a short diffusion path
- a good transport system to maintain maximum concentration gradients.

In animals, an efficient blood supply and continuous ventilation maintain the concentration gradient required for efficient gaseous exchange of oxygen and carbon dioxide.

Examples of specialised exchange surfaces include:

- alveoli (air sacs) in the lungs, which provide a large surface area and thin membrane for gaseous exchange
- root hair cells in plants, which have a large surface area for absorbing water and mineral ions from the soil.

> Find out more about adaptations on pages 58 (lungs) and 47 (plant roots).

(5) Worked example — Grade 5

1 Give **three** factors that affect the rate of diffusion into and out of cells. **[3 marks]**

> The difference in concentration (i.e. the concentration gradient), the temperature and the surface area of the membrane.

> Another suitable answer is the thickness of the membrane.

2 **Figure 2** shows three cells, **A**, **B** and **C**, which contain different concentrations of oxygen. The darker the shading, the higher the oxygen concentration. Draw arrows on the diagram to show how oxygen will diffuse between the cells. Explain your answer. **[2 marks]**

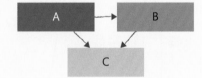

Figure 2

> Oxygen will diffuse from areas of higher concentration to areas of lower concentration.

(5) Exam-style practice — Grade 5

1 Explain why a good blood supply increases the rate of absorption of oxygen in the lungs. **[2 marks]**

2 Alveoli (air sacs) in the lungs have a large surface area. Explain the effect this has on the rate of gas exchange. **[2 marks]**

Made a start **Feeling confident** **Exam ready**

Osmosis

You need to understand the process of osmosis and be able to draw and interpret labelled diagrams that model the diffusion of water molecules.

 Diffusion of water molecules

Osmosis is the diffusion of a solvent's molecules, from a **dilute solution** to a **concentrated solution**, through a **partially permeable membrane**.

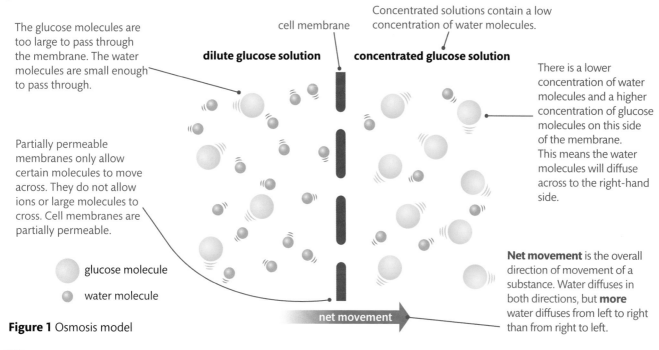

The glucose molecules are too large to pass through the membrane. The water molecules are small enough to pass through.

Partially permeable membranes only allow certain molecules to move across. They do not allow ions or large molecules to cross. Cell membranes are partially permeable.

- glucose molecule
- water molecule

cell membrane

dilute glucose solution　　**concentrated glucose solution**

Concentrated solutions contain a low concentration of water molecules.

There is a lower concentration of water molecules and a higher concentration of glucose molecules on this side of the membrane. This means the water molecules will diffuse across to the right-hand side.

net movement

Net movement is the overall direction of movement of a substance. Water diffuses in both directions, but **more** water diffuses from left to right than from right to left.

Figure 1 Osmosis model

 Worked example 　　　　　　　　　　　　　　　　　　　**Grade 7**

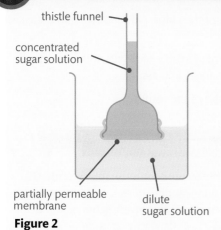

thistle funnel

concentrated sugar solution

partially permeable membrane

dilute sugar solution

Figure 2

Figure 2 shows the apparatus a student uses in an osmosis experiment.

(a) Describe the result that the student observes. 　　**[1 mark]**

The level of the solution will rise up the tube.

(b) Use your knowledge of osmosis to explain this result. 　**[3 marks]**

In the dilute solution there is a higher concentration of water molecules than in the concentrated sugar solution. Sugar molecules are too large to pass through the partially permeable membrane. Water molecules are able to pass through the membrane and will move from the dilute solution to the concentrated solution. There will be a net movement of water molecules into the thistle funnel, so the volume of liquid inside the thistle funnel will increase.

You need to think about how the concentration gradient will change. Go to page 10 to revise this topic.

 Exam-style practice 　　　　　　　　　　　　　　　　　**Grade 7**

1 Explain what happens to the rate of osmosis in **Figure 1** if the concentration of glucose on the right-hand side of the partially permeable membrane is increased. 　**[3 marks]**

2 The higher the temperature, the faster molecules move. Explain what happens to the rate of osmosis as the temperature is increased. 　**[2 marks]**

Practical: Osmosis

You need to know how to investigate the effect of different concentrations of sugar solution on osmosis in potatoes.

(10) Worked example — Grade 8

A student placed equal-sized raw potato chips in different concentrations of sugar solution for two hours. The table shows the change in mass of each of the potato chips.

Sugar solution concentration ($g\,dm^{-3}$)	Initial mass of chip (g)	Final mass of chip (g)	Percentage change in mass (%)
0	2.50	2.95	+18
80	2.50	2.45	−2
160	2.50	2.20	
240	2.50	2.05	−18
320	2.50	1.98	−21

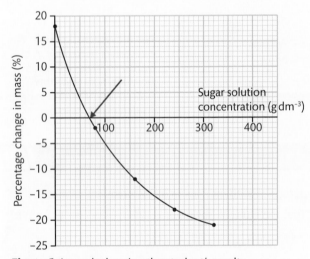

Figure 1 A graph showing the student's results

(a) One of the results is missing from the table.
Determine the missing result. **[2 marks]**

$$100 \times \frac{(2.20 - 2.50)}{2.50} = -12\%$$

(b) Explain **one** way the student could improve the method. **[2 marks]**

The student could do the investigation several more times under the same conditions to see whether the results are repeatable.

(c) Use **Figure 1** to determine the concentration of sugar solution inside the potato cells. **[2 marks]**

The concentration of the cytoplasm will be the same as the sugar solution when there is no change in mass. From the arrow on the graph, this is about 68 g dm⁻³.

(2) Apparatus

- ☑ five equal-sized potato chips
- ☑ five different concentrations of sugar solution:
  - ● 0 g dm⁻³
  - ● 80 g dm⁻³
  - ● 160 g dm⁻³
  - ● 240 g dm⁻³
  - ● 320 g dm⁻³
- ☑ ruler
- ☑ balance

Maths skills

You can calculate percentage change in mass by subtracting the initial mass from the final mass, then dividing by the initial mass and multiplying by 100.

$$\text{percentage change} = \frac{\text{change in mass} \times 100}{\text{original mass}}$$

(5) Method

1 Using the balance, measure the masses of five **equal-sized** potato chips.

2 Place each potato chip in a different concentration of sugar solution.

3 Leave the chips for two hours.

4 Remove each of the chips, pat them dry and measure their masses.

5 Record the data in a table of results and calculate the percentage changes in mass.

6 Plot a line graph of the results.

(1) Working scientifically

You should be able to produce a suitable hypothesis based on your understanding of osmosis. For example, a student's hypothesis for this investigation could be:

The higher the concentration of sugar solution, the greater the change in mass.

(5) Exam-style practice — Grade 5

1 The potato chips were equal in size at the start of the investigation. Explain why this was important. **[2 marks]**

2 State and explain whether the hypothesis in the box above was supported or disproved. **[2 marks]**

☑ **Made a start** ☑ **Feeling confident** ☑ **Exam ready**

Active transport

You need to understand how substances are transported by active transport and be able to describe how it differs from osmosis and diffusion.

 Active transport

Active transport is the movement of a substance from an area of low concentration to a higher concentration against the **concentration gradient**. It requires energy from respiration.

Plants require mineral ions for healthy growth. The uptake of minerals in a plant requires active transport. Root hair cells absorb minerals from the soil, where the concentration is very low.

In humans, active transport allows glucose to be absorbed through the wall of the small intestine during digestion. The concentration of glucose is usually higher in the blood than in the gut so the glucose does not enter by diffusion. The glucose is then used for respiration.

Go to page 47 for more about specialised root hair cells.

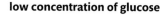
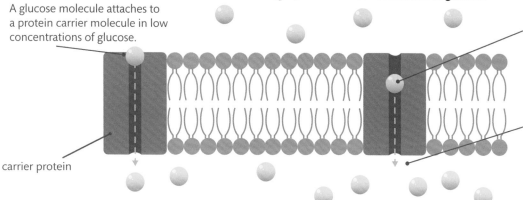

A glucose molecule attaches to a protein carrier molecule in low concentrations of glucose.

inside the small intestine (gut)   low concentration of glucose

The carrier molecule carries the glucose molecule across the cell membrane. This requires energy from respiration.

The carrier molecule releases the glucose molecule into an area with a higher concentration of glucose.

carrier protein

inside the blood   high concentration of glucose

Figure 1 Membrane of cell lining small intestine showing active transport in the human gut

 Worked example   Grade 6

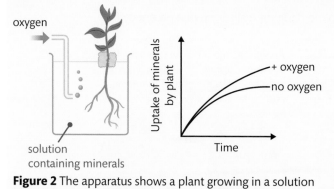

oxygen

Uptake of minerals by plant

+ oxygen
no oxygen

Time

solution containing minerals

Figure 2 The apparatus shows a plant growing in a solution of mineral ions. Oxygen is bubbled through the solution.

1 Explain the shape of the graph in **Figure 2**.   [2 marks]

The graph shows an increase in mineral uptake when extra oxygen is added by being bubbled through the solution. This is because oxygen is used for respiration and respiration provides energy for the active transport of mineral ions.

2 State **one** factor that slows down the rate of active transport.   [1 mark]

A reduction in the availability of oxygen.

 **Exam focus**

If you are ever asked to explain how one thing is different from another, make sure you use the names of the things you are comparing. Do not refer to either as just 'it' as it may not be obvious which one you mean.

 Exam-style practice   Grade 6

1 Explain the differences between diffusion and active transport.   [3 marks]

2 Describe **two** different examples of active transport in living organisms.   [2 marks]

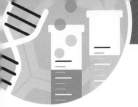

Mitosis and the cell cycle

Multicellular organisms grow and develop using a type of cell division called mitosis. You need to know how this occurs.

5 Chromosomes: key facts

- Chromosomes are found in the nucleus of nearly all types of cell.
- There are two copies of each chromosome in nearly all body cells. In humans, there are 23 pairs of chromosomes giving a total of 46 chromosomes in each cell (but not in the sex cells – see page 24).
- Chromosomes consist of long strands of DNA coiled up.
- The full number of chromosomes, found in nearly all body cells, is called the **diploid** number. For humans the diploid number is 46.
- Chromosomes carry many **genes**, sections of DNA which control our characteristics.

10 The cell cycle

The life-cycle of a cell is called the **cell cycle** and it is made up of different stages.

1 Interphase

The cell grows and the number of sub-cellular structures such as ribosomes and mitochondria increases. The DNA replicates (copies) itself in preparation for cell division. The chromosomes are not yet visible because the DNA is uncoiled.

2 Mitosis

There are four stages of mitosis (**prophase**, **metaphase**, **anaphase** and **telophase**) during which the genetic material is split up so each new cell will have a full diploid set of chromosomes.

3 Cytokinesis

The cell itself divides into two daughter cells – this is called **cytokinesis** – and the cells begin interphase again.

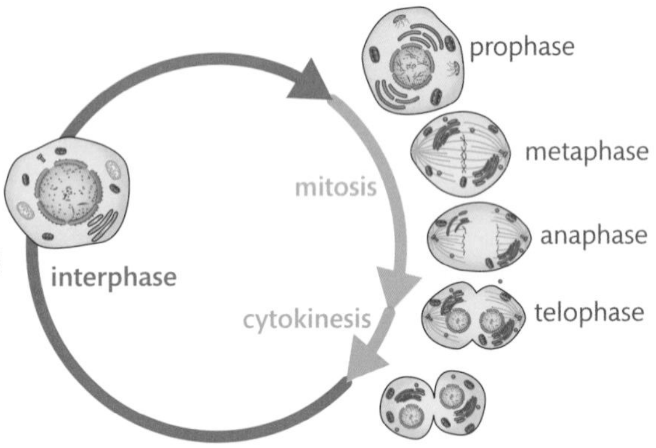
prophase
metaphase
anaphase
telophase
mitosis
interphase
cytokinesis

Figure 1 The cell cycle

10 Stages in mitosis

Mitosis leads to the production of two genetically identical diploid daughter cells from one parent cell.

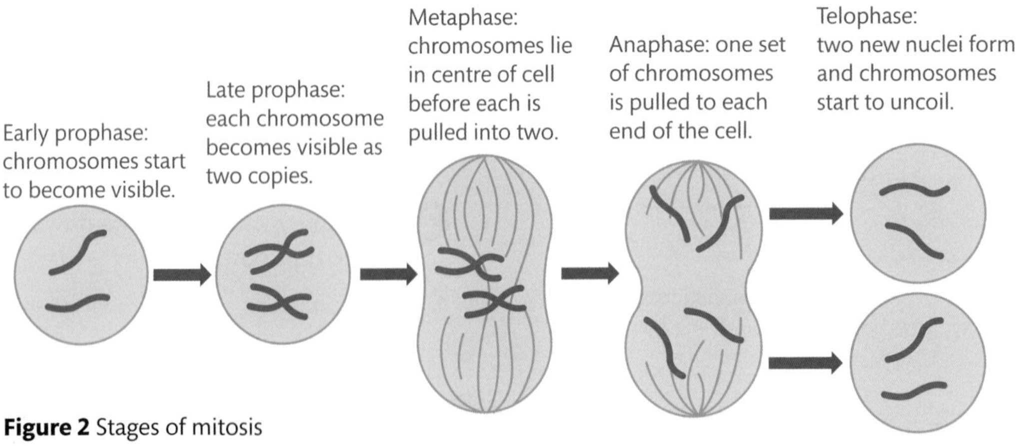
Early prophase: chromosomes start to become visible.
Late prophase: each chromosome becomes visible as two copies.
Metaphase: chromosomes lie in centre of cell before each is pulled into two.
Anaphase: one set of chromosomes is pulled to each end of the cell.
Telophase: two new nuclei form and chromosomes start to uncoil.

Figure 2 Stages of mitosis

5 Exam-style practice — Grade 6

1. Describe what must happen to a cell before it can divide. **[2 marks]**
2. Give the number of chromosomes in a body cell from a human baby. **[1 mark]**

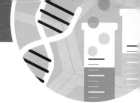

Importance of mitosis

You need to know the importance of mitosis for growth, repair and asexual reproduction. Sometimes cells can divide uncontrollably. This is called cancer.

[2] The importance of mitosis

Mitosis is the process of cell division involved in body growth, in repair (the replacement of damaged cells) and asexual reproduction. The new daughter cells produced by mitosis are genetically identical to each other and to the parent cell. They are all diploid cells.

[5] Asexual reproduction

Asexual reproduction only involves one parent. There is no fusion of male and female gametes. (A **gamete** is a sex cell which contains genetic information.)

This means that there is no mixing of genetic information, so when the cells divide, all the offspring are genetically identical to the parent.

The only type of cell division involved in asexual reproduction is mitosis. These offspring are called clones. Organisms which can produce asexually include bacteria, fungi, potatoes and daffodils.

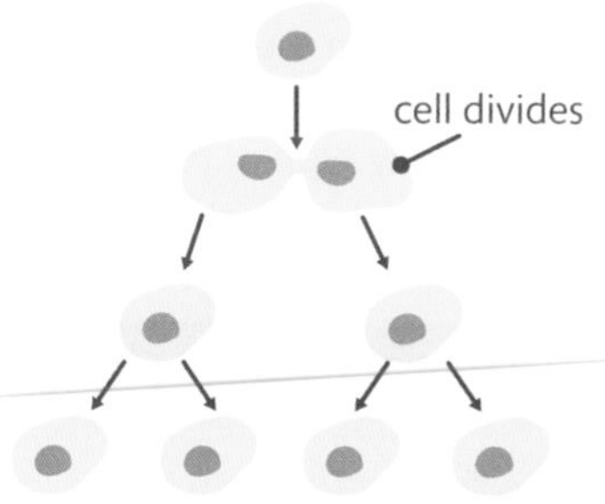

Figure 1 Asexual reproduction involves only mitosis.

Nuclei is the plural of nucleus.

[5] Cancer

Cancer is caused by changes to genes in the DNA inside cells that lead to uncontrolled cell division and tissue growth. A change in the DNA of a cell is called a **mutation** (page 25).

Risk factors

Some people inherit alleles that are more likely to mutate (change) than other alleles. This means these people are born with certain genetic risk factors which make them more likely to develop cancer later in life.

Lifestyle factors linked to cancer include sunbathing, smoking, heavy drinking and working with carcinogenic (cancer-causing) materials such as asbestos.

Go to page 22 for more about alleles.

[5] Sexual reproduction

Sexual reproduction involves the joining of male (pollen or sperm) and female (ova or egg) gametes. Gametes in reproductive organs are produced by a type of cell division called meiosis (see page 19).

During fertilisation, the nuclei of the male and female gametes fuse together to make a fertilised egg cell called a **zygote**.

The zygote divides many times by mitosis (page 14), eventually forming an embryo. The mixing of genetic information from the male and the female parent provides variation.

Go to page 25 for more about variation.

[5] Worked example — Grade 5

Compare sexual and asexual reproduction. **[4 marks]**

Sexual reproduction involves gametes (sex cells) produced by meiosis, whereas asexual reproduction involves one parent cell dividing by mitosis. Sexual reproduction produces variety in offspring but asexual reproduction leads to genetically identical clones. This is because sexual reproduction involves the mixing of genetic information from male and female gametes.

Exam questions could refer to sexual or asexual reproduction. Make sure you know the differences between the two types of reproduction.

[5] Exam-style practice — Grade 6

1. Explain **three** reasons why mitosis is important. **[3 marks]**
2. Explain what happens in cells to cause cancer. **[2 marks]**

Made a start | Feeling confident | Exam ready

Cell differentiation and growth

You need to understand the importance of cell **differentiation** in plants and animals. You also need to understand how percentile charts can be used to monitor human growth.

 Cell differentiation

As an organism develops, cells differentiate to form different types of specialised cells. When a cell differentiates, it acquires different sub-cellular structures to enable it to perform specific functions. For example:

- muscle cells need to be able to contract to cause movement
- nerve cells need to be able to transmit electrical impulses to communicate with other parts of the organism
- plant root hair cells need to have a large surface area to absorb water and nutrients from the soil.

> Stem cells are able to differentiate into different kinds of cell. Human stem cells can come from human embryos or from adult bone marrow. Go to page 17 for more about stem cells.

> Go to page 4 to revise how cells have become specialised to perform their function.

Differentiation in animal cells

Most types of animal cell are formed by differentiation at an early stage in the life of an organism. In mature animals, cell division is restricted mainly to repair and replacement, such as generating new blood cells, healing skin cuts, hair and fingernail growth, and healing broken bones.

Differentiation in plant cells

Many types of plant cell retain the ability to differentiate throughout the life of an organism. Cells can differentiate to grow new leaves, flowers, branches, xylem and phloem. This is why plants can regrow branches that are cut off during pruning. Cells in meristems (page 17) in plants can divide, elongate and then differentiate into any type of plant cell, throughout the life of the plant.

 Monitoring growth

The weight and height of babies and children are regularly measured to make sure they are growing properly and are healthy. Percentile charts show the normal range of variation. **Figure 1** shows a **percentile chart** for boys' heights. For example, if a child is on the 75th percentile line at a particular age, then they are the same height or taller than 75% of boys of the same age.

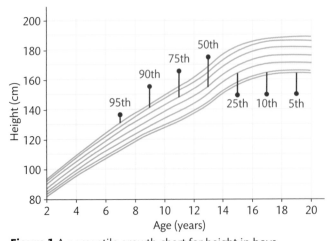

Figure 1 A percentile growth chart for height in boys

 Worked example　　Grade 6

Describe **two** examples of cell differentiation in mature animals. **[4 marks]**

In mature animals, cell division is mainly restricted to providing new cells to repair and replace damaged or lost tissue. For example, new red blood cells are constantly being generated to replace old and damaged red blood cells. Cell differentiation is also integral to the repair of skin and bone after injury.

 Exam-style practice　　Grades 5–6

1. Describe **two** examples of repair and replacement in humans, not including the creation of red blood cells or the healing of cut skin. **[2 marks]**

2. Explain the advantage of some cells retaining the ability to differentiate throughout the life of the organism. **[1 mark]**

3. Look at **Figure 1**. At age 12 years, what is the height of the 10th percentile? **[1 mark]**

 Made a start　　 **Feeling confident**　　 **Exam ready**

Stem cells

Stem cells are undifferentiated cells. They can develop into different types of body cell. You need to know how stem cells are obtained and how they can be used.

 Stem cell applications ✓

Stem cells may one day be used to cure diseases by replacing faulty cells. They could cure diseases such as diabetes, paralysis, hearing and vision loss, and Parkinson's disease. If the stem cells are used to treat the donor, then there is no danger of the cells being rejected.

Embryonic stem cells

Stem cells from human embryos can be cloned and made to differentiate into most types of human cell when instructed. They have the potential to cure many genetic conditions by replacing damaged cells. However, embryos cannot choose to donate and they are destroyed in the process. Unwanted embryos from fertility clinics are often used.

Adult stem cells

Adult human stem cells can be taken from bone marrow. They can form many, but not all, types of cell, as they are used naturally in the body for repair and replacement of some tissues. Adult stem cells are useful in the treatment of people suffering from blood disorders as they can form new blood cells.

An advantage is that donation of adult stem cells is a choice and no life is destroyed, but it can be a painful procedure.

Meristem tissue in plants

In animals, growth can occur anywhere in the body. However, plants only grow in certain areas called **meristems**. Meristems consist of stem cells that can differentiate into any type of plant cell throughout the life of the plant. Growth occurs in meristems as they are the only points on the plant with actively dividing cells. Meristems are found, for example, at the tips of shoots and roots. They can be used to quickly and cheaply produce cloned plants (by taking cuttings) and are useful for growing rare species of plants to protect them from extinction. They can be used to grow lots of identical crops exhibiting desired traits such as disease resistance.

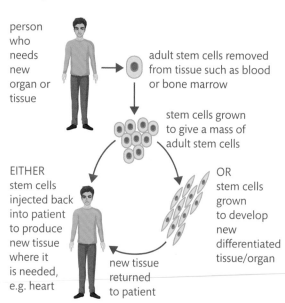

Figure 1 How adult stem cells can be used

 Working scientifically ✓

Stem cell research is controversial. Some people have ethical and religious objections to the process since human embryos are being destroyed in the process, but others believe the advantage of using stem cells to cure diseases or injured people outweighs the rights of an embryo.

 Worked example | **Grade 7** ✓

Scientists are developing a treatment for paralysis using embryonic stem cells.

Why are stem cells used? **[2 marks]**

Stem cells are unspecialised, so they can differentiate into any type of cell. Therefore, they can differentiate and replace the damaged cells causing the paralysis.

 Exam focus ✓

You do not need to know details about stem cell techniques for the exam, but you are expected to be able to evaluate the risks and benefits. You also need to know about social and ethical issues in science.

 Exam-style practice | **Grades 5–7** ✓

❶ Give **one** advantage for commercial growers using cloned plants. **[1 mark]**

❷ Describe the ethical considerations involved with embryonic stem cell therapy. **[2 marks]**

The human nervous system

The nervous system senses a stimulus (a change in the environment) and coordinates the body's response. You need to be able to explain the structure and function of the human nervous system.

(5) Coordination

When **sensory receptors** are stimulated, for example when light stimulates receptors in the retina in the eye, **electrical impulses** are sent to the **central nervous system (CNS)**, which consists of the brain and spinal cord. The CNS coordinates suitable responses to stimuli by sending impulses to **effectors** (muscles or glands). This pathway is known as a **reflex arc**:

stimulus → receptor → coordinator → effector → response

> Examples of stimuli include: touch, substances in food, temperature and light.

(10) Types of neurone

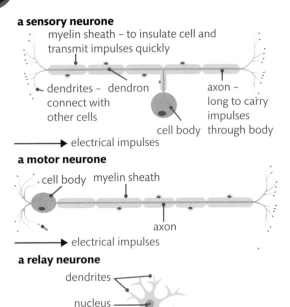

Figure 1 Neurones

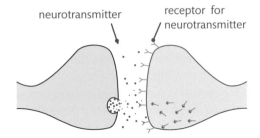

Figure 2 A synapse

Neurones are cells in the nervous system. Sensory neurones carry information from sensory receptors to the CNS. Motor neurones carry instructions from the CNS to effectors. Sensory and motor neurones are covered in an insulating **myelin sheath** which speeds up the transmission of the impulses. **Synapses** are gaps between neurones. When electrical impulses arrive at a synapse they cause the release of chemical messengers called **neurotransmitters** which diffuse across the gap and cause an electrical impulse in the next neurone.

(5) Reflex arcs

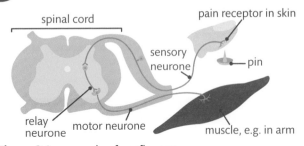

Figure 3 An example of a reflex arc

Reflex arcs are automatic and do not involve the conscious part of the brain. This is important to speed up reaction times.

Not all impulses go via the brain: some impulses just go to into the spinal cord and straight back out to an effector. Sensory and motor neurones are connected by **relay neurones**.

receptor → sensory neurone → relay neurone → motor neurone → effector

(5) Exam-style practice   Grade 6

Describe and explain **two** ways that the structure of a motor neurone is adapted for its function.   **[4 marks]**

Made a start   Feeling confident   Exam ready

Meiosis

Meiosis is the type of cell division that produces the cells called gametes, which are needed for sexual reproduction. You need to know how this occurs.

(10) The stages of meiosis

Meiosis in humans and other animals results in sperm and egg cells (**gametes**).

Although similar to mitosis (see page 14), it is a two-stage cell division process, resulting in the production of four cells, each containing a single set of chromosomes.

The gametes produced by meiosis are genetically different from each other.

During fertilisation, one male gamete and one female gamete join up to form a cell with the typical number of chromosomes in a body cell (in humans, 46 chromosomes arranged in 23 pairs). This cell is called a **zygote**.

The zygote will then divide by mitosis forming a ball of cells called the **embryo**. As the embryo develops, cells differentiate.

The final stage of division during meiosis will always produce cells containing half the number of chromosomes (**haploid** number) as the parent cell (which has the full or **diploid** number). The chromosomes can be either chromosome from each pair of chromosomes contained in the parent cell.

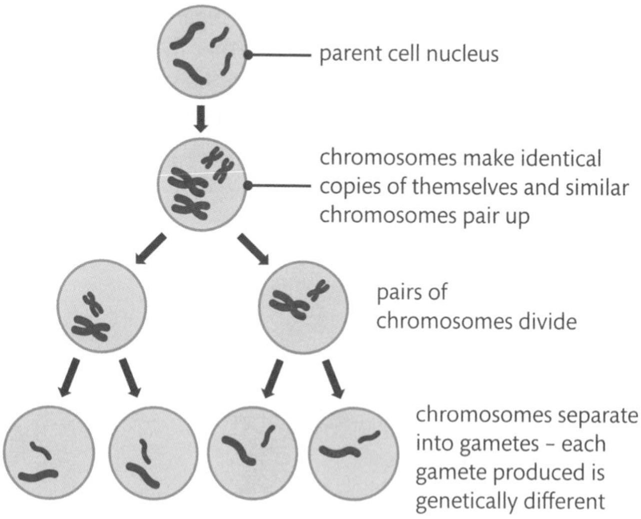
parent cell nucleus
chromosomes make identical copies of themselves and similar chromosomes pair up
pairs of chromosomes divide
chromosomes separate into gametes – each gamete produced is genetically different

Figure 1 The stages of meiosis

(5) Worked example — Grade 7

1 Describe what happens to the chromosomes when a cell divides by meiosis. **[4 marks]**

The chromosomes duplicate; the cell then divides twice to form four gametes, each with a single set of chromosomes.

The first cell division occurs after chromosomes have made identical copies of themselves and paired up.

The second round of cell division splits the 46 chromosomes in one cell into two cells, each containing only half the number of chromosomes (23).

2 Complete the diagram to show the nucleus of a parent cell. **[1 mark]**

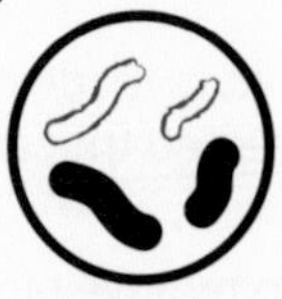

3 Complete the diagram to show one of the four nuclei produced from the cell above during meiosis. **[1 mark]**

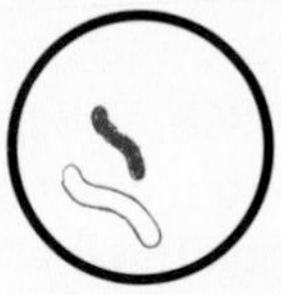

(2) Key terms

- **gametes** – sex cells: sperm and egg cells
- **diploid** – a cell containing two sets of chromosomes
- **haploid** – a cell containing a single set of unpaired chromosomes

(1) Exam focus

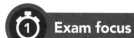

In your exam, be very careful with your spellings of 'mitosis' or 'meiosis', so it is clear which one you are writing about. If it is not clear, you may lose marks.

(5) Exam-style practice — Grades 4–6

1 Describe how variation occurs due to meiosis and sexual reproduction. **[3 marks]**

2 **(a)** Describe how the number of chromosomes in a human sex cell differs from the number of chromosomes in a human body cell. **[1 mark]**

(b) Give the number of chromosomes found in a human egg cell. **[1 mark]**

Made a start | Feeling confident | Exam ready

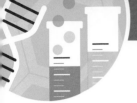

The structure of DNA

You need to know about the substance that makes up genetic material: DNA or deoxyribonucleic acid.

(10) DNA

DNA (deoxyribonucleic acid) is the genetic material – the substance that genes are made of. Understanding its structure has allowed advances such as genetic engineering (page 30) and 'DNA fingerprinting'.

DNA consists of two strands made of sugars and phosphates. The strands are coiled to form a **double helix**. The strands are linked by pairs of bases held together by weak intermolecular bonds called **hydrogen bonds**. There are four different bases: A, T, C and G. They always form the same pairs: A-T and C-G. These are known as **complementary base pairs**. Each gene has a different sequence of base pairs along its length.

DNA is a **polymer**, meaning that it is a very long molecule made up of repeating sub-units (see page 94). Each sub-unit is made of a sugar molecule attached to a phosphate group and a base, and is known as a **nucleotide**.

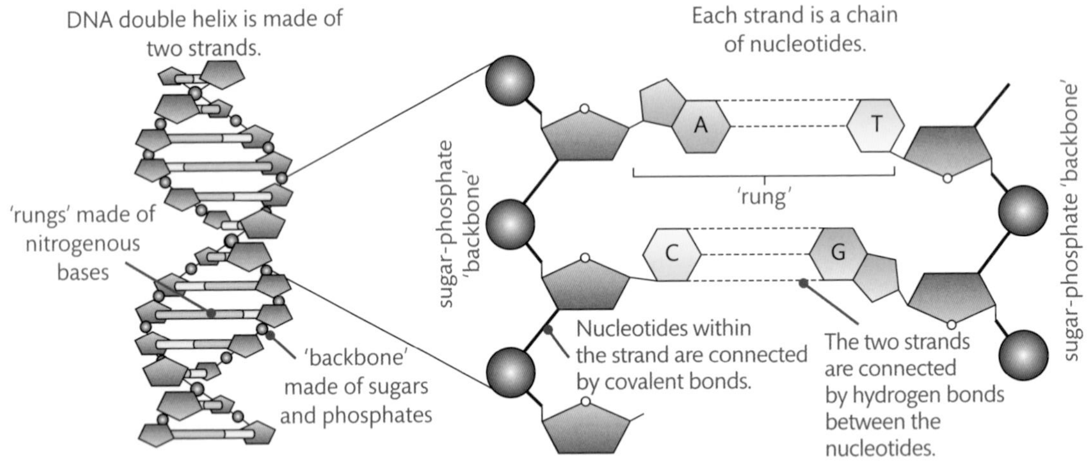
DNA double helix is made of two strands.
'rungs' made of nitrogenous bases
'backbone' made of sugars and phosphates
sugar-phosphate 'backbone'
Each strand is a chain of nucleotides.
A
T
'rung'
C
G
Nucleotides within the strand are connected by covalent bonds.
The two strands are connected by hydrogen bonds between the nucleotides.
sugar-phosphate 'backbone'

Figure 1 The structure of DNA

(5) Worked example — Grade 5

1. State why DNA is described as a 'polymer'. **[1 mark]**

Each strand is a repeating series of nucleotides.

2. Everyone has a unique 'DNA fingerprint'. Suggest an explanation for what makes one person's DNA different from someone else's. **[2 marks]**

DNA contains a sequence of base pairs. Each person has a slightly different sequence.

(2) Working scientifically

The structure of DNA was worked out in 1953 by James Watson and Francis Crick, using research from other scientists like Rosalind Franklin to help them. In 1962, together with Maurice Wilkins, Watson and Crick were awarded a Nobel prize, recognising the importance of their discovery.

(10) Extracting DNA

DNA can be extracted from fruit and vegetables. The process works well with kiwi, bananas and strawberries.

Method

1. Remove any tough skin and mush up the fruit.
2. Add a prepared mixture made of water, salt and detergent to the mushed fruit and leave for about 20 minutes.
3. Filter the mixture to remove pips and pulp, collecting the liquid in a test tube.
4. Carefully pour some cold alcohol or methylated spirits down the side of the test tube so it collects on top of the fruit extract. The alcohol needs to have been kept in a freezer so that it is very cold.
5. After about 10 minutes, white 'stringy' material will appear in the alcohol. This is DNA.

(10) Exam-style practice — Grade 6

Describe the structure of DNA. **[6 marks]**

DNA and the genome

The whole genetic material of an organism is called its genome. You need to know about how genes work and the importance of the Human Genome Project.

 Genes and the genome

The whole genetic material of an organism is called its **genome**.

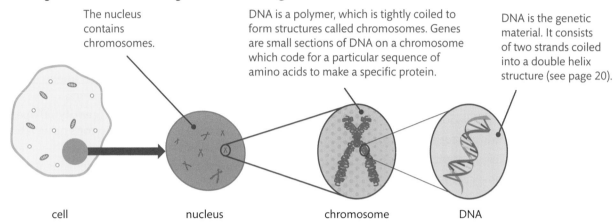

The nucleus contains chromosomes.

DNA is a polymer, which is tightly coiled to form structures called chromosomes. Genes are small sections of DNA on a chromosome which code for a particular sequence of amino acids to make a specific protein.

DNA is the genetic material. It consists of two strands coiled into a double helix structure (see page 20).

cell　　　nucleus　　　chromosome　　　DNA

Figure 1 DNA in a cell

 The Human Genome Project

Completed by 2003, the purpose of the **Human Genome Project** was to map and identify all the genes in the human genome.

Information about DNA can be very useful for forensic science, tracing human migration patterns, and for the understanding and treatment of inherited genetic disorders. The project helps scientists to:

- diagnose diseases before symptoms develop
- identify the genetic changes that are responsible for an already diagnosed disease
- help doctors to determine the best treatment
- identify genetic mutations that may increase the risk of developing a disease
- identify gene changes that could be inherited
- screen babies for treatable conditions.

 Worked example | Grade 6–7

1 Describe the role of a gene. **[1 mark]**

A gene codes for a sequence of amino acids to make a protein.

2 Explain how the human genome and genetic markers have enabled scientists to trace human migration back to Africa. **[3 marks]**

Genetic markers are areas of variation in the sequence of human DNA. Mapping the occurrence of these markers around the world shows the movement of human population. As human populations migrated, their genome mutated, showing small changes in different populations. These changes can be traced back, showing the patterns of migration of human populations from their ancestors in Africa.

Virtually all human DNA is identical – only around 1 in 1000 DNA base pairs varies from one individual to the next. These variations are known as genetic markers, caused by mutations in DNA.

 Exam-style practice | Grade 7

1 Cystic fibrosis is an inherited disorder. Explain how the human genome can be used to identify whether or not an unborn baby carries the disorder. **[3 marks]**

2 Describe how an understanding of the human genome is useful for developing treatments for diseases caused by mutations in genes. **[2 marks]**

3 Give **three** ways in which knowledge of the sequence of the human genome can be used. **[3 marks]**

Genetic inheritance

Many of our characteristics are controlled by the genes we inherit. You need to know how alleles, the different forms of each gene, cause variation between individuals.

5 Key terms

- **gene** – a short section of DNA which codes for a protein
- **allele** – different version of a gene
- **dominant** – only one dominant allele is needed for a characteristic to be expressed
- **recessive** – two recessive alleles are needed for the characteristic to be expressed
- **homozygous** – both alleles for a gene are identical
- **heterozygous** – the alleles for a gene are different
- **genotype** – the alleles present for genes
- **phenotype** – the physical characteristics, determined by the alleles

5 Genes

Some characteristics are controlled by a single **gene**, such as red-green colour blindness in humans, and fur colour in mice.

Most characteristics are controlled by multiple genes interacting. For example, multiple genes affect eye colour and skin colour.

The different forms of a gene are called **alleles**; alleles for each gene are inherited from each parent.

The combination of alleles present (**genotype**) operates at a molecular level to develop a person's observable characteristics (**phenotype**).

The appearance of a characteristic is dependent on both the type of alleles present and whether they are **dominant** or **recessive**.

10 Worked example — Grade 6

The allele **m** causes a rare blood-linked condition.

(a) What type of allele is responsible for the disease? **[1 mark]**

A recessive allele

(b) Two parents produce offspring. Parent A has the alleles **Mm** and parent B has the alleles **mm**.

Produce a Punnett square to calculate the percentage chance of their offspring inheriting the disease. Draw a circle around any offspring who have the disease. **[4 marks]**

		Parent A: M	Parent A: m
Parent B	m	Mm	[mm]
	m	Mm	[mm]

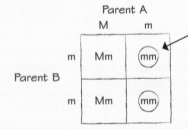

There is a 50% chance of having a child with the disease.

One mark is awarded for correctly identifying the alleles. The second mark is for four correct crosses. The third mark is for identifying the offspring who have the disease. The final mark is for the correct percentage given.

Dominant alleles are represented by a capital letter, while recessive alleles are shown by a lower case letter.

2 Working scientifically

You need to know how to draw genetic cross diagrams, such as **Punnett squares**, to predict the probability of the results of a single gene cross. (A different type of genetic diagram is shown on page 24.) The results of genetic crosses are usually represented as either a ratio or a percentage.

2 Exam focus

If a question asks you to draw a 'genetic diagram' then it is up to you which type you draw. However, a Punnett square is usually the easiest type to draw.

Go to page 23 to read about the inheritance of polydactyly.

5 Exam-style practice — Grade 6

Polydactyly is an inherited condition which causes a person to have extra fingers or toes. It is caused by a dominant allele.

(a) Draw a Punnett square to show the inheritance of polydactyly between a mother who is homozygous for polydactyly, and a father who does not have the polydactyly allele.

Use **D** for the polydactyly allele and **d** for the normal allele. **[3 marks]**

(b) Give the percentage of the offspring that will inherit the condition. **[1 mark]**

Inherited disorders

You need to know how genetic diagrams, such as Punnett squares and family pedigrees, show how genetic disorders are inherited.

5 Family pedigree diagrams

Family pedigree diagrams are family trees showing how inherited disorders are passed down through different generations. The example in **Figure 1** shows the inheritance of polydactyly.

Polydactyly is a disorder where the person has extra fingers or toes. It is caused by a dominant allele.

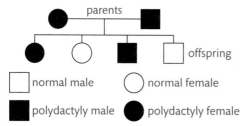

Figure 1 This family pedigree diagram shows the inheritance of polydactyly within a family.

1 Exam focus

In the exam, you could be asked to:

- complete a Punnett square diagram
- extract and interpret information from genetic cross and family pedigree diagrams.

2 Maths skills

When explaining the results of genetic diagrams, you may be asked to give your answers as:

- percentages (%)
- probabilities
- ratios.

A chance of 100% is the same as a probability of 1.0, and a chance of 50% is the same as a probability of 0.5.

Always give ratios in the lowest form. For example, if the ratio is 2:2, then write this as 1:1.

10 Worked example — Grade 8

1 Polydactyly is an inherited disorder.

(a) Explain what is meant by 'an inherited disorder'. **[1 mark]**

An inherited disorder is a genetic disorder that has been passed on from either one or both parents.

(b) Explain how **Figure 1** shows that polydactyly is caused by a dominant allele and not by a recessive allele. **[4 marks]**

Two of the offspring do not have polydactyly, but both of the parents do. This means that polydactyly is caused by a dominant allele and each of the parents must be heterozygous. The offspring without polydactyly must have inherited a normal recessive allele from each parent.

If polydactyly was caused by a recessive allele, then both parents would have to be homozygous recessive and therefore all the offspring would have polydactyly too.

2 Draw and complete a Punnett square to show how two people with polydactyly can have a child without polydactyly. Use **D** for the allele causing polydactyly and **d** for the recessive allele. Identify any children without polydactyly by drawing a circle around them. **[3 marks]**

	D	d
D	DD	Dd
d	Dd	(dd)

10 Exam-style practice — Grade 7

Cystic fibrosis is a disorder of cell membranes leading to the production of a thick sticky mucus which affects organs, particularly the lungs. It is caused by a recessive allele.

The allele for cystic fibrosis can be represented by **f**, while the allele for the normal gene is represented as **F**.

(a) Give the genotype of a person who is unaffected and is not a carrier of the condition. **[1 mark]**

(b) Explain whether a person who has cystic fibrosis will be heterozygous or homozygous for the condition. **[2 marks]**

(c) Determine the probability of a child being affected if both parents are unaffected carriers. Use a Punnett square to show your answer. **[3 marks]**

Sex determination

You need to know how sex is determined by chromosomes.

Sex chromosomes

Human body cells each contain 23 pairs of chromosomes, 22 of which control characteristics that do not depend on whether you are male or female.

The 23rd pair carries the genes that determine whether a person is male or female.

The female sex chromosomes are XX. The male sex chromosomes are XY.

Sex cells (gametes) only contain 23 chromosomes, one of each pair. Female sex cells (gametes) therefore only contain one X chromosome. The male sex cells (gametes) can either contain one X or one Y, depending on how the chromosomes are separated during meiosis. Therefore an X chromosome is always inherited from the egg but there is a 50% chance of inheriting either an X or a Y chromosome from the sperm, which determines the sex of the offspring.

Genetic diagrams

A genetic diagram can be used to determine the sex of offspring.

1 To construct a genetic diagram, the phenotype of each parent must be given on the top line.

2 The next stage is to provide the genotype for each parent, underneath their phenotype.

3 The next line shows the genotype of all the gametes which can be passed on to the offspring.

4 The final stage in the genetic cross diagram is to show all of the combinations of gametes which could occur which gives the different genotypes possible.

You are expected to know the genotype for a male and a female:
- In males, the two sex chromosomes are different. They are XY.
- In females, the two sex chromosomes are the same. They are XX.

Working scientifically

Although it is possible to identify the sex of an unborn baby, it is illegal to choose the sex of a baby unless you have a serious genetic condition which could put a child at risk if inherited, such as haemophilia or muscular dystrophy. (The alleles for these conditions are carried on the sex chromosomes.)

Worked example | Grade 7

There is a 1 : 1 chance of a child being a boy or a girl. Draw a suitable diagram to explain this. **[4 marks]**

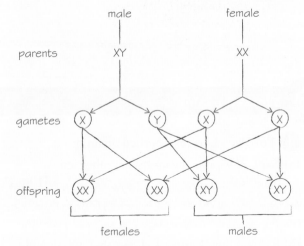

The diagram shows that there is a 2 : 2 chance of female : male offspring, which equates to a 1 : 1 ratio.

You could also show your answer as a Punnett square diagram:

		Male	
	gametes	X	Y
Female	X	XX	XY
	X	XX	XY

Exam-style practice | Grade 5

Humans have two different sex chromosomes: X and Y.

(a) Give the genotype of a female. **[1 mark]**

(b) Give the number of chromosomes, passed on from the egg, that help determine the sex of a baby. **[1 mark]**

(c) Give the probability of having a male child. Explain your answer. **[2 marks]**

Variation and mutation

You need to know how both variation and mutation occur in a species.

⑩ Causes of variation

Although a lot of characteristics are inherited, the interaction of genes with the environment will also influence the phenotype (physical features) of an individual (see page 22).

Variation between individuals occurs due to differences in:

- inherited genes
- the environment in which the person grew up
- the interaction of genes with the environment.

Some characteristics brought about by genetic variation include Down's syndrome, blood group and eye colour.

Some characteristics brought about by environmental variation include language spoken and the presence of scars. Characteristics caused by the environment are sometimes called **acquired characteristics**.

Most examples of variation are influenced by both environmental and genetic factors. For example, a person may have the potential to be tall, but an unhealthy diet can cause poor growth.

There is usually a lot of genetic variation within a population of a species.

Genetic variation in individuals is caused by sexual reproduction (see pages 15 and 19) and by **mutations**. Most mutations will have no effect on the phenotype; some mutations have a small effect on the phenotype; rarely, a single mutation will significantly affect the phenotype. Mutations occur continuously. If the new phenotype is suited to an environmental change it can lead to a relatively rapid change in the species.

> Mutations can have positive or negative effects:
> 👍 improve chances of survival
> 👍 increase genetic diversity
> 👎 can lead to diseases, such as cancer (pages 15 and 41)
> 👎 can lead to genetic disorders (page 23).

⑤ Mutations: key facts

- ☑ A mutation is a change in genetic material (DNA).
- ☑ Mutations occur naturally and continuously, usually when DNA is being copied before cell division takes place.
- ☑ Mutations usually have no effect on an individual's characteristics. However, sometimes they can be harmful or useful.
- ☑ Mutations cause variation within a species, which can be vital to ensure the survival of the species.
- ☑ Some mutations are caused by substances such as tar from cigarettes.
- ☑ Radiation, including gamma rays, X-rays and UV rays, can also cause genetic mutations.

⑩ Worked example — Grades 4–6

Identical twins are individuals who developed from a single fertilised ovum (egg cell). As a result, they have identical DNA. Explain why identical twins may or may not be identical when they reach adulthood. **[3 marks]**

Phenotype is controlled by genetic inheritance, environmental factors and the interaction between them. Identical twins will inherit the same DNA and so are genetically identical. However, environmental factors such as their diet will also affect their phenotypes so their appearances could be different.

Remember, the phenotype (appearance) is determined by a combination of factors.

⑤ Exam-style practice — Grade 7

1. Give **two** examples of genetic variation and **two** examples of environmental variation. **[2 marks]**

2. Describe what is meant by a mutation. Give **two** causes of mutation. **[3 marks]**

3. Give **one** way in which a mutation can be beneficial. **[1 mark]**

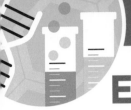

Evolution by natural selection

You need to know how the theory of evolution explains the development of species over time.

5 Natural selection

The theory of **evolution** states that all species of living things have evolved, over more than three billion years, from simple life forms, through a process called natural selection. **Natural selection** is the theory that organisms which are best suited to their environment are more likely to survive and reproduce. Therefore, their offspring are more likely to inherit genes that give rise to phenotypes (see pages 22 and 25) most suited to the environment, causing changes to the population over time.

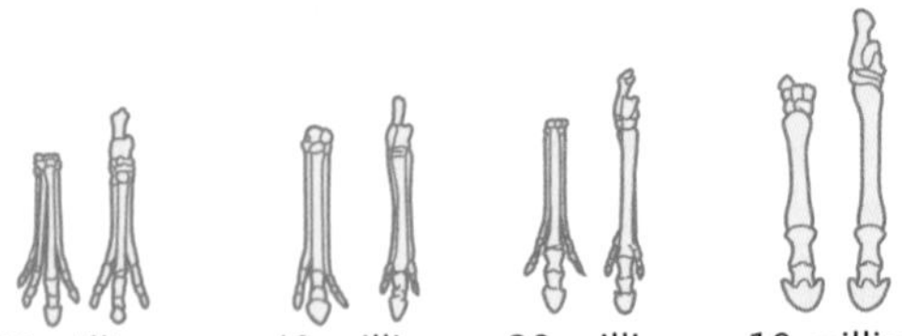
60 million years ago
40 million years ago
30 million years ago
10 million years ago

Figure 1 All the main stages of horse evolution have been preserved in fossil records.

5 Working scientifically

Alongside other scientists, **Charles Darwin** developed the theory of natural selection after observing many examples of variation, for example, between species of tortoises and finches, while voyaging around South America and the Galapagos Islands.

Darwin realised that the animals that exhibited a variation that made them more successful were more likely to survive and breed, passing on the genes (alleles) for this feature to their offspring. As later generations reproduce, the successful feature continues to be passed on to the next generation.

As more evidence surrounding genetic inheritance (page 22) has been discovered and more of the fossil record continues to be discovered, the theory of evolution by natural selection has become widely accepted by scientists. There is further evidence for evolution in the process by which bacteria become resistant to certain antibiotics over time (page 39), and in how some pests, such as rats or mosquitoes, become resistant to particular poisons or insecticides.

The theory of evolution by natural selection was only gradually accepted because:

- the theory challenged the idea that God made all the animals and plants that live on Earth
- there was insufficient evidence at the time the theory was first published to convince all scientists
- the mechanism of inheritance and variation was not known until 50 years after the theory was published.

10 Worked example — Grade 4

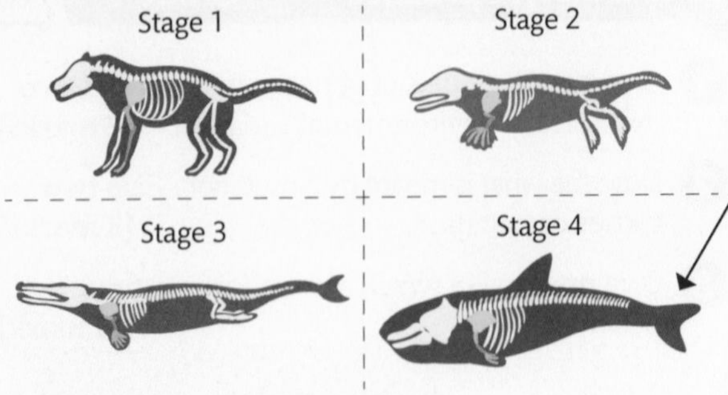
Stage 1
Stage 2
Stage 3
Stage 4

Figure 2 Evolution of the whale

Figure 2 shows how the whale is thought to have evolved from its land-dwelling ancestors.

Give **two** ways in which the whale has evolved since Stage 1. **[2 marks]**

The early ancestor had four limbs, and the whale alive today doesn't.

The whale has a fin on its back unlike its ancestors.

New species can form when the genes of individuals within a species become so different that their phenotype changes and they can no longer interbreed to form fertile offspring. This is known as **speciation**.

You are not expected to recall evolutionary stages in the development of species; you need to use the information provided in the question.

You could also be asked to explain why the feature has evolved. For example, the whale's fin developed so that the whale could swim efficiently.

5 Exam-style practice — Grade 7

1. Define the theory of evolution. **[2 marks]**
2. Some species have evolved to look like another species; for example, the scarlet king snake, which is harmless, has evolved to look like the deadly coral snake. Explain why this is considered to be a successful adaptation. **[2 marks]**
3. Describe the process of natural selection suggested by Darwin. **[4 marks]**

Made a start | Feeling confident | Exam ready

Evidence for human evolution

Fossils are the preserved remains of organisms that lived millions of years ago. You need to know that fossils can show us how life, including humans, has evolved on Earth. Stone tools provide further evidence of human evolution.

 Evidence for human evolution

Evidence for how humans have evolved includes fossils and stone tools.

Fossils

- Ardi is a fossil of a female human-like animal from 4.4 million years ago. She could probably walk upright but had much longer arms than a human, which would help with moving through trees.
- Lucy is another human-like fossil from 3.2 million years ago. She also could walk upright but her feet were more similar to modern humans than Ardi's.

- Turkana Boy is a fossil discovered by a team led by Richard Leakey. It is about 1.6. million years old and is more similar to modern humans than Ardi or Lucy, for example in having a much larger brain size.

Stone tools

The oldest known fossil remains of modern humans, *Homo sapiens*, are about 0.3 million years old. However, stone tools have been found that are 3.3 million years old and so were almost certainly made by human-like creatures living at that time. Scientists have worked out the age of the tools from the surroundings and environment where they were found.

 Worked example Grade 5

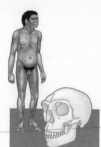

Ardipithecus ramidus ('Ardi')
Brain volume: 350 cm³

Australopithecus afarensis ('Lucy')
Brain volume: 400 cm³

Homo erectus ('Turkana Boy')
Brain volume: 850 cm³

Figure 1 Fossil skulls

Describe **two** ways, shown by the fossil skulls in **Figure 1**, that early humans changed as they evolved.

[2 marks]

Their brains became larger and their faces became more flattened.

 Exam-style practice Grade 6

Using **Figure 2**, explain how the development of stone tools over time provides evidence for human evolution. **[2 marks]**

The question is worth 2 marks, so you are not expected to write a long answer. Keep your answer succinct and ensure you link the changes in the tool design to what this must mean in evolutionary terms.

Figure 2 Over time, stone tools are better designed and show more skill in their construction.

Classification

Classification is the process used to arrange living organisms into groups based on their similar structures and characteristics. You need to know how species are classified and how the process of classification has changed over time.

⏱ 10 The five kingdoms ✓

In the 18th century, Carl Linnaeus introduced a hierarchical system for classifying living organisms and giving them scientific names. Linnaeus divided all living things into large groups called **kingdoms** according to the organisms' features. Then he divided the kingdoms into smaller and smaller groups, as shown in **Figure 1**.

You need to know about five kingdoms:

1. Animals – eukaryotic organisms that move around to get their food
2. Plants – eukaryotic organisms that photosynthesise to make their own food
3. Fungi – eukaryotic organisms that feed on dead materials
4. Protists – single-celled eukaryotic organisms
5. Prokaryotes – bacteria.

> As the classification groups get smaller, the organisms have more characteristics in common.

Kingdom	animal
Phylum	chordate
Class	mammal
Order	primate
Family	hominid
Genus	*Pongo*
Species	*albelii*

Figure 1 Classification of a Sumatran orangutan

> Page 2 has more information about prokaryotic and eukaryotic cells.

Naming species

It is important for a species to have a unique scientific name as it allows scientists to identify and refer to individual species quickly and accurately. Organisms are named after the genus and species that they belong to. This double name is called the **binomial system** of naming. The scientific name for the Sumatran orangutan is *Pongo albelii*.

Figure 2 A Sumatran orangutan

⏱ 5 The three domains ✓

Over time, scientists' understanding of biochemistry and cell structure has changed as scientific equipment and techniques have developed. Advances, such as more powerful microscopes and DNA analysis and sequencing, have led to several new classification systems.

In 1977, Carl Woese proposed, on the basis of genetic analysis, that all living organisms can be divided into three **domains**:

- **archaea** – primitive bacteria, many of which live in extreme environments
- **bacteria** – true bacteria
- **eukaryota** (or eukaryotes) – protists, fungi, plants and animals.

The archaea and bacteria have prokaryotic cells, which, unlike eukaryotic cells, do not contain nuclei and many other organelles. (Revise pages 2 and 3 for more about these different types of cell.) The differences between the archaea and bacteria are in their chemical makeup and cannot be seen with a microscope.

> This mnemonic can help you remember the classification hierarchy:
> **K**ing **P**hilip **c**ame **o**ver **f**rom **g**reat **S**pain

⏱ 5 Worked example   Grade 5 ✓

For a long time, the domains archaea and bacteria were classified together in the same kingdom.

(a) Name the kingdom that corresponds with the archaea and bacteria.   **[1 mark]**

Prokaryotes

(b) Explain why it took until 1977 to separate the archaea and bacteria into two different groups.   **[2 marks]**

The differences between them can only be shown by genetic analysis, which was not available before then.

⏱ 5 Exam-style practice   Grade 5 ✓

1. Give **two** advantages of using the binomial system of classification.   **[2 marks]**

2. Give **two** reasons why we now have more information to classify organisms.   **[2 marks]**

✓ **Made a start**   ✓ **Feeling confident**   ✓ **Exam ready**

Selective breeding

You need to know about selective breeding and the positive and negative impacts it can have.

Selective breeding

Selective breeding is like natural selection (page 26), except it is humans who choose the desired characteristics to produce the best offspring. Selective breeding is also called **artificial selection**. It involves selecting and breeding together parents with the desired characteristic from a mixed population. Those offspring that have the desired characteristic are then used for breeding. This continues over many generations, until all the offspring show the desired characteristic. Selective breeding can lead to inbreeding, where problems are caused by inherited defects or being prone to certain diseases.

Impacts of selective breeding

Positive	Negative
plants 👍 improved crop yield 👍 improved disease resistance 👍 large or unusual flowers. **animals** 👍 improved quality of meat 👍 increased milk production 👍 increased meat production 👍 sociable domesticated animals 👍 large eggs.	👎 A new disease could put the whole species at risk as the lack of genetic diversity makes them all equally vulnerable. 👎 The reduction in the stock of different alleles in the population would restrict the ability to produce new varieties in the future. 👎 Inbreeding can lead to inherited defects or susceptibility to disease.

wild cabbage plant (*Brassica oleracea*)

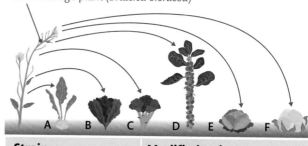

Strain	Modified trait
A kohlrabi	stem
B kale	leaves
C broccoli	flower buds and stem
D Brussels sprouts	lateral leaf buds
E cabbage	terminal leaf bud
F cauliflower	flower buds

Figure 1 Wild cabbage has been selectively bred to produce a variety of modern crops.

Worked example Grade 7

1 Describe the stages of selective breeding in cattle to produce an increased milk yield.

[4 marks]

Choose cows that have a high milk yield and a bull that is the offspring of a female with a high milk yield. Breed them together. Select the highest milk-yielding offspring that are produced and breed them. For each generation, select the males from the highest milk-yielding females and breed them with the highest milk-yielding females. Continue this over many generations until all cows show the desired characteristic.

2 Selective breeding leads to a reduction in variety in genetic material. Explain the advantage of this for cattle farming. **[1 mark]**

A reduction in the variety of genetic material in cattle would increase the chance of inheriting the desired feature.

This also applies to any other example of selective breeding.

You would also choose bulls that are healthy (free from any genetic diseases).

Exam-style practice Grades 5–7

1 Explain how selective breeding differs from natural selection. **[2 marks]**

2 Describe **two** problems that could be caused by selective breeding. **[2 marks]**

3 Selective breeding is often used to improve features of crop plants. Give **two** features that are selected for. **[2 marks]**

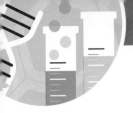

Genetic engineering

You need to know how genetic engineering is used to change the genome of an organism.

5 Genetic engineering

Genetic engineering (also known as **genetic modification** or **GM**) is a process used to alter the genetic material (genome) of an individual organism, by inserting a gene from another organism to give a desired characteristic. For example, bacterial cells can be genetically modified to produce substances that are useful to humans, such as insulin for the treatment of diabetes. Scientists are working on cures for genetic disorders based on genetic engineering. However, there are ethical concerns, for example, some people have concerns about animal welfare and believe that it is unethical to genetically modify living things.

GM crops are crops that have had genes inserted into them to alter their characteristics. For example, some GM plant crops have been genetically engineered to produce higher-quality plants with increased yield, for example by being disease-, herbicide- and insect-resistant. Crops can also be engineered to grow containing additional nutrients, such as golden rice, which provides high levels of vitamin A. This is useful for countries where vitamin deficiencies are common.

10 Stages in genetic engineering

1. The required gene is cut out from the source DNA, using **restriction enzymes**, which leave single-stranded sections at each end. These are called **sticky ends** because they can attach to other corresponding single-stranded sections.
2. The gene is inserted into a **vector**, such as a bacterial plasmid (see page 2) or a virus. The same type of restriction enzyme as used in stage 1 is used to cut open the vector, again leaving sticky ends. **Ligase enzymes** insert the required gene (from stage 1) into the vector by joining the sticky ends together.
3. The vector is put into the cells of the desired organism (animal, plant or microorganism) at an early stage of development.
4. The organism develops exhibiting the desired characteristics.

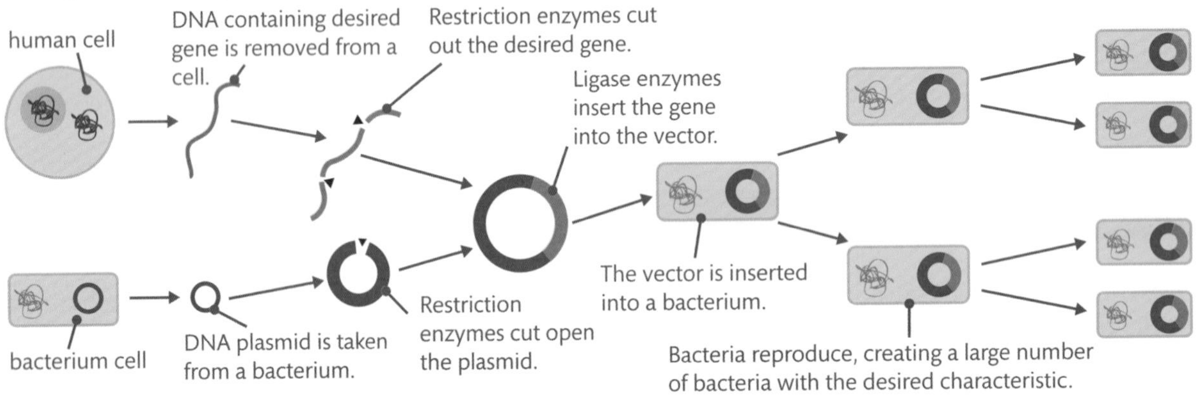

Figure 1 An example of genetically engineering bacteria

5 Worked example — Grade 5

1. Give **three** reasons why some people are against the growth of GM crops. **[3 marks]**

They might cross-pollinate with wild plants. We do not know if there are potential health risks for humans. They may pass on their herbicide resistance to wild plants or weeds.

2. Give **one** advantage to growing herbicide-resistant crops. **[1 mark]**

Farmers can spray the crops with herbicide as the crops will not be harmed (only the weeds).

5 Exam-style practice — Grade 5

Give **two** concerns associated with GM crops being herbicide resistant. **[2 marks]**

Health issues

According to the World Health Organization (WHO), health is the complete state of physical, mental and social well-being, including being free from disease. You need to know about the things that can affect health.

(5) Types of disease

Some diseases are communicable and some are not.

Communicable diseases

Communicable diseases are diseases that can be spread from one person to another. They are often called **infectious diseases**. They are caused by **pathogens** – microorganisms which cause disease.

> Examples include flu, measles and food poisoning. Go to page 32 for more about communicable diseases and their causes.

Non-communicable diseases

Non-communicable diseases are diseases that cannot be passed on from one person to another.

They are usually caused by lifestyle factors, such as diet, stress, drinking alcohol or smoking, and/or failures within the body's own systems, such as auto-immune diseases or old age.

(5) Disease interaction

Some diseases are more complex and may be caused by multiple factors. Different types of disease may interact.

- Defects in the immune system mean a person is more likely to suffer from infectious diseases.
- Viruses living inside cells can sometimes be the cause of cancer.
- The immune system, which is designed to destroy invading pathogens, can sometimes be the cause of allergies and asthma.
- Severe illnesses can lead to depression and other mental illnesses.

> Go to pages 41, 42 and 43 for more about non-communicable diseases and their causes. Examples include cardiovascular disease, cancer and diabetes.

(5) Worked example Grade 4

The table shows the number of cases of Ebola and the number of deaths caused in four different countries during a recent outbreak.

Country	Number of cases of Ebola	Number of deaths caused by Ebola	Case fatality rate
Guinea	2871	1876	0.65
Liberia	8478	3605	0.43
Mali	8	6	0.75
Sierra Leone	10 340	3145	

The case fatality rate is calculated using the formula

$$\text{case fatality rate} = \frac{\text{number of deaths}}{\text{number of cases}}$$

(a) The case fatality rate for Sierra Leone is missing.

Calculate the case fatality rate for Sierra Leone. **[2 marks]**

$$\frac{3145}{10\,340} = 0.30 \text{ (2 decimal places)}$$

(b) One newspaper reported that three quarters of all the people who catch Ebola die. Does the data support this conclusion? Explain your answer. **[2 marks]**

In countries with a substantial number of cases the death rate is much lower than three-quarters, so this conclusion is not supported.

(1) Exam focus

In the exam, you could be expected to interpret data from a table, graph or chart. Before answering any questions, make sure you know what the data is, what its units are, and if there are any trends.

(10) Exam-style practice Grade 5

1 Explain the differences between communicable and non-communicable diseases. **[2 marks]**

2 Explain what is meant by a pathogen. **[2 marks]**

Communicable diseases

Communicable diseases are diseases that can be spread from one person to another. They are sometimes called infectious diseases. You need to know how infections spread.

(5) Pathogens

Pathogens are microorganisms such as **bacteria** and **viruses** that cause infectious diseases.

Once inside the body they reproduce rapidly. Viruses enter cells, and force them to make more copies of the virus. This causes the cells to die and other cells are then invaded by the viruses.

Bacteria produce poisonous waste products called toxins. These toxins damage tissue and can make you feel ill.

(2) Four types of pathogen

1. viruses
2. bacteria
3. fungi
4. protists

For more about diseases caused by the different types of pathogen go to pages 33 (viral diseases), 34 (bacterial diseases), 35 (fungal diseases) and 36 (protist diseases).

(5) Spread of communicable diseases

Communicable diseases can be spread by:

1. **direct contact**, which involves touching or coming into contact with the diseased person

2. **indirect contact**, which involves touching objects that have been contaminated with the disease-causing organism, breathing in airborne disease-causing organisms, or eating or drinking contaminated food or water.

The spread of communicable diseases can be reduced or prevented by:

- reducing contact with the microorganism which causes the disease
- using physical barriers such as surgical masks
- using the immune system to destroy the pathogen
- using drugs such as antibiotics to destroy bacteria
- immunisation (vaccination).

Go to page 37 to revise human defence systems.

(5) Worked example

Grade 6

Some bacteria can divide once every 20 minutes.
The table shows the number of bacteria produced from a single bacterium after 180 minutes.

(a) The number of bacteria for 120 minutes is missing from the table. Calculate the missing number. **[1 mark]**

64 (double 32)

(b) Calculate the number of bacteria a single bacterium could produce in 4 hours. **[1 mark]**

4096 (doubling every 20 minutes means there are 1024 after 200 minutes, 2048 after 220 minutes, and 4096 after 240 minutes)

(c) Suggest an explanation for why it is important to treat infectious diseases at an early stage. **[2 marks]**

Fewer bacteria are present at an early stage of an infectious disease so it is easier to treat, and less harm has been caused by toxins.

Time in minutes	Number of bacteria
20	2
40	4
60	8
80	16
100	32
120	
140	128
160	256
180	512

(5) Exam-style practice

Grades 4–5

1. Give the meaning of the word 'infectious'. **[1 mark]**

2. Airborne diseases spread much faster than diseases which are spread through contact. Suggest an explanation for this. **[2 marks]**

Made a start | Feeling confident | Exam ready

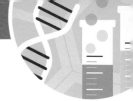

Viral diseases

A virus is an infective agent that is too small to be seen using a light microscope. You need to know about the characteristics and some examples of viruses.

5 Viruses

Viruses are much smaller than bacteria. They are so small that for many years scientists did not know that they existed.

They consist of small fragments of DNA enclosed by protein.

They invade other cells and the DNA in the virus takes over the cell. The DNA instructs the host cell to make more copies of the virus.

This kills the cell and millions more viruses are released into the body to invade other cells.

10 Viral diseases

Measles

Measles is a viral disease which affects humans. It is spread by breathing in airborne droplets from sneezes and coughs.

Symptoms include a fever, sore eyes and a red skin rash. Most people recover from the disease but fatal complications can sometimes arise. These complications include swelling of the brain, called encephalitis, and ear and eye infections. One in 20 children who get measles also get pneumonia. This is why most young children are vaccinated against measles.

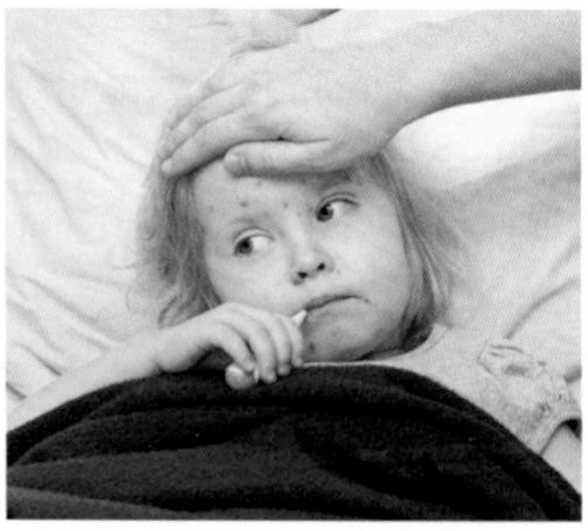

Figure 1 Measles is usually accompanied by a fever and a red skin rash.

Human Immunodeficiency Virus (HIV)

HIV causes flu-like symptoms. The virus attacks the human immune system by destroying white blood cells, which is why the body cannot destroy the virus.

In the final stage of HIV infection, when the immune system is badly damaged, it can no longer protect the body from other pathogens or cancers. This is called Acquired Immune Deficiency Syndrome (AIDS). The infected person will develop other diseases. It is these diseases that can kill a person with HIV.

People infected with HIV can take antiviral drugs to prevent the virus from damaging their immune system.

HIV is spread by sexual contact or other exchanges of bodily fluids, such as blood when drug users share needles.

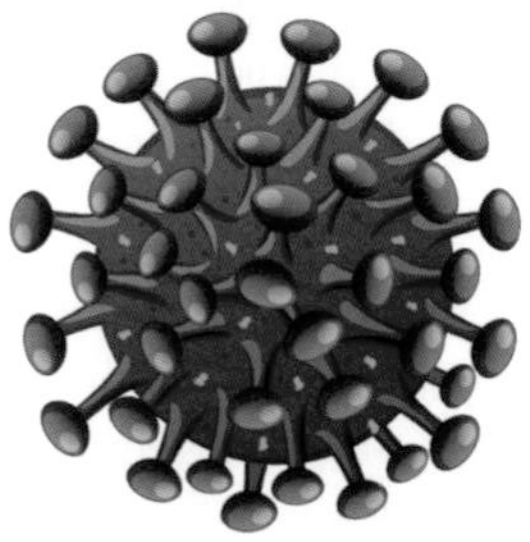

Figure 2 A highly magnified view of the HIV virus

Diseases spread by sexual contact are known as sexually transmitted infections (STIs). The spread of STIs can be reduced in several ways, for example, by avoiding sexual contact, or by using condoms.

Go to page 34 for another example of an STI.

2 Worked example — Grade 6

Describe the differences between how HIV and the measles virus are spread. **[2 marks]**

HIV can only be passed from one person to another through the transfer of body fluids. Measles can be spread by droplets coughed or sneezed out by an infectious person, which are then breathed in by someone else.

5 Exam-style practice — Grade 5

Give **three** characteristics of viruses. **[3 marks]**

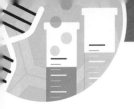

Bacterial diseases

You need to know about the different kinds of bacteria. Most are harmless, some are very useful and some can cause diseases in humans.

2 Bacteria

Bacteria are microscopic organisms. Once they have entered the body, they reproduce rapidly.

Some produce toxins that kill tissues and make us feel unwell.

Unlike viruses, bacteria can be treated with antibiotics. However, many strains of bacteria have become resistant to antibiotics. Scientists are trying to find new antibiotics that will be effective against disease-causing bacteria.

5 Bacterial diseases

Cholera

Cholera is caused by a bacterium spread through unclean water, for example, water contaminated by sewage.

Symptoms include severe diarrhoea, vomiting and cramps. It can be treated with antibiotics and rehydration.

The spread of cholera can be prevented by good water sanitation.

Tuberculosis

Tuberculosis (TB) is caused by a bacterium spread through the air when people with TB cough or sneeze.

Tuberculosis mainly affects the lungs, and can cause blood to be coughed up. Other symptoms include fever and weight loss.

The disease can be treated with antibiotics. Although TB is very common in some parts of the world, in the UK most children are vaccinated against it.

Chlamydia

Chlamydia is a bacterium that is spread through sexual contact.

Some infected people show no symptoms but it can cause painful discharges in both sexes and can lead to infertility in women. If diagnosed at an early stage, it can be treated successfully with antibiotics.

Like other STIs (see page 33), its spread can be prevented by avoiding sexual contact, by using condoms and by regular screening.

10 Worked example — Grade 7

In 1854, before the cause of cholera was known, there was an outbreak in London. A doctor, John Snow, realised that affected people got their water from a pump in Broad Street. He persuaded the local council to remove the pump handle so it could not be used.

Look at **Figure 1**. Evaluate the suggestion that water from the Broad Street pump caused the cholera outbreak. **[3 marks]**

The number of deaths fell after the pump handle was removed, which supports the suggestion. However, the number of deaths was already falling when the handle was removed, which does not support the suggestion. Also, the graph only shows the number of deaths, not the number of cases, so more information is needed.

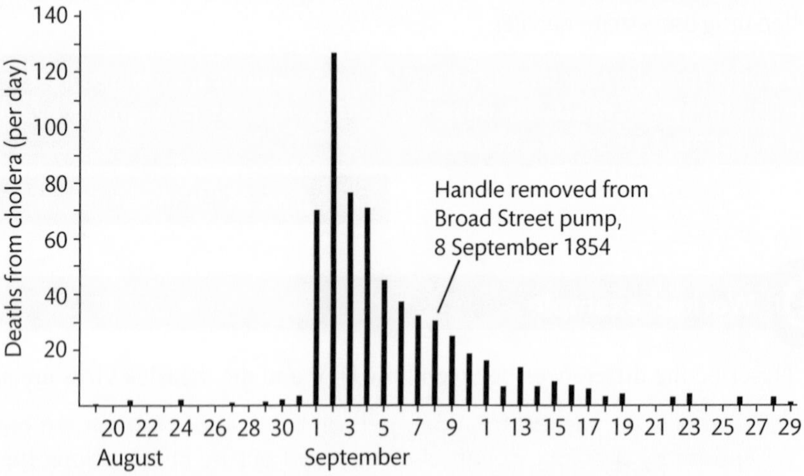

Figure 1 Number of deaths due to cholera during the 1854 outbreak

5 Exam-style practice — Grades 5–6

1. Explain how bacteria cause the symptoms of a disease. **[2 marks]**
2. Describe how the spread of *Chlamydia* can be prevented. **[3 marks]**

Fungal diseases

You need to know about fungal diseases and how they can affect other living things.

 Fungus

A **fungus** is a living organism, but it is neither a plant nor an animal. Fungi include moulds, yeast, mushrooms and toadstools.

Unlike plants, they do not contain chlorophyll so cannot make their own food. Instead they secrete enzymes onto organic matter, and then absorb the digested organic products. Fungi can live on dead organisms or invade living ones.

How are fungal diseases spread?

Fungi reproduce by producing microscopic spores, which can grow into a new fungus. The spores can be spread in droplets of rainwater or may be blown by the wind.

 Chalara ash dieback

Chalara ash dieback is a fungal disease affecting ash trees. Ash trees are an important species because they provide habitats for many other species, as well as being widely used for timber. The disease causes death of the growing shoots of the tree, loss of leaves, and lesions (openings) in the bark. It can be fatal in itself, but death can also be caused by the weakened trees being attacked by other fungi or pests.

The fungus causing chalara ash dieback is spread through the air by wind. Its spread can be prevented by cutting down infected plants, and collecting up, burning, burying or composting infected leaves.

Scientists have discovered that some ash trees are naturally resistant to the disease, and that this resistance has a genetic cause.

Figure 1 Chalara ash dieback

 Worked example 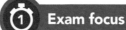 **Grade 5**

1 How is the chalara ash dieback fungus spread? **[1 mark]**

☐ **A** by insects
✓ **B** through air
☐ **C** through soil
☐ **D** through water

2 Scientists have discovered that some ash trees are genetically resistant to chalara ash dieback. Explain how this knowledge can be used to combat the spread of chalara ash dieback. **[2 marks]**

Collect cuttings or seedlings from the resistant trees. Plant these to replace infected or dead trees.

 Exam focus

One way to check your answers to multiple-choice questions are correct is by using a process of elimination to rule out the other options.

Remember that multiple-choice questions can be more difficult than you might at first think because the other options may seem like plausible answers at first glance.

> Think about the structure of plant and animal cells (page 3) compared with fungal cells.

 Exam-style practice **Grade 6**

1 Suggest an explanation why fungi are classified as neither a plant nor an animal. **[3 marks]**

2 Explain why leaves infected with chalara ash dieback should be collected and burned or buried. **[2 marks]**

 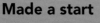

Protist diseases

Protists are a group of organisms that are usually unicellular (made of just one cell) and have a nucleus. You need to know how protist diseases like malaria are spread.

 Malaria

Malaria is spread from person to person by mosquitoes. If left untreated, malaria can be fatal.

The spread of malaria can be controlled by using mosquito nets and insect repellents to avoid being bitten. Mosquitoes can also be controlled by killing them with insecticides. They can be prevented from breeding by draining the stagnant water, for example in ditches, where they lay their eggs.

The infection starts when a person is bitten by a vector, an infected mosquito. The protist is injected into the person's bloodstream. It rapidly enters the liver where it reproduces.

The protists leave the liver and enter the bloodstream. They then invade red blood cells where they reproduce once more.

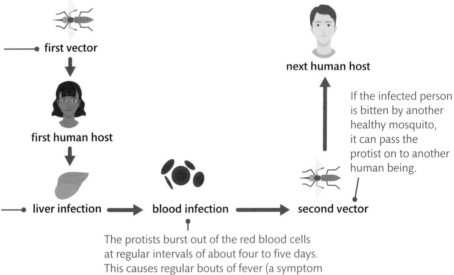

first vector

first human host

liver infection → blood infection → second vector

next human host

If the infected person is bitten by another healthy mosquito, it can pass the protist on to another human being.

The protists burst out of the red blood cells at regular intervals of about four to five days. This causes regular bouts of fever (a symptom of the disease).

Figure 1 The life-cycle of the malarial protist

 Worked example | Grades 5–6

Figure 2 shows malarial protists invading human blood.

(a) Label **Figure 2** to show: a malarial protist and a red blood cell. **[2 marks]**

(b) Explain what is meant by 'protist'. **[2 marks]**

An organism made of a single cell with a nucleus.

(c) A person suffering from malaria gets regular bouts of fever. Explain why. **[2 marks]**

The fever is caused by the protists bursting out of red blood cells every four to five days.

(d) The malarial protist is transferred from one person to another. Explain how. **[2 marks]**

An infected person is bitten by a mosquito, which then bites another person, infecting them with the protist.

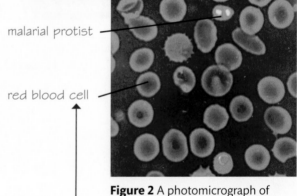

malarial protist

red blood cell

Figure 2 A photomicrograph of malarial protists in human blood

When labelling diagrams always make sure your lines start and finish at the correct points.

 Exam-style practice | Grade 5

1 Name the vector involved with the transfer of malaria. **[1 mark]**

2 Explain why it is incorrect to say that mosquitoes cause malaria. **[2 marks]**

 Made a start **Feeling confident** **Exam ready**

Human defence systems

You need to know about the human body's defence mechanisms and how they protect us from invading pathogens.

 Physical defences

Tears, and the liquid covering the eye, contain an enzyme called **lysozyme** which kills pathogens.

The nose is lined with hairs and mucus to trap pathogens to stop them getting to the lungs.

The stomach produces **hydrochloric acid** to help kill any pathogens in food.

Sticky **mucus** in the trachea and bronchi traps pathogens. **Cilia** on the cells lining these passages move in a wave-like motion, moving mucus and trapped pathogens out of the lungs towards the back of the throat where they are swallowed.

The **skin** is the organ that covers the outer surface of the body. It acts as a barrier to pathogens and has other features that defend against them. It secretes antimicrobial substances that kill pathogenic bacteria or inhibit their growth. Many species of non-pathogenic bacteria live on the skin. They secrete substances that kill pathogenic bacteria, and compete with them for nutrients. Scabs form over damaged skin, keeping pathogens out while the skin repairs itself.

Figure 1 The body's non-specific defences make it difficult for pathogens to enter the body.

 The immune system

When a person is infected with a pathogen, the pathogen starts to reproduce. Symptoms of the illness only appear when there are a large number of pathogens present in the body producing toxins and killing cells.

When a pathogen enters the body the **immune system** tries to destroy it. There are several ways it does this:

- **Phagocytosis** – some white blood cells engulf the pathogen and digest it.
- **Antibody production** – some white blood cells produce **antibodies**. These are proteins that recognise and target specific molecules called **antigens** on the pathogen and destroy it. When the infection has passed, some white blood cells remain in the blood as **memory lymphocytes** (also known as 'memory cells'). If a person is re-infected by the same pathogen, the memory lymphocytes enable the immune system to react more rapidly, which reduces the risk of the symptoms. This is called the **secondary response**.
- **Antitoxin production** – some white blood cells produce **antitoxins**. Antitoxins are proteins that attach to the poisonous toxins produced by pathogens and neutralise them.

 Worked example **Grade 5**

Look at **Figure 2**.

(a) State how long it took for the body to start producing the antibody after infection. **[1 mark]**

7.5 hours

(b) Give the number of hours the person felt ill for. **[1 mark]**

23 hours

(c) Give the concentration of antibodies in the blood when the pathogen started being destroyed faster than it was reproducing. **[1 mark]**

28 arbitrary units

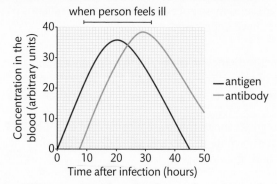

Figure 2 The concentration of antigens of a pathogen in the blood and the concentration of antibodies that the body produces in response.

 Exam-style practice **Grade 6**

1 White blood cells help to protect the body against disease-causing microorganisms. Explain how. **[2 marks]**

2 Explain why a person who has had an infectious disease is less likely to get the same disease again. **[3 marks]**

Immunisation

You need to know how immunisation (or vaccination) can build up immunity to a disease.

(5) Immunisation ✓

Immunisation (or **vaccination**) is the process of using dead or inactive pathogens to ensure that the immune system can recognise and quickly respond to the live pathogen if a person becomes infected with a disease.

1 Dead or inactive pathogens are injected into the body (the **vaccine**).

2 The body responds by white blood cells producing antibodies specific to the pathogen.

3 If the live pathogen infects the body in the future, white blood cells in the blood rapidly produce large quantities of antibodies to destroy the pathogens.

Go to page 37 for more about antibodies.

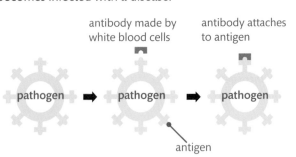

Figure 1 How antibodies attack pathogens

(2) Working scientifically 🧪⚗️ ✓

The more people that are immunised against a disease, then the less chance of that disease being able to spread. In the UK, young babies and children are routinely immunised against such diseases as polio, diptheria and measles. Before the widespread use of immunisation, such potentially life-threatening diseases were much more common.

(2) Working scientifically 🧪⚗️ ✓

Smallpox is a disease that has killed millions of people around the world. The World Health Organization organised a global immunisation programme. In 1977, Ali Maow Maalin had the last recorded case of smallpox. No one has had the disease since that date. Smallpox is the only disease that has been totally eradicated by science and immunisation. Millions of lives have been saved.

Use information in the graph to help you answer the question. The graph shows the concentration of antibodies increasing after the first vaccination.

The graph shows that the concentration of antibodies increases more quickly and significantly following the second vaccination.

(10) Worked example — Grade 7 ✓

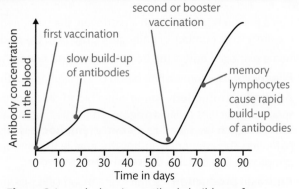

Figure 2 A graph showing antibody build-up after immunisation.

Look at **Figure 2**.

(a) Explain how the body responds after a vaccine is injected. **[2 marks]**

White blood cells produce antibodies to destroy the antigens in the vaccine.

(b) Describe the difference in response when a second or booster dose of vaccine is injected. **[2 marks]**

Memory lymphocytes in the blood produce the antibodies much faster and in greater quantities.

(10) Exam-style practice — Grades 6–7 ✓

1 Some people think that it is their social responsibility to have their children immunised. Suggest an explanation for this point of view. **[2 marks]**

2 Explain why you need a different immunisation for each disease. **[2 marks]**

3 Explain why the pathogens used in immunisations must be either dead or inactive. **[2 marks]**

4 Describe the function of memory lymphocytes. **[2 marks]**

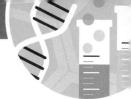

Antibiotics

You need to know how **antibiotics** can be used to treat some diseases.

2 Antibiotics: key facts

- Antibiotics are a group of drugs that kill bacteria.
- Antibiotics work by inhibiting cell processes in the bacteria but not in the host organism.
- Specific bacteria should be treated using specific antibiotics but antibiotics do not destroy viruses.
- Since their discovery, antibiotics have significantly reduced deaths from infectious bacterial diseases.
- However, many bacteria are now developing strains which are resistant to antibiotics. This has serious implications for treating bacterial diseases.

10 Bacterial resistance

Bacteria can develop resistance to antibiotics by natural selection (page 26).

- Some bacteria have mutations which make them resistant to an antibiotic.
- Bacteria that are susceptible to the antibiotic get killed.
- Bacteria that are resistant to the antibiotic survive and reproduce rapidly.
- Soon all the surviving bacteria are resistant to the antibiotic.
- Resistant strains can then spread because people are not immune to them and there are no effective treatments.

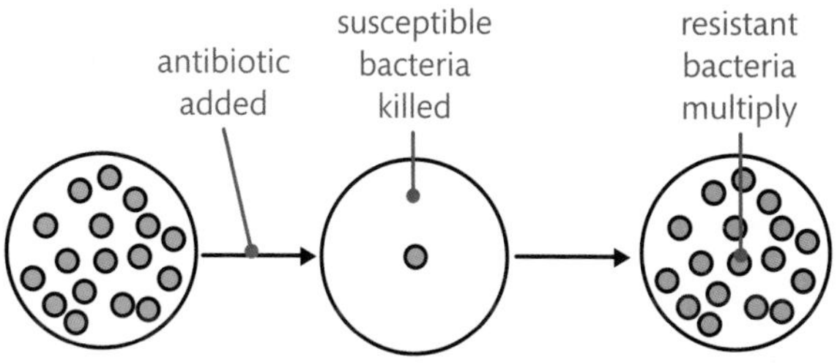

bacteria susceptible to antibiotic

bacteria resistant to antibiotic

Figure 1 Bacteria developing resistance to an antibiotic

5 Worked example — Grade 5

Penicillin was the first antibiotic to be discovered.
The discovery was made by Alexander Fleming.
Fleming was growing bacteria in a Petri dish.
The Petri dish was contaminated by the mould *Penicillium*.
Look at Fleming's Petri dish in **Figure 2**. Suggest an explanation of how looking at this Petri dish led to Fleming discovering penicillin. **[3 marks]**

Fleming noticed that no bacteria were growing near the mould. He realised that the mould must be producing a substance that killed bacteria. He isolated the substance which is called penicillin. This substance became the first antibiotic.

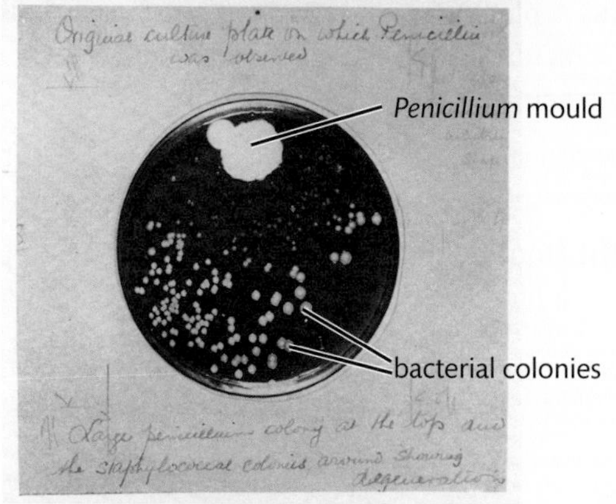

Figure 2 Fleming's Petri dish

10 Exam-style practice — Grade 5

1. Antibiotics do not kill viruses. Suggest an explanation why. **[2 marks]**
2. Describe how antibiotic resistance develops in bacteria. **[4 marks]**
3. Before prescribing an antibiotic, a doctor will often take a sample from the patient so the bacteria causing the illness can be identified. Explain the advantage of identifying the type of bacteria. **[2 marks]**

Development of drugs

You need to know how medicinal drugs are developed.

⑩ Development of medicinal drugs

Research & development 3–6 years	Pre-clinical studies 1 year	Clinical trials 4–7 years	Review & approval 1–2 years
This is when potential new drugs are made or discovered.	This is when the drug is tested in the laboratory.	This is when the drug is tested on healthy human volunteers, starting with very low doses for toxicity and efficacy.	This is when new drugs are approved to be used on patients.
Scientists first decide what drugs are needed.	In vitro ('in glass') tests on cells and tissues (the drug is tested in Petri dishes and test tubes).	**Phase 1** It is tested on about 50 people to check for side effects and to see how quickly the body breaks down the drug.	If the drug is effective, it is sent to regulating bodies for approval.
Scientists then look for compounds that might do the job they are looking for.	Testing in animals	**Phase 2** It is tested on about 200 patients with the condition.	The governing body fast tracks drugs that are desperately needed. If the benefits outweigh the risks, it is approved.
Thousands of chemical compounds are then tested or modified to improve their action.	Testing in mammals	**Phase 3** If the drug is found to be safe, it is tested on about 2000 people to see how well the drug works and its optimum dose.	When the drug is available for doctors to use it is monitored for side effects indefinitely.

⑤ Worked example　　Grade 5

New drugs are tested using placebos and double blind trials.

(a) A placebo is designed to appear exactly the same as the drug itself, but it does **not** contain any of the actual drug. Suggest an explanation why some patients in a drugs trial are given a placebo instead of the actual drug. **[2 marks]**

The placebo acts as a 'control'. It is used to check if any effects are caused by the drug or by something else.

(b) Double blind trials are when neither the patient nor the doctor knows if they are getting the drug or a placebo. Suggest an explanation why double blind trials are used. **[2 marks]**

To avoid any bias by either the patient or the doctor if they know whether or not the actual drug is being used.

② Working scientifically

All the results from testing and trialling new drugs are published. Other scientists then peer review the data.

The other scientists check the results and the theories suggested. They may also carry out further tests to check the data provided is correct.

Peer review in this way helps to ensure that new drugs are as safe and effective as possible.

⑩ Exam-style practice　　Grade 5

❶ Explain what is meant by peer review. **[2 marks]**

❷ Give the approximate time needed for a new medical drug to be developed. **[1 mark]**

❸ Describe the differences between clinical trials and pre-clinical trials in the development of a new medicine, including the purposes of each. **[4 marks]**

  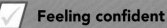

Non-communicable diseases

You need to know that many non-communicable diseases are caused by the interaction of a number of **risk factors**. (Non-communicable diseases cannot be passed on from one person to another – see page 31.)

 10 Non-communicable diseases

Many non-communicable diseases are caused by the interaction of different factors.

Cardiovascular disease

This is the general name for conditions affecting the heart or blood vessels, such as heart attacks or strokes. It is one of the main causes of death in the UK. It is common because there are so many risk factors:

- high blood pressure
- smoking
- high blood cholesterol levels
- diabetes
- lack of exercise
- being overweight
- genetic factors
- unhealthy diet.

Risk factors interact to increase the risk of cardiovascular disease. The chances of getting coronary heart disease increase dramatically for someone who smokes, drinks heavily, is obese and takes little exercise.

Liver disease

Interacting risk factors include:

- genetic factors
- drinking alcohol
- drug abuse
- diabetes
- being overweight.

Lung disease

Interacting risk factors include:

- genetic factors
- smoking
- air pollution.

Cancer

Cancer is caused by changes to the genes that control cell growth, leading to uncontrolled cell division and tissue growth.

 See page 15 for more about cancer.

Some people are genetically more at risk of developing cancer, but the risk is also increased by:

- sunbathing – risk factor for skin cancer
- smoking – risk factor for lung cancer
- heavy drinking – risk factor for liver and other cancers
- working with carcinogenic (cancer-causing) materials such as asbestos – risk factor for lung and other cancers
- living in unventilated buildings in areas where radioactive radon is released from the ground.

Nutritional diseases

Unhealthy diets increase the risk or severity of many diseases, such as cardiovascular disease. Unhealthy diets may consist of eating too much or too little in total, or too much or too little of particular types of food. For example:

- scurvy is caused by a lack of vitamin C
- anaemia is caused by a lack of iron
- rickets is caused by a lack of vitamin D or calcium.

 5 Worked example **Grade 7**

Although scientists have found cures for many diseases, it has not been possible so far to find cures for all cancers. Suggest an explanation of why it is especially difficult to find cures for cancer. **[3 marks]**

There are many different types of cancer, and there may be many different and interacting risk factors for each type. Unlike communicable diseases, most cancers are not caused by pathogens so cannot be prevented with immunisations nor treated with medicines like antibiotics.

10 Exam-style practice **Grades 4–5**

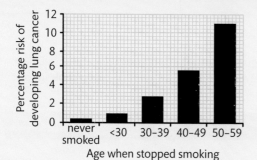

Figure 1 A chart showing the risk of cancer for people who stop smoking

Look at **Figure 1**.

(a) Explain what is meant by <30 on the x-axis. **[1 mark]**

(b) Give **two** conclusions that can be made from the data shown by the graph. **[2 marks]**

(c) Give the risk of getting cancer for people who have:

(i) never smoked **[1 mark]**

(ii) stopped smoking at the age of 45 years. **[1 mark]**

Effects of lifestyle

You need to know how lifestyle factors, acting at local, national and global levels, can affect whether or not people develop some non-communicable diseases.

(5) Risk factors

- Smokers are more likely to develop lung cancer and cardiovascular diseases.
- Heavy alcohol drinkers are more likely to suffer from cirrhosis of the liver.
- Smoking and drinking during pregnancy increases the risk of growth and development impairments in embryos.
- Obese people are more likely to develop Type 2 diabetes.
- Lack of exercise and eating too many fatty foods can lead to malnutrition, obesity and coronary heart disease.

These lifestyle risk factors are having a global impact, affecting people in many different countries.

(2) Measuring obesity

BMI (Body Mass Index) is a measure of whether a person is a healthy weight for their height. It is calculated using the formula:

$$BMI = \frac{mass\ in\ kg}{(height\ in\ m)^2}$$

However, factors other than weight and height can affect a person's BMI and anyone with any concerns should consult their doctor.

Another indication of whether a person is a healthy weight is to compare measurements around their waist and hips. Generally, the hips measurement should be greater than the waist measurement.

(5) Implications

Impact of lifestyle
Having a lifestyle that includes many risk factors may not only affect an individual, but their family and the wider community as well.

Cost implications
Non-communicable diseases which are contributed to by lifestyle factors also affect the government's spending on the National Health Service.

(5) Worked example   Grade 4

1 (a) A man has a height of 1.75 m and a mass of 80.5 kg. Calculate his BMI. **[2 marks]**

$$BMI = \frac{mass\ in\ kg}{(height\ in\ m)^2} = \frac{80.5}{1.75^2} = 26.3$$

> Make sure the figures used are in kg for mass and in m for height.

(b) The same man has a waist measurement of 990 mm and a hip measurement of 1.02 m. Calculate his waist : hip ratio. Give your answer to two decimal places. **[2 marks]**

$$waist : hip\ ratio = 0.99 : 1.02 = \frac{0.99}{1.02} : 1 = 0.97 : 1$$

> For a ratio it does not matter what units you use as long as they are the same unit. In this case both figures are in m.

2 Look at **Figure 1**.

(a) State what conclusion can be made from the data. **[1 mark]**

There is a positive correlation between blood cholesterol levels and Body Mass Index.

(b) Name **one** type of non-communicable disease that high body mass index and high blood cholesterol could lead to. **[1 mark]**

Heart disease

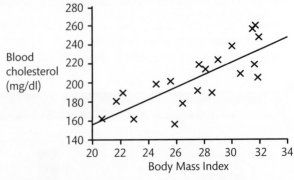

Figure 1 Scatter diagram showing the correlation between body mass index and blood cholesterol levels

(10) Exam-style practice   Grades 4–5

1 Suggest why BMI measurements may **not** be a good indicator of healthy weight in a teenager. **[2 marks]**

2 Describe how poor diet affects health. **[2 marks]**

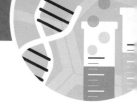

Cardiovascular disease

You need to know how different diseases of the cardiovascular system can be treated by lifestyle changes, life-long medication or surgery.

5 Diseases of the cardiovascular system

Blocked coronary arteries

The coronary arteries supply the heart muscle with blood containing oxygen and glucose.

The build-up of fatty deposits, such as cholesterol, in the coronary arteries can narrow or even block them, starving the heart muscle of oxygen. This can cause a heart attack. A heart attack can also occur when the supply of blood to the heart is suddenly blocked, for example by a blood clot. Heart attacks are life threatening because they can seriously damage the heart muscle or cause it to die from lack of oxygen.

Faulty valves

Heart valves prevent blood from flowing backwards when the heart pumps blood. Sometimes the valves in the heart become faulty, preventing the valve from opening fully, or the valve may develop a leak. This makes it harder for the heart to pump blood around the body.

Heart failure

Heart failure occurs when the heart is unable to pump blood around the body properly.

Go to page 61 for more about the heart.

5 Treatment

Treatments for cardiovascular disease can include life-long medication, surgical procedures and lifestyle changes.

Treating blocked coronary arteries

- Stents can be inserted into arteries to keep them open.
- Drugs such as statins can be used to lower the blood cholesterol. Other drugs such as warfarin can be used to reduce the chances of blood clots. Patients may need to take such drugs for the rest of their lives.
- Lifestyle changes such as exercising more or eating less fatty food can help to lower blood cholesterol, and reduce the risk of blood clots forming.

Treating faulty valves

- Biological or mechanical valves can replace faulty ones.

Treating heart failure

- Heart or heart and lung transplants can be performed.
- If the damage is extensive, the whole heart can be replaced with an artificial heart. These are sometimes used to keep patients alive while they are waiting for a heart transplant or to allow the heart to rest to help it recover.

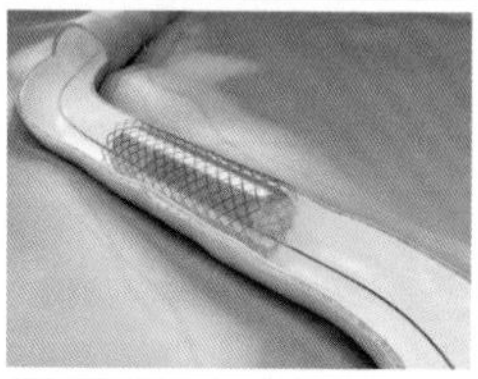

Figure 1 A stent used to keep an artery open

2 Worked example — Grade 6

Warfarin and aspirin are two drugs that have a similar effectiveness in reducing blood clot formation. This reduces the risk of heart attacks and strokes (a lack of blood to the brain). However, both drugs can also cause side effects such as internal bleeding. Warfarin is better than aspirin at reducing the risk of a stroke, although the risk of major bleeding is higher with warfarin.

A doctor has a patient who is at a high risk of a stroke because of other risk factors. The doctor is considering prescribing the patient warfarin or aspirin. Evaluate the choices. **[2 marks]**

Although both drugs can cause side effects, for this patient, the dangers of side effects are outweighed by the risk of a stroke, so one of the drugs should be prescribed. In this case, warfarin is probably the best choice. Although there is more risk of internal bleeding with warfarin, the patient is already at risk of a stroke and warfarin is better at reducing that risk.

5 Working scientifically

Evaluation of treatments

- Heart surgery is risky and not all surgery is successful.
- Sometimes the patient's body rejects the new heart or valve.
- Artificial hearts need a source of power, such as batteries, to make them work.
- Long-term treatment using drugs such as statins may have unwanted side effects in some people.
- Mechanical replacement valves can wear out.

5 Exam-style practice — Grades 5–6

1 'No surgery is 100 per cent safe.' Explain what this statement means. **[2 marks]**

2 Give **two** treatments for a blocked artery. **[2 marks]**

Photosynthesis

You need to understand the process of **photosynthesis**.

 Photosynthesis ✓

During the process of photosynthesis, plants and algae use energy from sunlight to build large complex organic molecules from simple inorganic ones. Cells in green leaves contain small structures called chloroplasts. Chloroplasts contain **chlorophyll**, a green pigment that absorbs the energy from sunlight. This energy is needed for photosynthesis.

Photosynthesis is an **endothermic reaction**. This means that it absorbs energy.

The chemical equation for photosynthesis

Water is absorbed by root hair cells. Go to page 47 for more about how this happens.

Glucose is used to make lots of other substances such as sucrose. Go to page 47 for more about how sucrose is transported around the plant.

$$\text{carbon dioxide} + \text{water} \xrightarrow[\text{chlorophyll in green leaves}]{\text{light from the Sun}} \text{glucose} + \text{oxygen}$$

$$6CO_2 + 6H_2O \xrightarrow[\text{chlorophyll in green leaves}]{\text{light from the Sun}} C_6H_{12}O_6 + 6O_2$$

Carbon dioxide diffuses from the air into the leaf cells. Oxygen diffuses from the cells into the air. Go to page 10 to revise diffusion.

Light energy is absorbed by chloroplasts in plant cells.

Go to page 3 to revise the structure of plant cells.

 Importance of photosynthesis ✓

Photosynthetic organisms, such as plants and algae, are the main producers of food on the planet. This food is used to make not only plants and algae grow; it is also used by all the other organisms, such as animals, in the food chains that begin with plants and algae. The mass of material in living organisms is known as **biomass**. Most biomass on Earth is therefore produced by photosynthesis.

Figure 1 Algae have a simpler structure than plants but photosynthesise in the same way.

 Worked example | Grades 5–7 ✓

1 Most chloroplasts are found in cells towards the upper surface of leaves. Suggest an explanation why. **[2 marks]**

More light reaches the upper surface of leaves, enabling more photosynthesis to take place.

Read more about respiration on page 62.

2 Explain how animals and plants are interdependent. Use the processes of respiration and photosynthesis in your answer. **[2 marks]**

Through photosynthesis plants provide animals with oxygen and food. In respiration animals provide plants with carbon dioxide.

3 Photosynthesis is an endothermic reaction. State what is meant by the term 'endothermic'. **[1 mark]**

It is a reaction that takes in energy.

 Exam-style practice | Grade 7 ✓

1 A teacher tells a student that 'almost all life on Earth depends on photosynthesis'. Explain the teacher's statement. **[2 marks]**

2 Most animals have to move around to find their food. However, most plants stay in one place. Suggest an explanation for this difference. **[2 marks]**

 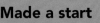

Rate of photosynthesis

The rate of photosynthesis is determined by three factors: temperature, light intensity and carbon dioxide concentration. You need to know how these factors affect the rate of photosynthesis.

 Graphs of limiting factors

Limiting factors are environmental conditions that have an impact on the rate of a process. There are three factors that affect the rate of photosynthesis.

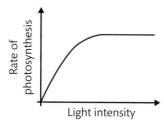 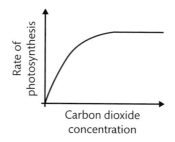 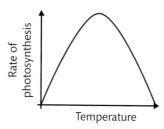

Figure 1 Graphs showing limiting factors

When light levels are low, the rate of photosynthesis will be slow as it is limited by the lack of light. As light intensity increases, the rate of photosynthesis increases until it reaches an optimum level when any further increase in light intensity has no effect. As light cannot be a limiting factor when at a high intensity, there must be another factor affecting the rate of photosynthesis.

Carbon dioxide is a common limiting factor affecting the rate of photosynthesis because it is at a low level in the atmosphere. Plants cannot photosynthesise without carbon dioxide. The level of carbon dioxide can be increased if plants are grown in a greenhouse.

As temperature increases, the rate of photosynthesis increases until it reaches a maximum and then begins to decrease until it reaches zero. This is because at high temperatures the enzymes that control photosynthesis are denatured.

 Worked example | **Grade 5**

Figure 2 The apparatus shown can be used to measure the rate of photosynthesis in pondweed.

1 Describe how the apparatus in **Figure 2** can be used to work out the rate of photosynthesis. Give a reason for your answer. **[2 marks]**

Count the bubbles over a certain period of time. Pondweed gives off bubbles of oxygen as it photosynthesises.

2 A student wants to investigate the effect of carbon dioxide on the rate of photosynthesis. Describe how they could do this. **[2 marks]**

Dissolve different amounts of sodium hydrogencarbonate in the water to vary the concentration of carbon dioxide.

Working scientifically

Commercial growers can use knowledge of limiting factors to improve yields by raising temperature, carbon dioxide and light levels, although doing so costs money and they must find a balance between maximising photosynthesis and making a profit.

 Exam-style practice | **Grade 7**

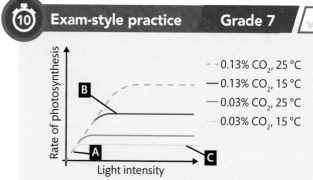

Figure 3 The effect of limiting factors on growing tomatoes in a greenhouse

Use **Figure 3** to answer the following questions.

(a) Identify the **three** limiting factors shown on the graph. **[3 marks]**

(b) Name the limiting factor at point A on the graph. Explain your answer. **[2 marks]**

(c) Name the limiting factor at point B on the graph. Explain your answer. **[2 marks]**

(d) Identify the factor that is definitely **not** limiting at point C. **[1 mark]**

Practical: Photosynthesis

You need to know how to investigate the effect of light intensity on the rate of photosynthesis.

Method

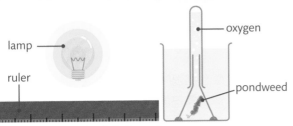

Figure 1 Investigating light intensity

1 Change the light intensity by altering the distance of the lamp from the pondweed.

2 Record the distance and the number of bubbles counted in one minute in a table.

Worked example — Grades 5–8

The rate of photosynthesis is measured by counting the number of bubbles given off by pondweed each minute.

Distance of pondweed from lamp (cm)	Rate of photosynthesis (bubbles/minute)
10	63
20	16
30	
40	4
50	3

(a) Look at the table. Calculate an estimate for the missing number. You need to use the inverse square law. Show your working. **[3 marks]**

Increasing distance from 10 cm to 30 cm (by a factor of 3), changes the intensity by a factor of $\frac{1}{3^2} = \frac{1}{9}$

Number of bubbles is directly related to intensity, so the estimate for number of bubbles $= \frac{1}{9} \times 63 = 7$ bubbles when lamp is at 30 cm from pondweed.

(b) Explain how the accuracy of the results could be improved. **[2 marks]**

Repeat the measurements several times and calculate the means.

(c) A student repeated the experiment but placed a sheet of glass between the beaker and the lamp. The glass absorbed the heat from the lamp. Suggest a reason why the student did this. **[1 mark]**

To control the temperature.

Working scientifically

This practical investigates the effect of light intensity on the rate of photosynthesis. This means that light intensity is the **independent variable**.

The rate of photosynthesis is determined by counting oxygen bubbles in a given period of time. This is the **dependent variable**.

Key experimental skills

☑ Use of correct apparatus to record measurements accurately.

☑ Safe use of hot devices, such as a lamp.

☑ Consider ethical issues by removing any small invertebrates on the pondweed before starting the investigation.

☑ Measure rate of photosynthesis by counting oxygen bubbles.

Inverse square law

Light intensity is proportional to the inverse square of the distance.

$$\text{intensity} \propto \frac{1}{\text{distance}^2}$$

If you double the distance between the lamp and the plant, the light intensity is reduced by one-quarter.

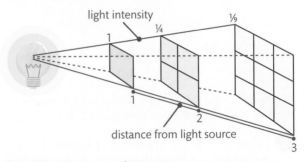

Figure 2 Inverse square law

The rate of photosynthesis is **directly proportional** to light intensity, but **inversely proportional** to the square of the distance from the light source.

Exam-style practice — Grade 7

State and explain a more accurate method of measuring the gas produced than counting bubbles. **[2 marks]**

Made a start ☑ Feeling confident ☑ Exam ready ☑

Specialised plant cells

You need to know about the structural adaptations of specialised plant cells that enable them to transport substances, including food molecules, by translocation.

 Specialised plant cells ✓

You need to know how the following plant cells are specialised to carry out a particular function.

Go to page 4 for specialised animal cells.

Xylem is made of columns of dead cells with **lignified** walls (contain lignin) which transport water and minerals up from the roots to the rest of the plant.

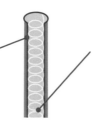

Lignin walls provide strength and support – pits in the walls allow water and mineral ions to move in and out of the xylem.

A hollow lumen (space) enables water and mineral ions to flow easily through the plant.

Root hair cells absorb water and mineral ions from the soil.

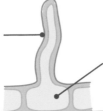

The cell has a large surface area to maximise osmosis (see page 11).

Cytoplasm contains a lot of mitochondria which release energy to increase the rate of active transport (see page 13) of mineral ions.

Phloem is made of living cells which transport dissolved sucrose (sugar) from the leaves and storage regions to the other parts of the plant where it is used for growth or is stored.

Holes in the end walls allow solutions to move from cell to cell.

Some cells contain many mitochondria for active transport.

Figure 1 Specialised plant cells

 Transport in plants ✓

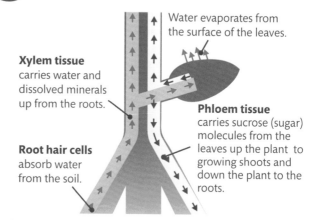

Water evaporates from the surface of the leaves.

Xylem tissue carries water and dissolved minerals up from the roots.

Phloem tissue carries sucrose (sugar) molecules from the leaves up the plant to growing shoots and down the plant to the roots.

Root hair cells absorb water from the soil.

Figure 2 Plant tissues involved in the transport of substances

Water and mineral ions move through plants, through **xylem** tissue, by a process called **transpiration**.

There is more about this on page 48.

Food moves through plants by a different process, called **translocation**. This occurs in **phloem** tissue. Food can move from leaves, where glucose sugar has been made by photosynthesis, to places where it is stored, for example as starch in the roots. It can also be moved to growing regions such as new shoots or buds. The food is transported as **sucrose** (another type of sugar) dissolved in cell sap, which moves from one phloem cell to the next.

 Worked example Grade 6 ✓

Compare and contrast xylem tissue and phloem tissue. **[4 marks]**

The similarities are that both xylem and phloem are specialised cells which transport substances through plants. The differences are that xylem is made of dead cells and transports water and mineral ions from the roots up the plant, whereas phloem is made of living cells which transport sucrose up and down the plant.

 Exam-style practice Grades 5–6 ✓

1 Explain **two** adaptations a root hair cell has to allow it to function efficiently. **[4 marks]**

2 Describe the differences between translocation and transpiration. **[4 marks]**

Transport in plants

You need to know how water and mineral ions move through a plant by transpiration.

 Transpiration

Transpiration is the movement of water through a plant from the roots to the leaves. Water evaporates from the surface of cells inside the leaves and diffuses out through open pores called **stomata**. This causes more water to be drawn upwards against gravity through **xylem** cells in the plant. Water is absorbed from the soil into root hair cells by osmosis.

As water moves up through the plant by transpiration, it carries with it dissolved mineral ions that were also absorbed from the soil by root hair cells. The movement of water is called the **transpiration stream**. This is shown in **Figure 1**.

Go to page 47 to revise root hair cells and xylem.

 Stomata

Stomata (singular: **stoma**) are small pores, found mostly on the underside of leaves, formed by specialised cells called **guard cells**. Guard cells can swell up (by absorbing water by osmosis) which opens the stoma. At other times, the guard cells shrink slightly (because of losing water by osmosis) which closes the stoma. Stomata usually open during the daytime to allow carbon dioxide and oxygen to diffuse in and out of the leaf during photosynthesis.

The stomata also control the loss of water through transpiration. Although transpiration is important, for example for moving mineral ions through a plant, losing too much water is harmful if plants cannot readily replace it. Since plants cannot photosynthesise at night, the guard cells close the stomata at night to prevent water from evaporating from the leaf. Stomata can also close during the day if the plant is in danger of dehydrating.

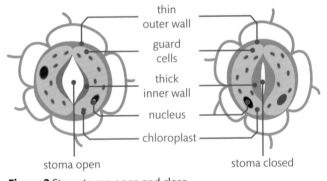

thin outer wall
guard cells
thick inner wall
nucleus
chloroplast
stoma open
stoma closed

Figure 2 Stomata can open and close

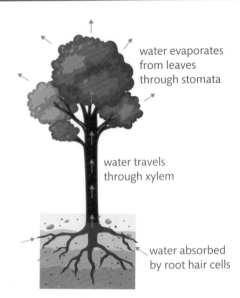

water evaporates from leaves through stomata

water travels through xylem

water absorbed by root hair cells

Figure 1 The transpiration stream

 **Worked example** **Grade 7**

1 Suggest **one** explanation why stomata are commonly found on the underside of leaves. **[3 marks]**

The underside of a leaf is shaded and so cooler than the upper surface. This means transpiration occurs more slowly, reducing water loss.

2 The leaves of water lilies float on the surface. Unlike most plants, their stomata are on the upper surface of their leaves. Suggest a reason why. **[2 marks]**

So the leaves can exchange carbon dioxide and oxygen with the air, because the lower surface is in the water.

 Exam-style practice **Grade 5**

Describe the passage of water through plants from the root hair cells to the stomata. **[3 marks]**

Made a start | Feeling confident | Exam ready

Water uptake in plants

You need to know how different environmental factors can affect the rate of transpiration.

 Factors affecting transpiration

Different environmental factors affect the rate of transpiration and therefore the rate of water uptake by a plant.

- **Temperature** – as temperature increases, water molecules have more kinetic energy. This means evaporation from the leaves increase, so transpiration is faster in higher temperatures.

- **Air movement** – as wind speed increases, the water molecules which have just left the stomata get blown away. This maintains a greater concentration gradient so water molecules diffuse out of the leaves more rapidly, increasing the rate of transpiration.

- **Light intensity** – at night, the guard cells close the stomata to retain valuable water resources, so transpiration stops. In bright light, the stomata open wider to allow more carbon dioxide to enter the leaf for photosynthesis, so the rate of transpiration increases.

Measuring the rate of transpiration

The rate of transpiration can be measured by measuring the rate of water loss from a plant, or the rate of water uptake.

One way to measure the rate of water loss is by weighing a plant in a pot over a period of time. If the soil is covered so water can only evaporate from the leaves, any decrease in mass must be due to transpiration.

One way to measure the rate of water uptake is to use a potometer such as that shown in **Figure 1**. How quickly the air bubble moves is a measure of the rate of water uptake.

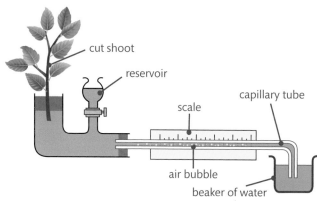

Figure 1 A potometer

 Worked example — **Grade 8**

1 The graph shows how the rate of transpiration in a plant changes as light intensity increases.

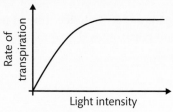

Explain the shape of the graph. **[3 marks]**

The graph shows that the rate of transpiration increases with light intensity until it reaches a

maximum. This is because the stomata open wider at greater light intensities, up to a maximum width.

2 A student investigates the uptake of water using a potometer like that shown in **Figure 1**. The water uptake is measured by recording the time taken for a bubble to move a set distance in the capillary tube. The bubble moves 34 mm in 15 minutes. Calculate the rate of water uptake. Give your answer in mm/minute. **[2 marks]**

$$\text{rate of water uptake} = \frac{\text{distance moved by bubble}}{\text{time}}$$

$$\frac{34}{15} = 2.3 \text{ mm/minute}$$

 Exam-style practice — **Grade 6**

1 Describe the kind of weather in which transpiration takes place most quickly. **[3 marks]**

2 A student measures transpiration using a potometer. The bubble moves 27 mm in 10 minutes. Calculate the rate of water uptake in cm/hour. **[3 marks]**

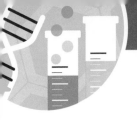

Human endocrine system

You need to know how the release and distribution of hormones is controlled by the human endocrine system.

10 Hormones

Hormones are sometimes called chemical messengers. They are secreted by **endocrine glands**, which release hormones directly into the blood. The blood carries the hormone to a target organ where the hormone causes an effect. The effects of the hormone system are much slower than the nervous system as it takes time for hormones to be transported around the body by the blood. However, the effects of a hormone last longer than those of an impulse sent by the nervous system.

There is more about adrenalin and thyroxine on page 51.

There is more about hormones produced by the ovaries and pituitary on page 52.

There is more about insulin and glucagon on page 55.

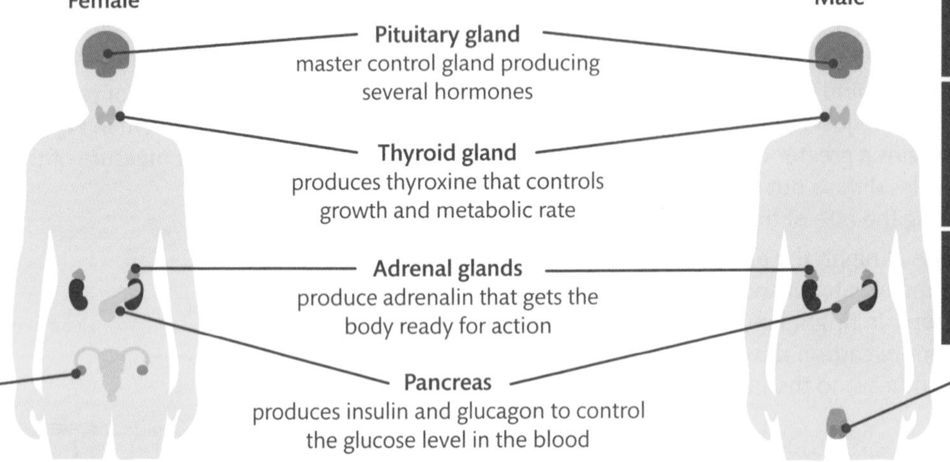
Female
Male
Pituitary gland
master control gland producing several hormones
Thyroid gland
produces thyroxine that controls growth and metabolic rate
Adrenal glands
produce adrenalin that gets the body ready for action
Pancreas
produces insulin and glucagon to control the glucose level in the blood
Ovaries
control female sexual characteristics
Testes
control male sexual characteristics

Figure 1 The endocrine (hormone) glands

The pituitary gland

The **pituitary gland** is located in the brain and is sometimes called the master gland. It secretes several different hormones.

Some of these hormones control other hormonal glands by stimulating the gland to release its own hormone. It does this as the concentration of the hormone from the gland begins to fall.

This system that involves two different hormones controlling each other is an example of **negative feedback**.

There is more about negative feedback on page 51.

5 Worked example — Grade 5

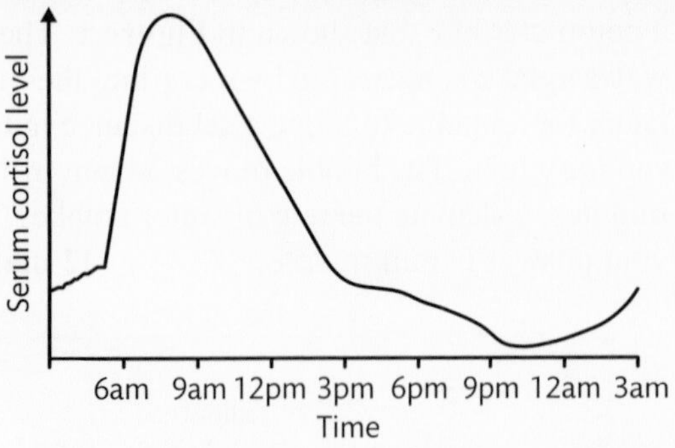
Serum cortisol level
6am
9am
12pm
3pm
6pm
9pm
12am
3am
Time

Figure 2 Graph showing the level of serum cortisol (a hormone) in the blood

1. Look at **Figure 2**. State the time of day when the serum cortisol level is at its highest and its lowest. **[1 mark]**

Highest: 8 am
Lowest: 10 pm

2. The effects of hormones are longer lasting than the effects of nerve impulses. Explain why. **[2 marks]**

Hormones are substances which remain in the blood until they are eventually broken down, whereas nerve impulses are electrical impulses which do not last long.

5 Exam-style practice — Grades 4–5

1. Name the gland which produces the hormone insulin. **[1 mark]**
2. Describe what is meant by a hormone. **[3 marks]**

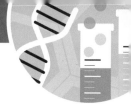

Adrenalin and thyroxine

You need to know how negative feedback works and how it controls hormone levels within the body.

5 Negative feedback

Negative feedback happens where an output of a process feeds back into the system to reverse changes and bring them back to a set level.

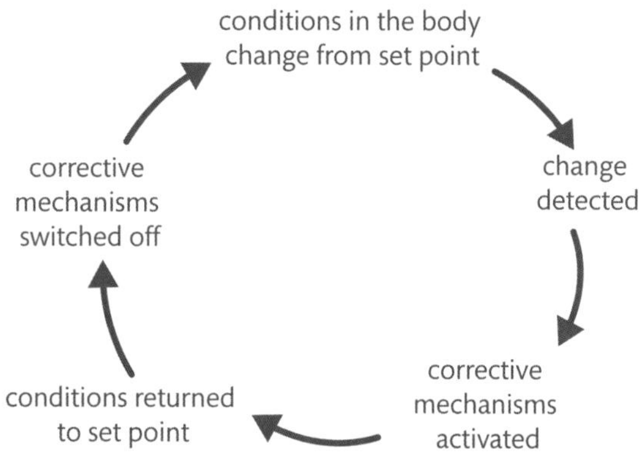

Figure 1 A negative feedback system

5 Thyroxine

Thyroxine is a hormone produced in the thyroid gland. It does several different jobs:

- It controls metabolic rate.
- It plays an important role in growth and development.

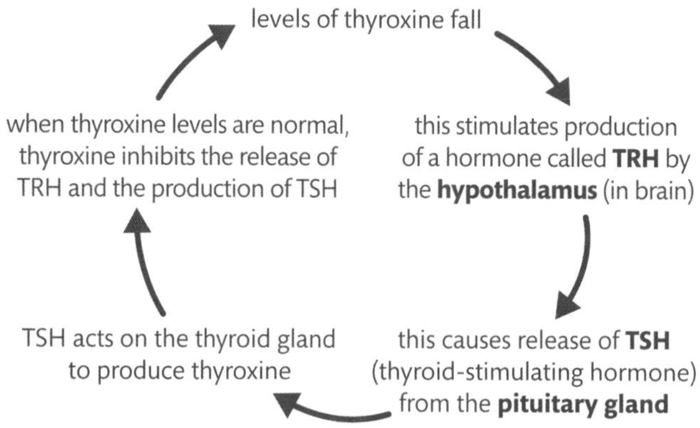

Figure 2 Thyroxine levels are controlled by negative feedback.

5 Adrenalin

Adrenalin is sometimes called the fight, flight or fright hormone. It is the hormone that causes the feeling of 'butterflies in your stomach' when you are frightened.

Adrenalin prepares the body for rapid action. It:

- increases the heart rate, which also increases the blood pressure and therefore the rate of blood flow, pumping blood containing oxygen and glucose more rapidly to the brain and muscle cells
- increases the level of sugar in the blood by stimulating the liver to change stored glycogen (see page 55) into glucose
- diverts blood from the gut to the muscles
- increases sweating
- dilates the pupils of the eyes.

10 Worked example — Grade 7

1 Tomatoes can be grown in a greenhouse. To keep the greenhouse at a constant temperature, farmers use a thermostatic heater and windows that automatically open and close. The thermostat controls the heater and the windows to maintain a constant temperature using negative feedback.
Explain how this works. **[4 marks]**

When the temperature drops, the thermostat turns the heater on and closes the windows. This causes the temperature to rise. When the temperature rises too much the thermostat turns the heater off and opens the windows, making the temperature fall.

2 Explain why adrenalin increases heart rate. **[2 marks]**

Adrenalin increases the heart rate so blood containing oxygen and glucose is transported to the brain and muscles more quickly.

5 Exam-style practice — Grade 6

1 Explain why thyroxine is needed by the body. **[2 marks]**

2 Explain what is meant by negative feedback. **[2 marks]**

Hormones in reproduction

During puberty, hormones cause secondary sexual characteristics to develop. These include the production of sperm in males and the beginning of the menstrual cycle in females. You need to know the roles of different hormones in the menstrual cycle.

The menstrual cycle

The **menstrual cycle** is a recurring process in which the uterus lining is prepared for pregnancy. There are several hormones involved in this cycle.

Follicle stimulating hormone (FSH) is secreted by the pituitary gland. It stimulates the ovaries to release oestrogen and it causes an egg to mature.

Oestrogen is secreted by the ovaries. It affects the pituitary gland where it inhibits the production of FSH, causing only one egg to mature during each monthly cycle. It stimulates the pituitary gland to release **luteinising hormone (LH)**, which triggers **ovulation**, the release of the mature egg from the ovary.

Progesterone builds up ('repairs') and maintains the uterus lining during the middle part of the cycle and pregnancy. The uterus lining is important during pregnancy because this is where the fertilised egg develops and grows. During pregnancy, progesterone also inhibits production of FSH and LH to prevent the release of new eggs at this time.

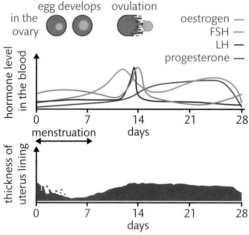

Figure 1 Changes during the menstrual cycle

Worked example — Grade 8

During puberty, eggs begin to mature in the ovaries. One egg is released about every 28 days. This is called ovulation. The whole 28-day cycle is called the menstrual cycle. Hormones play an important part in the menstrual cycle.

Describe the roles of the hormones oestrogen, progesterone, and the pituitary hormones FSH and LH.　**[4 marks]**

Oestrogen repairs and thickens the lining of the uterus.

Progesterone maintains the wall of the uterus and prevents menstruation from starting.

FSH stimulates the production of an egg in an ovary.

LH triggers ovulation, causing the egg to be released from an ovary ready for fertilisation.

Exam-style practice — Grades 7–8

1 Explain how hormonal control ensures that usually only one egg is released every 28 days.　**[2 marks]**

2 Describe **one** example of negative feedback in the hormones involved with the menstrual cycle.　**[2 marks]**

3 Menstruation, a 'period', is the monthly breakdown of the uterus lining. It stops during pregnancy.
Suggest an explanation of which hormone prevents menstruation from happening during pregnancy.　**[2 marks]**

Contraception

You need to know how hormonal and barrier methods of contraception can be used to prevent pregnancy.

(5) Methods of contraception

Hormonal

- Oral contraceptives (the 'pill') contain the hormones oestrogen or progesterone or a combination of both. These hormones inhibit FSH production and therefore stop eggs maturing and being released ready for fertilisation. Oral contraceptives are very effective if taken correctly. Some forms of the pill can lead to side effects such as weight gain or mood changes.
- Injections, skin patches or implants contain slow release oestrogen or progesterone or both to prevent the maturation and release of eggs for months or years.

Barrier

- Methods such as the condom and diaphragm act as a physical barrier between the sperm and egg. Condoms are easy to use, but can sometimes tear or come off. Diaphragms have to be inserted just before sex and left in place afterwards for several hours.

(5) Working scientifically

Ethics

There are some questions that science can answer, such as: 'How can you stop a sperm fertilising an egg?'

There are some questions that science cannot answer, such as: 'When should we stop a sperm from fertilising an egg?'

Individuals have to decide whether or not to use contraception to prevent pregnancy. They also have to decide which methods of contraception to use.

Science can provide data to help you decide which methods are the most reliable, and understand the advantages and disadvantages of each method.

However, some people think that contraception is wrong.

Each person should evaluate personal, social, economic and religious implications, and make a decision about contraception based on evidence and argument.

(5) Worked example — Grade 6

The table summarises four different methods of contraception.

	The contraceptive pill	Diaphragm	Patch	Condom
Reliability	very reliable	reliable	very reliable	reliable
Level of risk to health	some risk	little risk	some risk	little risk
Are effects reversible?	reversible	reversible	reversible	reversible

A young, newly married couple want children but decide to postpone having them for ten years.

Evaluate the different methods of contraception, explaining if one method is best for the couple. **[4 marks]**

Any of the methods could be suitable because they are all reversible and so the couple will still be able to have children in the future. The contraceptive pill and patch are the most reliable, so may be best for the couple, although they lead to higher health risks than the diaphragm and condom. The diaphragm and condom have lower health risks but might not be as reliable.

Exam focus

Always read exam questions carefully. This question asks you to 'evaluate', which means you should explain the advantages and disadvantages of each method, before coming to a final decision if possible.

(10) Exam-style practice — Grade 6

1. Science can help people decide which method of contraception to use. Explain how science can help. **[2 marks]**

2. When deciding whether to use contraception, suggest **two** questions that science **cannot** answer. **[2 marks]**

 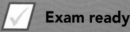

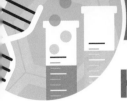

Hormones to treat infertility

You need to know how reproductive hormones can be used to treat **infertility** (where it is not possible to conceive a child naturally) – these methods are examples of **Assisted Reproductive Technology (ART)**.

5 Fertility treatments

Some women have difficulty releasing eggs from their ovaries. This means they might not be able to become pregnant naturally.

Some fertility drugs contain extra FSH and LH (see page 52) to increase the production and release of eggs (ovulation). **Clomifene** is another fertility drug that stimulates ovulation. Clomifene therapy is used especially for women who do not ovulate at all.

In vitro fertilisation

Some women produce eggs but still cannot become pregnant, perhaps because there are problems with the man's sperm, or the tubes carrying the eggs (oviducts) are blocked.

In vitro fertilisation (**IVF**) is sometimes used to help these women become pregnant. *In vitro* means 'in glass'. The woman's eggs are fertilised in a Petri dish before being placed back into her uterus to develop.

To increase the chances of success with IVF, fertility drugs are used to make the woman's ovaries release more eggs than usual.

5 IVF process

1. The woman is injected with a fertility drug to make her ovaries release eggs.
2. The eggs are collected and mixed with her partner's sperm in a Petri dish.
3. The eggs are fertilised and begin to divide and form tiny embryos.
4. The most viable embryos are selected and transplanted back into the woman's uterus (womb).
5. The embryos are then left to develop into foetuses in the mother's uterus.

Developments in microscopes (page 5) have helped IVF treatments to develop.

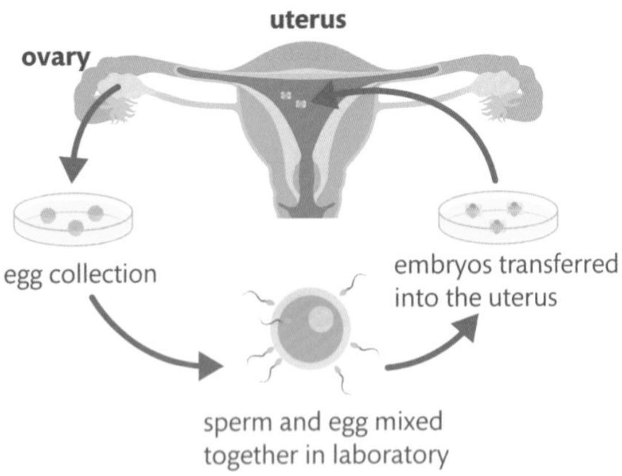

Figure 1 The stages in IVF

5 Working scientifically

You should be aware of some of the social and ethical issues associated with fertility treatments like IVF.

- Sometimes, this can lead to multiple pregnancies, which can reduce the chances of any one embryo developing and is a risk to the health of the mother.
- Some people think it is wrong to 'play God' and create life like this.
- It is very emotionally and physically stressful for the potential parents.
- The success rate is not very high.
- If several embryos are implanted, it can lead to multiple pregnancies.
- Some of the embryos are discarded and not used, which some people think is unethical.
- IVF can be very expensive.

2 Worked example — Grade 6

People undergoing IVF often find the experience very stressful. Suggest **two** reasons why. **[2 marks]**

It can be stressful because success is not guaranteed. Additionally, the procedure is invasive, requiring injections of hormones and the collection of eggs.

5 Exam-style practice — Grade 6

1. Explain why the IVF process usually begins with the use of fertility drugs. **[2 marks]**
2. Give the names of **two** hormones that are used to treat fertility and explain what they do. **[4 marks]**

Control of blood glucose

Controlling blood glucose concentration is an example of **homeostasis** (keeping a constant internal environment). The level of glucose in the blood is important because glucose is needed for respiration. You need to know how glucose levels are controlled in the human body.

 Controlling blood glucose

After a meal, carbohydrates are digested into simple sugars, such as glucose. Glucose is important as it is used during respiration.

Go to page 62 to revise respiration.

The role of insulin

When glucose enters the blood after a meal, the blood glucose concentration begins to rise. The **pancreas** detects the increase in blood glucose and releases the hormone **insulin**. Insulin causes glucose to move from the blood into cells. It also causes excess glucose to be converted into **glycogen** and stored in muscles and the liver. This ensures that glucose in the blood remains at the correct concentration.

The role of glucagon

If the concentration of glucose in the blood is too low, the pancreas detects this and releases the hormone **glucagon**. Glucagon causes glycogen, stored in the liver and muscles, to convert back into glucose. The glucose is then released into the bloodstream, bringing the concentration back to a normal level. The control of blood glucose by insulin and glucagon is an example of negative feedback.

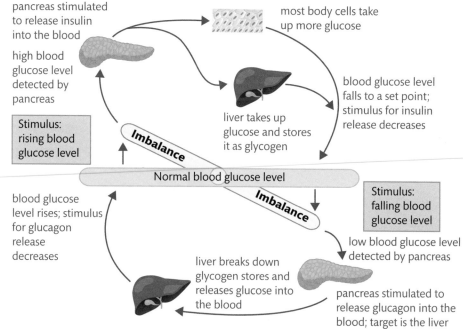

Figure 1 The control of blood glucose by negative feedback

 Worked example Grade 7

A student has an energy drink containing sugar. Explain what will happen to his blood glucose concentration after having the drink. **[6 marks]**

The blood glucose concentration starts to increase as glucose is absorbed into the blood. This increase is detected by the pancreas which secretes the hormone insulin. The insulin causes the excess glucose to be converted to glycogen and stored in the liver and muscles. This reduces the blood glucose concentration and returns it to normal.

 Exam-style practice Grade 7

Explain why the control of blood glucose by the pancreas is described as a 'negative feedback' process. **[3 marks]**

 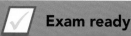

Diabetes

Type 1 and Type 2 diabetes are conditions that affect the body's ability to control blood glucose levels. You need to know about these type of diabetes and how they are controlled.

 Diabetes

Type 1 diabetes

Type 1 diabetes is a disease caused by the pancreas not producing enough insulin. This means that after a meal, the amount of glucose in the blood may rise to dangerously high levels. The condition is normally controlled by injections of the hormone insulin.

Type 2 diabetes

Type 2 diabetes is a disease caused by cells in the body no longer responding to the insulin produced by the pancreas.

People with Type 2 diabetes must eat a controlled diet to prevent glucose levels in their blood rising too high. Exercise helps to reduce the glucose levels in the blood. It is not possible to treat people with Type 2 diabetes with insulin injections.

Obesity is a major risk factor for this condition. Scientists know this because there is a correlation between the occurrence of Type 2 diabetes and different measurements of body mass such as **BMI** and **waist : hip calculations**.

(See page 42 for more about these measurements.)

BMI (Body Mass Index) is a measure of whether a person is a healthy weight for their height. It is calculated using the formula:

$$BMI = \frac{mass\ in\ kg}{(height\ in\ m)^2}$$

Another indication of whether a person is a healthy weight is to compare measurements around their waist and hips. Generally, the hips measurement should be greater than the waist measurement.

 Worked example **Grade 4**

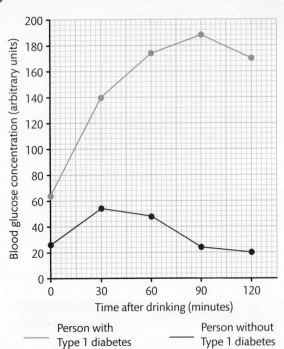

Person with Type 1 diabetes

Person without Type 1 diabetes

Figure 1 A graph showing the changing blood glucose concentration of two people after they each drank a sugar solution.

1 The hormone insulin is a protein.

Suggest a reason why people with Type 1 diabetes inject themselves with insulin rather than take insulin tablets. **[1 mark]**

The insulin protein would be digested.

2 Look at **Figure 1**. Compare the blood glucose concentrations of the two people. Include similarities and differences in your answer. **[4 marks]**

The blood glucose concentration rises and falls in the person with Type 1 diabetes and the person without it. At the start, the blood glucose concentration is higher in the person with Type 1 diabetes and rises higher and more rapidly than in the person without diabetes. The concentration stays high for longer in the person with diabetes.

 Exam-style practice **Grade 5**

Describe **three** of the differences between Type 1 and Type 2 diabetes. **[3 marks]**

 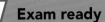

Transport in animals

You need to know how multicellular organisms have adaptations to enable the effective exchange of substances.

(10) Exchange surfaces

All living organisms need to exchange substances with their surroundings. For example, animals need to absorb oxygen and food from their surroundings and then transport them to their cells. Animals also need to transport waste substances like carbon dioxide and urea from their cells, and remove these substances from their bodies.

Plants need to absorb water and mineral ions through their roots, before transporting them to cells that need them. When they photosynthesise, plants absorb carbon dioxide into cells in their leaves and give out oxygen.

Different substances are absorbed into, or removed from, bodies, organs, tissues or cells by the processes of diffusion, osmosis or active transport.

Go to pages 10–13 to revise these processes.

The places where organisms absorb or remove substances are called **exchange surfaces**. For small unicellular organisms their exchange surface is their cell membrane. Larger multicellular organisms have specially adapted organ systems to maximise absorption. This difference is because of their different **surface area : volume ratios**.

Small unicellular organisms have a large surface area to volume ratio so processes like diffusion can occur rapidly. Whereas multicellular organisms have a small outer surface area to volume ratio, which slows down the rate of diffusion. To overcome this problem, multicellular organisms have evolved to have specialised exchange surfaces and transport systems that maximise diffusion by having:

- a large surface area
- a thin membrane for a short diffusion path
- a good transport system (e.g. blood system) to maintain maximum concentration gradients.

(5) Surface area to volume ratio

Think of a cube with sides of length 1 cm:
- the total surface area is $6\,cm^2$ (there are six sides each of area $1\,cm^2$)
- the volume is $1\,cm^3$ $(1 \times 1 \times 1)$
- the ratio of surface area to volume is $6:1$.

If the cube now has sides of length 2 cm:
- the total surface area is $24\,cm^2$ (there are six sides each of area $4\,cm^2$)
- the volume is $8\,cm^3$ $(2 \times 2 \times 2)$
- the ratio of surface area to volume is $3:1$.

There is a greater volume for more chemical reactions in the larger cube but proportionately less surface area for the molecules to diffuse through. This limits the maximum size of a cell.

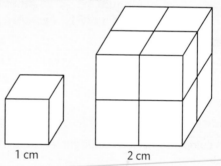

1 cm | 2 cm

Figure 1 Cubes of different sizes have different surface area : volume ratios.

Go to page 58 for more about how alveoli in the lungs are adapted for efficient gas exchange.

Go to page 47 to revise how plant root hair cells are adapted for efficient absorption of water and mineral ions.

(5) Worked example
Grades 5–7

(a) The table shows measurements for cubes of different sizes. Complete the table. **[4 marks]**

(b) Describe the trends in the table. **[2 marks]**

As the cubes get bigger, their total surface areas and volumes increase, but their surface area : volume ratios decrease.

Length of one side (cm)	Total surface area (cm^2)	Volume (cm^3)	Surface area : volume ratio
1	6	1	6 : 1
3	54	27	2 : 1
5	150	125	1.2 : 1

(5) Exam-style practice
Grades 5–6

1 Calculate the surface area : volume ratio of a cube of side length 4 cm. **[2 marks]**

2 The small intestine is covered with small projections called villi. Suggest an explanation for how villi are an adaptation. **[2 marks]**

Alveoli

You need to know how the alveoli in the lungs are adapted for efficient gas exchange.

⑤ The lungs

The lungs are adapted for efficient gas exchange of oxygen and carbon dioxide. This takes place between the **alveoli** (singular: **alveolus**) and their surrounding blood capillaries. There is a higher concentration of oxygen in the air we breathe into the alveoli than in the blood, so oxygen diffuses across the alveoli walls to be transported around the body by the red blood cells. Carbon dioxide is transported to the lungs in the blood plasma. There is a higher concentration of carbon dioxide in the blood than in the alveoli, so it diffuses from the blood into the alveoli to be breathed out.

> See page 59 for more about how the blood transports different substances.

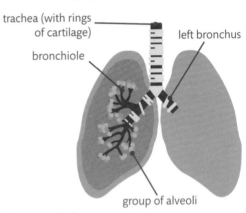
Figure 1 The lungs

Gas	Amount in inhaled air (%)	Amount in exhaled air (%)
Nitrogen	78	78
Oxygen	21	17
Carbon dioxide	0.04	4
Water vapour	variable	variable
Other gases	approx. 1	approx. 1

Table 1 A comparison of the composition of inhaled and exhaled air

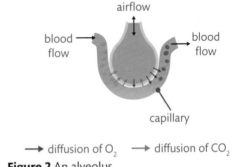
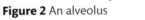
Figure 2 An alveolus

⑤ The alveoli

Alveoli, the small air sacs in the lungs, are adapted for efficient gas exchange by diffusion:

- The large number of alveoli provide a large surface area to absorb oxygen into the blood and remove carbon dioxide.
- Thin, moist membranes allow gases to diffuse quickly.
- The capillary network provides a good blood supply to transport the gases to and from the rest of the body.
- Concentration gradients for both oxygen and carbon dioxide are maintained by ventilation (breathing) and blood flow.

> Go to page 10 to revise the factors affecting the rate of diffusion, and to page 57 to revise exchange surfaces.

⑤ Worked example — Grade 7

Emphysema is a lung condition that can be caused by smoking. Emphysema damages the lungs by breaking down some of the alveoli walls, so the air sacs are fewer in number and bigger in size. Suggest an explanation for what effect this would have on someone with emphysema. **[4 marks]**

Someone with emphysema would be short of breath and get tired easily. This is because fewer air sacs results in a lower surface area for gas exchange. This means less oxygen can be absorbed into the blood, and so respiration is reduced.

⑤ Exam-style practice — Grades 5–7

1. Explain how alveoli are adapted to their function. **[3 marks]**
2. Explain why a rapid breathing rate increases the rate of gas exchange. **[3 marks]**

Made a start | Feeling confident | Exam ready

The blood

You need to be able to recognise the different components of blood and describe their functions.

⑩ Key components of the blood

Blood is a tissue. It consists of a fluid called plasma in which red blood cells, white blood cells and platelets are suspended.

Plasma is the liquid part of the blood. It is mainly made of water but also contains dissolved carbon dioxide, dissolved food, urea (waste), hormones and heat which it transports around the body.

Platelets are cell fragments that help blood to clot. This helps to seal wounds.

Red blood cells (also called **erythrocytes**) absorb oxygen from the lungs and carry it to muscles and tissue around the body. They are adapted for this function in several ways:

- They contain the red pigment **haemoglobin** which combines with oxygen to carry it around the body.
- They have no nucleus, which increases the space available for haemoglobin.
- They have a **biconcave disc** shape to increase the surface area for oxygen to diffuse in and out.
- They are small and flexible, which allows them to pass easily through the smallest capillaries.
- They have a large surface area to volume ratio to increase the rate of diffusion of oxygen in and out.

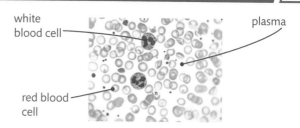

Figure 1 Blood viewed through a light microscope

White blood cells fight disease by producing antibodies and destroying bacteria and viruses. White blood cells have three main roles:

- Many of them are **phagocytes**, which ingest and destroy pathogens (by phagocytosis).
- Others are **lymphocytes**, which produce **antibodies**, specialised proteins produced in response to an **antigen**. An antigen is a substance that induces an immune response. Antibodies recognise when an antigen is foreign to the body and bind to them to destroy them.
- Lymphocytes also produce **antitoxins**. Bacteria produce harmful toxins, and lymphocytes can produce antitoxins to neutralise specific toxins.

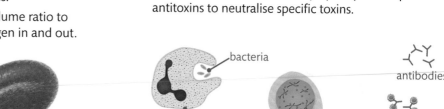

Figure 2 Red blood cells transport oxygen.

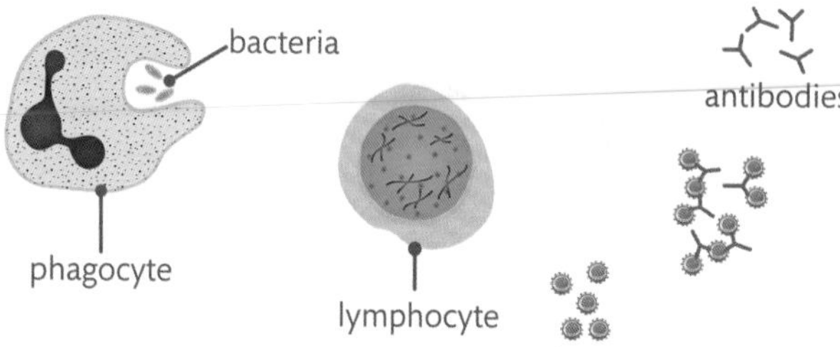

> Go to page 37 to revise the immune system and sealing wounds.

Figure 3 White blood cells destroy pathogens.

⑤ Worked example — Grade 7

Suggest explanations why:

(a) there are more red blood cells than white blood cells in the body **[2 marks]**

Large numbers of red blood cells are needed to carry oxygen to every part of the body so all cells can respire. White blood cells are not needed in every part of the body.

(b) the number of white blood cells is more variable than the number of red blood cells. **[2 marks]**

White blood cells are only needed in large numbers when there are pathogens to destroy. Their numbers fall when there is no infection.

⑤ Exam-style practice — Grade 7

1 Explain how the structure of a red blood cell is adapted to its function. **[4 marks]**

2 Describe the function of phagocytes. **[2 marks]**

Blood vessels

You need to know how blood is transported around the body by three different types of blood vessel.

 Arteries, veins and capillaries

Blood flows around the body through a series of different types of blood vessel: arteries, veins and capillaries.

Arteries
Arteries carry blood at high pressure away from the heart. They have thick walls containing muscle and elastic tissue, enabling them to stretch and then return to their original shape, withstanding and maintaining the high blood pressure.

Capillaries
Capillaries join the ends of arteries to the ends of veins. This is where exchange of materials between the blood and body tissues occurs. Capillaries have very thin walls, usually only one cell thick, to allow oxygen, carbon dioxide, glucose and urea to diffuse to and from surrounding tissues.

Veins
Veins carry blood at low pressure back to the heart. They have **valves** to prevent the blood flowing backwards, and keep it flowing in one direction towards the heart. They have a large **lumen** (space inside the vessel) to maximise blood flow.

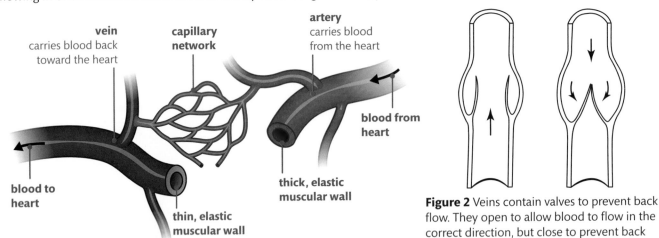

Figure 1 An artery, vein and capillaries

Figure 2 Veins contain valves to prevent back flow. They open to allow blood to flow in the correct direction, but close to prevent back flow.

 Worked example **Grade 7**

The table shows the volume of blood flowing in each of three blood vessels over a period of one minute. Complete the table to show the rate of blood flow per second. **[3 marks]**

Vessel	Volume of blood (cm³)	Rate of blood flow (cm³/s)
Artery	24	0.400
Capillary	4.5	0.075
Vein	3.3	0.055

To calculate the rate of blood flow, divide the volume of blood by time. For example:

$$\frac{24cm^3}{60s} = 0.400$$

 **Exam-style practice** **Grades 4–5**

1. Explain why the blood in arteries is at a higher pressure than the blood in veins and why this is important. **[3 marks]**

2. Explain why valves are found in veins but **not** in the other vessels. **[3 marks]**

The heart

You need to know how the structure of the heart is adapted to its function within the circulatory system.

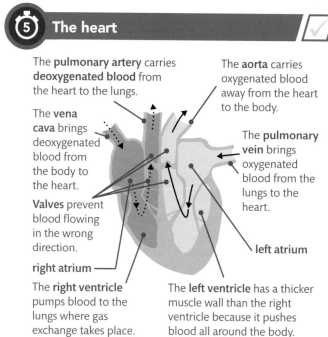

The **pulmonary artery** carries **deoxygenated blood** from the heart to the lungs.

The **aorta** carries oxygenated blood away from the heart to the body.

The **vena cava** brings deoxygenated blood from the body to the heart.

The **pulmonary vein** brings oxygenated blood from the lungs to the heart.

Valves prevent blood flowing in the wrong direction.

left atrium

right atrium

The **right ventricle** pumps blood to the lungs where gas exchange takes place.

The **left ventricle** has a thicker muscle wall than the right ventricle because it pushes blood all around the body.

·····▶ deoxygenated blood ⟶ oxygenated blood

Figure 1 Structure of the heart

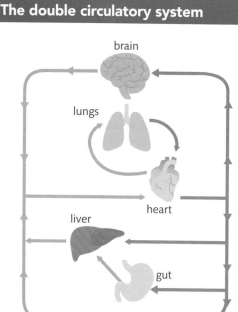

brain

lungs

heart

liver

gut

rest of body

Figure 2 The heart pumps blood around the body in a double circulatory system.

The **coronary arteries** supply **oxygenated blood** to the heart from the lungs. The blood enters the right and left atria, which contract, forcing blood into the ventricles. The left and right ventricles contract, forcing blood into the arteries. The valves ensure that blood does not flow in the wrong direction.

1 Give the names of the four chambers of the heart. **[2 marks]**

Left and right atria, left and right ventricles.

2 Explain why the left ventricle has a thicker wall than the right ventricle. **[2 marks]**

The right ventricle only has to pump blood to the lungs. The left ventricle has to pump blood around the whole of the rest of the body.

3 Most arteries in the body carry oxygenated blood. Name the **one** artery that carries deoxygenated blood and explain why this is different from all the other arteries. **[3 marks]**

The pulmonary artery carries deoxygenated blood. All arteries carry blood away from the heart, and most carry oxygenated blood around the body pumped by the left ventricle. However, the blood in the pulmonary artery is pumped by the right ventricle sending deoxygenated blood from the body to the lungs to collect more oxygen.

1 Describe the path taken by a red blood cell from the left ventricle to the left atrium. **[4 marks]**

2 Some animals, for example fish, only have one ventricle and one atrium in their hearts. Suggest an explanation of the advantage for humans, and all other mammals, of having two ventricles and two atria in their hearts. **[3 marks]**

Aerobic and anaerobic respiration

Respiration is a chemical reaction that takes place inside all living cells, releasing energy into and around the body. You need to know about two types of respiration – aerobic and anaerobic.

Aerobic respiration

Cellular respiration is an **exothermic reaction** that releases energy needed for **metabolic** processes (the processes that take place inside living things to maintain life – also called **metabolism**).

Muscle contractions and movement

Nerve impulses ← **Uses of energy** → Keeping warm

Chemical reactions to build larger molecules

Figure 1 The energy released by respiration has several different uses.

Aerobic respiration
Aerobic respiration requires oxygen.

glucose + oxygen ➜ carbon dioxide + water

$C_6H_{12}O_6 + 6O_2 \rightarrow 6CO_2 + 6H_2O$

Most of the reactions involving aerobic respiration happen inside mitochondria (see page 2) in cells.

The rate of aerobic respiration can be measured by how quickly oxygen is being used.

Anaerobic respiration

Anaerobic respiration does **not** require oxygen. Less energy is released by anaerobic respiration, the incomplete oxidation of glucose, than by aerobic respiration.

There are two forms of anaerobic respiration that you should know for the exam.

Anaerobic respiration in muscles
Anaerobic respiration takes place in muscles when there is not enough oxygen available for aerobic respiration, such as when an animal is running away from a predator.

glucose ➜ lactic acid

The muscle ache felt during exercise is due to a build-up of lactic acid.

Anaerobic respiration in microorganisms and plants
Anaerobic respiration also takes place in microorganisms and plant cells, such as in plant root cells in very wet soil.

Anaerobic respiration in microorganisms such as yeast can be shown by the following equation:

glucose ➜ ethanol (alcohol) + carbon dioxide

This type of anaerobic respiration is sometimes called **fermentation**. This is how alcoholic drinks are made.

Yeast is also used to make bread, as the carbon dioxide released in respiration makes the dough rise.

Worked example — Grades 4–6

1 Give the meaning of the term 'aerobic respiration'. **[2 marks]**

Aerobic respiration is the breaking down of glucose using oxygen to release energy.

2 Explain the meaning of the term 'exothermic reaction'. **[2 marks]**

This is a chemical reaction in which energy is transferred to the surroundings.

Exam focus

You will be expected to recall the definitions of certain key terms in the exam. Make sure you know the meaning of all the terms used in this revision guide.

Exam focus

In an exam, take care you do not mistake similar scientific terms such as 'aerobic' and 'anaerobic'. Try to think of ways to remember which is which. For example, 'aerobic' sounds like 'air', which contains oxygen.

Exam-style practice — Grade 6

Compare and contrast aerobic and anaerobic respiration in humans. **[5 marks]**

 Made a start **Feeling confident** **Exam ready**

Practical: Rate of respiration

You need to know how to investigate the rate of respiration in living organisms.

(10) Method

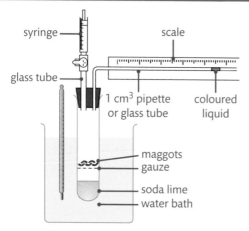

Figure 1 A simple respirometer

This apparatus can be used to investigate how temperature affects the rate of aerobic respiration:

1 Place small organisms, such as maggots, into the boiling tube.

2 Place a drop of coloured liquid at the right hand end of the glass tube.

3 Make a note of the starting position of the drop of liquid.

4 Make a note of the temperature in the water bath.

5 Close the tap.

6 Make a note of the position of the drop of liquid after five minutes.

7 Open the tap and use the syringe to move the liquid back to the start of the scale.

8 Repeat the experiment but with different temperatures of water in the water bath.

(2) Working scientifically

A **respirometer** is used to measure the rate of respiration. **Soda lime** (containing sodium hydroxide) is used to absorb any carbon dioxide present. This means as an organism respires aerobically, it removes oxygen from the air in the apparatus, and the carbon dioxide it gives out is absorbed. This causes the drop of liquid to move towards the organisms.

(5) Key experimental skills

- ☑ Use of apparatus to make and record measurements accurately.
- ☑ Safe use of appropriate heating techniques.
- ☑ Safe and ethical use of living organisms.
- ☑ Measure rate of respiration by measuring uptake of oxygen.

(10) Worked example Grade 5

A student carried out the experiment above. The table shows their results.

Temperature (°C)	Distance moved by drop of liquid in 5 minutes (mm)
10	5
15	7
20	9
25	12
30	30

(a) Describe and explain the pattern shown by these results. **[2 marks]**

As the temperature increases, the distance moved increases because the rate of respiration increases.

(b) Suggest why no temperatures higher than 30 °C were investigated. **[1 mark]**

A higher temperature could have harmed the maggots.

(c) The student uses the results to plot a graph. Explain **two** advantages of doing that. **[2 marks]**

To see the pattern more clearly. To see if there are any anomalies.

(d) Suggest how the accuracy of the results could be improved. **[2 marks]**

Repeat the experiment several times and take a mean of the results at each temperature.

(10) Exam-style practice Grade 8

1 Explain why the drop of liquid moves along the glass tube during the experiment. **[3 marks]**

2 Explain what would happen to the drop of liquid in **Figure 1** if the boiling tube did **not** contain soda lime. **[3 marks]**

 ☑ **Made a start** ☑ **Feeling confident** ☑ **Exam ready**

Response to exercise

You need to know how the human body responds to the increased demand for energy during exercise.

⑤ Responses to exercise

During exercise the human body responds to the increased demand for energy by supplying more glucose and more oxygen to the muscles. The human body responds to exercise in different ways:

❶ The rate of breathing increases.

❷ Breaths are deeper so the volume of each breath increases.

❸ The heart rate increases.

The heart beats faster so glucose and oxygenated blood are pumped to the muscles more quickly, and carbon dioxide is removed more quickly.

② Investigating the effects

There are various ways that you can investigate the effect of exercise on the human body. You can:

- measure the number of breaths per minute before and immediately after exercise
- measure the volume of each breath, using a device called a spirometer before and immediately after exercise
- measure the heart rate by counting the pulse rate in the wrist before, during and after exercise.

⑤ Cardiac output

During exercise, heart rate, stroke volume and cardiac output all increase.

Heart rate is the number of times the heart beats per minute. This is the same as your pulse rate. It is usually measured in beats per minute.

Stroke volume is the volume of blood pumped by the left ventricle in each heart beat. It is usually measured in ml.

Cardiac output is the total volume of blood pumped by the left ventricle per minute. It is usually measured in l per minute.

cardiac output (in l/min) = stroke volume (in l) × heart rate (in beats/min)

⑩ Worked example | Grade 7

❶ A man's heart beats every 0.8 seconds, and he has a stroke volume of 70 ml. Calculate his cardiac output in litres per minute. **[4 marks]**

If each heart beat lasts 0.8 seconds, then his heart rate = $\frac{60}{0.8}$

= 75 beats per minute.

His stroke volume = 70 ml = 0.07 litres.

His cardiac output = stroke volume × heart rate

= 0.07 × 75

= 5.25 litres per minute.

❷ Describe the trends shown in **Figure 1**. **[3 marks]**

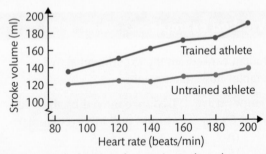

Figure 1 A graph showing changes in stroke volume and heart rate in two athletes during exercise

The trained athlete has a higher stroke volume than the untrained athlete. For both athletes, as heart rate increases the stroke volume increases, but it increases much more in the trained athlete, and only slightly in the untrained athlete.

⑤ Exam-style practice | Grades 6–7

❶ Explain how cardiac output changes before, during and after exercise. **[3 marks]**

❷ A woman has a cardiac output of 4 litres per minute, and a heart rate of 60 beats per minute. Calculate her stroke volume in ml to three significant figures. **[3 marks]**

 Made a start **Feeling confident** 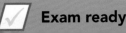 **Exam ready**

Communities

A community is made up of all the living organisms within an ecosystem. You need to know how the species within a community depend on one another.

 Features of an ecosystem

A **population** is all the **organisms** of one species within an ecosystem.

A **community** consists of all the populations of different species living in the same habitat. A **habitat** is the place where organisms live.

An **ecosystem** is the interaction of a community of living organisms (**biotic factors**, page 67) with the non-living (**abiotic factors**, page 66) parts of their habitat.

Plants in a community may compete for:

- light
- water
- space
- minerals.

Animals in a community may compete for:

- food
- a mate
- water
- territory.

organism

population

community

ecosystem

Figure 1 The different levels of organisation in an ecosystem

Worked example Grades 4–6

Figure 2 shows interdependence and competition between species.

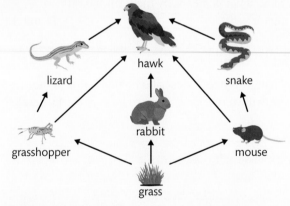

Figure 2 A food web for a grassland ecosystem

(a) Name **three** species that are competing for grass as a source of food. **[1 mark]**

Grasshopper, rabbit and mouse

(b) Suggest an explanation for how the populations of the lizards and the rabbits would be affected if all the grasshoppers were killed by a disease. **[3 marks]**

The number of lizards would decrease as there would be less food available for them.

As the number of lizards and grasshoppers decreases, the hawks would need an alternative source of food and so would probably start to eat more rabbits, causing the population of rabbits to decrease.

Interdependence

Within a community, each species depends upon other species for the things they need, including food, shelter, pollination and seed dispersal. This is known as **interdependence**.

If a change occurs, such as the removal of a species, then the whole community could be affected. If all the species and environmental factors in a community are balanced, then the community is stable and the sizes of populations remain fairly constant.

Exam-style practice Grades 5–6

Look at **Figure 3**.

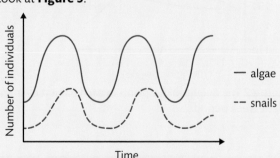

Figure 3 The changing populations of snails and algae

(a) Explain how changes in the population of algae affect the population of snails. **[4 marks]**

(b) Suggest an explanation for how the appearance of the graph would alter if a new predator (of the snails) was introduced to the ecosystem. **[2 marks]**

Abiotic factors

You need to know how abiotic (non-living) factors can affect a community and its survival.

 Abiotic factors

Abiotic factors are non-living factors, including:

- temperature
- pH and mineral content of soil
- wind intensity and direction
- light intensity
- carbon dioxide levels (mainly affects plants)
- oxygen levels (e.g. for aquatic animals)
- moisture levels.

The oxygen content of the water in rivers, streams and lakes can be greatly reduced if it is polluted by sewage or nitrates from farming. The amount of dissolved oxygen usually determines the number and types of organisms living in that body of water. For example, mayfly larvae need water with a high oxygen content, whereas rat-tailed maggots can thrive in low oxygen levels.

Figure 1 Changes in abiotic factors, such as temperature, can have a serious impact on the environment. Rising temperatures are causing sea ice in the Arctic to melt, which is having a negative effect on polar bears which are adapted to hunt and breed there.

 Worked example — Grades 4–6

A study into the growth of ivy plants in different habitats was conducted. The pH of the soil was different in each habitat.

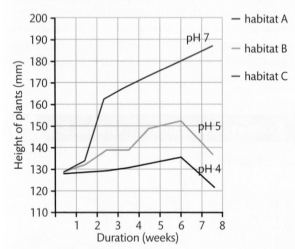

Figure 2 The heights of ivy plants in each habitat over an eight-week period

(a) Soil pH is an example of an abiotic factor. State what is meant by the term 'abiotic factor'. **[1 mark]**

Abiotic factors are the non-living factors that can affect a community.

(b) Using **Figure 2**, describe how pH affects the growth of ivy. **[3 marks]**

The graph shows that as the pH becomes less acidic, the growth of the ivy plant increases. For example, after 6 weeks the ivy plant in pH 7 soil had grown to a height of 180 mm, whereas the plant in pH 5 had only grown around 152 mm and in soil of pH 4 the ivy plant had reached a lower height of 135 mm.

 **Exam focus**

In the exam, you could be expected to extract and interpret information from charts, tables and graphs. Use specific data to help describe or explain any patterns shown.

Exam-style practice — Grades 4–6

1. Give **three** abiotic factors in a rainforest. **[3 marks]**

2. Explain, giving an example, how a change in an abiotic factor could affect the stability of an ecosystem in the Arctic. **[4 marks]**

Biotic factors

You need to know how biotic (living) factors can affect a community and its survival.

 Biotic factors

Communities can be affected by **biotic factors** such as:

- **predation**
- **competition**
- **associations**.

Predation

Predators depend on their prey for food. Predators also control the sizes of the prey populations.

Competition

Living things compete for the resources they need. For example, plants compete for light and water, and animals compete for food, mates or territory. Competition can occur both between members of the same species, and between different species.

Associations

There are other interactions between organisms apart from predation or competition. Some species form close relationships in which both benefit. This is called **mutualism**. **Figure 1** shows oxpecker birds on a rhinoceros. The birds eat ticks (insects) on the rhinoceros' skin. The birds gain food and the rhinoceros gets the ticks removed.

Parasitism is an association in which only one of the species (the parasite) benefits and the other (the host) is harmed. **Figure 2** shows a parasitic flea feeding on the blood of its host.

Figure 1 Oxpeckers and rhinoceros in a mutualistic association

Figure 2 Fleas are parasites, feeding on the blood of their host but not killing it.

 Worked example   Grade 7

A hedgerow is an example of an ecosystem.

(a) Suggest **one** biotic factor that could affect this ecosystem. Explain how a change in this biotic factor might affect the community within the hedgerow. **[4 marks]**

> A biotic factor could have a positive effect on the hedgerow, for example, a new species of plant growing could provide more food and allow populations to thrive.

If a new insect-eating species was introduced into the ecosystem, this would affect the stability of the ecosystem as the number of organisms preying upon the insects would increase. This could cause a dramatic drop in the population of other insect-eating species. It could also affect other species, as there might be less food available for the original predators in the ecosystem and so they might starve and die out.

(b) Suggest and explain how clearing the rainforest for biofuel production is affecting communities of birds within the rainforest. **[3 marks]**

Deforestation removes habitat for insects and small organisms. This leads to a decline in the population sizes of prey for birds. Therefore, the populations of birds will also decrease.

 Exam-style practice   Grades 4–5

1 Give **two** biotic factors affecting an Arctic ecosystem. **[2 marks]**

2 State which of the following factors are biotic, and which are abiotic. **[2 marks]**

    temperature

    carbon dioxide levels

    new pathogens

    wind intensity

    food availability

    predators

3 Suggest an explanation for how the introduction of the grey squirrel to the UK has caused the red squirrel to become endangered. **[2 marks]**

 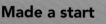

Practical: Population studies

The size of a population in a habitat can be measured using quadrats. You need to know how quadrats can also be used along a belt transect to investigate the effect of an abiotic factor on the distribution of a species.

(10) Using a belt transect and quadrats

This method describes the process of **sampling** the plants as you move away from the trunk of a large tree. One abiotic factor that would change is the light intensity, which would be greater further away from the trunk.

1 Set up a line, called a **belt transect**, from the base of the tree trunk to beyond the shade of the tree, using a tape measure (or string marked out with the required distances).

2 Place a **quadrat** against the transect line, ensuring the corner of the quadrat is lined up with 0 on the tape measure.

3 Count how many plants of each different species are within the quadrat and record your findings in a suitable table.

4 Place the quadrat 1 metre along the transect; count and record your findings of plants of each species.

5 Repeat the steps above until you have results for every metre until you are beyond the shade of the tree.

6 Go back to the tree trunk, set up a new transect line in a different direction and repeat the steps given above.

(2) Maths skills

In some investigations you may need to calculate the **mean** number of plants of a particular species per quadrat.
The mean is calculated by:

$$\frac{\text{total number of plants}}{\text{number of quadrats}}$$

The mean is one type of average. Two other types of average are:

- the **mode**, which is the most common value in a range of values
- the **median**, which is the middle value when all the values are put in order.

(5) Worked example — Grade 6

The table shows the number of buttercups found in four different areas of a habitat.

Quadrat number	1	2	3	4
Number of buttercups	12	14	17	13

(a) Calculate the mean number of buttercups per quadrat. **[1 mark]**

$$\text{mean} = \frac{\text{total number of buttercups}}{\text{number of quadrats}}$$
$$= \frac{56}{4} = 14$$

(b) Using your answer from **(a)**, estimate the population of buttercups in the field. The quadrat used has an area of 0.25 m² and the field has an area of 125 m². **[2 marks]**

$$\frac{125}{0.25} = 500 \text{ quadrats for the whole field}$$
$$14 \times 500 = 7000 \text{ buttercups in the field}$$

> There are an average of 14 buttercups per quadrat.

Working scientifically

To ensure the data collected is accurate:

- place the quadrats down at specified coordinates
- identify all the different species present
- count the number of individual plants of each species, not the number of flowers for example.

(2) Key terms

☑ A **quadrat** is a square frame, often 0.25 m²; they are used to sample the distribution of plants or animals. Quadrats are either placed in a line (belt transect) or placed randomly to compare two different areas.

☑ A **belt transect** is a series of quadrats in a line across a habitat.

☑ **Sampling** means using information from several places to make **estimates** of the results for the whole area. The more samples taken the more accurate the estimates will be.

☑ **Random** coordinates can be taken from random number tables. Placing quadrats at random coordinates avoids **bias**.

(5) Exam-style practice — Grade 7

1 When using quadrats to estimate the number of plants in a large area, it is important that the quadrats are placed at random coordinates. Explain why this is important. **[2 marks]**

2 When using a belt transect, quadrats are **not** placed randomly. Explain why. **[2 marks]**

> First, work out the number of quadrats it would take to cover the whole field.

☑ **Made a start** ☑ **Feeling confident** ☑ **Exam ready**

Biodiversity

Biodiversity refers to the variety of plant and animal species within a habitat, in a larger area or on Earth. You need to be able to discuss the benefits of and threats to **biodiversity**, both locally and on a global scale.

(5) Advantages of biodiversity

The greater the number of species in a community, the greater the biodiversity.

An ecosystem (page 65) is much more stable if there is greater biodiversity because organisms can depend upon multiple species for food and shelter. This gives them a greater chance of survival compared with relying on just one species.

Working scientifically
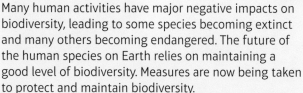
Many human activities have major negative impacts on biodiversity, leading to some species becoming extinct and many others becoming endangered. The future of the human species on Earth relies on maintaining a good level of biodiversity. Measures are now being taken to protect and maintain biodiversity.

(2) Key threats to biodiversity

- deforestation
- pollution, e.g. eutrophication
- climate change
- destruction of habitats
- landfill
- changes in agricultural methods
- increasing human population
- over-exploitation, e.g. fishing
- introduction of **non-indigenous** (non-native) species

(5) Eutrophication

Eutrophication is a problem involving extra nutrients entering the water in rivers and lakes. This could be caused by sewage pollution or by mineral ions from fertiliser put on fields to help crop plants grow. The extra nutrients cause excessive growth of algae, which reduces the light entering the water, causing the death of water plants. As the plants die, they decay due to the action of bacteria, which in turn use up oxygen from the water, killing fish and other water animals.

Fish farming can also contribute to eutrophication. If fish are kept in large cages in open water, then waste from the large number of fish can enter the natural ecosystem, damaging it.

(10) Worked example   Grades 5–6

1 Give the meaning of the term 'biodiversity'.   **[1 mark]**

The variety of all the different species in an ecosystem.

2 Explain how deforestation is leading to a decrease in biodiversity.   **[3 marks]**

Loss of habitat, food and shelter will lead to smaller populations, which makes species more vulnerable.

3 **Figure 1** shows the harlequin ladybird, which was introduced in the USA as a predator to control whitefly on crops.

Explain why scientists are concerned that the appearance of this ladybird in the UK would have severe detrimental effects on biodiversity.   **[3 marks]**

Figure 1 This species of ladybird is particularly competitive and aggressive.

All species of ladybird are competing for similar food sources. The more aggressive species will take much of the food available, leaving the less competitive species to starve and die, reducing biodiversity.

(5) Exam-style practice   Grade 6

1 Over-exploitation of cod (a type of fish) has led to vastly reduced cod supplies in the ocean. Describe **two** methods that could be used to reverse this.   **[2 marks]**

2 Explain why biodiversity is vital for the stability of ecosystems.   **[2 marks]**

Maintaining biodiversity

It is important to reverse the negative effect the growing human population has had on biodiversity, to improve the stability of ecosystems. You need to know the methods used and the difficulties involved with conserving species and maintaining biodiversity.

(10) Maintaining biodiversity

- **Captive breeding programmes** increase the population of endangered species until they are no longer vulnerable and can be released to re-establish wild populations.
- **Reducing the rate of deforestation** in some areas, and **increasing the rate of reforestation** by replanting in other areas, reduces the negative impacts on the climate, habitats and food supply which aids organisms' survival.
- **Reducing carbon dioxide emissions** slows down global warming which is already reducing the populations of Arctic and Antarctic animals.
- **Recycling waste** reduces the use of landfill and saves energy. Landfill sites produce 'landfill gas', a mixture of greenhouse gases which contribute to climate change. Dumping waste at landfill also wastes land and destroys ecosystems.
- **Protecting and regenerating habitats** prevents harm to the ecosystem. Coral reefs are protected to prevent further damage and to allow the coral to recover.
- **Reintroducing field margins and hedgerows** to the edges of fields of crops increases biodiversity in these areas, especially where farmers grow only one type of crop.

Figure 1 A giant panda, born and raised in a captive breeding programme, being released into the wild

(5) Working scientifically

Running programmes to maintain biodiversity effectively can be very expensive – national parks and protected habitats all cost money to maintain.

Some revenue can be generated by opening protected areas to the public and charging them for entry.

Governments may offer incentives to businesses to reduce their carbon emissions and reduce their waste, or they may tax heavily polluting industries.

Farmers may be offered benefits for replanting hedgerows such as an increased price for their crops and livestock.

(5) Worked example — Grade 5

Explain why it is important to prevent organisms from becoming extinct. **[3 marks]**

Species should be preserved so future generations can see them. Extinctions can have a dramatic effect on food chains, causing other species to become endangered.

Most species directly or indirectly impact our food supply.

Another suitable answer is that certain plants are sources of vital medical treatment. It may be difficult or even impossible to find replacements.

(5) Exam-style practice — Grade 6

1. Give **two** methods that can be used to reduce carbon emissions. **[2 marks]**
2. Describe **one** advantage and **one** disadvantage for reintroducing hedgerows in farmland. **[2 marks]**

Carbon cycle

You need to know how materials in the living world are recycled to provide the building blocks for future organisms. The **carbon cycle** is one example of how substances are cycled through an ecosystem.

⏱10 The carbon cycle

Most of the different substances that living organisms are made up of, such as carbohydrates, proteins, lipids and DNA, contain the element **carbon**. Without carbon, life as we know it could not exist. There is only a certain amount of carbon on the Earth, and carbon atoms are constantly being recycled through both the biotic (living) and abiotic (non-living) parts of ecosystems.

Carbon dioxide (CO_2) is removed from the atmosphere by photosynthesis (see page 44) in plants and algae. The plants and algae use the carbon to make glucose which is later converted to other substances such as starch, protein and lipids. When animals eat plants, they take in these substances and convert them to other carbon-containing compounds in their own bodies. When animals and plants respire (see page 62), carbon is returned to the atmosphere as carbon dioxide again.

There are other processes in the carbon cycle. For example, dead animals and plants, or their waste, are decayed by **decomposers**, returning carbon dioxide to the atmosphere. Sometimes, over millions of years, the remains of dead organisms form fossil fuels such as coal and oil. When these fuels are burnt, again carbon returns to the atmosphere as carbon dioxide.

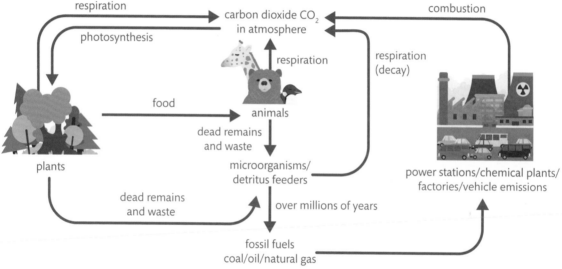

Figure 1 The carbon cycle

⏱5 Decomposers

Decomposers are microorganisms, such as certain bacteria or fungi, that **decay** (decompose) dead remains and waste (**detritus**). As the decomposers respire, they release carbon dioxide into the atmosphere. Decay also releases mineral ions, such as nitrates, into the soil for new plant growth.

Go to page 73 to see how nitrates are involved in the nitrogen cycle.

⏱5 Worked example — Grade 5

Explain how microorganisms help to provide plants with the mineral ions they need. **[2 marks]**

Microorganisms feed on dead plant and animal matter. As they break down the waste they return mineral ions to the soil.

⏱5 Exam-style practice — Grade 6

1 When an animal dies, the carbon it contains is recycled through the carbon cycle. Describe how the carbon is released back into the atmosphere. **[2 marks]**

2 Explain why the carbon cycle is vital to life on Earth. **[3 marks]**

Water cycle

The water cycle is another example of a substance that is cycled through an ecosystem.

⏱ The water cycle

The water cycle is important because every living organism on Earth depends on water to survive. Without water, all living organisms would die very quickly. The water cycle recycles water and nutrients, bringing fresh water to people, animals and plants all around the world. There are four main stages to the water cycle.

1 **Evaporation** – (heat) energy from the Sun causes water in the oceans, lakes and rivers to evaporate, forming water vapour in the atmosphere.

2 **Condensation** – as water vapour cools high up in the atmosphere it condenses to form clouds.

3 **Precipitation** – as clouds become more condensed water falls as rain, snow, ice or hail.

4 **Collection** – water may fall straight into rivers, lakes and oceans ready for the process to begin again, or it may be absorbed into the soil and taken up by vegetation to eventually evaporate from the leaves (by **transpiration**). Water that is not absorbed will flow across the ground (surface run-off) until it reaches a river or other area of water.

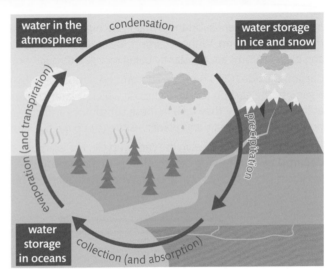

Figure 1 The water cycle

Plants also produce more water when they respire.

⏱ Worked example — Grades 4–6

1 Describe the ways water enters the atmosphere. **[3 marks]**

Some water evaporates from rivers, lakes and seas. Water is produced when living organisms respire and is given out, for example, when animals breathe. Water is lost from plant leaves during transpiration.

2 Explain **two** advantages and **two** disadvantages of producing potable water by the desalination of sea water compared with other methods. **[4 marks]**

Two disadvantages are that desalination plants are expensive to build and they use a lot of energy to run which causes pollution such as carbon emissions. Two advantages are that they are a way of obtaining potable water in places where there is drought and fresh water is scarce, and that the water produced is safe to drink and does not contain pathogens or toxins.

⏱ Potable water

People need clean water that is safe to drink (**potable water**). This can be a particular problem in areas of drought. Potable water can be obtained in different ways including:

- from springs and wells
- treating previously used water
- from sea water (**desalination**).

Desalination is the removal of salts from sea water usually by some form of distillation.

There is more about desalination on page 110.

⏱ Exam-style practice — Grades 4–5

1 Give **two** reasons why water might **not** be potable. **[2 marks]**

2 Explain why the water cycle is vital to life on Earth. **[2 marks]**

 Made a start **Feeling confident** **Exam ready**

Nitrogen cycle

Plants take in **nitrate ions** for healthy growth. You need to know how **nitrogen** compounds like nitrates are cycled through ecosystems by the nitrogen cycle.

 Fertilisers and crop rotation

Growing the same type of crop plant in the same soil for many years reduces the levels of nitrates and other mineral ions. **Fertilisers** and **crop rotation** can restore the levels:

- **Natural fertilisers** such as compost or manure slowly decompose in the soil to release nitrates and other minerals. **Artificial fertilisers**, which may be liquid or powder, contain nitrates and other minerals that can be quickly taken up by plants.

- **Crop rotation** means that different crop plants, with different mineral requirements, are grown each year. Often one of the crops in the rotation is peas, beans or clover. Their roots have swellings called **root nodules** which contain **nitrogen-fixing bacteria**. The bacteria provide the plant with nitrates and also increase nitrate levels in the soil.

Go to page 69 to revise how excessive use of artificial fertilisers can cause eutrophication.

Figure 1 Root nodules

 The nitrogen cycle

Plants and animals need nitrogen to make compounds such as proteins, but they cannot use nitrogen gas as it is too unreactive. Different types of soil bacteria are involved in making nitrates available for uptake by plants.

Go to pages 47 and 48 to revise how mineral ions are taken into, and transported through, plants.

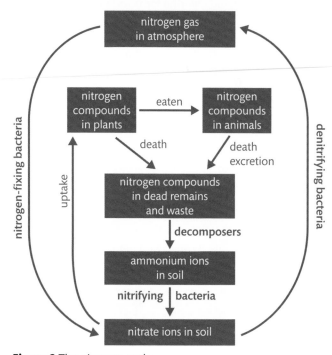

Figure 2 The nitrogen cycle

 Worked example Grade 7

A farmer uses the following four-year crop rotation: wheat, turnips, barley, clover.
The farmer does **not** harvest the clover, but instead ploughs the plants back into the soil.
Explain why. **[3 marks]**

Clover contains nitrogen-fixing bacteria in its root nodules.

These bacteria cause nitrogen gas from the air to be converted into nitrogen compounds such as nitrates.

Ploughing back the clover adds nitrogen compounds to the soil to improve crop plant growth in the following years.

Exam-style practice Grade 8

When plants and animals die, the nitrogen they contain is recycled through the nitrogen cycle. Explain how some nitrogen can return to the atmosphere. **[6 marks]**

Atoms, elements and compounds

You need to be able to apply your knowledge of atoms, elements and compounds to name substances and write balanced chemical equations.

 Elements and compounds

Everything, whatever its state of matter, is made of atoms. An **atom** is the smallest part of an **element** that can exist. Go to page 76 to revise the structure of the atom.

Elements

There are over 100 different elements, which are shown in the **periodic table**. Each element is made of atoms that have the same atomic number (number of protons). Each type of atom can be represented by an atomic symbol, e.g. Na for an atom of sodium.

An element is a pure substance that cannot be chemically broken down into anything simpler. The atoms of a particular element are chemically identical to each other.

Compounds

Compounds form when two or more elements chemically combine in fixed proportions. The name or symbol of a compound is derived from the elements reacting. For example, sodium and chlorine form sodium chloride.

Compounds can only be separated into elements by chemical reactions. Chemical reactions always involve the formation of new substances. The reactions also often involve an energy change.

> If only a metal element and a non-metal element react, the compound name ends in **-ide**.

> If a compound also contains oxygen, its name will end in **-ate**.

 Key skills

✅ Identify the names and symbols of the first 20 elements in the periodic table, and the elements in Groups 1 and 7.

✅ Name compounds from given formulae or chemical equations.

✅ Write word equations and produce balanced chemical equations for given reactions.

> Go to page 77 to find out about protons and atomic number.

> Atoms do not have the bulk properties of molecular substances.

 Worked example | **Grade 4**

1 Name the compounds formed by the combination of the following elements.
  (a) Cu and F   **[1 mark]**

Copper fluoride

  (b) Cu, O and F   **[1 mark]**

Copper fluorate

2 Write a word equation for the reaction between magnesium and oxygen.   **[1 mark]**

magnesium + oxygen → magnesium oxide

> To write a word equation, put the reactants on the left, then an arrow leading to the products on the right. The name of the metal comes first in the name of a compound.

 Exam-style practice | **Grade 4**

1 Explain why aluminium is an element.   **[1 mark]**

2 Give the correct atomic symbol for aluminium.   **[1 mark]**

3 **Figure 1** shows a section of the periodic table.
  (a) Name the labelled element in Group 1.   **[1 mark]**
  (b) (i) Give the name and symbol of the element in the blue box.   **[1 mark]**
      (ii) Write a word equation showing this element reacting with chlorine.   **[1 mark]**

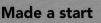

Figure 1 A section of the periodic table

The model of the atom

The work of many scientists has led to our current model of the atom. You need to know the theories (outlined below) that have developed over time due to the discovery of subatomic particles.

(10) Developing the model of the atom

1800s

1. Dalton thought that an atom was a solid sphere. He stated that all matter is made of atoms that cannot be split into anything simpler or destroyed. All atoms of a given element are identical, with the same mass and properties; however, atoms of different elements are different.

2. The model of the atom changed when subatomic particles were discovered. After electrons were observed, scientists proposed the **plum pudding model**: atoms are like a positively-charged 'pudding', with electrons like 'plums' embedded in it.

3. Rutherford, Geiger and Marsden tested the plum pudding model by aiming a beam of positively-charged alpha particles at a very thin sheet of gold foil (scattering experiment). Some of the alpha particles were repelled by positively-charged particles (the nucleus). Most alpha particles passed through unaffected, showing that the nucleus was only a very small part of the atom. This evidence gave rise to the **nuclear model**.

4. Bohr adapted the nuclear model. Using theoretical calculations alongside experimental observations, he suggested that electrons travel in circular orbits around the nucleus. Further research showed that the nucleus was actually composed of smaller particles with equal amounts of positive charge. These became known as protons.

Approximately 20 years after the nuclear model became accepted, Chadwick discovered that neutrons also existed in the nucleus.

1930s

(5) Scientific theory

You need to know how scientific theories develop over time. New experimental evidence may lead to a scientific model being changed or replaced. The **scientific method** is a systematic, logical approach used to discover how science works. It may be modified but ultimately it is used to gather experimental and theoretical evidence and observations to solve a problem.

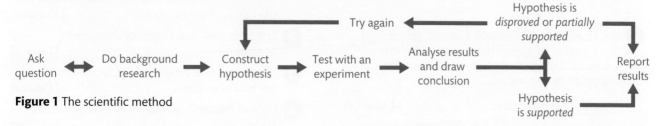

Figure 1 The scientific method

(2) Worked example — Grade 5

Describe the differences between the plum pudding model and the nuclear model of the atom. **[2 marks]**

The electrons orbit a positive central nucleus in the nuclear model, whereas, in the plum pudding model, the electrons are dotted around the nucleus 'like plums in a pudding'.

(5) Exam-style practice — Grade 5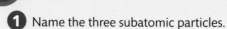

1 Name the three subatomic particles. **[1 mark]**

2 Explain how Dalton's model of the atom changed with the discovery of subatomic particles. **[2 marks]**

Subatomic particles

You need to know about the size and structure of atoms.

 Structure of an atom

Everything is made of atoms. Atoms contain subatomic particles, some of which are charged.

Within the atom, there is a central **nucleus** that contains the protons and neutrons. As the number of protons (the atomic number) identifies the element, all atoms of the same element must have the same number of protons.

The **atomic number** is the number of protons the atom contains. The number of electrons in an atom is equal to the number of protons in its nucleus.

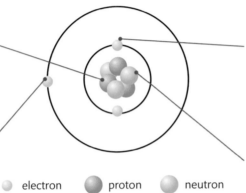

electron   proton   neutron

The tiny negatively-charged electrons are found in electron shells surrounding the nucleus. They are attracted to the positively-charged protons.

Atoms are electrically neutral as they have an equal number of protons and electrons and neutrons are not charged.

Figure 1 The nuclear model of the atom

 Size of an atom

The atom is the smallest part of an element. Atoms have a radius of about 0.1 nanometres (nm) (1×10^{-10}). A nanometre is equal to one-billionth of a metre (1×10^{-9} m). The nucleus of an atom has a radius of about 0.00001 nm (1×10^{-14} m).

Go to page 77 for more about the size of an atom.

Maths skills

You need to know how to convert nanometres to metres using standard form.

$1\,nm = 1 \times 10^{-9}$ m

 Worked example **Grade 5**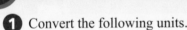

1 Convert the following units.

(a) 15 nm to m **[1 mark]**

1.5×10^{-8} m

(b) 3.4×10^{-6} m to nm **[1 mark]**

3.4×10^{3} nm

2 An atom has a radius of 0.134 nm. Its nucleus has a radius of approximately 1×10^{-14} nm. Estimate the fraction of the volume of the atom occupied by the nucleus.

Volume $= \dfrac{4}{3} \pi \times \text{radius}^3$ **[4 marks]**

Radius of atom in m $= 1.34 \times 10^{-10}$ nm, approximately $= 1 \times 10^{-10}$ nm

Volume of atom approximately $= \dfrac{4}{3} \pi \times (1 \times 10^{-10}\,\text{nm})^3$

Volume of nucleus approximately
$= \dfrac{4}{3} \pi \times (1 \times 10^{-14}\,\text{nm})^3$

$\dfrac{\text{Fraction of volume nucleus}}{\text{atom approximately}} = \dfrac{\frac{4}{3} \pi \times (1 \times 10^{-14}\,\text{nm})^3}{\frac{4}{3} \pi \times (1 \times 10^{-10}\,\text{nm})^3}$

(cancelling) $= \dfrac{(1 \times 10^{-14}\,\text{nm})^3}{(1 \times 10^{-10}\,\text{nm})^3} = \dfrac{10^{30}}{10^{42}} = \dfrac{1}{10^{12}}$

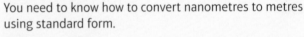 **Exam-style practice** **Grade 4**

1 The nucleus of an atom has a radius of 1×10^{-14} m. Given that one nanometre is 1×10^{-9} m, calculate how many nanometres the radius of the nucleus is. **[2 marks]**

2 State the electrical charge of the nucleus of an atom. **[1 mark]**

3 Name the subatomic particles found in the nucleus of an atom. **[1 mark]**

4 Look at **Figure 2**, a diagram of a helium atom.

(a) Give the atomic number of helium. **[1 mark]**

(b) Explain why an atom of helium has no overall charge. **[2 marks]**

(c) Use **Figure 2** to explain the nuclear model of helium. **[2 marks]**

Figure 2 An atom of helium

 Made a start **Feeling confident** **Exam ready**

Size and mass of atoms

You need to be able to calculate the numbers of protons, neutrons and electrons in atoms when you are given the atomic number and mass number.

(5) Representing atoms

The sum of the number of protons and neutrons in an atom is its **mass number**. Almost all the mass of an atom is in the nucleus.

The **atomic number** is the number of protons in an atom. Atoms contain the same number of protons and electrons.

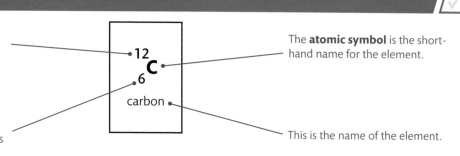

$^{12}_{6}\text{C}$

carbon

The **atomic symbol** is the short-hand name for the element.

This is the name of the element.

(10) Worked example — Grade 5

(a) Name the three subatomic particles in an atom of aluminium and give their relative charge and relative masses. **[3 marks]**

Protons have a relative mass of 1 and a charge of +1.
Electrons have a very small relative mass and a charge of –1.
Neutrons have a relative mass of 1 and a charge of 0.

(b) An atom of aluminium is represented by $^{27}_{13}\text{Al}$. Calculate the number of protons, electrons and neutrons in an atom of aluminium. **[3 marks]**

number of protons = atomic number = 13
number of electrons = number of protons = 13
number of neutrons = mass number – atomic number
= 27 – 13 = 14

(c) An unknown atom, X, has 8 electrons and 9 neutrons. Give the atom symbol. **[2 marks]**

number of electrons = number of protons = 8
mass number = protons + neutrons = 17
Therefore atom symbol is $^{17}_{8}\text{X}$

(1) Maths skills

You need to know how to use mass number and atomic number to work out the number of protons, neutrons and electrons.

For sodium:

number of protons = atomic number = 11

number of electrons = number of protons = 11

number of neutrons = mass number – atomic number
= 23 – 11 = 12

Exam focus

When giving the mass of an atom in an exam you do not need to state the units.

mass number – atomic number

In an atom, the number of electrons is equal to the number of protons.

(10) Exam-style practice — Grade 5

(a) Atoms have different atomic numbers and mass numbers. In terms of subatomic particles, describe the differences between an atom's atomic number and its mass number. **[4 marks]**

(b) Complete the table. **[6 marks]**

Subatomic particle	Relative mass	Relative charge
	$\dfrac{1}{1835}$	
neutron		
	1	

(c) Use the periodic table to complete the table. **[1 mark]**

Atom	Number of protons	Number of neutrons	Number of electrons
fluorine	9		9

Isotopes and relative atomic mass

Isotopes are atoms of the same element that have different numbers of neutrons. You need to be able to calculate relative atomic mass given the percentage abundance.

 ## Isotopes

Isotopes are atoms with the same atomic number but a different atomic mass. This means they have the same number of protons and electrons but a different number of neutrons. Most elements have two or more isotopes. Isotopes of an element have the same chemical properties. Isotopes of the same element are usually specifically identified by their mass number, e.g. hydrogen-3.

Isotopes of hydrogen

	Hydrogen ^1_1H	Deuterium ^2_1H	Tritium ^3_1H	
Number of protons	1	1	1	Atoms can be represented in this way. The top number is the mass number. The bottom number is the atomic number.
Number of electrons	1	1	1	
Number of neutrons	0	1	2	

Radioactive isotopes

Some radioactive isotopes have useful applications. For example, cobalt-60 is used in cancer treatment.

Fluorine-18 is used as a tracer for detecting cancers and in cardiac and brain imaging.

 ## Worked example   Grades 5–7

1 Two isotopes of lithium are ^7_3Li and ^8_3Li. Describe the similarities and differences between them, referring to the number of subatomic particles in each isotope.

[3 marks]

The atoms of both isotopes possess the same number of protons and electrons – three of each.

They have a different number of neutrons – ^7_3Li has four neutrons and ^8_3Li has five neutrons.

2 The percentage abundances of three lithium isotopes are:

^7_3Li 55%

^8_3Li 25%

^6_3Li 20%.

Calculate the relative atomic mass of lithium. **[3 marks]**

$$A_r = \frac{(7 \times 55) + (8 \times 25) + (6 \times 20)}{100}$$

$$A_r = \frac{(385 + 200 + 120)}{100}$$

$$A_r = 7.05$$

 ## Relative atomic mass

The relative atomic mass (A_r) is the average mass of one atom of an element compared with $\frac{1}{12}$ of a carbon-12 atom. The relative atomic mass of an element is the average value of the mass of all isotopes of the element, taking into account their abundance.

The percentage abundance of an element's isotopes is needed to calculate the A_r.

Maths skills

To calculate the relative atomic mass (A_r):

1. Multiply the atomic mass of each isotope by its percentage abundance.

2. Add these values together and divide by 100.

 ## Exam-style practice   Grade 5

Look at the atomic symbols below. The letters are **not** the symbols for these elements.

^6_3R ^7_3S $^{23}_{11}T$ $^{39}_{19}U$ $^{85}_{37}V$

(a) State and explain which **two** atoms are isotopes of the same element. **[3 marks]**

(b) Name the element that they are isotopes of. **[1 mark]**

 Made a start **Feeling confident** **Exam ready**

Developing the periodic table

You need to be able to describe the development of the periodic table over time, in terms of the scientific theories and instruments available.

 Mendeleev's periodic table

In 1869, Mendeleev arranged the elements in a table in order of increasing relative atomic mass, split into rows so that elements (and their compounds) with similar properties were grouped vertically. In some cases, he changed the order of the elements to fit the pattern better. For example, he placed iodine after tellurium although the relative atomic mass of iodine is slightly lower. He thought that the masses must be wrong. In fact, they are correct – tellurium has a high abundance of isotopes of high mass.

Mendeleev also left gaps to maintain the pattern, predicting that new elements would be discovered to fill the gaps. Over the next 20 years more elements were discovered and their properties were found to match Mendeleev's predictions.

Row	Group							
	1	2	3	4	5	6	7	8
1	H	-	-	-	-	-	-	-
2	Li	Be	B	C	N	O	F	-
3	Na	Mg	Al	Si	P	S	Cl	-
4	K	Ca	?	Ti	V	Cr	Mn	Fe, Co, Ni, Cu
5	(Cu)	Zn	?	?	As	So	Br	-
6	Rb	Sr	Yt	Zr	Nb	Mo	?	Ru, Rh, Pd, Ag

Figure 1 The periodic table developed by Dmitri Mendeleev

 **Exam focus**

To answer a multiple-choice question, you need to apply the following principles.

- You must put a cross in only **one** box. If you do not cross any boxes or cross more than **one** box, you will score zero.
- Read all of the answers before selecting which one to cross; several answers may seem correct at first until you have read through all of the options.
- If you are unsure, eliminate the answers you know are wrong and then make a considered decision on the options left.

 Working scientifically

To develop new scientific ideas, predictions need to be tested. If the evidence supports the prediction, a scientific idea will develop.

The development of the periodic table is an example of how scientific ideas develop. Many scientists suggested possible arrangements of the elements but others rejected them as they weren't supported by evidence.

 Worked example **Grade 4**

In Mendeleev's periodic table, the elements lithium, sodium and potassium were all placed into Group 1.

Explain why he grouped them together. **[2 marks]**

Because they have similar properties – for example, react with water to give alkaline solutions.

Exam-style practice **Grade 4**

Look at **Figure 1**.

(a) Name **three** elements Mendeleev put into Group 4. **[1 mark]**

(b) Which property did Mendeleev use to arrange his periodic table? **[1 mark]**

   ☐ **A** atomic mass

   ☐ **B** atomic number

   ☐ **C** atomic size

(c) Suggest an explanation for the use of question marks in Mendeleev's table. **[1 mark]**

(d) Explain why ordering atoms by increasing relative atomic mass does not create a periodic table with the correct order. **[2 marks]**

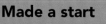 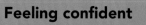

The periodic table

The modern periodic table is based on Mendeleev's work, but the elements are arranged in order of atomic number rather than atomic mass. You will be given a copy of the periodic table in your exam.

 Groups and periods

The periodic table is so-called because similar properties occur at regular intervals. Originally the atomic number simply gave the number of where the atom was placed. It was only later realised that this was also the number of protons in the nucleus. An element's position in the periodic table indicates how it reacts and how reactive it is likely to be.

alkali metals — Hydrogen is a non-metal but has the same electronic configuration as the alkali metals and so is often put in the top middle area of the periodic table. — halogens — noble gases

1	2											3	4	5	6	7	0
						1 **H** Hydrogen 1											4 **He** Helium 2
7 **Li** Lithium 3	9 **Be** Beryllium 4											11 **B** Boron 5	12 **C** Carbon 6	14 **N** Nitrogen 7	16 **O** Oxygen 8	19 **F** Fluorine 9	20 **Ne** Neon 10
23 **Na** Sodium 11	24 **Mg** Magnesium 12											27 **Al** Aluminium 13	28 **Si** Silicon 14	31 **P** Phosphorus 15	32 **S** Sulfur 16	35.5 **Cl** Chlorine 17	40 **Ar** Argon 18
39 **K** Potassium 19	40 **Ca** Calcium 20	45 **Sc** Scandium 21	48 **Ti** Titanium 22	51 **V** Vanadium 23	52 **Cr** Chromium 24	55 **Mn** Manganese 25	56 **Fe** Iron 26	59 **Co** Cobalt 27	59 **Ni** Nickel 28	63.5 **Cu** Copper 29	65 **Zn** Zinc 30	70 **Ga** Gallium 31	73 **Ge** Germanium 32	75 **As** Arsenic 33	79 **Se** Selenium 34	80 **Br** Bromine 35	84 **Kr** Krypton 36
85 **Rb** Rubidium 37	88 **Sr** Strontium 38	89 **Y** Yttrium 39	91 **Zr** Zirconium 40	93 **Nb** Niobium 41	96 **Mo** Molybdenum 42	98 **Tc** Technetium 43	101 **Ru** Ruthenium 44	103 **Rh** Rhodium 45	106 **Pd** Palladium 46	108 **Ag** Silver 47	112 **Cd** Cadmium 48	115 **In** Indium 49	119 **Sn** Tin 50	122 **Sb** Antimony 51	128 **Te** Tellurium 52	127 **I** Iodine 53	131 **Xe** Xenon 54
133 **Cs** Caesium 55	137 **Ba** Barium 56	139 **La** Lanthanum 57	178 **Hf** Hafnium 72	181 **Ta** Tantalum 73	184 **W** Tungsten 74	186 **Re** Rhenium 75	190 **Os** Osmium 76	192 **Ir** Iridium 77	195 **Pt** Platinum 78	197 **Au** Gold 79	201 **Hg** Mercury 80	204 **Tl** Thallium 81	207 **Pb** Lead 82	209 **Bi** Bismuth 83	[210] **Po** Polonium 84	[210] **At** Astatine 85	[222] **Rn** Radon 86
[223] **Fr** Francium 87	[226] **Ra** Radium 88	[227] **Ac** Actinium 89	[261] **Rf** Rutherfordium 104	[262] **Db** Dubnium 105	[266] **Sg** Seaborgium 106	[264] **Bh** Bohrium 107	[277] **Hs** Hassium 108	[268] **Mt** Meitnerium 109	[271] **Ds** Darmstadtium 110	[272] **Rg** Roentgenium 111							

Elements with similar properties are found in vertical columns known as **groups**. The group number is given on the periodic table above each column. All elements in the same group have the same number of electrons in their outer shell, for example, oxygen is in Group 6 and has six electrons in its outer shell.

Rows of elements are called **periods**. All elements in the same period have the same number of electron shells. For example, sodium is in Period 3 and has three electron shells. Across a period, the number of outer-shell electrons increases by 1. For example, lithium (Period 2) has the electronic configuration of 2.1.

 Worked example | **Grade 5**

When lithium metal is added to water it fizzes, producing lithium hydroxide and hydrogen gas. Predict the reaction between sodium and water and name the products formed. **[2 marks]**

Sodium would react with water by fizzing, hydrogen and sodium hydroxide would be produced.

Find sodium and lithium in the periodic table above or on page 245 and compare their position with the answer. When counting rows, remember that the first row (or period) only contains two elements, H and He.

Exam-style practice | **Grade 5**

1 An element has an electronic configuration of 2.8.5.

  (a) State which group the element is in. **[1 mark]**

  (b) State which period the element is in. **[1 mark]**

  (c) Name another element which would react in a similar way to this element. **[1 mark]**

2 An element has 12 electrons.

  (a) State which group the element is in. **[1 mark]**

  (b) State which period the element is in. **[1 mark]**

3 Explain the arrangement of the first 20 elements in the periodic table. You should answer in terms of atomic structure. **[2 marks]**

| ✓ **Made a start** | ✓ **Feeling confident** | ✓ **Exam ready**

Electronic structure

You need to be able to recognise and represent the electronic configurations of the first 20 elements of the periodic table.

 Electronic configuration

Negatively-charged electrons are held in electron shells surrounding the positively-charged nucleus of an atom.

Electrons occupy the lowest available electron shell first, starting with the innermost electron shell. The innermost electron shell is very small and can only hold two electrons. Each subsequent shell can hold up to eight electrons.

The electronic configuration of an atom can be represented by a diagram or by listing the number of electrons in each shell, starting with the innermost shell.

- The atomic number is the same as the number of electrons in an atom.
- The number of electrons in the outermost electron shell is the same as the element's group number in the periodic table. The exception to this is elements in Group 0, which have complete outer shells.
- The number of electron shells is the same as the element's period number in the periodic table.

Examples of electronic configuration

Element	fluorine	neon	sodium
Electronic configuration	2.7	2.8	2.8.1
Periodic table group	7	0	1

> Although electrons repel each other, and should be spread evenly around the shell, it is helpful to pair the electrons up so that you can clearly see how many are in each shell.

> Go to page 76 for more about the properties of electrons.

 Worked example Grades 5–6

(a) Give the electronic configuration of nitrogen (atomic number 7). **[1 mark]**

2.5

> Nitrogen is in Group 5 so it has five electrons in its outer electron shell.

(b) Complete the diagram to show the electronic configuration of nitrogen. **[2 marks]**

> The number of electron shells is equal to the period the element is in (2). The number of electrons in the outer shell is equal to the group (5).

(c) The electronic configuration of lithium is 2.1 and of sodium is 2.8.1. Explain how these electronic configurations can be used to determine their position in the periodic table. **[3 marks]**

The number of electrons in an element's outer shell is the same as its group number, so both lithium and sodium must be in Group 1.

The number of occupied shells is the same as an element's period number, so lithium must be in Period 2 and sodium must be in Period 3.

 Exam-style practice Grade 6

The electronic configurations of four elements are:

A 2.5 **B** 2.7 **C** 2.8.8 **D** 2.8.8.1

Use the periodic table to answer these questions.

Identify which element, **A, B, C** or **D**:

(a) is a Group 0 gas

(b) is fluorine

(c) is found in Group 1

(d) is in Period 3. **[4 marks]**

> Go to page 245 to see the periodic table.

 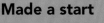

Metals and non-metals

You need to know about the electronic configuration, reactivity and properties of non-metals and metals.

 Differences between metals and non-metals

An element can be classified as a metal or non-metal. Metals are found on the left and centre of the periodic table (**Figure 1**). There are more metal elements than non-metal elements.

- Metals lose electrons when they react, forming positive ions.
- Non-metals gain or share electrons when they react, forming negative ions or covalent compounds (page 87).

As you move across the periodic table, from left to right, the number of outer electrons increases. The elements become less metallic, as they are more likely to share or gain electrons. The more electron shells an element has the more easily it loses outer electrons. The outer electrons are further from the positive charge of the protons in the nucleus, so less energy is needed to remove them.

Go to pages 84–86 to revise ionic bonding and compounds.

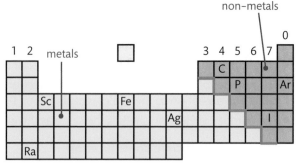

Figure 1 Metals are on the left of the periodic table and non-metals are on the right.

 Worked example **Grade 6**

1 Predict the electron configurations of the following elements. **[3 marks]**

(a) Magnesium (atomic number 12)

2.8.2

(b) Silicon (atomic number 14)

2.8.4

(c) Chlorine (atomic number 17)

2.8.7

2 Explain how the electron configuration of an element can be used to find its position in the periodic table. Use potassium (atomic number 19) to explain. **[4 marks]**

The number of electrons in the outermost shell is equal to the group number.

The number of shells is equal to the period number.

Potassium has an electron configuration of 2.8.8.1.

Therefore it is in Group 1, Period 4.

> You are expected to predict the electronic configurations for the first 20 elements in the periodic table (hydrogen to calcium).
>
> You could be asked to show electronic configurations as diagrams or numerically, as shown in the worked example.

> If the question asks for the diagram, this would be the answer.
>
>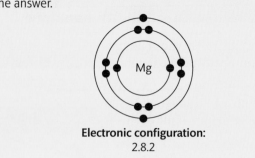
>
> Electronic configuration:
> 2.8.2

 Exam-style practice **Grade 3**

1 (a) Describe what the zigzag line in **Figure 1** represents. **[1 mark]**

(b) Using **Figure 1**, explain whether carbon (C) is a metal or a non-metal. **[1 mark]**

2 Use the electronic configurations provided below to explain which element is most likely to be a metal and which is most likely to be a non-metal. **[2 marks]**

Element A: 2.2

Element B: 2.6

 Made a start **Feeling confident** **Exam ready**

Chemical bonds

You need to be able to apply knowledge about the types of chemical bonds to the physical and chemical properties of substances.

 Types of bonding

You need to know about three types of chemical bond: ionic, covalent and metallic (page 94).

Chemical bonding occurs because atoms need a full outer shell of electrons to become stable.

Atoms can join together by **transferring** electrons (page 84) or by **sharing** electrons (page 87).

Ions

An **ion** is an atom or group of atoms with a positive or negative charge. Ions form when atoms lose or gain electrons, often to result in a full outer shell (page 81). For example, a chlorine atom (electron configuration 2.8.7) gains one electron to become a chloride ion, Cl^- (2.8.8), and a sodium atom (2.8.1) loses one electron to become a sodium ion, Na^+ (2.8).

 Comparing types of bonding

Type of bonding	ionic bonding	covalent bonding	metallic bonding
Occurs between	metals and non-metals	non-metallic elements or compounds of non-metals	metallic elements
Diagram	chloride ion (Cl^-) ... sodium ion (Na^+)	H — O — H	delocalised electrons
How the bonds form	Oppositely charged ions are attracted by electrostatic attraction.	Atoms share a pair of electrons.	Positive ions are surrounded by delocalised electrons.
Examples	NaCl and MgO	CO_2 and H_2O	Cu and Al

 Worked example **Grade 5**

1 State and explain which type of bonding occurs in each of the following substances. **[3 marks]**

(a) Sodium chloride

Ionic bonding because sodium is a metal and chlorine is a non-metal.

(b) Magnesium metal

Metallic bonding because there are only metal atoms present.

(c) Hydrogen gas

Covalent bonding because hydrogen is a non-metal.

> Delocalised electrons are electrons that are free to move. The negatively-charged electrons are attracted to the positively-charged metal ions by electrostatic attraction.

2 Describe each type of bonding with reference to the electrons involved and electrostatic forces. **[6 marks]**

Ionic bonding involves the transfer of electrons from one atom to another. This causes the ions to have opposite charges and so to be electrostatically attracted to each other.

Covalent bonding involves the sharing of a pair of electrons to form a covalent bond. The positively-charged nuclei of the bonded atoms are electrostatically attracted to the bonding pair of electrons.

Metallic bonding is formed by the electrostatic attraction between the positive metal ions and the delocalised electrons (from the outer shell of the metal atoms).

Exam-style practice **Grade 4**

(a) State what is meant by the term 'delocalised'. **[1 mark]**

(b) Name the type of bonding that involves delocalised electrons. **[1 mark]**

Ionic bonding

You need to know how to describe ionic bonding and represent it using dot and cross diagrams.

⑤ Ionic bonding

An ion is an atom (or group of atoms) with a positive or negative charge.

Metal atoms lose electrons to form positively-charged ions, called **cations**. Non-metal atoms gain electrons to form negatively-charged ions, or **anions**.

Positive and negative ions attract each other, forming ionic bonds.

The ions formed from the metals in Groups 1 and 2 and the non-metals in Groups 6 and 7 have the electronic configuration of a Group 0 element.

⑩ Worked example — Grade 5

Look at **Figure 1**.

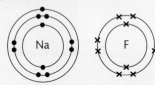

Figure 1 The electronic configurations of sodium and fluorine.

(a) Describe how fluorine atoms and sodium atoms form sodium fluoride. **[2 marks]**

Sodium atoms lose one electron to form ions with a +1 charge. Fluorine atoms gain one electron to form ions with a −1 charge.

(b) Draw each of the ions formed during the reaction. Give the charge on each of the ions formed. **[3 marks]**

sodium ion   fluoride ion

(c) Determine the number of protons, neutrons and electrons in each of the ions formed in **(b)**. **[4 marks]**

Sodium ion (Na⁺) = 11 protons, 12 neutrons, 10 electrons

Fluoride ion (F⁻) = 9 protons, 10 neutrons, 10 electrons

Use your periodic table to work out the number of protons and neutrons. Go to page 77 to revise calculating the number of protons, neutrons and electrons.

⑤ Electron transfer

Ionic bonds are formed by the transfer of electrons from metal atoms to non-metal atoms, so both gain a stable arrangement of electrons. Electron transfer is represented by dot and cross diagrams.

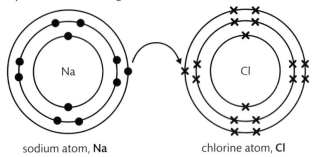

sodium atom, **Na**   chlorine atom, **Cl**

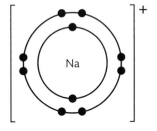
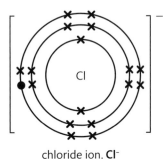

sodium ion, **Na⁺**   chloride ion, **Cl⁻**

Figure 2 The dot and cross diagrams show the formation of sodium chloride, an ionic compound. Go to page 85 to revise ionic compounds.

Fluorine is in Group 7 so it needs to gain one electron to have a full outer shell. Because fluorine gains an electron the fluoride ion is negatively charged.

① Exam focus

In the exam, you could be asked to draw dot and cross diagrams for ionic compounds formed between metals in Groups 1 and 2 and non-metals in Groups 6 and 7. Make sure you know the charge on the ions formed.

Group	Charge of ion formed
1	1+
2	2+
6	2−
7	1−

⑤ Exam-style practice — Grade 6

Draw each of the ions formed during the reaction between magnesium and fluorine. Give the charge on each of the ions formed. **[3 marks]**

Ionic compounds

You need to be able to identify ionic compounds from different types of diagrams.

Ionic compounds are comprised of many ions, which are held together by strong electrostatic forces of attraction. Ionic compounds form giant structures called **lattices**. The **electrostatic forces of attraction** between the ions are strong due to the attraction between the oppositely charged ions.

Ionic lattices are three-dimensional structures. The forces of attraction act in all directions throughout the lattice. Ionic compounds can be represented by:

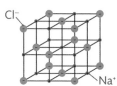

Figure 1 A ball and stick diagram

Figure 2 A dot and cross diagram

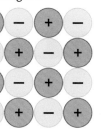

Figure 3 A two-dimensional diagram

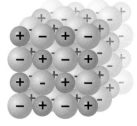

Figure 4 A three-dimensional diagram

The crossover method can be used to work out formulae. Write the ions, positive first. Then cross over the numbers for each charge:

$$Mg^{2+} + Cl^- \rightarrow MgCl_2$$

(Remember, when the charge is 1, no number is needed in the formula.)

Magnesium is in Group 2 so the ion will have a charge of +2. Chloride ions (and all halide ions) have a charge of −1. In the neutral compound the positive and negative charges must balance; therefore, two chloride ions are needed to balance the +2 charge on the magnesium ion.

Using **Table 1**, deduce the formulae of the following ionic compounds.

Negative ions (anions)	Formula	Ionic formula	Charge
Hydroxide	OH	OH^-	1−
Nitrate	NO_3	NO_3^-	1−
Sulfate	SO_4	SO_4^{2-}	2−
Carbonate	CO_3	CO_3^{2-}	2−
Halide	Cl, Br, I	Cl^-, Br^-, I^-	1−
Oxide	O	O^{2-}	2−

Table 1 Formulae of ions

(a) Magnesium chloride [1 mark]

$MgCl_2$

(b) Potassium sulfate [1 mark]

K_2SO_4

(c) Sodium carbonate [1 mark]

Na_2CO_3

(d) Calcium hydroxide [1 mark]

$Ca(OH)_2$

When an ion is made up of several atoms (like OH^-), and there are two or more in a compound, use brackets () to show that the subscript number applies to the whole ion.

1 Describe the structure and bonding of the ionic compound sodium chloride. **[2 marks]**

2 Use **Figure 1** to answer the following questions.

    (a) State the type of bonding shown. **[1 mark]**

    (b) Give **one** limitation and **one** advantage to using this type of model. **[2 marks]**

Properties of ionic compounds

You can use the structure and type of bonding in an ionic compound to determine its properties.

 Properties of ionic compounds

The type of bonding in a compound affects its properties. Scientists can design new materials with tailored properties using their understanding of structure and bonding.

Structure	giant lattices
Melting point	generally high
Boiling point	generally high
Electrical conductivity	excellent conductors when molten or aqueous
Solubility in water	generally soluble

Go to page 85 to revise ionic bonding and the structure of ionic compounds.

Ionic compounds have high melting and boiling points because a large amount of energy is required to break the strong electrostatic forces that hold the oppositely charged ions together in all directions within the giant lattice structure.
Go to page 105 for more about state changes.

Ionic compounds can conduct electricity when melted (molten) or dissolved in water (aqueous) because the ions are free to move, allowing charge to flow.

 Worked example Grade 6

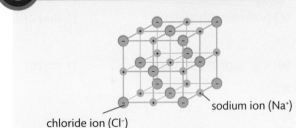
sodium ion (Na⁺)
chloride ion (Cl⁻)

Figure 1 The structure of sodium chloride

1 Explain why sodium chloride cannot conduct electricity when solid. **[2 marks]**

To conduct electricity, ions need to be free to allow the charge to flow. When solid, sodium ions and chloride ions are in fixed positions, held by strong ionic bonds, and so are unable to conduct electricity.

2 Explain why sodium chloride melts when heated strongly. **[2 marks]**

When heated, the ions gain enough energy to overcome the forces of attraction and move apart.

3 Explain why sodium chloride has a high melting point (801 °C). **[2 marks]**

Sodium chloride is made of oppositely charged ions, which are held together by strong electrostatic forces of attraction in all directions that require a large amount of energy to overcome.

 **Exam focus**

In your exam, you may need to explain why ionic compounds have high melting points and boiling points (in terms of forces between ions), and whether or not they conduct electricity (when they are solids, molten or in aqueous solution).

 Exam-style practice Grade 6

1 Chlorine reacts with sodium to produce sodium chloride (NaCl).

(a) Write a balanced chemical equation for the reaction. **[2 marks]**

(b) Draw a dot and cross diagram to show the bonding in sodium chloride. **[2 marks]**

2 Magnesium oxide has a similar structure to sodium chloride. Use your understanding of ionic compounds to answer the following questions about magnesium oxide.

(a) Describe the structure of magnesium oxide. You may use a diagram. **[2 marks]**

(b) Give a reason why magnesium oxide can conduct electricity when molten. **[1 mark]**

(c) Give a reason why magnesium oxide has a high melting point. **[2 marks]**

 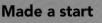

Covalent bonding

You need to be able to identify and draw covalent bonds for simple molecules, polymers and giant covalent structures.

Go to page 85 for the visual representations of these models.

(5) Forming covalent bonds

A covalent bond is a strong bond, which forms between atoms that share a pair of electrons. Covalent bonds are found in simple molecules (page 88), polymers (page 93) and giant covalent structures (page 89).

Covalent bonds form between non-metal atoms, which combine together by sharing outer-shell electrons. The shared pair of electrons holds the two atoms together. When atoms bond together in this way, they are called a molecule.

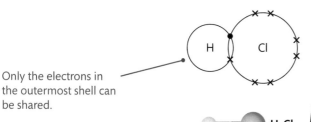

Only the electrons in the outermost shell can be shared.

H-Cl

Figure 1 The covalent bonding in hydrogen chloride can be displayed in different ways.

A hydrogen atom has one electron in its outer shell. Carbon has four electrons in its outer shell.

The bond must clearly show a **shared pair** of electrons, one being a dot and one being a cross.

The covalent compound must show each atom correctly bonded with a full outer shell.

(2) Exam focus

For the exam, you need to know how to do the following:

- ☑ Draw dot and cross diagrams for H_2, O_2, HCl, H_2O, CO_2 and CH_4.
- ☑ Show a single covalent bond as a line between two atoms.
- ☑ Describe the limitations of dot and cross, ball and stick, 2D and 3D models to represent covalent molecules and giant structures.
- ☑ Deduce the molecular formula of a substance from a given diagram.

Look at **Figure 3** and count how many shared pairs of electrons there are.

(10) Worked example — Grades 5–6

1. Draw a dot and cross diagram to show the bonding in methane, CH_4. **[4 marks]**

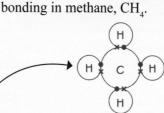

2. Give the limitations of each of the following models for representing compounds.

(a) Ball and stick diagram **[2 marks]**

Ball and stick diagrams show a three-dimensional representation of the compound and indicate the bonds between the atoms. However, as the models are not to scale, the size of the atoms is incorrect.

(b) Dot and cross diagram **[2 marks]**

Dot and cross diagrams only give a two-dimensional representation of the atoms in a bond. It is not possible to see the actual arrangement of the atoms in the compound.

(c) Two-dimensional diagram **[2 marks]**

Two-dimensional diagrams don't show the electronic structure of the atoms or the arrangement of giant structures.

(d) Three-dimensional diagram **[2 marks]**

Three-dimensional diagrams show the size of the atoms and give a more realistic idea of their position; however, they do not show the bonds or the internal structure.

(10) Exam-style practice — Grade 6

1. Each of the lines in **Figure 2** represents a covalent bond. Describe a covalent bond. **[2 marks]**

Figure 2 Water

2. Look at **Figure 3**. Determine how many bonds there are between the atoms. **[1 mark]**

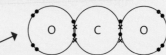

Figure 3 A molecule of carbon dioxide

3. Draw a dot and cross diagram to show the bonding in oxygen, O_2. **[2 marks]**

Properties of simple molecular substances

Simple molecules, such as carbon dioxide and water, consist of two or three atoms bonded together. You need to use your knowledge of forces and bonding to predict the properties of simple molecular substances.

Structure of simple molecular substances

Simple molecules, sometimes referred to as simple covalent molecules, have strong covalent bonds **within** the molecule.

Simple molecular substances have weak intermolecular forces **between** the molecules. The intermolecular forces increase with the size of the molecules, so larger molecules have stronger intermolecular forces.

Go to page 87 to revise covalent bonds.

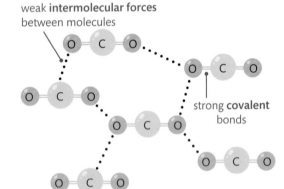

weak **intermolecular forces** between molecules

strong **covalent** bonds

Figure 1 Carbon dioxide is a simple covalent molecule.

Properties of simple molecular compounds

Simple molecular substances are usually liquids or gases at room temperature. Their relatively low melting and boiling points are due to the weak intermolecular forces between the molecules. Larger molecules have higher melting and boiling points because there are stronger intermolecular forces to overcome.

Simple molecular substances do not conduct electricity when solid or in solution because there are no charged particles or free electrons able to move to carry an electrical current.

Simple molecular substances are mainly insoluble or slightly soluble in water.

Worked example — Grade 6

1 The boiling point of chlorine, Cl_2, is relatively low ($-34\,°C$). Explain this fact, relating your answer to both intermolecular forces and covalent bonds. **[3 marks]**

Only the intermolecular forces between the Cl_2 molecules need to be overcome to boil chlorine, not the strong covalent bonds between the atoms.

Intermolecular forces are very weak, so only a small amount of energy is needed to overcome them.

2 **Figure 2** shows the structural formulae of two alkane molecules.

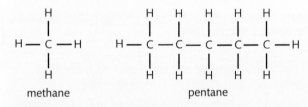

methane   pentane

Figure 2

Using ideas about intermolecular forces, explain which alkane has the higher boiling point. **[2 marks]**

Intermolecular forces increase with the size of molecules. As pentane is a larger molecule it will have a higher boiling point.

The covalent bonds are not broken when a substance melts or boils; only the intermolecular forces are.

Exam-style practice — Grade 6

1 State the properties of simple molecular compounds. **[2 marks]**

2 State the type of bonding that occurs within a simple molecular compund. **[1 mark]**

3 Explain, in terms of forces, what must happen for a simple molecular liquid to boil. **[2 marks]**

 Made a start   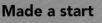 **Feeling confident**   **Exam ready**

Giant covalent structures

You need to be able to recognise a giant covalent structure from a diagram that shows its structure and bonding.

5 Two types of giant covalent structures

Giant covalent structures are covalently bonded solids that contain many atoms. The atoms are usually arranged in lattices. Examples of giant covalent structures include graphite and diamond.

Each carbon atom in graphite forms three covalent bonds. Carbon has a 2.4 electron configuration, so each carbon atom in graphite has one electron that delocalises, like in a metal (page 94). Each carbon atom in diamond forms four covalent bonds.

For more on the structure of graphite see page 91

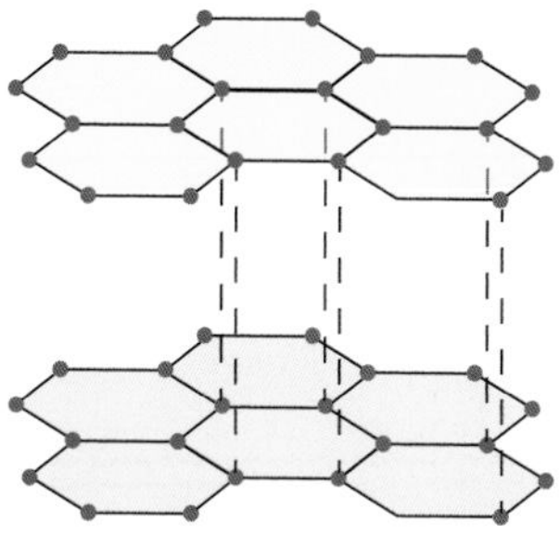

Figure 1 Graphite

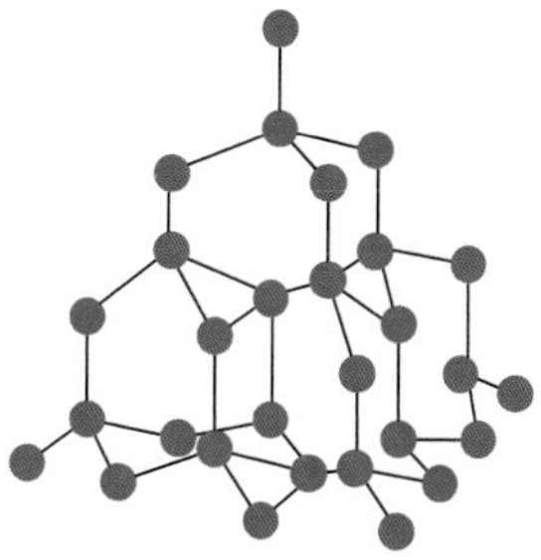

Figure 2 Diamond

For more on the structure of diamond see page 90

Giant covalent structures have very high melting and boiling points because a lot of energy is required to break the numerous strong covalent bonds. Giant covalent structures are insoluble in water (the attraction to the water molecules is not strong enough to overcome the covalent bonds in order to allow the substance to dissolve).

Some giant covalent structures can conduct electricity and others cannot (as solids and in solution). As there are no mobile charged particles in diamond, it is unable to conduct electricity. Graphite contains charged particles (electrons) that can move, so can conduct electricity.

5 Worked example — Grade 5

Figures 1 and **2** show the structures of two forms of carbon. Using **Figures 1** and **2** and your knowledge of structure and bonding, explain why:

(a) graphite is very soft **[2 marks]**

Graphite contains strong covalent bonds between the carbon atoms in each layer. However, between the layers there are only weak forces of attraction, so the layers can slide over each other.

(b) diamond is very hard. **[2 marks]**

The atoms in diamond are bonded together in a three-dimensional structure, so the structure is harder to break.

Exam focus

Make sure you look at any diagrams, images or photos provided in the exam. If you're unsure of the answer to the question, a diagram can help.

Graphite is soft as the layers can slide. This is because they are only held together by weak forces of attraction.

All the carbon atoms in diamond are held together by strong covalent bonds, which require a large amount of energy to break.

10 Exam-style practice — Grades 5–7

1. State the number of bonds each carbon atom forms in graphite. **[1 mark]**
2. State the number of bonds each carbon atom forms in diamond. **[1 mark]**
3. Name the type of bonding that occurs in both diamond and graphite. **[1 mark]**
4. Explain each of the following in terms of structure and bonding:
   (a) why graphite and diamond are described as having giant covalent structures **[2 marks]**
   (b) why graphite and diamond have high melting and boiling points. **[2 marks]**

Diamond

Diamond is a rare and expensive form of carbon. You need to explain its many useful properties in terms of its structure and bonding.

Structure of diamond

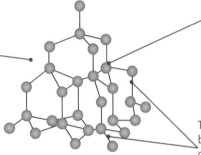

Diamond is a giant covalently bonded lattice of carbon **atoms**.

Each carbon atom is bonded to **four** other carbon atoms. They form the shape of a **tetrahedron**.

There are strong covalent bonds between each of the atoms in all different directions.

Figure 1 Molecular structure of diamond

Properties and uses of diamond

The properties of diamond, such as high melting point, are related to its giant covalent structure. A lot of energy is required to overcome the strong covalent bonds between the carbon atoms in diamond.

State at room temperature	solid
Appearance at room temperature	transparent
Hardness	very hard
Melting and boiling points	very high
Electrical conductivity	does not conduct
Solubility in water	insoluble

The weak attraction between water molecules and carbon atoms is not strong enough to overcome the strong covalent bonds in diamond.

The unique structure and properties of diamond make it suitable for many different uses. For example, it is used in **cutting tools**. Diamond is one of the hardest naturally occurring substances. It can be used to cut a wide range of materials. Its high melting point prevents the tools from melting under the heat generated by cutting (**Figure 2**).

Figure 2 Cutting discs are coated in tiny diamonds.

Worked example — Grade 7

Explain how the structure of giant covalent compounds contribute to their characteristic properties. Using diamond as an example, your answer must refer to the melting point and lack of electrical conductivity. **[6 marks]**

Each carbon atom in diamond forms four strong covalent bonds and all of the bonds must be broken to melt diamond. A lot of energy is required to break the large number of strong covalent bonds. Therefore diamond has a very high melting point.

Diamond cannot conduct electricity as all of the outer electrons are involved in covalent bonding, meaning there are no charged particles free to move.

Exam-style practice — Grade 6

1 (a) Explain why diamond has a very high melting point. **[2 marks]**

(b) Explain why diamond does not conduct electricity. **[2 marks]**

2 Drill bits, used for cutting through rock, often have diamonds on the end.

Explain why diamond is used to make cutting tools. **[5 marks]**

Graphite

Graphite is another form of carbon. It is a non-metal that can conduct electricity due to its structure. You need to know about the structure and properties of graphite and how they relate to its many uses.

 Structure of graphite

Graphite is made up of covalently bonded carbon **atoms**.

Each carbon atom has three covalent bonds and one electron put between the layers.

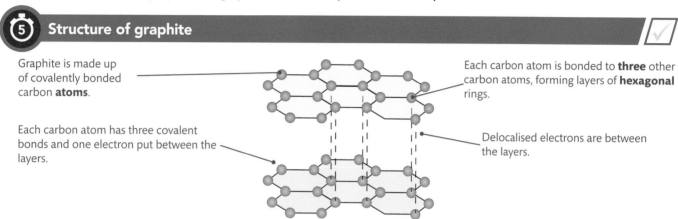

Each carbon atom is bonded to **three** other carbon atoms, forming layers of **hexagonal** rings.

Delocalised electrons are between the layers.

Figure 1 Molecular structure of graphite

 Properties and uses of graphite

Like diamond, graphite is made up of many strong covalent bonds, which require a lot of energy to be broken. This means that graphite has high melting and boiling points.

State at room temperature	solid
Appearance at room temperature	grey / black
Hardness	soft
Melting and boiling points	very high
Electrical conductivity	good conductor
Solubility in water	insoluble

Graphite is a good conductor because its delocalised electrons enable it to conduct electricity.

The weak attraction between water molecules and carbon atoms is not strong enough to overcome the strong covalent bonds in graphite.

The structure and properties of graphite make it suitable for many different uses.

- **Pencil lead** – the forces between the layers are weak, so the layers easily slide onto paper, leaving a mark.
- **Lubricant** – graphite is slippery, which makes it a perfect dry lubricant for machine parts and metal locks.
- **Electrodes for electrolysis (and batteries)** – graphite has a high melting point and conducts electricity, making it a suitable electrode.

Worked example — Grade 6

1 Use your knowledge and understanding of the structure of graphite to explain why graphite can be used as an electrical conductor. **[2 marks]**

Graphite is a good conductor of electricity as there are delocalised electrons free to move within its structure.

2 Explain how the structure and bonding in graphite gives it a high melting and boiling point. **[3 marks]**

Graphite has a giant covalent (molecular) structure. There are many strong covalent bonds which must be overcome to separate the atoms. This would take a lot of (heat) energy.

Exam-style practice — Grade 5

(a) Give **two** properties that make graphite suitable for use as electrodes in electrolysis. **[2 marks]**

(b) State the type of bonding present between carbon atoms in graphite. **[1 mark]**

(c) Why is graphite slippery and soft? **[1 mark]**

- [ ] **A** It is made of layers.
- [ ] **B** It is an ionic compound.
- [ ] **C** It is made of simple molecules.

(d) Graphite is slippery. Name **two** uses for graphite related to this property. **[2 marks]**

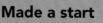 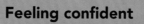

Graphene and fullerenes

Graphene and fullerenes are carbon structures based on covalently bonded rings of carbon atoms. You need to know about the structure and properties of graphene and fullerenes and how they relate to their uses.

Structure and properties

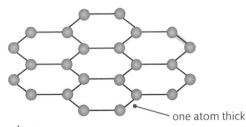

Figure 1 Graphene

Graphene is a single layer of graphite formed from carbon atoms, each bonded to three other carbon atoms in a hexagonal ring arrangement. It is a two-dimensional structure. This arrangement gives graphene the following properties:

- good conductor of electricity (due to the delocalised electrons)
- strong (due to lots of covalent bonds to break)
- flexible (only one atom thick)
- transparent (as only one atom thick).

Uses of graphene

Potential uses of graphene include: display screens, electric circuits and solar cells. It can also be used in medical, chemical and industrial processes. Graphene is a relatively recent discovery and scientists are learning more about its uses each day.

Explain, in terms of structure and bonding, the properties of fullerenes including C_{60} and graphene. **[6 marks]**

Fullerenes consist of hexagonal rings of carbon atoms arranged as single sheets (graphene); spheres (C_{60}) or tubes (fullerene nanotubes). To achieve this arrangement each carbon must bond covalently with three other carbon atoms. This also gives fullerenes a high melting point and high tensile strength.

This structure also allows fullerenes to conduct electricity, as there are delocalised electrons within the structure. Delocalised electrons can move throughout the structure.

Use scientific terminology to show your understanding.

Structure and properties

Figure 2 Fullerene

Fullerenes are hollow cages or tubes made of carbon atoms. Just like in graphene, each carbon is bonded to three other carbon atoms, but unlike graphene, fullerenes have a three-dimensional structure. Cylindrical fullerenes (**carbon nanotubes**) form tubes based on hexagonal rings of carbon. Fullerenes have the following properties:

- good conductor of electricity (due to the delocalised electrons)
- strong (due to the strong covalent bonds)
- high melting and boiling points (due to the high number of covalent bonds to break).

The first fullerene to be discovered was a sphere containing 60 carbons (named Buckminsterfullerene).

Figure 3 Buckminsterfullerene C_{60}

Uses of fullerenes

Fullerenes may be used for transporting drugs within the body because of their hollow structure.

Fullerenes are useful for nanotechnology, electronics and in drug delivery systems for fighting cancers. Tube fullerenes (nanotubes) are used for reinforcing structures, for example tennis racket frames, as they are very light but very strong.

Split the question into sections to help you answer it; discuss the structure and the bonding of the fullerenes, relating their properties to these features.

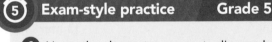
1. Name the element common to diamond, graphite, fullerenes and graphene. **[1 mark]**
2. Give **two** similarities and **one** difference between the structure of fullerenes and graphite. **[3 marks]**

Polymers

You need to know that simple polymers consist of large molecules containing chains of carbon atoms, and to be able to describe their structure and bonding.

⏱ 10 Polymers

Polymers are very large molecules. The atoms in a polymer molecule are joined together by strong covalent bonds in long chains. There are variable numbers of atoms in the chains of a particular polymer. One example of a polymer is poly(ethene).

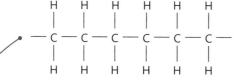

Figure 1 Three ethene molecules join to make part of a poly(ethene) molecule

Go to page 87 for more about covalent bonds.

The intermolecular forces between the large surfaces of polymer molecules are stronger compared with the intermolecular forces between small molecules, so polymers melt at higher temperatures. Polymers are solids at room temperature.

Polymers have fairly high melting points due to the intermolecular forces between their large molecules.

⏱ 5 Worked example — Grades 5–6

1 Describe the formation and structure of the polymer poly(ethene). **[3 marks]**

Poly(ethene) is produced when many ethene ($CH_2{=}CH_2$) molecules react together, forming a very large molecule made up from a long chain of carbon atoms. The carbon atoms are joined together by strong covalent bonds.

2 Explain how the strength of the intermolecular forces is affected by the length of the polymer chain. **[1 mark]**

The longer the polymer chain, the more surface area available for intermolecular fores to act on and so the stronger the forces become.

Repeat units

Polymer molecules consist of lots of identical, repeat units in a chain.

The word poly means 'many' so poly(ethene) is made from many ethene molecules joined together.

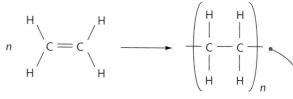

Figure 2 Ethene and the repeat unit of poly(ethene)

Go to page 156 for more about the formation of polymers from alkenes.

Figure 3 Uses of poly(ethene)

⏱ 5 Exam-style practice — Grade 6

1 Draw a section of the polymer poly(ethene) containing three repeat units. **[2 marks]**

2 State what is meant by the term 'polymer'. **[1 mark]**

3 State what type of bond joins the atoms together in a polymer molecule. **[1 mark]**

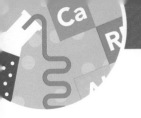

Metallic bonding

Metals have very strong bonds due to the presence of free electrons. You need to be able to recall the structure and arrangement of metal particles.

5 Structure of metals

Most metals have one, two or three electrons in their outer shell. These electrons are said to be 'delocalised', which means they are not in fixed positions but instead are free to move throughout the metal structure.

As the electrons can move, they are shared within the structure, giving rise to strong metallic bonds.

The metallic bonds are formed from the strong attraction between positively-charged metal ions and the negatively-charged electrons.

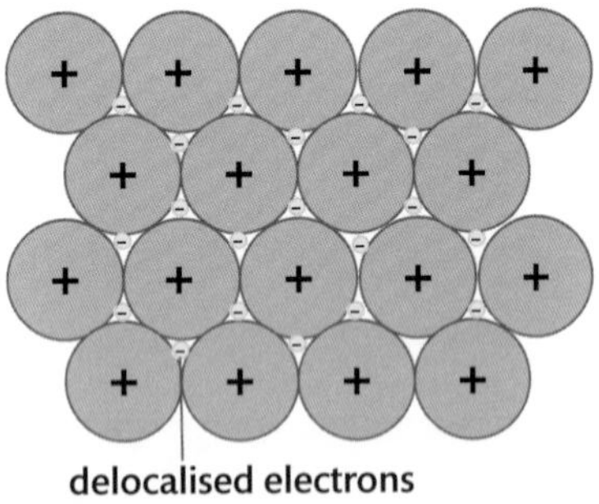

Figure 1 The arrangement of metal ions and electrons in metallic bonding

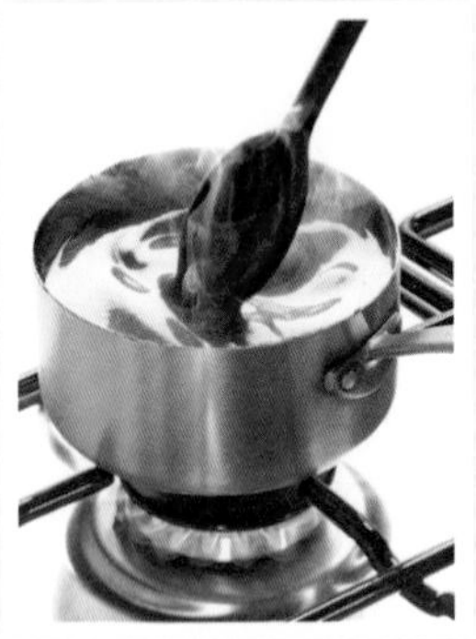

Figure 2 Metals, such as copper, are used to make saucepans because of their high strength and thermal conductivity.

10 Worked example — Grade 7

1 Describe the structure of a metal. **[3 marks]**

Metals consist of giant structures of metal ions arranged in a regular pattern, with delocalised electrons.

2 Draw a diagram to show the arrangement of particles in a metal. Label the diagram. **[3 marks]**

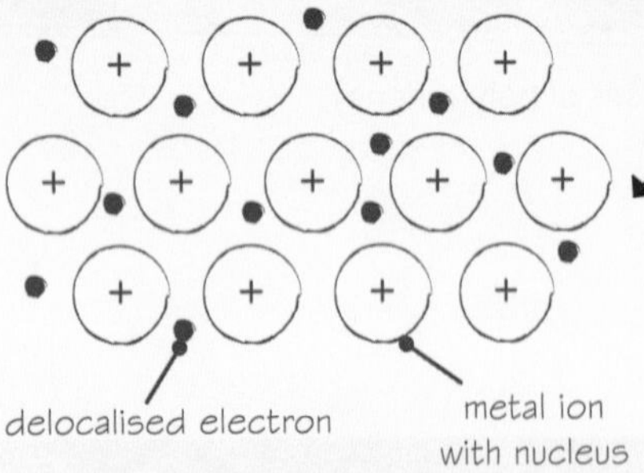

3 State what is meant by the term 'delocalised electron'. Identify which electrons, in a metal atom, become delocalised. **[2 marks]**

Delocalised electrons are not fixed to one atom, they are free to move. Only the electrons in the outer shell of a metal atom are delocalised.

Exam focus

Make sure you use key scientific terminology, such as 'delocalised electrons', in your answer.

Show the regular arrangement of the metal ions as positively-charged particles surrounded by negative electrons.

5 Exam-style practice — Grade 6

1 Which of these statements best describes metallic bonding? **[1 mark]**

- ☐ **A** transfer of electrons
- ☐ **B** sharing electrons
- ☐ **C** attraction of positive nuclei and electrons
- ☐ **D** atoms form hexagonal rings

2 Explain why metal particles are shown as positively charged in metallic bonding. **[2 marks]**

3 Explain how a metallic bond forms. **[2 marks]**

Properties of metals

You need to be able to describe the physical properties of metals and how these differ to non-metals.

⑤ Properties of metals

Metals form giant structures with strong metallic bonds, in which electrons in the outer shells of the metal atoms are free to move. This gives them the following properties.

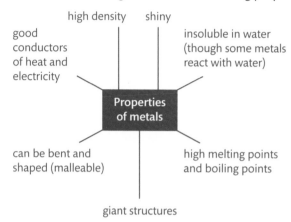

high density   shiny

good conductors of heat and electricity

insoluble in water (though some metals react with water)

Properties of metals

can be bent and shaped (malleable)

high melting points and boiling points

giant structures

Go to page 94 to revise the structure of metals.

⑩ Worked example   Grades 5–6

1 Copper is a metal. Explain why copper is a good electrical conductor. **[2 marks]**

The electrons in the outer shell are delocalised, so they are free to move.

2 Explain why a blacksmith can work iron into different shapes by hitting it with a hammer. **[3 marks]**

Metals such as iron are malleable because their atoms are in layers which can slide easily over each other; this makes them easy to bend and shape.

3 Explain why aluminium, a Group 3 metal, is a better conductor than sodium, a Group 1 metal. **[2 marks]**

Aluminium has more electrons in its outer shell, so more free electrons are available to conduct heat and electricity.

⑤ Metals as conductors

Metals are good conductors of electricity because they have delocalised electrons within their metallic structure.

The more electrons available in the outer shell, the more efficient a conductor the metal is. This is because there are more electrons available to carry electrical charge.

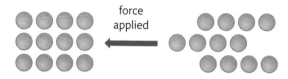

force applied

Figure 1 Malleability of metals. The metallic layers can 'slide' when force is applied, meaning that unlike non-metals, they can be shaped.

② Comparison of metals and non-metals

Non-metals	Metals
Dull	Shiny
Low melting points	High melting points
Poor electrical conductors	Good electrical conductors
Low density	High density
Brittle	Malleable

> Remember, it is only the electrons in the outer shell that are free to move throughout the metallic structure. These delocalised electrons enable the metal to conduct electricity and heat efficiently.

> Think about how the electron structure of elements changes in different groups in the periodic table.

⑩ Exam-style practice   Grades 5–6

1 Give the term used to describe materials that allow energy transfer to take place within the material. **[1 mark]**

2 Give a reason why metals are better thermal conductors than non-metals. **[1 mark]**

3 Explain why metals have high melting and boiling points. **[2 marks]**

 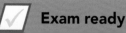

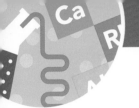

Relative formula mass

The relative formula mass of a compound is found by adding together the relative atomic masses of all the atoms in the compound.

5 Relative formula mass

Relative formula mass (M_r) is the sum of the relative atomic masses of all the atoms in the formula of a substance. For example, to find the M_r of sodium hydroxide (NaOH), you add together the A_r values of all the atoms in its formula:

A_r of Na is 23

A_r of O is 16

A_r of H is 1

so the M_r of NaOH is 23 + 16 + 1 = 40.

In a balanced equation, the sum of the M_r of the reactants is equal to the sum of the M_r of the products.

10 Worked example — Grade 5

Go to page 78 to revise relative atomic mass.

1 Calculate the relative formula mass of carbon dioxide. (A_r values: C = 12; O = 16) **[2 marks]**

$CO_2 = C + (2 \times O)$

$= 12 + (2 \times 16)$

$= 44$

Look at the periodic table to find the relative atomic mass of each atom.

The relative formula mass has no units.

2 Calculate the relative formula mass of zinc nitrate.

The formula for zinc nitrate is $Zn(NO_3)_2$.

(A_r values: Zn = 65; N = 14; O = 16) **[2 marks]**

When there are brackets, the subscript number that follows means everything inside the brackets is multiplied by that number.

A_r of Zn = 65

M_r of $(NO_3)_2$ =

$2 \times N + 2 \times O_3$

$2 \times 14 + 2 \times (3 \times 16)$

$28 + 2 \times 48$

$28 + 96$

$= 124$

M_r of $Zn(NO_3)_2 = 124 + 65 = 189$

The '2' in O_2 refers to a pair of atoms that are joined together. Whereas, the '2' in $(NO_3)_2$ means there are two separate NO_3 ions, so you need to multiply each atom in NO_3 by two.

10 Exam-style practice — Grades 6–7

1 **Figure 1** represents a molecule of aspirin.

(a) State how many of each type of atom is present in aspirin. **[1 mark]**

(b) Calculate the relative formula mass of aspirin.

(A_r values: C = 12; H = 1; O = 16) **[2 marks]**

2 Calculate the relative formula mass of aluminium sulfate. The formula for aluminium sulfate is $Al_2(SO_4)_3$.

(A_r values: Al = 27; S = 32; O = 16) **[2 marks]**

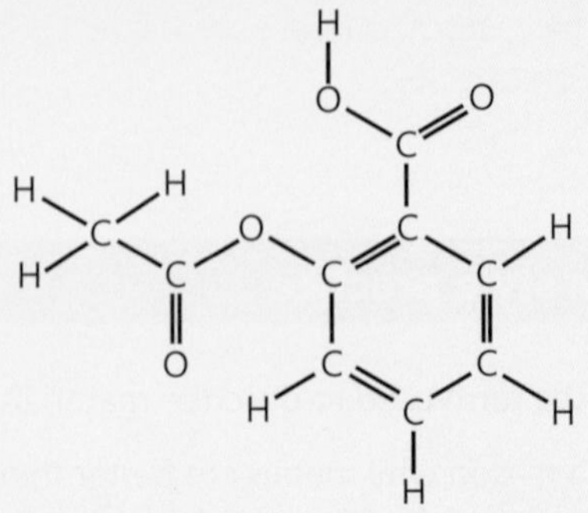

Figure 1 Aspirin

Empirical formulae

You need to be able to deduce the empirical formula of a compound from its molecular formula, and the molecular formula of a compound from its empirical formula and relative atomic mass.

⑤ Formulae

- Atoms of different elements combine, in specific ratios, to form compounds.
- The empirical formula gives the simplest whole-number ratio of atoms in an element or compound.
- The molecular formula of a compound contains the numbers of each of the atoms present in a compound.
- Experimental data can be used to identify the empirical formula of a compound.

⑩ Worked example — Grade 6

1 A compound has a molecular formula of $C_{12}H_{16}O_8$. Deduce its empirical formula. **[1 mark]**

$C_3H_4O_2$

2 The relative molecular mass of a compound is 84 and the empirical formula is CH_2.

Calculate the molecular formula of the compound. **[3 marks]**

Carbon = 12; hydrogen = 1

so CH_2 = 12 + 2 = 14

$\frac{84}{14} = 6$

The molecular formula is C_6H_{12}

3 A compound contains 40 g carbon, 6.72 g hydrogen and 53.28 g of oxygen.

Calculate the empirical formula of the compound. **[3 marks]**

	C	**H**	**O**
Mass	40	6.72	53.28
Divide by A_r	/12	/1	/16
Calculate moles	= 3.33	= 6.72	= 3.33
Divide by smallest	/3.33	/3.33	/3.33
	= 1	= 2	= 1

Empirical formula = CH_2O

To calculate empirical formula, first divide the mass of the element by the relative atomic mass (A_r, from the periodic table) to find the number of moles.

Divide the number of moles of each element by the element with the smallest number of moles – this will give you a whole number ratio.

⑤ Experimental determination of empirical formula

1 Weigh an empty crucible and lid. Add some magnesium and reweigh.

2 Set up the equipment as shown in **Figure 1**.

3 Heat the crucible strongly, lifting the lid occasionally to allow more oxygen to react with the magnesium.

4 When no further change takes place allow to cool.

5 Reweigh the crucible. Calculate the increase in mass of the crucible.

The increase in mass of the crucible is due to oxygen combining with the magnesium.

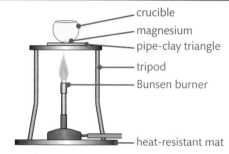

- crucible
- magnesium
- pipe-clay triangle
- tripod
- Bunsen burner
- heat-resistant mat

Figure 1

Each number (of atoms) is divided by the highest common factor, 4, to give the simplest whole-number ratio of atoms.

To calculate the molecular formula, first work out the mass of the atoms in the empirical formula.

Next, divide the relative molecular mass by the empirical mass.

The molecular formula is the empirical formula × 6.

⑩ Exam-style practice — Grade 7

A student carried out the experiment described above. The results are given below.

Mass of crucible and lid (g)	2.61
Mass with magnesium added (g)	5.00
Mass when reaction is completed (g)	6.39

(a) Use the first and second readings to calculate the mass of magnesium used. **[1 mark]**

(b) Use the second and third readings to calculate the mass of oxygen gained. **[1 mark]**

(c) Use your answers to parts **(a)** and **(b)** to calculate the empirical formula of magnesium oxide. **[3 marks]**

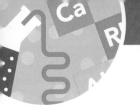

Balancing equations

You need to be able to balance a chemical equation given the masses of reactants and products, using the law of conservation of mass.

5 Balancing equations

Chemical reactions can be represented by balanced chemical equations. In a balanced chemical equation, there must always be the same number of each element on either side of the arrow. This is because no atoms are lost or made in a chemical reaction.

Chemical equations can only be balanced by putting multipliers in front of the formulae of elements or compounds. You cannot change the formulae of elements or compounds to balance an equation.

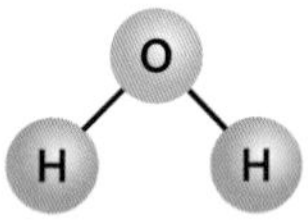

Figure 1 H_2O is a molecule with one oxygen and two hydrogens.

If you tried to balance an equation by adding a 2 to the end of the formula, you would end up with a new substance – hydrogen peroxide H_2O_2 (**Figure 2**).

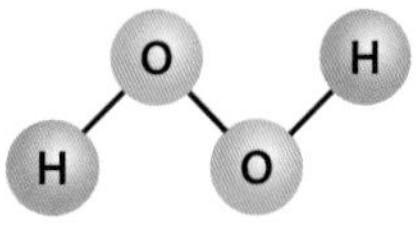

Figure 2 Hydrogen peroxide, H_2O_2

5 Worked example — Grade 6

Balance the following equations.

(a) $CH_4 + \underline{2}O_2 \rightarrow CO_2 + \underline{2}H_2O$ **[1 mark]**

Carbon: 1 → 1 ✓

Oxygen: 2 → 3 ✗

Hydrogen: 4 → 2 ✗

(b) $\underline{2}Na + \underline{2}H_2O \rightarrow \underline{2}NaOH + H_2$ **[1 mark]**

Sodium: 1 → 1 ✓

Hydrogen: 2 → 3 ✗

Oxygen: 1 → 1 ✓

5 Checking balanced equations

You can check that an equation is balanced using the law of conservation of mass. For example, aluminium reacts with bromine to create aluminium bromide in the equation:

$2Al + 3Br_2 \rightarrow 2AlBr_3$

To check that the equation is balanced, use relative formula mass (M_r) to find the total mass of the reactants and products.

Reactants		
2Al	2 × 27	= 54
$3Br_2$	3 × (80 × 2)	= 480
$2Al + 3Br_2$	54 + 480	= 534

Products		
$2AlBr_3$	2 × (27 + (3 × 80))	= 534

The total masses for the reactants and products are equal, so the equation is balanced.

Go to page 99 for more about the law of conservation of mass.

Chemical equations show the balanced chemical formulae of reactants and products. Word equations show names of the reactants and products but are not balanced.

Work out how many atoms of each element are present on each side of the equation. You need to have the same total number of each type of atom in front of the arrow as there are after the arrow.

Adding a 2 before H_2O balances the hydrogen atoms. There are now 4 oxygen atoms on the right side of the reaction and 2 on the left. Adding a 2 before O_2 balances the oxygen atoms.

Adding a two in front of Na, H_2O and NaOH balances the hydrogen and oxygen atoms. There are now two sodium atoms on the left and right sides of the reaction, four hydrogen atoms on both sides and two oxygen atoms on both sides.

10 Exam-style practice — Grade 7

1. Iron reacts with oxygen to produce iron(III) oxide, Fe_2O_3.
   Write a balanced chemical equation to show the reaction that takes place. **[2 marks]**
2. Give **two** reasons why a balanced equation is more useful than a word equation for describing a reaction. **[2 marks]**
3. Give a reason why chemical equations should always balance. **[1 mark]**

Conservation of mass

In a closed system, the mass of the products equals the mass of the reactants. Some chemical reactions seem to involve a change in mass. This is usually because one of the reactants or products is a gas.

⑤ Change in mass

If a reactant or a product is a gas, its mass is often not included in calculations. This occurs when a reaction does not take place in a **closed system**. There are two possibilities:

1 A gaseous product escapes while the reaction takes place. The product mass will be lower than the reactant mass.

2 Gases from the air enter a reaction. They have not been measured with the reactants so the mass will appear to increase.

Change in mass can be calculated using the law of conservation of mass (page 100). For example, after heating 6.2 g of copper carbonate (**Figure 1**), the product (copper oxide) has a mass of 4 g. This means that 2.2 g of gas was produced and lost to the atmosphere during the reaction.

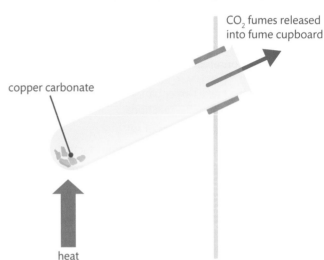

Figure 1 Heating copper carbonate will cause it to decompose and release carbon dioxide. If the gas is not collected, there will appear to be a loss in mass during the reaction.

⑤ Worked example   Grade 5

For each of the following reactions, explain how and why the mass may appear to change during each reaction.

(a) magnesium + oxygen → magnesium oxide

[2 marks]

The mass appears to increase because oxygen from the air is gained in the reaction.

(b) calcium carbonate → calcium oxide + carbon dioxide

[2 marks]

The mass appears to decrease because carbon dioxide is given off in the reaction.

When a metal is heated, it may react with oxygen from the air. The mass of the magnesium oxide will be greater than the mass of the magnesium.

When a substance undergoes thermal decomposition, the mass of the products may appear to have decreased as the gas produced can escape, leaving only the metal oxide as the product.

Think about the conditions required for the law of conservation of mass (page 100).

⑩ Exam-style practice   Grade 6

1 When heated, zinc carbonate thermally decomposes to produce zinc oxide and carbon dioxide.

(a) Write the word equation for this reaction.   [1 mark]

(b) A student decomposed 50 g of zinc carbonate in an unsealed container. After the reaction, there was only 32 g of product. Suggest a reason why.   [1 mark]

(c) Explain how a closed system could be used to improve accuracy when measuring the mass of the products.   [2 marks]

2 When ethanol, C_2H_5OH, burns it reacts with oxygen from the air to produce carbon dioxide and water. Complete the balanced chemical equation, with state symbols, to show the reaction.   [2 marks]

_____ + _____ → _____ + _____

Calculating masses in reactions

The law of conservation of mass enables scientists to make predictions about chemical reactions before carrying them out.

10 Conservation of mass and balanced chemical equations

The law of conservation of mass states that in a closed system, the mass of the products equals the mass of the reactants. This means that no atoms are lost or made during a chemical reaction – only their arrangement changes. For example, hydrogen and oxygen react to form water (**Figure 1**). The total number of hydrogen and oxygen atoms is unchanged in the reaction. There are four hydrogen atoms and two oxygen atoms before the arrow (reactants) and after the arrow (products).

For mass to be conserved the reaction must take place in a **closed system** where none of the reactants or products can escape.

You can write the law as an equation and use it to find missing masses in chemical reactions:

mass of A + mass of B → mass of AB

total mass of reactants = total mass of products

> The law of conservation of mass applies to changes of state (page 105). This includes precipitation, when a solid product settles out of liquid reactants, and sublimation. **Sublimation** is the process by which a solid turns directly into a gas.

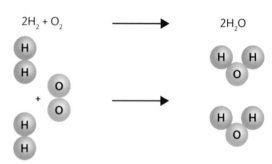

$$2H_2 + O_2 \longrightarrow 2H_2O$$

Figure 1 Hydrogen reacts with oxygen to form water in a balanced chemical equation.

10 Worked example — Grade 5

1 112 g of iron reacts with oxygen to produce 160 g of iron oxide. Calculate the mass of oxygen used in this reaction. **[2 marks]**

iron + oxygen → iron oxide

112 g +   ?   = 160 g

160 − 112 = 48 g

2 Magnesium and chlorine react to produce magnesium chloride in the following reaction.

$Mg + Cl_2 \rightarrow MgCl_2$

Show that mass is conserved in this reaction.

(Atomic masses: Mg = 12; Cl = 35.5) **[3 marks]**

$Mg + Cl_2 \rightarrow MgCl_2$

12 + (2 × 35.5) → 12 + (2 × 35.5)

     83   →   83

Exam focus

In the exam, you may need to use the law of conservation of mass to work out the unknown mass of a substance in a reaction.

1. Write the word equation for the reaction.
2. Write the masses provided in the question under the correct substance.
3. Rearrange the masses to calculate the missing substance. Don't forget to include units in your answer.

Conservation of mass can be shown by adding up the relative atomic mass (see pages 78 and 96) of each of the atoms on either side of a balanced chemical equation.

The total mass of the atoms on the left-hand side (the reactants) will always equal the total mass of the atoms on the right-hand side in a balanced equation.

10 Exam-style practice — Grade 5

1 When iodine is heated, it sublimes (changes from a solid to a gaseous state). If 50 g of iodine is heated, calculate the mass of the iodine vapour produced. **[2 marks]**

2 When heated, magnesium carbonate thermally decomposes, producing magnesium oxide and carbon dioxide.
   (a) Write a word equation for this reaction. **[1 mark]**
   (b) If 84 g of magnesium carbonate is used and 40 g of magnesium oxide is produced, calculate the mass of carbon dioxide produced in the reaction. **[2 marks]**

  Made a start **Feeling confident** **Exam ready**

Concentrations of solutions

Many chemical reactions take place in solution. The concentration of a solution depends on the mass of solute and the volume of solution.

5 Calculating concentrations

A solution is prepared by dissolving a solute (solid) in a solvent (liquid).
The concentration of a solution is how much solute is dissolved into the solvent.

Concentration can be calculated using the formula given below:

$$\text{concentration } (\text{g dm}^{-3}) = \frac{\text{mass (g)}}{\text{volume (dm}^3)} \qquad c = \frac{m}{V}$$

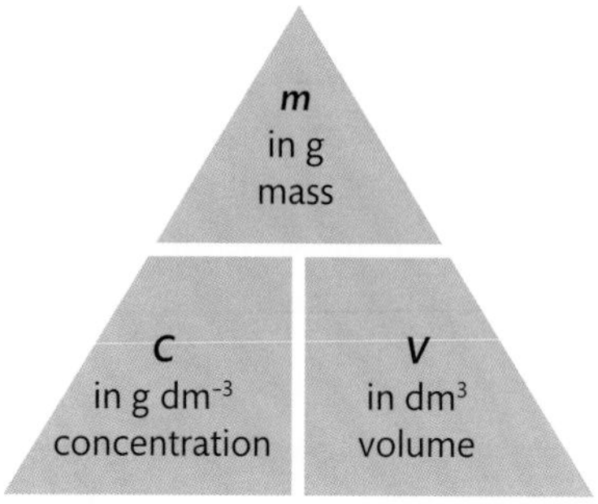

To find the mass of solute, you need to rearrange the formula:

mass (g) = concentration (g dm^{-3}) × volume (dm^3)

If the mass of solute is increased but the volume of solvent stays the same, the concentration of the solution will increase.

If the volume of solvent is increased but the mass of solute stays the same, the concentration of the solution will decrease.

10 Worked example — Grades 5–6

1 Calculate the mass of solute needed to be dissolved in 1.5 dm of a solvent to produce a concentration of 3 g dm^{-3}. **[3 marks]**

mass = concentration × volume

3 × 1.5 = 4.5 g

2 58 g of sodium hydroxide was dissolved in water. Calculate the volume of solution used to produce a concentration of 16.11 g dm^{-3}. **[3 marks]**

$V = \frac{m}{c} = \frac{58}{16.11} = 3.6\ \text{dm}^3$

3 Calculate the concentration of a solution of sodium carbonate, when 37.0 g of sodium carbonate is dissolved in 4.25 dm^3 of solvent. **[3 marks]**

$c = \frac{m}{V} = \frac{37.0}{4.25} = 8.70588235$

$= 8.71\ \text{g dm}^{-3}$

Use the formula triangle to rearrange the calculation for mass.

You can use the units as a clue to work out the formula. The units of concentration are g dm^{-3}. This tells you that concentration = mass ÷ volume.

Give your answer to no more than 2 or 3 significant figures.

Remember to give the correct units.

2 Maths skills

You need to know how to convert units from cm^3 to dm^3 and vice versa.

1 dm^3 = 1000 cm^3 (multiply by 1000)

1 cm^3 = 0.001 dm^3 (divide by 1000)

10 Exam-style practice — Grades 5–6

1 A student dissolves 60 g of sodium chloride in 1.5 dm^3 of water.
Calculate the concentration of the solution of sodium chloride produced. **[2 marks]**

2 Calculate the mass of calcium chloride needed to produce a solution with a concentration of 10 g dm^{-3} when dissolved into 5 dm^3 of water. **[3 marks]**

3 Explain how increasing the mass of solute used affects the concentration of the solution produced, when the same volume of solvent is used. **[1 mark]**

Moles

It is impossible to weigh a single atom because they are too small, so scientists measure amounts of substances in moles. This enables scientists to compare the amount of each substance in a reaction.

10 Measuring substances

Chemical amounts are measured in **moles**. The symbol for mole is **mol**. One mole of a substance has the same number of particles as one mole of another substance, regardless of their different properties. Moles can refer to the number of particles, atoms, ions or molecules in a substance. For example, one mole of helium (He) has the same number of atoms as the number of molecules in one mole of water (H_2O).

One mole (mol) of any substance contains the same number of particles (6.02×10^{23} particles – see page 103). This means one mole of a substance will have a mass in grams equal to the relative formula mass of the atoms or molecules.

15 Worked example — Grade 6

The relative atomic masses (A_r) of hydrogen, oxygen and helium are: H = 1; O = 16; He = 4.

1 State the mass of one mole of helium. **[1 mark]**

4 g

The mass of one mole of an element is equal to its relative atomic mass (A_r) in grams.

2 (a) Calculate the relative formula mass (M_r) of water (H_2O). **[1 mark]**

16 + 1 + 1 = 18

(b) State the mass of one mole of water. **[1 mark]**

18 g

3 Calculate the number of moles of water in 99 g. **[3 marks]**

$$\text{moles} = \frac{m}{M_r} = \frac{99}{18} = 5.5 \text{ mol}$$

4 Calculate the mass, in grams, of lithium oxide (Li_2O) in 5 mol. **[3 marks]**

Li = 7 Li_2 = 2 × 7 = 14

O = 16

M_r = 30

mass = 5 × 30 = 150 g

Maths skills

You can use this formula triangle to calculate the number of moles, mass or relative formula mass by substituting in the known values.

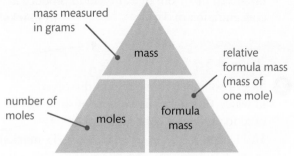

mass measured in grams

mass

relative formula mass (mass of one mole)

number of moles

moles

formula mass

Draw a formula triangle, and cover up the quantity you need to find. For example, to find mass, you multiply the number of moles by the relative formula mass (M_r). In your exam, make sure you write out the formula, not just the triangle.

The mass of one mole of a molecule is equal to its relative formula mass (M_r) in grams.

Calculate the M_r of Li_2O.

5 Exam-style practice — Grade 6

1 State the mass of one mole of O_2. **[1 mark]**

2 State how many moles of each reactant are in the equation given below.
$Mg + 2HCl \rightarrow MgCl_2 + H_2$ **[2 marks]**

3 Calculate the number of moles in 10 000 g of calcium carbonate ($CaCO_3$).
A_r: Ca = 40; C = 12; O = 16 **[3 marks]**

Made a start   Feeling confident   Exam ready

Amounts of substances

You need to know how to calculate mass, moles or the number of particles of a substance given the other two values, and how to calculate masses of reactants and products from balanced equations.

5 The Avogadro constant

The **Avogadro constant** gives the number of particles in one mole (1 mol) of a substance. It is equal to 6.02×10^{23} particles.

The constant can be used to calculate:

1. the number of particles of a substance in a given number of moles of that substance (and vice versa)
2. the number of particles of a substance when given the mass of that substance (and vice versa).

10 Worked example — Grade 8

1. Calculate the number of moles (of particles) in 12 g of carbon. **[1 mark]**

$\frac{12}{12} = 1$ mol

2. Calculate the number of atoms in 5 mol sodium. **[1 mark]**

$6.02 \times 10^{23} \times 5 = 3.01 \times 10^{24}$

3. Calculate the number of atoms in 80 g calcium. **[2 marks]**

$\frac{80}{40} = 2$ mol calcium

$6.02 \times 10^{23} \times 2 = 1.204 \times 10^{24}$

4. Calculate the mass of sodium chloride produced by 0.35 g of sodium hydroxide reacting with an excess of hydrochloric acid. **[4 marks]**
(A_r: Na = 23, Cl = 35.5, O = 16, H = 1)

$NaOH(aq) + HCl(aq) \rightarrow NaCl(aq) + H_2O(l)$

1 mol (excess) 1 mol

0.35 g

$M_r = 40$ $M_r = 58.5$

$\frac{0.35}{40} = 0.00875$ mol

$0.00875 \times 58.5 = 0.51$ g

Multiply the Avogadro constant (the number of particles in 1 mol) by the number of moles.

Step 1 – divide mass (g) by A_r.
Step 2 – multiply the number of moles by the Avogadro constant.

An excess of hydrochloric acid is used. This means you know that the sodium hydroxide is the limiting reactant. That is, all the sodium hydroxide is used up, so you can use the amount of sodium hydroxide to calculate the amount of sodium chloride produced.

Write the balanced equation so you can see how many moles of product you get from 1 mol of the limiting reactant. Then work out how many moles of the limiting reactant were used up. Finally, work out how many moles of product were made, and thus how many grams.

5 Balanced equations and limiting reactants

Atoms of different elements combine, in specific ratios, to form compounds. Balanced equations tell you how many moles of each reactant and each product are involved in a reaction.

$2Cu(s) + O_2(g) \rightarrow 2CuO(s)$

This equation tells you that two moles of copper (solid) react with one mole of oxygen (gas) to produce two moles of copper oxide (solid).

If you have only two moles of copper, no matter how much oxygen you add you will not get more than two moles of copper oxide. In other words, copper is the limiting reactant in this case. In practice, oxygen would be used in excess (more than one mole) to ensure that all of the copper is used up.

1 Exam focus

You may need to use the value for the Avogadro constant in your exam and explain what it represents.

10 Exam-style practice — Grade 8

1. Calculate the mass, in g, of 0.050 mol of NO_2. **[2 marks]**
2. Calculate M_r for a substance when 2.65 g contains 0.025 mol of the substance. **[1 mark]**
3. If 55 g of magnesium reacts with excess oxygen, calculate how much magnesium oxide will be produced, in grams. (A_r: Mg = 24, O = 16) **[4 marks]**

Using mass to balance equations

The masses of reactants and products can be used to deduce the stoichiometry of a reaction.

5 Using reacting masses to balance equations

A chemical reaction is a rearrangement of atoms. Atoms are separated and rearranged to form new substances during a chemical reaction. The number of each type of atoms does not change, and so the mass of all the reactants is the same as the mass of all the products. If you have the masses of reactants and products in an equation, you can use these values to determine the stoichiometry (i.e. balance the equation) to show how many moles of each substance react.

To balance equations using given masses you should follow these steps:

1. Calculate the relative formula mass, M_r.
2. Rearrange the mole calculation triangle and calculate the number of moles of each substance.
3. Use the ratio of moles to determine the stoichiometry of the reaction.

Divide the given mass, in grams, of each substance by its M_r to get the number of moles of each substance.

Stoichiometry is the ratio of the amounts of each substance in a balanced chemical equation.

10 Worked example — Grade 7

1. 12 g of magnesium reacts completely with 8 g of oxygen to produce 20 g of magnesium oxide. Determine the balanced equation for the reaction. **[4 marks]**

A_r: Mg = 24; O_2 = 32; MgO = 40

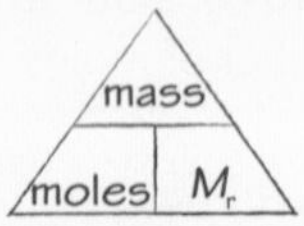

Mg = 12 ÷ 24 = 0.5 mol

O_2 = 8 ÷ 32 = 0.25 mol

MgO = 20 ÷ 40 = 0.5 mol

0.5 ÷ 0.25 = 2Mg

0.25 ÷ 0.25 = $1O_2$

0.5 ÷ 0.25 = 2MgO

$2Mg + O_2 \rightarrow 2MgO$

The lowest value is 0.25. Dividing the highest values (0.5) by the lowest value gives the ratio 2:1:2. This means two moles of magnesium react with one mole of oxygen to form two moles of magnesium oxide.

2. 7 g of N_2 reacts with 1.5 g of hydrogen to produce 8.5 g of NH_3. Determine the balanced equation for the reaction. **[4 marks]**

M_r: N_2 = 28; H_2 = 2; NH_3 = 17

N_2 = 7 ÷ 28 = 0.25 mol

H_2 = 1.5 ÷ 2 = 0.75 mol

NH_3 = 8.5 ÷ 17 = 0.5 mol

0.25 ÷ 0.25 = $1N_2$

0.75 ÷ 0.25 = $3H_2$

0.5 ÷ 0.25 = $2NH_3$

$N_2 + 3H_2 \rightarrow 2NH_3$

Divide all the values by the lowest value. If the values derived are not whole numbers, multiply all the values by the same amount to get whole numbers.

When writing balanced equations, you don't need to put a number before the formula if there is one mole of the substance.

15 Exam-style practice — Grade 7

1. 15.9 g of copper(II) oxide (CuO) was reduced by 0.4 g of hydrogen to produce 12.7 g copper and 3.6 g of water. Use the masses provided to determine the balanced equation for the reaction. **[4 marks]**
2. Give the formula which relates moles, relative formula mass and mass. **[2 marks]**
3. A student reacted 13 g of zinc with 14.6 g of hydrogen chloride gas, producing 27.2 g of zinc chloride and 0.4 g of hydrogen gas. Use the masses provided to determine the balanced equation for the reaction. **[4 marks]**
4. Describe what the numbers in front of the chemical formulae represent. **[1 mark]**

States of matter

You need to be able to predict the states of substances at different temperatures and explain changes of state using the particle model.

10 Changing state

The three states of matter, solid, liquid and gas, can be represented by the **particle model**. This simple model shows the interconversions that occur when energy is supplied or removed from the particles. When substances are heated or cooled the forces **between** particles change. The density, arrangement and motion of particles change when a substance changes state.

Particles in a substance **gain energy** when the substance turns from a solid to a liquid (**melting**) or from a liquid to a gas (**boiling**).
- The distance between particles increases.
- The strength of the forces between particles decreases.
- The particles have more energy so move faster.

Particles in a substance **lose energy** when the substance turns from a gas to a liquid (**condensing**) and from a liquid to a solid (**freezing**).
- The distance between particles decreases.
- The strength of the forces between particles increases.
- The particles have less energy so move more slowly.

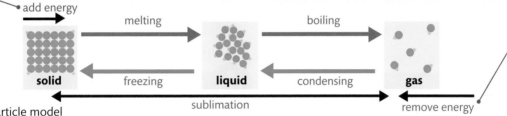

Figure 1 The particle model

The amount of energy needed to change state from a solid to a liquid and from a liquid to a gas varies. The energy must be great enough to overcome the forces of attraction **between** the particles. The strength of forces vary according to the type of bonding and structure of the substance. The stronger the forces between the particles, the higher the **melting point** and **boiling point** of the substance.

2 Physical and chemical change

Physical changes do not affect the chemical composition of a substance. Changing the state of matter, for example freezing a liquid into a solid, is an example of a physical change.

In a chemical change, a new substance is formed.

2 State symbols

Symbols are used in a chemical equation to represent states of matter:
- (s) for solids, e.g. ice
- (l) for liquids, e.g. water
- (g) for gases, e.g. steam
- (aq) for aqueous solutions, e.g. NaCl in water.

For example:

$$2Na(s) + 2H_2O(l) \rightarrow 2NaOH(aq) + H_2(g)$$

5 Worked example — Grade 5

1 Explain, in terms of particles and energy, how a liquid evaporates. **[3 marks]**

The particles in a liquid have different energies. An increase in energy (boiling) causes the forces of attraction between some particles to break. These particles will escape from the surface of the liquid and form a gas.

2 Explain why more energy is required to change the state of a solid than to change the state of a liquid. **[2 marks]**

The forces of attraction are much greater in a solid due to the regular lattice arrangement. The particles in a solid are much closer together than in a liquid so the forces of attraction are greater and more difficult to overcome.

5 Exam-style practice — Grade 7

Compound	Melting point (°C)	Boiling point (°C)
LiCl	610	1382
BeCl$_2$	405	488
CCl$_4$	−23	77
NCl$_3$	−40	71
OCl$_2$	−20	4

1 Look at the table. For each of the compounds, identify whether they are a solid, liquid or gas at room temperature (25 °C). **[2 marks]**

2 Predict the state of LiCl at 900 °C. **[1 mark]**

3 Predict whether OCl$_2$ is solid or liquid at −19 °C. **[1 mark]**

Pure substances

You need to be able to distinguish pure from impure substances using melting and boiling points.

⑤ What is a pure substance?

In everyday language, a pure substance is a substance that has had nothing added to it, for example, pure milk. In Chemistry, it is a substance that contains only atoms or molecules of that particular substance, for example, pure water must contain only H_2O molecules.

Impure substances can be mixtures of elements, compounds, or mixtures of elements and compounds.

Pure substances cannot be separated by physical methods, such as filtration. Impurities in a substance will affect its properties. The values for melting point, boiling point and density obtained for a sample can be compared with data to identify its purity.

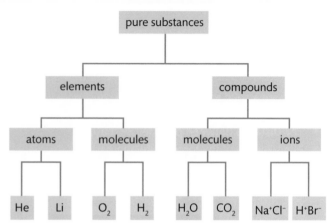

Figure 1 Examples of pure substances

⑩ Worked example · Grades 5–6

The table shows the boiling points of three samples of water.

Sample	Boiling point (°C)
A	98
B	100
C	103

(a) State and explain which sample is pure water. **[2 marks]**

Sample B is pure water because it boils at 100 °C, which is the boiling point of water.

(b) Suggest a reason why the other two samples do not boil at the expected temperature. **[1 mark]**

They contain impurities.

(c) When manufacturing pharmaceutical drugs, the drugs need to be as pure as possible to reduce the chance of side effects.

Devise one method that could be used to check the purity of a sample of aspirin. **[2 marks]**

Measure the melting point of the sample and compare it to the known melting point of pure aspirin.

Other possible methods involve measuring the boiling point or the density, and then comparing them with known data.

① Working scientifically

Melting point apparatus can be used to investigate the purity of a sample. The sample is heated along with a thermometer until it begins to melt. The temperature range over which it melts is recorded. The sharper the temperature range the more pure the sample is likely to be.

If a substance is pure, every sample of that substance will have the same properties, including:
- melting point
- boiling point
- density.

⑩ Exam-style practice · Grade 6

1 Describe how you could prove that a sample of hexane is pure. **[2 marks]**

2 **Figure 1** shows a table of melting points for substances **A–E**.

Substance	Melting point (°C)
A	0
B	228–230
C	17
D	117–119
E	–63.5

State and explain which of the substances **A–E** are pure and which are impure. **[3 marks]**

3 The boiling point of pure ethanol is 78 °C. A student measures the boiling point of a sample of ethanol and records a value of 79 °C. State whether the sample is pure or impure. **[1 mark]**

Made a start · Feeling confident · Exam ready

Mixtures

You need to know the different types of mixtures and how they can be separated using physical methods.

 Separating mixtures

A mixture contains two or more substances that are not chemically bonded together, which means they can be separated by physical methods. The chemical properties of the substances in the mixture are unchanged as they haven't reacted with each other.

- **Filtration** separates an insoluble solid from a liquid. A mixture is passed through filter paper in a filter funnel. The liquid can pass through the gaps in the filter paper but the solid cannot.
- **Simple distillation** separates a solvent from a solution. A mixture is heated and the liquid evaporates, re-condenses and is collected.
- **Fractional distillation** separates a mixture of liquids. It is covered in more detail on page 152.
- **Crystallisation** separates a soluble solid from a liquid. A mixture is heated until the solvent evaporates, leaving a crystallised solid behind.
- **Paper chromatography** separates a mixture of several liquids. It is covered in more detail on page 108.

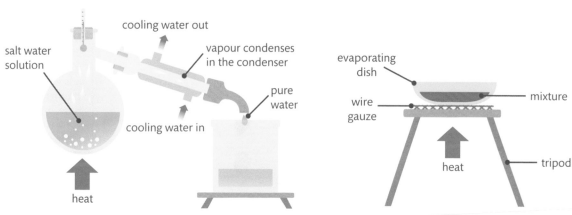

Figure 1 Simple distillation

Figure 2 Crystallisation

 Worked example — Grade 5

A student is given a mixture containing a liquid that evaporates at 65 °C, a soluble solid and a second liquid that evaporates at 98 °C. Describe the steps the student should follow to separate the soluble solid. **[4 marks]**

Step 1: The two liquids can be separated by fractional distillation. The liquid with a boiling point of 65 °C will evaporate first and be collected in the beaker.

Step 2: The remaining mixture should be heated in an evaporating dish to evaporate the liquid. It is then left to cool to allow crystals to form.

 Exam-style practice — Grade 4

1 Draw one straight line from each mixture to its method of separation. **[4 marks]**

Mixture	Separation method
ink and water	filtration
sand and water	simple distillation
sugar and water	evaporation

2 Name the apparatus labelled **W**, **X** and **Y** in **Figure 3**. **[3 marks]**

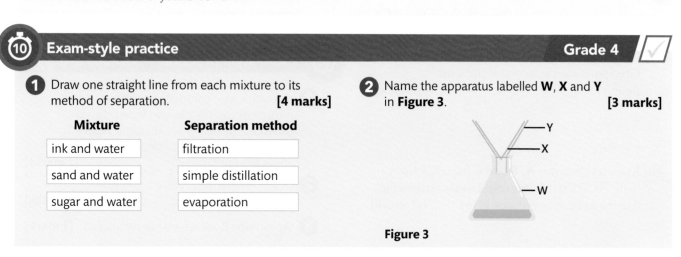

Figure 3

Chromatography

Chromatography is a technique used to separate the components of a mixture so they can be identified. You need to understand how chromatography works and be able to calculate R_f values using chromatograms.

 Paper chromatography

Chromatography is usually used to separate coloured substances, such as inks, food colourings and dyes. It can also be used to separate colourless mixtures with the use of a locating agent, which adds pigment to otherwise colourless substances. Chromatography is important in the manufacturing of pharmaceutical drugs. The process can be used to assess the purity of drugs and medicines, enabling scientists to reduce the risk of unnecessary side effects. Go to page 109 to revise how to set up chromatography apparatus to produce a chromatogram.

Paper chromatography involves two phases:

- The chromatography paper, on which a spot of the unknown substance or mixture is placed, contains the **stationary phase**.
- The liquid solvent, which moves through the chromatography paper carrying the components of the mixture, is the **mobile phase**.

Mixtures are separated because different substances travel different distances depending on their attractions to the stationary phase or the mobile phase.

R_f values

The **R_f value** is the ratio of the distance moved by a substance (from the centre of its spot at the base line) to the distance moved by the solvent.

The R_f value of a particular substance will always be the same if the same type of chromatography paper and solvent are used. This means that R_f values can be used to identify unknown substances.

The more soluble a substance, the further it will travel up the chromatography paper and the higher the R_f value will be. The less attracted the substance is to the stationary phase, the further it will travel up the paper and the higher the R_f value will be.

Pure compounds produce a single spot on the chromatogram.

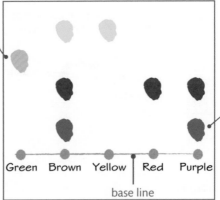

Mixtures separate into several spots in different positions on the chromatogram. Here, the purple dye has a red spot at the same height as the red dye, showing that the purple is a mixture of the red and another substance.

Figure 1 A chromatogram of different food colourants

Maths skills

R_f values can be worked out using the formula:

$$R_f = \frac{\text{distance moved by substance}}{\text{distance moved by solvent}}$$

 **Worked example** — **Grade 5**

A substance travels 78 mm from the base line while the solvent travels 150 mm.

(a) Calculate the R_f value for this substance. Give your answer to two significant figures. **[3 marks]**

$$R_f = \frac{78}{150}$$

$$R_f = 0.52$$

(b) Known substances **A**, **B** and **C** have R_f values 0.485, 0.515 and 0.760, respectively. State which one might be the substance in **(a)**. **[1 mark]**

B

 Working scientifically

In paper chromatography:

- a pencil is used to draw the base line because ink may run and interfere with the chromatogram
- the base line should sit above the solvent level so that the substance does not dissolve in the solvent
- you should wear eye protection to protect your eyes from harmful substances.

 Exam-style practice — **Grades 5–6**

1 A scientist uses chromatography to see what mixture of colours a brown food colourant contains. The results are shown in **Figure 1**. Describe what the chromatogram tells you about the food colourant. **[2 marks]**

2 Describe what an R_f value is and why it is useful. **[2 marks]**

3 Explain why R_f values are not given units. **[1 mark]**

| Chemistry | States of matter and mixtures | Separating and purifying | Practical skills |

Practical: Investigating inks

The aim of this practical is to find out the composition of inks, using paper chromatography and simple distillation.

10 Paper chromatography

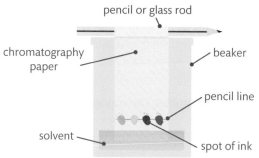

Figure 1 Paper chromatography apparatus

1. Use a ruler to draw a horizontal pencil line 2 cm from the bottom of the chromatography paper (the base line).

2. Using glass capillary tubes, put a small spot of each of the known colourings on the pencil line, 1 cm apart. Make sure each spot is no more than 5 mm in diameter.

3. Using another glass capillary tube, put a small spot of the unknown mixture on the paper.

4. Label each spot in **pencil**.

5. Tape the end edge of the chromatography paper to the glass rod so that the paper hangs with the base line at the bottom.

6. Pour water into the beaker so that the water level is **below** the base line.

7. Rest the rod on the top edge of the beaker. The bottom edge of the paper should dip into the water.

8. Use a ruler to measure the distance the solvent has moved up the paper (from the bottom edge of the paper) and the distance the spot has moved (from the base line).

2 Worked example — Grade 6

Explain how paper chromatography is used to separate substances. **[3 marks]**

As the solvent travels up the paper, it carries substances different distances. The distance a substance travels depends on its solubility and attraction to the paper.

10 Simple distillation of inks

Simple distillation is a method which can be used to separate ink from pure water.

The apparatus is set up as shown in **Figure 2**.

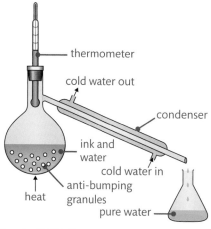

Figure 2 Simple distillation apparatus

1. Pour some ink into a round-bottomed flask.

2. Attach a condenser to the top and connect it to a cold water supply.

3. Heat the flask using a Bunsen burner until the solution boils gently, then maintain the temperature.

4. Collect a sample of the distilled solvent in the conical flask.

2 Working scientifically

Hazard symbols are found on containers to indicate the dangers associated with the contents and to inform people about how to use the substances safely in the laboratory. You could be asked to evaluate the risks of an experiment and suggest suitable precautions based on the hazards indicated for the substances you will be using.

Flammable	Irritant	Corrosive

10 Exam-style practice — Grade 6

1. Simple distillation can be used to separate liquids such as inks and water.

   (a) Describe **one** hazard and **one** suitable precaution for the hazard for the distillation experiment. **[2 marks]**

   (b) Explain why a thermometer is needed in the distillation investigation. **[2 marks]**

2. A substance travels 23 mm from the base line while the solvent travels 74 mm. Calculate the R_f value for this substance. Give your answer to two significant figures. **[3 marks]**

Potable water

You need to know how potable water (drinking water) is produced.

(15) Pure water and potable water

Pure water only contains water molecules. Pure water, often produced by distillation, must be used when scientists carry out analyses. Otherwise dissolved salts in the water will affect the results. **Potable**, or drinking, water is not pure as it still contains dissolved substances (at safe levels), such as minerals. The origin of the term 'potable' is the Latin word *potare* which means to drink.

Producing potable water

For water to be suitable for human consumption, it must be treated to remove microbes. The concentration of dissolved salts must be low enough to not cause harm.

The processes used to produce potable water depend on the water source and the local conditions. If supplies of fresh water are limited, desalination of salt water may be required. Desalination processes are expensive because they require large amounts of energy.

Type of water	Source	Treatment processes
waste water and groundwater	rainwater, which collects underground (the most common source of potable water in the UK) or in lakes and rivers	**Filtration** The waste water or groundwater is filtered through layers of gravel, then sand, to remove any solid waste. Smaller particles can be coagulated using chemical substances in **sedimentation**. They can then be filtered out. **Chlorination** The final stage of water treatment is to use chlorine to kill any microbes present in the water.
sea water	from the oceans	**Distillation** The sea water is heated until it evaporates, leaving the salt behind. The water is then condensed to give fresh water. Go to page 107 for more information on distillation.

(5) Worked example　　Grade 6

1 There are **two** main steps involved in the treatment of rainwater to produce potable water. State and explain the role of each step. **[2 marks]**

Filtration removes solid particles. This is followed by chlorination, which kills microbes.

2 Distillation of salt water is expensive due to the high amounts of energy required. State why energy is needed for distillation. **[1 mark]**

The water must be heated until it evaporates.

3 Describe how waste water is treated to produce potable water. **[2 marks]**

It can be filtered to remove any solid particles, then treated with chlorine to remove microbes.

(10) Exam-style practice　　Grades 5–7

1 Name a method that can be used to produce potable water from salt water. **[1 mark]**

2 Name **one** substance that can be used to sterilise rainwater. **[1 mark]**

3 Give a reason why unprocessed sea water is not used as drinking water. **[1 mark]**

4 Name the main source of potable water in the UK. **[2 marks]**

5 Give **three** sources of water that can be used to produce potable water. **[3 marks]**

6 Besides microbes, what else may need to be removed from water (if in high concentration) which could then be used for analysis? **[1 mark]**

 Made a start　　 **Feeling confident**　　 **Exam ready**

The pH scale and neutralisation

You need to know how to use the pH scale to measure how acidic or alkaline a solution is.

10 Acids, bases and alkalis

Acids

An acid is a substance that produces hydrogen (H^+) ions when dissolved in water.

Acids have a pH of less than 7. The lower the pH, the stronger the acid.

Bases and alkalis

Bases react with acids and neutralise them to make a salt and water only. They are usually metal oxides or metal hydroxides.

Alkalis are soluble bases. Copper oxide is a base but not an alkali, whereas sodium hydroxide is an alkali and a base because it dissolves in water.

acid | neutral | alkaline

Indicator pH:	0	1	2	3	4	5	6	7	8	9	10	11	12	13	14
Methyl orange				··· change ···											
Litmus								······ change ······							
Phenolphthalein										··· change ···					

Figure 1 Colours of indicators in acids and alkalis

An alkali is a substance that produces hydroxide (OH^-) ions when dissolved in water.

Aqueous solutions of alkalis have a pH greater than 7. The higher the pH number, the stronger the alkali.

Neutralisation reactions

A solution with pH 7 is neutral. When acids and bases react, a neutralisation reaction occurs.

The hydrogen ions from acid react with the hydroxide ions from alkali to produce water:

$H^+(aq) + OH^-(aq) \rightarrow H_2O(l)$

Indicators change colour to show the pH of a substance. pH can also be measured using a pH probe.

5 Working scientifically

If there is the same concentration (e.g. 3.65 $g\,dm^{-3}$) of a strong acid, such as HCl, and a strong alkali, such as NaOH, that react in a 1 : 1 ratio, then it takes the same volume of NaOH to neutralise a particular volume of HCl (e.g. 25 cm^3).

$NaOH + HCl \rightarrow NaCl + H_2O$

1 : 1

mass = volume (dm^3) × concentration ($g\,dm^{-3}$)

= (25 ÷ 1000) × 3.65

= 0.09125 grams of HCl

volume of NaOH = grams ÷ concentration

= 0.09125 ÷ 3.65

= 0.025 dm^3

= 25 cm^3

1 Maths skills

Divide by 1000 to convert from cm^3 to dm^3.

5 Worked example — Grade 5

Vinegar has a pH of about 2.5.

(a) State what pH is a measure of. **[1 mark]**

How acidic or alkaline a substance is

(b) Explain, using the pH value of vinegar, what type of substance vinegar is. **[2 marks]**

Its pH is lower than 7 so vinegar is an acid.

(c) State what ion is responsible for the pH at 2.5. **[1 mark]**

H^+

5 Exam-style practice — Grade 6

1. Write a word equation for the neutralisation reaction between hydrochloric acid and sodium hydroxide. **[1 mark]**
2. An unknown solution is tested using phenolphthalein. The indicator changes to a bright pink colour.
   (a) Identify the type of solution being tested. **[1 mark]**
   (b) Name the type of ions present in the solution tested. **[1 mark]**
3. Suggest a piece of equipment that could be a used to accurately measure the pH of a solution. **[1 mark]**

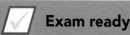

Strong and weak acids

You need to know what is meant by a strong or weak acid and how the strength of an acid is measured.

⑤ Acid strength

Ionisation occurs when acid particles dissociate, releasing hydrogen ions. The strength of an acid depends on the degree of ionisation that occurs when the acid is in aqueous solution.

A strong acid is more easily able to lose a hydrogen ion and will completely ionise in aqueous solution. The concentration of H^+ released in the solution is a measure of the strength of an acid. Strong acids include:

- sulfuric acid
- nitric acid
- hydrochloric acid.

A weak acid will only partially ionise in aqueous solution.

Weak acids include:

- citric acid
- ethanoic acid
- carbonic acid.

> Go to page 111 for more about acids.

⑤ Working scientifically

An acid such as nitric acid (HNO_3) can be represented as HA, where H represents the hydrogen in the acid and A represents the type of acid. You can show the ionisation of an acid in solution with the equation:

$$HA \rightarrow H^+ + A^-$$

The stronger the acid, the higher the hydrogen ion concentration of its solution (as more of the acid particles dissociate to release H^+ in the solution).

For every 1 unit decrease on the pH scale, the hydrogen ion concentration $[H^+]$ of the solution increases by a factor of 10.

pH 0 1 2 3 4 5 6 7 8 9 10 11 12 13 14
$[H^+]$ 1 10^{-1} 10^{-2} 10^{-3} 10^{-4} 10^{-5} 10^{-6} 10^{-7} 10^{-8} 10^{-9} 10^{-10} 10^{-11} 10^{-12} 10^{-13} 10^{-14}

So pH 7 $[H^+]$ (1×10^{-7}) = 0.0000001 $g\,dm^{-3}$

pH 6 $[H^+]$ (1×10^{-6}) = 0.000001 $g\,dm^{-3}$.

② Strength vs concentration

The strength of an acid refers to the degree of ionisation. The opposite of strong is weak.

The concentration of an acid refers to the number of moles of acid in a given volume of acid solution (usually 1 dm^3). The more moles of an acid in solution, the more concentrated the acid. The opposite of concentrated is dilute.

An acid can be concentrated and weak at the same time.

⑩ Worked example — Grades 5–7

① (a) State the ions produced when hydrochloric acid is in solution. **[2 marks]**

H^+ and Cl^-

(b) Explain how the ions produced show that it is an acidic solution. **[1 mark]**

Hydrogen ions (H^+) are produced.

② Describe the observations made if a pH probe is used to compare the strength of ethanoic acid with hydrochloric acid, if both acids are the same concentration. **[2 marks]**

Hydrochloric acid is a strong acid so it will ionise completely. The concentration of hydrogen ions in the hydrochloric acid solution is therefore higher than that from the weak ethanoic acid, which ionises only partially. Therefore the hydrochloric acid has a lower pH.

③ (a) State what the pH scale measures. **[1 mark]**

The concentration of hydrogen ions in solution.

(b) Explain the difference between a strong acid and a weak acid. **[2 marks]**

The stronger an acid is the more dissociation takes place. This means that the acid can more readily lose a hydrogen ion (H^+).

> You could also answer this in terms of ionisation – pH is a measure of the degree of ionisation which occurs to an acid in aqueous solution.

⑤ Exam-style practice — Grades 5–7

① Describe what is meant by a strong acid. **[2 marks]**

② Give **two** examples of strong acids. **[1 mark]**

③ (a) Write the ionic equation for the neutralisation reaction between sodium hydroxide and nitric acid (HNO_3). **[2 marks]**

(b) Name the ion responsible for the strength of an acid. **[1 mark]**

(c) Explain how the concentration of these ions affects the pH of a solution. **[1 mark]**

Made a start | Feeling confident | Exam ready

Practical: pH change

You need to know how to investigate the change in pH when adding an alkali to a fixed volume of acid.

 Neutralisation reactions

During a neutralisation reaction in which alkali is added to an acid, the pH of the solution will change from a low pH to a high pH.

When hydroxide ions are added to an acid they react with the hydrogen ions and reduce their concentration, causing the pH to increase.

A graph can be plotted to show how the pH changes as more alkali is added.

Indicators, such as universal indicator, are used to measure the approximate pH of a solution. Universal indicator changes colour to show the pH of a substance. pH can also be measured using a pH probe.

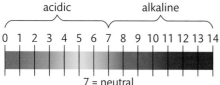

This is the point at which the amount of acid is equal to the amount of alkali.

7 = neutral

Figure 1 The pH scale

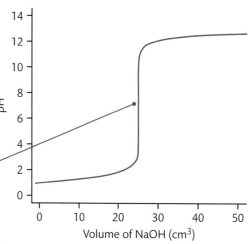

Figure 2 A pH curve

 Worked example — Grade 6

A student was provided with the following equipment:

measuring cylinder, beaker, glass rod, universal indicator, spatula, white tile.

1 Describe how the reaction between calcium hydroxide powder and hydrochloric acid can be used to investigate the pH change during the reaction. **[6 marks]**

1 Measure volume of the dilute hydrochloric acid, using the measuring cylinder, add to the beaker.

2 Place small pieces of the indicator paper onto a white tile.

3 Use the glass rod to transfer a drop of the solution in the beaker onto one piece of the paper.

4 Compare the colour to a pH chart and record its value.

5 Add a level spatula of calcium hydroxide powder to the beaker and mix.

6 Repeat steps 3 to 5 until there are no further changes in pH, recording how many spatulas of calcium hydroxide are added.

2 Suggest a piece of equipment that could be used to improve the accuracy of the pH reading. **[1 mark]**

A pH probe

> You could be asked to suggest other ways to improve the accuracy of the experiment – a burette or pipette would give a more accurate measurement of the acid; using a balance would enable the exact mass of the alkali added each time to be determined.

 Maths skills

You could be asked to draw a graph of pH data from an experiment. To show the relationship between two variables, you need to draw a scatter graph with a smooth line drawn between the points. Remember, the variable that you change – the **independent variable** – goes on the x-axis; the variable that you measure – the dependent variable – goes on the y-axis.

 Exam-style practice — Grade 6

Spatula measures of sodium oxide were added to hydrochloric acid and the pH changes were recorded. The table shows the results.

(a) Plot a graph of the results. **[3 marks]**

(b) Identify on your graph the pH at which the amounts of acid and alkali are equal. **[1 mark]**

(c) State how much alkali was used to neutralise the acid.

Show on your graph how you have worked this out. **[2 marks]**

No. of spatulas	pH
0	2.2
1	2.6
2	3.0
3	3.2
4	3.4
5	3.6
6	3.7
7	3.9
8	4.2
9	4.4
10	5.0
11	9.6
12	10.6
13	11.0

Salt production

You need to know how salts are formed and the conventions used for naming them.

5 Forming salts

Salts are produced by the reaction between an acid and an alkali. When an acid is neutralised by an alkali, such as a soluble metal hydroxide, or by a base, the products are always a salt and water.

acid + metal oxide → salt + water

acid + metal hydroxide → salt + water

If a metal carbonate is neutralised, then carbon dioxide is also produced.

acid + metal carbonate → salt + water + carbon dioxide

These are redox reactions. The metal ions lose electrons (oxidation) and the H^+ ions gain electrons (reduction).

Go to page 120 for more about redoc reactions.

1 Test for CO_2

Limewater (aqueous calcium hydroxide) turns cloudy if carbon dioxide is passed through it.

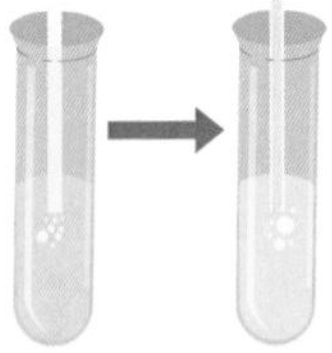

5 Worked example Grade 6

(a) Calcium oxide is added to hydrochloric acid; a neutralisation reaction occurs. Write a word equation for the reaction. **[1 mark]**

calcium oxide + hydrochloric acid → calcium chloride + water

(b) Write the balanced chemical equation for the reaction. **[2 marks]**

$CaO + 2HCl \rightarrow CaCl_2 + H_2O$

1. Identify the metal reacting. It is calcium.
2. Work out the salt name ending from the acid. The acid is hydrochloric acid, so the second part of the name of the salt is chloride.
3. Name the salt. It is calcium chloride.
4. Complete the equation.

When you are constructing the formula of a compound, remember the charges on each of the ions must balance. Ca is in Group 2 so has a charge of +2; Cl is in Group 7 so has a charge of −1. In order for the charges to balance, there needs to be two chloride ions with one calcium ion.

5 Naming salts

A salt has a name with two parts; the first part is just the name of the metal reacting.

For example, if the base is magnesium hydroxide, the first name of the salt is magnesium.

The second part comes from the type of acid reacting:

Acid reacting	Second part of salt name
sulfuric	sulfate
nitric	nitrate
hydrochloric	chloride

So, magnesium hydroxide and sulfuric acid would produce a salt called magnesium sulfate (and water).

If magnesium carbonate reacted with nitric acid, then magnesium nitrate would be produced (with water and carbon dioxide).

2 Working scientifically

When producing a balanced chemical equation, you will need to work out the formula of the salt produced. The overall charge on a compound of the salt is 0, so any charges must be balanced.

Charges on common ions

Ion	Charge
carbonate	CO_3^{2-}
sulfate	SO_4^{2-}
nitrate	NO_3^-
chloride	Cl^-

10 Exam-style practice Grades 5–6

1. Name the salt produced in the reaction between potassium hydroxide and nitric acid. **[1 mark]**
2. Name the type of reaction that produces a salt. **[1 mark]**
3. Name the acid reactant used to produce the salt copper chloride. **[1 mark]**
4. Write the ionic equation for the production of the salt zinc sulfate ($ZnSO_4$). **[2 marks]**
5. Give the formula for each of the following salts.
   (a) lithium sulfate **[1 mark]**
   (b) magnesium chloride **[1 mark]**
   (c) calcium nitrate **[2 marks]**

Reactions of acids with metals

When acids and some metals react, a salt and hydrogen gas are produced. You need to know the reactions of acids with metals in terms of oxidation and reduction.

5 Redox reactions

Acids react with some metals to produce salts and hydrogen. The following reaction takes place between a metal and an acid:

metal + acid → salt + hydrogen

Acid and metal reactions are classed as **redox reactions**; they involve a transfer of electrons:

The chloride ion (Cl^-) is a spectator ion (it exists in the same form on both sides of the reaction).

The metal is oxidised (as metals lose electrons when they react).

$$Zn(s) + 2HCl(aq) \rightarrow ZnCl_2(aq) + H_2(g)$$

The hydrogen ions (H^+) are reduced (gain electrons).

Go to page 117 to revise the process of reacting a metal and an acid to produce a salt.

When reacting acids with metals, hydrochloric acid makes chlorides and sulfuric acid makes sulfates.

5 Worked example — Grades 6–7

1 Deduce, for the following equations, which species are oxidised.

(a) $Mg + H_2SO_4 \rightarrow MgSO_4 + H_2$ **[1 mark]**

Mg is oxidised

(b) $2HCl + 2Fe \rightarrow 2FeCl_2 + H_2$ **[1 mark]**

Fe is oxidised

(c) $Zn + H_2SO_4 \rightarrow ZnSO_4 + H_2$ **[1 mark]**

Zn is oxidised

2 Explain why the equations in question 1 are redox reactions. **[2 marks]**

The metals are oxidised and lose electrons, while the hydrogen gains electrons and is reduced. The transfer of electrons makes these reactions redox reactions.

Remember, in this type of equation metals will always be oxidised. Mg is a Group 2 metal and so will lose two electrons.

Iron is oxidised to iron(II).

The same rules apply as in equation (b).

Remember OILRIG:

oxidation	**r**eduction
is	**i**s
loss	**g**ain.

5 Testing for hydrogen gas

A lit splint will make a squeaky pop noise when held near a test tube of hydrogen gas.

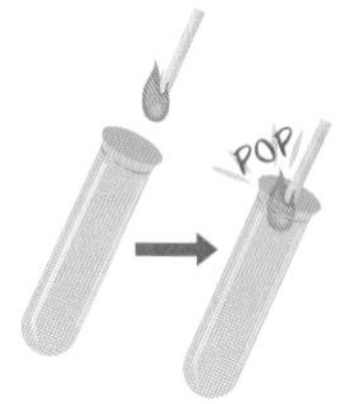

10 Exam-style practice — Grades 5–7

1 Write the balanced chemical equation, with state symbols, for the reaction between magnesium and hydrochloric acid. **[2 marks]**

2 State what is meant by the term 'reduction'. **[1 mark]**

3 Suggest an explanation for why metals are oxidised during a metal acid reaction. **[1 mark]**

4 Predict the name of the salt produced when calcium reacts with nitric acid. **[1 mark]**

Soluble salts

You need to be able to describe the preparation of a soluble salt.

 Making a soluble salt

A soluble salt can be produced by reacting an acid with solid insoluble substances, such as metals, metal oxides, hydroxides or carbonates.

1. Add solid, e.g. metal oxide, to the acid until no more reaction takes place.

2. Filter to remove excess solid.

3. Heat gently, then leave to crystallise into a solid salt. Soluble salts can be dissolved in water.

heat

Working scientifically

When using a Bunsen burner you should take the following precautions:

- Wear eye protection.
- Stand at a reasonable distance away from the flame.
- Place the Bunsen burner on a heat-resistant mat.

Remember, the solid is added in excess to the acid so that all the acid reacts, as the excess solid can then be filtered to remove it, leaving only the products (the salt and water).

 Different types of reactants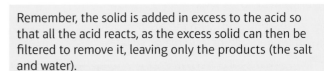

Some metals are too reactive, or not reactive enough, to be used to produce soluble salts. This is why metal oxides, hydroxides or carbonates are used.

- Sodium chloride – sodium is too reactive, so sodium hydroxide or sodium carbonate is used instead.
- Copper chloride – copper does not react with dilute hydrochloric acid so copper oxide or copper carbonate is used instead.

Crystallisation is a separation technique used to separate solids from liquids by evaporating some of the solvent. See page 107 for more information on separation techniques.

 Worked example **Grades 4–5**

1 A student reacts sodium carbonate with dilute sulfuric acid.

Describe how the student could ensure that all of the acid has completely reacted. **[2 marks]**

Keep adding sodium carbonate until the fizzing stops.

2 Name the process used to produce a sample of solid salt from a solution of soluble salt. **[1 mark]**

Crystallisation

 Exam-style practice **Grade 5**

1 When producing a soluble salt by reacting an acid with an insoluble metal hydroxide, describe how you would remove the excess solid. **[1 mark]**

2 Which reactants are used to safely produce sodium sulfate? **[1 mark]**

☐ **A** sodium hydroxide and hydrochloric acid

☐ **B** sodium and sulfuric acid

☐ **C** sodium hydroxide and sulfuric acid

3 Name the soluble salt produced when copper oxide reacts with nitric acid. **[1 mark]**

4 State what is meant by the term 'soluble'. **[1 mark]**

 Made a start **Feeling confident** **Exam ready**

Practical: Making salts

You need to know how to prepare a sample of pure, dry soluble copper sulfate from an insoluble oxide.

10 Making a salt ✓

1 Pour 200 cm³ sulfuric acid into a beaker and warm it.

2 Stir in copper(II) oxide powder until no more reacts. The liquid will turn blue.

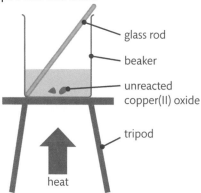

- glass rod
- beaker
- unreacted copper(II) oxide
- tripod
- heat

Figure 1 Adding copper(II) oxide to sulfuric acid

3 Allow the apparatus to cool.

4 Set up funnel and filter paper apparatus.

5 Filter the solution.

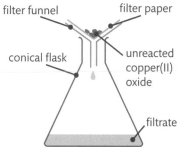

- filter funnel
- filter paper
- conical flask
- unreacted copper(II) oxide
- filtrate

Figure 2 Filtration

6 Collect the filtrate in a conical flask.

7 Transfer the filtrate to an evaporating basin, then gently heat.

8 Leave the filtrate somewhere warm to crystallise for 24 hours.

9 Remove crystals from evaporating dish, put onto filter paper and pat dry. The crystals can then be weighed if required.

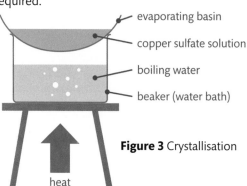

- evaporating basin
- copper sulfate solution
- boiling water
- beaker (water bath)
- heat

Figure 3 Crystallisation

10 Worked example   Grade 6 ✓

1 A salt can be made by reacting an acid and an alkali. Name this type of reaction.   **[1 mark]**

Neutralisation

2 (a) Write a balanced chemical equation for the reaction between sulfuric acid and copper(II) oxide.   **[1 mark]**

$H_2SO_4 (aq) + CuO(s) \rightarrow CuSO_4(aq) + H_2O(l)$

(b) Explain why the following steps are important in the production of the salt copper sulfate.   **[4 marks]**

Warming the acid: speeds up the reaction

Adding excess copper oxide: ensures all the acid reacts

The mixture is filtered: removes any excess copper oxide

The filtrate is heated to begin evaporation: encourages the formation of crystals

(c) Describe what you would observe during the reaction of copper oxide and sulfuric acid.   **[2 marks]**

The black solid copper oxide would disappear, and a blue solution would form.

2 Working scientifically ✓

A water bath may be used during the crystallisation process. To allow large crystals to form, crystallisation must occur slowly. If the solution is heated fast until it all evaporates, only a powdery solid would be left. The initial use of the water bath speeds up the evaporation process while still permitting large crystals to form.

10 Exam-style practice   Grade 6 ✓

1 Describe a method for the preparation of a salt using dilute sulfuric acid and copper oxide.   **[5 marks]**

2 Name the salt produced in Question 1.   **[1 mark]**

Titration

You need to know how to carry out an acid–alkali titration to determine the exact volume of an acid needed to neutralise a given volume of alkali or vice versa, and how to use this result to prepare a pure sample of a soluble salt.

(10) Titration method

1 Fill the burette with acid; record the initial volume.

2 Use the pipette and pipette filler to add a measured volume of alkali to the conical flask.

3 Add a few drops of indicator, swirl to mix; place the conical flask on a white tile.

4 Slowly add small portions of the acid from the burette into the conical flask, swirling to mix.

5 When the indicator just changes colour (permanently) stop adding the acid, as the end point has been reached. Record the final volume reading to calculate how much acid is used.

6 Repeat steps 1 to 5 until you get concordant titres.

'Concordant' refers to two or more results within 0.1 cm³ (or 0.2 cm³, depending on the marking on the burette) of each other.

(5) Preparing a soluble salt from a titration

7 Once you have achieved concordant results, measure out the same volume of alkali and the volume of acid determined by the titration and mix together. This time you do not need to add indicator.

8 Heat the solution gently in an evaporating dish until you have salt crystals.

9 Dry the crystals between two pieces of filter paper.

Look at page 97 for the evaporation technique.

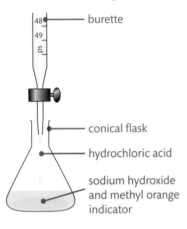

burette
conical flask
hydrochloric acid
sodium hydroxide and methyl orange indicator

Figure 1 Preparing a soluble salt using titration

(5) Worked example

Grades 4–5

The results of a titration to determine how much sulfuric acid is required to neutralise sodium hydroxide are given in the table below.

	Titration 1/ rough titration	Titration 2	Titration 3	Titration 4
Initial volume (cm³)	0.00	25.00	0.10	20.00
Final volume (cm³)	22.20	44.30	19.30	43.00
Volume used (cm³)	22.20	19.30	19.20	23.00
Tick if result used		✓	✓	

(a) Complete the table to give the volume used in titration 2. **[1 mark]**

(b) Complete the final row to show which values should be used to calculate the mean. **[1 mark]**

(c) Calculate the mean. **[2 marks]**

$$\frac{(19.30 + 19.20)}{2} = 19.25 \, cm^3$$

The volume used is calculated by subtracting the initial volume from the final volume.

The mean should always be calculated from the two (or three) most concordant results. It should not include any trial or rough titration values.

(5) Exam-style practice

Grade 6

In an acid–alkali reaction a soluble salt is produced when an acid reacts with a soluble base or alkali. In this type of reaction the metal ion of the alkali replaces one or more hydrogen ions from the acid.

(a) Write a balanced equation, with state symbols, to show the reaction between hydrochloric acid and sodium hydroxide (NaOH). **[2 marks]**

(b) Give the colour changes observed when phenolphthalein is used in this type of reaction. **[2 marks]**

 Made a start **Feeling confident** 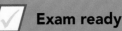 **Exam ready**

Solubility rules

You need to know the rules of solubility to be able to predict which mixed solutions will produce precipitates.

Solubility rules

The following substances are **soluble** in water:

- 👍 All nitrate salts.
- 👍 All common sodium, potassium and ammonium salts.
- 👍 Most sulfates.
- 👍 Most chlorides.

The following substances are **insoluble** in water:

- 👎 Most carbonates and hydroxides (but not those with sodium, potassium or ammonium ions, see left).
- 👎 Lead sulfate, barium sulfate and calcium sulfate.
- 👎 Silver chloride and lead chloride.

Preparation of insoluble salts

1 Mix together two solutions that will produce the precipitate you want (e.g. silver nitrate and sodium chloride to give silver chloride).

2 Filter the precipitate that forms, using filter paper and a filter funnel.

3 Wash the residue with a small amount of distilled water and allow the water to filter away.

4 Allow the residue to dry between some filter paper.

Worked example   Grades 4–6

1 A student mixed lead nitrate and ammonium sulfate solutions together in a test tube.

(a) Write a word equation for the reaction.   **[1 mark]**

lead nitrate + ammonium sulfate → lead sulfate + ammonium nitrate

(b) Explain any observations the student would make.   **[2 marks]**

The student would see a precipitate form, because lead sulfate is insoluble.

2 For each of the following pairs of solutions predict, using solubility rules, whether or not a precipitate will be formed when they are mixed. Name any precipitates.   **[4 marks]**

(a) sodium carbonate and calcium nitrate

Calcium carbonate precipitate formed

(b) potassium chloride and ammonium sulfate

No precipitate

(c) magnesium chloride and ammonium nitrate

No precipitate

(d) calcium chloride and silver nitrate

Silver chloride precipitate formed

3 Give the state symbol that would be given to a precipitate in a balanced equation.

Explain your answer.   **[2 marks]**

(s), because the precipitate is insoluble so is in the solid state.

Exam focus

You are expected to recall the rules for solubility given at the top of the page.

Try to invent a mnemonic to help you remember them.

Exam focus

You need to be able to name the precipitate formed when named solutions are mixed together. Remember you are looking at the products of the reaction, not the reactants, when determining solubility.

Exam-style practice   Grade 5

1 Explain the term 'solubility'.   **[1 mark]**

2 (a) Draw and label the equipment used to separate an insoluble salt from a solution.   **[2 marks]**

(b) Suggest why the residue is washed with distilled water.   **[1 mark]**

Oxidation and reduction

You need to be able to identify which substances are oxidised and reduced in a given reaction, chemical equation or half equation.

 Redox reactions

Oxidation and reduction reactions at their simplest involve a gain or loss of oxygen. For example, iron reacting with oxygen to give iron oxide is an oxidation (page 130). In a broader definition, oxidation and reduction (redox) reactions occur when the outer-shell electrons are lost or gained during a reaction.

Redox reactions involve the transfer of electrons:

- Oxidation is the **loss** of electrons.
- Reduction is the **gain** of electrons.

Many metals react with the oxygen in the air. They oxidise, losing electrons and forming **metal oxides** (see page 130).

Displacement reactions are examples of redox reactions; they involve simultaneous oxidation and reduction of the reacting species.

iron chloride + zinc → zinc chloride + iron
$FeCl_2$ + Zn → $ZnCl_2$ + Fe

Zinc is more reactive than iron, so pushes it out of its compound, forming zinc chloride.

The zinc metal is oxidised, forming a zinc ion.

The iron ion is reduced; it gains two electrons.

 Worked example Grades 6–7

1 Ionic equations can be used to represent redox reactions.

A redox reaction takes place when aqueous chlorine is added to potassium iodide solution.

The equation for this reaction is:

$$Cl_2(aq) + 2KI(aq) \rightarrow I_2(aq) + 2KCl(aq)$$

(a) Identify which species has been oxidised during the reaction. **[1 mark]**

The iodine is oxidised.

(b) Write the ionic equation for the reaction of chlorine with potassium iodide. **[2 marks]**

$2I^- + Cl_2 \rightarrow I_2 + 2Cl^-$

In this reaction, the **chlorine** has gained an electron. It has been **reduced** from Cl to Cl^-.
The **iodine** has lost an electron. It has been **oxidised** from I^- to I.

2 **(a)** Which **one** of the following reactions is a redox reaction? **[1 mark]**

☐ **A** $CuO + H_2 \rightarrow Cu + H_2O$

☐ **B** $HCl + NaOH \rightarrow NaCl + H_2O$

☐ **C** $MgO + 2HCl \rightarrow MgCl_2 + H_2O$

(b) Give the species that is reduced in the redox reaction in part **(a)**. **[1 mark]**

A – copper is reduced from Cu^{2+} to Cu

When writing an ionic equation, you don't need to include the spectator ions (see page 115). In this reaction, the potassium is a spectator ion and so is not included in the ionic equation.

 Exam-style practice Grade 6

(a) Write a balanced equation for the reaction between copper oxide and magnesium. **[2 marks]**

(b) Write an ionic equation to show the oxidation of magnesium in this reaction. **[2 marks]**

 Made a start Feeling confident Exam ready

Electrolysis

You need to understand the process of electrolysis and be able to write half equations for the reactions occurring at the electrodes.

(5) The process

In electrolysis, electrical energy from a direct current supply decomposes electrolytes. Electrolytes are compounds in which ions are free to move, allowing the substance to conduct electricity, so they are ionic compounds that are molten or dissolved in water.

> Ionic compounds cannot conduct when solid as the ions are in fixed positions.

Electrolysis causes the charged ions to move towards oppositely charged electrodes.

The ions are discharged at the electrodes, producing elements.

The reactions at the electrodes can be represented by half equations.

> Go to page 124 for more about half equations.

(5) Key words

- ☑ **Electrolysis** – using electricity to decompose a compound
- ☑ **Electrolyte** – the liquid or solution used in electrolysis, conducts electricity
- ☑ **Electrode** – a solid electrical conductor, usually metal or carbon
- ☑ **Anode** – the positively-charged electrode (remember **A**node **A**dd +)
- ☑ **Cathode** – the negatively-charged electrode

> The products of electrolysis may be reactive, so it is important to use inert (unreactive) materials for the electrodes.

> The command word 'explain' means you should state the electrode **and** give a reason for your answer.

(2) Working scientifically

Electrolysis is used to extract reactive metals from their ore if they cannot be extracted by reduction with carbon.

Electrolysis can also be used in making jewellery. Lower value metals are electroplated with precious metals to increase their value.

Electroplating can also be used to protect a metal from corrosion, for example, tin plating on steel food cans.

(10) Worked example — Grade 6

Look at **Figure 1**.

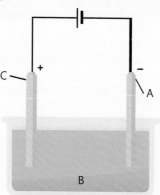

Figure 1 An electrolysis cell

(a) Use words from the box to identify A, B and C. **[3 marks]**

| electrolyte | cathode | anode | cell |

A: cathode

B: electrolyte

C: anode

(b) Give a reason why electrodes are normally made from inert substances. **[1 mark]**

Electrodes are normally made from inert materials so that they don't react with the electrolyte.

(c) State and explain which electrode metals are attracted to. **[2 marks]**

Metal ions are positively charged and the cathode is negatively charged. Metal ions are attracted to the cathode as opposite charges attract.

(5) Exam-style practice — Grades 4–5

1 Draw one straight line from each term to the correct definition. **[4 marks]**

electrolyte — electrode with positive charge
electrode — electrode with a negative charge
anode — solid, electrical conductor
cathode — liquid used for electrolysis

2 Metals form positive ions. Identify the electrode the ions will travel to. **[1 mark]**

Electrolysis of molten ionic compounds

You need to know how molten ionic compounds separate during electrolysis and be able to state the reactions that occur at each electrode.

5 Reactions at electrodes

Ionic compounds consist of positive metal ions and negative non-metal ions. These ions can move when the compound is in a molten state. This allows a current to flow when electricity is passed through the molten compound.

The positive metal ions will always travel to the negatively-charged cathode, where they gain electrons (reduce) to form the metal element.

At the anode, the non-metal ions will lose electrons (oxidise) forming the non-metal element.

5 Worked example — Grade 8

(a) Explain why sodium chloride must be molten or in solution for electrolysis. **[2 marks]**

The ions must move to conduct electricity, and they can only move when molten or in solution.

(b) Describe what happens at the positive electrode during the electrolysis of sodium chloride. **[3 marks]**

The chloride ions lose one electron each to form chlorine (gas).

(c) Write the half equation for the reaction at the negative electrode for molten sodium chloride. **[1 mark]**

$Na^+ + e^- \rightarrow Na$

5 Half equations

During electrolysis, metal ions will always be reduced and non-metals will be oxidised. This is an example of a redox reaction. Go to page 120 for more about redox reactions.

Half equations can be used to show the reactions of the ions at the electrodes (see page 124). For example, the half equations for the electrolysis of silver chloride (AgCl) are:

- Cathode: $Ag^+ + e^- \rightarrow Ag$ (reduction)
- Anode: $Cl^- \rightarrow Cl + e^-$ (oxidation)

Ionic compounds must be molten or in solution to have free ions. If the compound is dissolved in an aqueous solution, different products may form at the electrodes (page 123).

The negative non-metal ion is attracted to the positive electrode; here it becomes **oxidised** (loses electrons).

The half equation shows the reaction taking place at the cathode. Positive metal ions are attracted to the cathode where they are **reduced** (gain electrons) to form the metal element. In this case, because of the high temperature and production of sodium metal, this electrolysis would only ever be performed with strict safety precautions.

1 Exam focus

You could be asked to draw a labelled diagram of electrolysis in the exam. Go to page 125 to see what you should include in the diagram.

10 Exam-style practice — Grades 7–9

1 Lead is produced by the electrolysis of molten lead bromide.

(a) Draw a diagram of the apparatus that you could use for the electrolysis of lead bromide. **[4 marks]**

(b) Balance the half equations, to show the reactions that will take place at each electrode. **[2 marks]**

$Pb^{2+} + ___ \rightarrow Pb$

$2Br^- \rightarrow Br_2 + ___$

(c) Suggest what you would observe at the anode. **[2 marks]**

2 For each of the following ionic compounds, predict the product at the anode and at the cathode. **[4 marks]**

(a) lead iodide

(b) zinc bromide

(c) magnesium oxide

(d) lithium chloride

Electrolysis of aqueous solutions

You need to be able to describe what happens to aqueous solutions during electrolysis (where an ionic substance is dissolved in water).

Ions

When an electrical current is passed through an aqueous solution of ionic compounds, the water molecules break down so H^+ and OH^- ions are produced along with the solute ions. The ion that is discharged from each electrode is dependent upon the relative reactivity of the elements involved in the reactions.

At the anode: oxygen is produced, unless the solution contains a halide ion (Cl^-, Br^-, I^-) in which case the halogen is produced (Cl_2, Br_2, I_2).

At the cathode: hydrogen is produced, unless the metal in the solution is less reactive than hydrogen (lower position in the reactivity series, such as copper or platinum).

Worked example — Grade 7

Look at **Figure 1**.

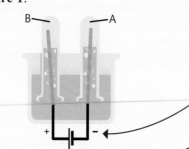

Figure 1 Method for the electrolysis of brine

(a) Name gases **A** and **B**. [2 marks]

A: chlorine

B: hydrogen

(b) State what substance is found in the solution in the beaker after the reaction has taken place. [1 mark]

Sodium hydroxide

(c) Write the half equation for the reaction at the cathode. [2 marks]

$2H^+ + 2e^- \rightarrow H_2$

Electrolysis of water

A small proportion of water molecules dissociate into ions, allowing it to conduct electricity. During the electrolysis of water (acidified with a little dilute sulfuric acid) hydrogen and oxygen are released at the electrodes:

- OH^- ions are attracted to the anode where they lose electrons and form oxygen gas and water.
- H^+ ions are attracted to the cathode where they gain electrons and form hydrogen gas.

The overall balanced equation for the process is:

$$2H_2O(l) \rightarrow 2H_2(g) + O_2(g)$$

The volume of hydrogen given off is twice the volume of oxygen given off.

Exam focus

If you are asked to draw the apparatus for electrolysis, make sure you include a power source as shown here.

Brine is a concentrated solution of salt (sodium chloride) in water. The ions present are Na^+, H^+, OH^- and Cl^-.

As sodium is more reactive than hydrogen, hydrogen will be discharged at the cathode.

Chlorine is a halogen and so will be discharged at the anode.

As hydrogen and chlorine have been discharged at the electrodes, Na^+ and OH^- are left in the solution, forming NaOH.

Remember to balance the number of charges with the correct number of electrons.

Go to page 124 to revise half equations.

Exam-style practice — Grade 7

Electrolysis can be used to show that aqueous copper chloride contains ions.

(a) State and explain what happens when an electrical current passes through the solution. [4 marks]

(b) Write the half equation for the reaction that takes place at the anode. [2 marks]

Made a start | Feeling confident | Exam ready

Half equations

You need to be able to represent the reactions occuring at each electrode during electrolysis using half equations.

⑤ Ionic equations ✓

The electrolysis of copper iodide can be represented by two half equations, showing the reactions at each electrode.

At the cathode: the positively-charged ion (Cu^{2+}) is reduced; it gains electrons:

$$Cu^{2+} + 2e^- \rightarrow Cu$$

At the anode: the negatively-charge ion (I^-) is oxidised; it loses electrons:

$$2I^- \rightarrow I_2 + 2e^-$$

⑤ Balancing half equations ✓

You should follow these steps to balance half equations:

❶ Write the formulae of the reactant (or reactants) and the product (or products).

❷ Balance the number of ions on either side of the arrow.

❸ Work out the number of charges and then balance with electrons so that both sides of the equation have the same overall charge.

⑩ Worked example — Grades 5–7 ✓

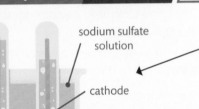
sodium sulfate solution
cathode
anode

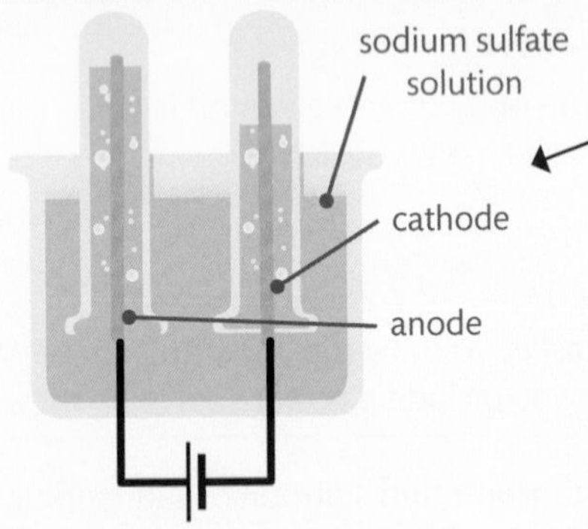

Figure 1 Electrolysis of sodium sulfate

A solution of dilute sodium sulfate is electrolysed as shown in **Figure 1**.

Oxygen gas is discharged at the anode.

(a) Give a reason why oxygen is produced at the anode. **[1 mark]**

Hydroxide ions discharge, forming oxygen and water.

(b) Write the half equation for the reaction at the anode. **[2 marks]**

$$4OH^- \rightarrow 2H_2O + O_2 + 4e^-$$

(c) Name the substance produced at the cathode. **[1 mark]**

Hydrogen gas

(d) Write the half equation for the reaction at the cathode. **[2 marks]**

$$2H^+ + 2e^- \rightarrow H_2$$

Exam focus 📌

Make sure you look at diagrams carefully in the exam. Look at any labels or keys, and pay attention to any details that may be important, e.g. gas bubbles.

Negative ions are attracted to the anode, so SO_4^{2-} ions and OH^- ions accumulate at the anode. Oxygen gas will always be discharged at the anode, unless a halide is present. OH^- ions give up their electrons more readily than SO_4^{2-} ions, so the sulfate ions are left in solution.

Hydroxide ions will react to produce oxygen gas and water: $4OH^- - 4e^- \rightarrow 2H_2O + O_2$ (or as shown in the worked example). Learn this equation.

Sodium is **more reactive** than hydrogen so hydrogen gas will be **discharged** at the cathode.

Hydrogen ions are reduced to form molecules of hydrogen gas.

Go to page 126 for more about the electrodes used in electrolysis.

⑤ Exam-style practice — Grades 6–7 ✓

❶ Copper chloride ($CuCl_2$) solution is electrolysed. Write the half equation for the reaction at each electrode. **[2 marks]**

❷ Give a reason why inert electrodes must be used when a molten substance is electrolysed. **[1 mark]**

 Made a start **Feeling confident** **Exam ready**

Practical: Electrolysis of copper sulfate

You need to know what happens during the electrolysis of copper sulfate using inert electrodes and copper electrodes.

② Apparatus

- ☑ 50 cm³ copper sulfate solution
- ☑ 100 cm³ beaker
- ☑ Petri dish lid
- ☑ two graphite rod electrodes, two copper electrodes
- ☑ two crocodile/4 mm plug leads
- ☑ low-voltage power supply
- ☑ blue litmus paper
- ☑ tweezers

Another suitable answer is platinum.

⑤ Electrolysis of copper sulfate

1 Pour copper sulfate solution into the beaker to about 50 cm³.

2 Add the Petri dish lid and insert carbon rods through the holes. **The rods must not touch each other.** Attach crocodile leads to the rods. Connect the rods to the **DC (red and black)** terminals of a low-voltage power supply.

3 Switch on the power supply (4 V).

4 Look at both electrodes. Is there bubbling at either, one or both of the electrodes?

5 Use tweezers to hold a piece of blue litmus paper in the solution next to the positive electrode.

6 Record your observations.

7 Repeat with copper electrodes: weigh both electrodes, dry, before and after electrolysis.

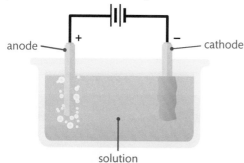

anode ——— + — ——— cathode

solution

Figure 2 Electrolysis apparatus

⑩ Worked example — Grade 7

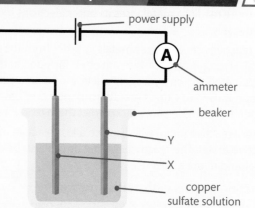

power supply — A — ammeter — beaker — Y — X — copper sulfate solution

Figure 1 Apparatus for the electrolysis of copper sulfate solution

(a) Give the names of the electrodes **X** and **Y**. [1 mark]

X is the anode; Y is the cathode.

(b) Name an inert element that can be used for the electrodes. [1 mark]

Carbon/graphite

(c) This process is used industrially to purify copper, by connecting impure copper as the anode and pure copper as the cathode. Describe the reaction taking place at each of the electrodes, giving any observations. [4 marks]

At the anode: copper atoms lose electrons, forming copper ions, $Cu^{2+}(aq)$

The electrode/anode gets smaller in size as the ions form.

$$Cu(s) \rightarrow Cu^{2+}(aq) + 2e^-$$

At the cathode, copper ions gain electrons to form copper metal:

$$Cu^{2+}(aq) + 2e^- \rightarrow Cu(s)$$

The electrode increases in size as copper is deposited.

If a gas is produced at the anode and it does **not** bleach blue litmus paper, it will be oxygen. If a gas is produced at the cathode, it will be hydrogen.

⑩ Exam-style practice — Grade 7

(a) Name the products at the electrodes when copper sulfate solution is electrolysed with inert electrodes. [2 marks]

(b) Explain which product is formed at the positive electrode and which product is formed at the negative electrode. [2 marks]

The reactivity series

You need to understand how the reactivity of metals with water or dilute acids and salt solutions is related to the tendency of the metal to form its cation, or positive ion, and be able to deduce an order of reactivity of metals based on experimental results.

⑩ Reactivity of metals

When metals react, they lose their outer-shell electrons to form cations (positive ions). The more readily a metal loses its outer electrons to form a positive ion, the more reactive it is.

The reactivity series places metals in order from the most reactive to the least reactive metal. Hydrogen and carbon are often included in the reactivity series, although they aren't metals. When hydrogen reacts it loses an electron in the same way that metals do. Carbon is used to extract metals from their ores based on their reactivity – the reactivity of carbon needs to be known to predict these reactions (see page 127).

A more reactive metal will displace a less reactive metal from a compound of the less reactive metal. The reactivity of metals can also be compared using their reactions with water and dilute acids.

potassium	most reactive	K
sodium		Na
calcium		Ca
magnesium		Mg
aluminium		Al
carbon		C
zinc		Zn
iron		Fe
hydrogen		H
copper		Cu
silver		Ag
gold	least reactive	Au

Figure 1 The reactivity series

Reacting metals with acids and water

The alkali metals all react vigorously with cold water (see page 137). Calcium and magnesium have less vigorous reactions with water. Less reactive metals, such as zinc and iron, need dilute acids to react. The reactivity can be compared by seeing how vigorously the hydrogen gas is released. The more vigorous the reaction, the more reactive the metal.

metal + acid → salt + hydrogen

metal + water → metal hydroxide + hydrogen

⑩ Worked example · Grades 5–7

A student investigates the reactivity of four different metals with salt solutions. The table shows the observations.

	Cu	Mg	Zn	Ag
CuSO$_4$	no reaction	**colour change**	**colour change**	no reaction
AgNO$_3$	**colour change**	**colour change**	**colour change**	no reaction
ZnSO$_4$	no reaction	**colour change**	no reaction	no reaction
MgSO$_4$	no reaction	no reaction	no reaction	no reaction

> You should be able to deduce the most reactive to the least reactive metals by either how many reactions they took part in or how vigorous their reactions were.

(a) Deduce the order of reactivity of zinc, copper and magnesium. **[1 mark]**

magnesium (most reactive)   zinc   copper (least reactive)

(b) Describe what the results suggest about the reactivity of silver in relation to the other metals given. **[1 mark]**

It is the least reactive of the four metals tested.

(c) Write a balanced chemical equation for the reaction between copper sulfate and magnesium. **[2 marks]**

CuSO$_4$ + Mg → MgSO$_4$ + Cu

⑩ Exam-style practice · Grades 6–7

1 **Figure 2** shows four metals reacting with dilute hydrochloric acid.

The four metals used are magnesium, iron, copper and calcium. Deduce, using your knowledge of reactivity, the names of metals **A**, **B**, **C** and **D**. **[2 marks]**

2 Explain how a metal's reactivity is determined by the tendency of the metal to form a positive ion. **[2 marks]**

3 Write a balanced equation, with state symbols, for the reaction between calcium and water, producing calcium hydroxide (Ca(OH)$_2$). **[2 marks]**

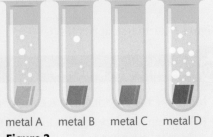

metal A   metal B   metal C   metal D

Figure 2

✓ **Made a start**   ✓ **Feeling confident**   ✓ **Exam ready**

Extraction of metals and reduction

You need to know how carbon is used to extract metals from their ores, found in the Earth's crust. Ores are naturally occurring rocks that contain a sufficient amount of metal or metal compounds.

Extracting metals

The method used to extract metals from their ore depends on their reactivity and the cost of the extraction process required. Metals that are less reactive than carbon can be extracted from their oxides by reduction; this process involves heating the metal oxide with carbon.

> For example: iron oxide + carbon → iron + carbon dioxide.

The extraction process removes the oxygen from the metal oxide. This means the metal is reduced. At the same time, the carbon is oxidised to form carbon dioxide.

Metals extracted by reduction with carbon include zinc, iron, tin, lead and copper.

Unreactive metals, such as gold, are found in the Earth's crust as uncombined elements, so chemical separation is unnecessary. However, chemical reactions may be needed to remove other elements that could contaminate the gold.

Some metals, such as aluminium, are so reactive that their oxides cannot be reduced by carbon. Go to page 128 for more about extracting these types of metals.

> Metals such as zinc, iron and copper are present in ores as their oxides.

Worked example — Grades 5–6

1 Iron can be extracted from its oxide.

(a) Name this type of process. **[1 mark]**

Reduction

> The iron loses the oxygen it is combined with and is **reduced**.

(b) Explain how oxygen can be removed from iron oxide to make iron. **[2 marks]**

Heat the iron oxide with carbon to reduce the iron and remove the oxygen.

> It may seem obvious that the iron oxide is heated but you need to always state the conditions used in a reaction. Although carbon is given in the answer, any element that is more reactive than iron could be used to extract it from its oxide.

(c) Explain why this process cannot be used to extract aluminium from its oxide. **[2 marks]**

Aluminium is above carbon in the reactivity series so carbon cannot remove oxygen from aluminium oxide.

> Only metals below carbon in the reactivity series can be extracted from their oxides using this process. As aluminium is further up the reactivity series than carbon, a different process is required.

2 The following equation is an example of a reduction reaction used to extract a metal from its ore.

$$2CuO + C \rightarrow 2Cu + CO_2$$

(a) Write the word equation for the reaction taking place. **[1 mark]**

copper oxide + carbon → copper + carbon dioxide

(b) Explain why this reduction reaction can take place. **[1 mark]**

Because copper is less reactive than carbon

Exam-style practice — Grade 7

1 Lead oxide reacts with carbon to form the products lead and carbon dioxide.

(a) Write a word equation to show the reduction of lead oxide using carbon. **[1 mark]**

(b) Name the type of reaction that occurs between carbon and oxygen during the reaction. **[1 mark]**

(c) Explain, in terms of electrons, how the lead in lead oxide (PbO) is reduced. **[3 marks]**

2 Explain why calcium cannot be reduced from calcium oxide using carbon. **[2 marks]**

 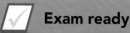

Electrolysis to extract metals

You need to know how reactive metals can be extracted from their compound using electrolysis.

⑤ Reactive metals

Metals that are more reactive than carbon cannot be extracted by reduction, so electrolysis is used instead.

The electrolysis of metals involves large amounts of energy as the metal compound must be in a molten state. Energy is also needed to produce the necessary electrical current.

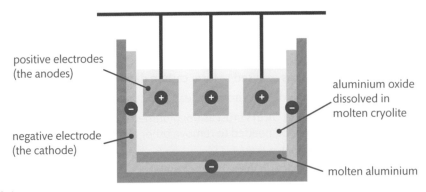

positive electrodes (the anodes)

aluminium oxide dissolved in molten cryolite

negative electrode (the cathode)

molten aluminium

Figure 1 Electrolysis of aluminium

⑩ Worked example   Grades 5–7

(a) Explain why the electrolyte for electrolysis of aluminium is a molten mixture of aluminium oxide dissolved in cryolite. **[2 marks]**

Cryolite melts at a lower temperature than aluminium oxide, so less energy is needed to form the electrolyte.

(b) Name the substance used for the electrodes in the electrolysis of aluminium. **[1 mark]**

Graphite (a form of carbon)

(c) Oxygen is produced at the anodes. Explain why the positive electrodes need replacing regularly. **[2 marks]**

The oxygen produced reacts with the carbon electrodes to produce carbon dioxide. This results in the electrodes gradually wearing away.

(d) Complete the half equation to show the reaction at the positive electrodes. **[2 marks]**

$2O^{2-} \rightarrow O_2 + 4e^-$

(e) Explain why aluminium forms at the negative electrode. **[3 marks]**

Aluminium ions are positive, therefore they are attracted to the negative electrode (the cathode) where they gain electrons and are reduced.

⑩ Exam-style practice   Grade 6

① **Figure 2** shows how magnesium can be produced from magnesium chloride using electrolysis.
Explain why large amounts of energy are used in the extraction process. **[2 marks]**

② The melting point of aluminium oxide is over 2000 °C.
Name the substance used to produce an electrolyte at a lower temperature. **[1 mark]**

③ Depending on their reactivity, metals can be extracted from their ores either by reduction with carbon or electrolysis. Reduction involves heating the ore to a very high temperature in a furnace with carbon. This reaction produces an impure sample of the metal and carbon dioxide.

Electrolysis requires a metal to be molten. Electricity is passed through the electrolysis cell to separate the metal from its impurities.

Evaluate the use of each of the processes. **[4 marks]**

cathode (–ve)   anode (+ve)

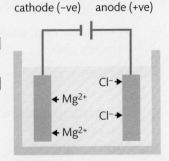

Cl^-
Mg^{2+}
Cl^-
Mg^{2+}

Figure 2 Extracting magnesium using electrolysis

Made a start | Feeling confident | Exam ready

Alternative methods of extracting metals

Earth's resources of metal ores, such as copper ores, are limited. You need to know about alternative methods that are being developed to extract metals from other sources.

 Bioleaching and phytoextraction

Traditional methods of metal extraction involve mining and digging. This produces vast amounts of waste rock that need to be removed from the mining sites.

Bioleaching (using bacteria) and **phytoextraction** are newer methods that can be used to extract metals, such as copper, from low-grade ores (ores that contain only a small percentage of copper).

The metal can then be obtained from the ore using scrap metal displacement or electrolysis.

Bioleaching

1 Bacteria feed on low-grade ore.

2 Biological and chemical processes are used to produce a leachate (a solution of copper ions).

3 Scrap iron displacement or electrolysis can be used to extract the copper from the leachate.

Phytoextraction

1 Plants are grown in copper-rich soils.

2 When the plants have absorbed the copper ions, they are harvested.

3 The plants are burned to produce an ash containing copper compounds.

4 Sulfuric acid is added to leach the copper ions (dissolve them).

5 Scrap iron displacement or electrolysis can be used to extract the copper.

 Worked example **Grade 6**

Figure 1 Opencast mine

1 Copper metal can be removed from the Earth's crust by opencast mining. State **one** environmental problem that is caused by the mining of copper ore. **[1 mark]**

It produces large amounts of waste rock, which will cause dust pollution.

2 Explain why scrap metal displacement is used to extract copper. **[2 marks]**

Scrap metal displacement is used as it is a cheaper method than electrolysis. Scrap iron displaces copper as iron is more reactive than copper.

3 Describe how bioleaching is used to obtain copper compounds. **[2 marks]**

Bacteria feed on low-grade copper compounds. Biological and chemical processes produce a leachate, which contains copper compounds.

 Exam-style practice **Grades 8–9**

1 Give **two** reasons why copper is now-extracted from low-grade ores. **[2 marks]**

2 Phytoextraction is used near mines to extract copper from soil that contains small concentrations of copper compounds. Describe how phytoextraction is used to obtain copper compounds. **[3 marks]**

3 Name the process which uses bacteria to extract metal. **[1 mark]**

4 Copper is a very useful metal. It can be extracted by mining and reduction with carbon or by phytoextraction.

The process involves mining for copper ore, crushing the rocks and separating the ore from the crushed rock. The ore is then processed before smelting with carbon in a furnace at around 1200 °C.

Phytoextraction usually takes place where copper ore has been mined, as there may be areas of land that contain very low percentages of copper compounds. One way to extract the copper is to grow specific plants on the land. The plants absorb copper compounds through their roots. The plants are then burned to produce an ash containing copper compounds. The ash is then reacted with sulfuric acid to extract the copper.

Compare and contrast each of these processes. Include the economic and environmental effect of each method in your answer. **[6 marks]**

Metal oxides

You need to be able to state the properties of metal oxides and give equations for their formation.

(2) Formation of metal oxides

Metal oxides are formed when a metal reacts with oxygen.

metal + oxygen → metal oxide

Metal oxides are examples of a giant ionic lattice structure. They are usually solid at room temperature. They generally have high melting and boiling points.

(5) Naming metal oxides

When metals react to form oxides, they gain oxygen so they are **oxidised**:

- copper + oxygen → copper oxide
- calcium + oxygen → calcium oxide
- lead + oxygen → lead oxide.

(5) The reactivity series

The reactivity of a metal is related to its reactivity towards water and acids to form the metal cation. The more reactive the metal, the more easily it can be oxidised (page 126).

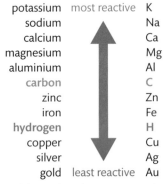

potassium	most reactive	K
sodium		Na
calcium		Ca
magnesium		Mg
aluminium		Al
carbon		C
zinc		Zn
iron		Fe
hydrogen		H
copper		Cu
silver		Ag
gold	least reactive	Au

Figure 1 The reactivity series: the more reactive a metal, the more easily it will be oxidised.

(10) Worked example   Grade 6

A student investigates magnesium oxide, a metal oxide.

(a) State what type of bonding is present in the magnesium oxide. **[1 mark]**

ionic bonding

(b) Using the equation below, show that the formation of a metal oxide is a redox reaction.

$$2Mg + O_2 \rightarrow 2MgO$$ **[2 marks]**

Mg loses 2 electrons as it is in Group 2, forming Mg^{2+}.

The magnesium has been oxidised (loss of electrons).

O gains 2 electrons as it is in Group 6, forming O^{2-}.

The oxygen has been reduced (gain of electrons).

Magnesium has lost electrons and oxygen has gained electrons. The reaction is a redox reaction.

(c) The student notices that shiny magnesium metal ribbon left out in air quickly develops a cloudy surface, whereas gold jewellery remains shiny. Explain what causes the observed change and why gold does not behave in the same way. **[2 marks]**

The magnesium surface reacts fast with oxygen in the air to form magnesium oxide, which changes the appearance of the metal. Gold is much lower in the reactivity series than magnesium, so it does not oxidise in air.

(5) Exam-style practice   Grade 6

(a) Write a word equation to identify the product formed in the reaction of iron and oxygen. **[1 mark]**
(b) Name this type of reaction. **[1 mark]**
(c) Name the substance that is reduced in this reaction. **[1 mark]**

  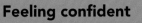

Recycling and life-cycle assessment

You need to know how a life-cycle assessment (LCA) is used to assess the environmental impact of a product, and the advantages of recycling metals to preserve metals and protect the environment.

Stages of an LCA

An LCA studies the environmental impact at several stages in the life of a product, including:

- extraction and processing of the raw material
- manufacture and packaging use during its lifetime
- disposal by incineration, landfill or recycling.

During each stage, energy is used, pollution is produced and waste is created.

LCAs are used to compare products with the same use but that are made from different materials, for example, paper cups and drinking glasses. In each case, the stages above need to be evaluated to identify which product has the least environmental impact.

Worked example — Grade 7

The table shows the energy used and waste created during the production of four different types of carrier bag. The figures shown are per 1000 carrier bags produced.

Bag type	Electricity used (kWh)	Waste (g)
conventional high-density polyethylene (HDPE)	6.15	418.4
starch-polyester blend (biopolymer)	17.24	94.8
poly(propene) (PP)	87.75	5850.0
cotton	11.00	1800.0

Evaluate, using the data provided, the environmental impact of producing the four carrier bags. **[4 marks]**

The starch-polyester bags produce the least waste, only 98.4 g, but they use nearly three times as much electricity in their production when compared with the HDPE bag.

The HDPE bags use the least amount of electricity, just over 6 kWh, but produce four times the waste of the biopolymer bags.

The poly(propene) bags would have the greatest environmental impact as they produce the most waste, nearly 6 kg, and use the most electricity, 87.75 kWh.

The cotton bags have the second lowest electrical usage. However, the production of cotton bags produces the second to largest amount of waste.

Recycling

Recycling reduces waste; however, energy is required to transform something into a new product, so pollution will still be created. The amount of energy required for recycling depends on the material and the final product. The levels of energy consumed and pollution produced by recycling are usually less than when the same product is made from raw materials.

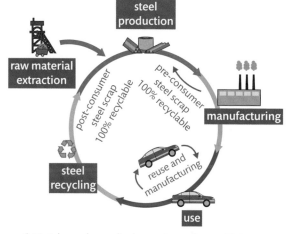

Figure 1 Metals can be melted, recast or reformed into new products. Scrap steel can be added to iron from the blast furnace to reduce the amount of iron that needs to be extracted.

The data illustrates the environmental impact of the production of the different bags. It doesn't indicate the environmental impact of people reusing the bags.

Working scientifically

You need to understand that LCAs cannot be classed as an objective process. It is straightforward to quantify the use of water, energy and production of waste. However, it is more difficult to give numerical values to the effect of pollutants. This can lead to LCAs being biased to misrepresent products for advertising.

Exam-style practice — Grades 5–7

1. It is estimated that two billion tonnes of iron ore are extracted every year. Explain why it is a good idea, environmentally, to recycle iron. **[3 marks]**

2. State the purpose of life-cycle assessments (LCAs). **[2 marks]**

3. Describe how recycling produces pollution, and the environmental impact of this pollution. **[4 marks]**

Reversible reactions

Many reactions, such as burning fuel, are irreversible – they go to completion and cannot be reversed. Other chemical reactions are easily reversible – the products of the reaction can react to form the original reactants.

5 Reversible reaction equations

A **reversible reaction** is indicated by a split arrow ($\rightleftharpoons$). This symbol means that the reaction can proceed in both directions.

A reversible reaction can be shown as:

$A + B \rightleftharpoons C + D$

In a closed system (one from which no substances can escape), both forward and back reactions can occur and equilibrium will be reached. **Equilibrium** occurs when the rate of the forward reaction is equal to the rate of the reverse reaction. The reactions continue in both directions, but the overall concentrations remain the same – dynamic equilibrium (see page 133).

An **irreversible reaction** is shown by

$A + B \rightarrow C + D$

The products, C and D, do not react to form the reactants, A and B.

2 A reversible reaction

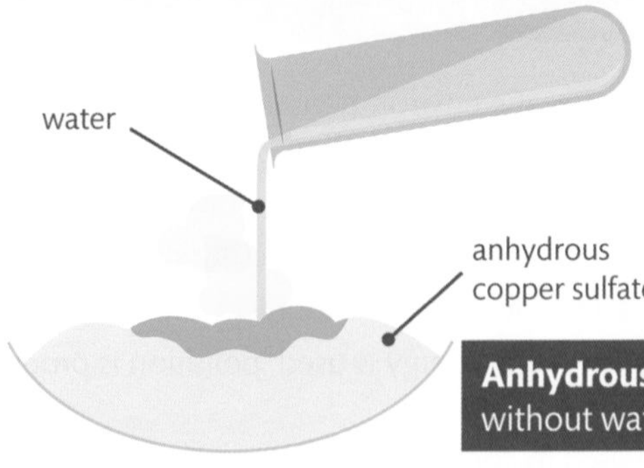

Anhydrous means without water.

Figure 1 When water is added to white anhydrous copper (II) sulfate, blue hydrated copper sulfate forms. When hydrated copper sulfate is heated, it loses water and anhydrous copper sulfate forms.

The reaction between anhydrous copper sulfate and water is reversible.

hydrated copper sulfate $\rightleftharpoons$ anhydrous copper sulfate + water

10 Worked example — Grade 6

1. Complete the word equation below, producing sulfur trioxide, to show that the reaction is reversible. **[1 mark]**

   sulfur dioxide + oxygen $\rightleftharpoons$ sulfur trioxide

2. Explain why equilibrium is only reached in a closed system. **[2 marks]**

   In an open system gaseous products can escape. If the system is closed, the gaseous products remain and can react to form the reactants.

3. The thermal decomposition of ammonium chloride, into ammonia and hydrogen chloride, is reversible.
   Write a word equation to show the reaction. **[2 marks]**

   ammonium chloride $\rightleftharpoons$ ammonia + hydrogen chloride

   The marks are awarded for correctly using the information from the question to write the word equation **and** for correctly showing the reaction is reversible.

4. When water is added to a sample of blue anhydrous cobalt chloride, pink hydrated cobalt chloride forms.

   (a) Write a word equation to show the reaction which took place. **[1 mark]**

   anhydrous cobalt chloride + water $\rightleftharpoons$ hydrated cobalt chloride

   (b) Devise an experiment to show that this reaction is reversible. **[2 marks]**

   Heat the hydrated cobalt chloride to drive off the water. The cobalt chloride will change colour back to blue showing that the reaction has reversed.

5 Working scientifically

The direction of a reversible reaction can be altered by changing the conditions, such as temperature, concentration and, if gases are involved in the reaction, pressure.

Some reactions involve a colour change or a change of state. For example, when solid white ammonium chloride is heated, it forms two colourless gases. When these gases are cooled, solid white ammonium chloride reforms.

10 Exam-style practice — Grade 6

1. The reaction between hydrogen and nitrogen is reversible. State what is meant by the term 'reversible'. **[2 marks]**

2. When hydrated copper sulfate is heated it changes colour from blue to white, producing anhydrous copper sulfate. When water is added, hydrated copper sulfate is reformed.

   (a) Describe the observation that proves this reaction is reversible. **[1 mark]**

   (b) Write a word equation to show the reaction taking place. **[2 marks]**

Dynamic equilibrium and the Haber process

You need to understand dynamic equilibrium reactions and know about the conditions that affect them.

(5) Reaching dynamic equilbrium

Dynamic equilibrium is reached in a reversible reaction when the forward reaction occurs at exactly the **same rate** as the reverse reaction. For equilibrium to be achieved the reaction must take place in sealed apparatus (**closed system**).

1 At the start of the reaction there is no product.

2 As the reaction proceeds in the forward direction (to the right), moles of reactant are being used up and moles of product are formed.

3 Some of the newly formed products react. Their reaction moves in the reverse direction (to the left), favouring the production of the reactants.

4 The reaction reaches equilibrium when the rate of the forward reaction is equal to the rate of the reverse reaction. The reactions continue in both directions, but the total amounts stay the same.

The amount of reactants and products at any one time are not equal but the proportions of each reactant and product remain constant. There is usually more of one than the other.

- If the concentration of the reactants is greater than the products, the position of the equilibrium is on the left.
- If the concentration of the products is greater than the reactants, the position of the equilibrium is on the right.

(5) The Haber process

Ammonia is an important raw material in the manufacture of fertilisers, explosives, plastics and cleaning products.

Ammonia is manufactured by reacting nitrogen and hydrogen in the Haber process:

> Go to page 152 to revise fractional distillation.

$$N_2(g) + 3H_2(g) \rightleftharpoons 2NH_3(g)$$

Nitrogen is extracted from the air by fractional distillation and hydrogen can be obtained from natural gas.

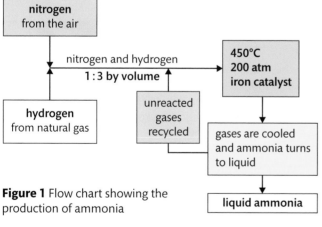

Figure 1 Flow chart showing the production of ammonia

(5) Conditions for the Haber process

The reaction for producing ammonia is reversible. The conditions used are a compromise between yield and speed – manufacturers need to produce enough ammonia in a suitable length of time.

Temperature: 450°C

The higher the temperature, the faster the reaction, **but** because the reaction is exothermic in the forward direction, higher temperatures will drive equilibrium to the left, reducing the yield.

Pressure: 200 atmospheres

Increasing pressure causes the equilibrium position to move to the lower number of moles of gas. There are four on the left-hand side of the equation and two on the right, so the higher the pressure, the greater the yield of ammonia, **but** increasing pressure means increased cost, as the reaction vessel must be built strong enough to withstand the high pressure.

Catalyst: iron

A catalyst is used to speed up the rate of the reaction; it does not affect the yield but will make the production of ammonia quicker.

(2) Worked example   Grade 4

State what is meant by the term 'dynamic equilibrium'.   **[1 mark]**

In a reversible reaction, the forward reaction occurs at exactly the same rate as the reverse reaction. (For equilibrium to be achieved, the reaction must take place in sealed apparatus – a closed system.)

(5) Exam-style practice   Grades 6–8

1 Explain why a relatively low temperature is used in the manufacture of ammonia.   **[2 marks]**

2 Explain why this low temperature is classed as a 'compromise'.   **[2 marks]**

3 Suggest why removing ammonia as it is produced increases its yield.   **[1 mark]**

Temperature and equilibrium

In a reversible reaction at equilibrium, if you change the temperature, the system will oppose the change until equilibrium is restored. You need to know how changes in temperature will affect the position of the equilibrium in endothermic and exothermic reactions.

 Changing temperature

If a reversible reaction is exothermic (gives out thermal energy) in one direction, it will be endothermic (takes in thermal energy) in the opposite direction. The amount of energy given out is always equal to the amount of energy taken in.

The system will oppose an increase in temperature by taking in thermal energy, favouring the endothermic reaction. The amount of products at equilibrium will increase in the endothermic reaction and decrease in the exothermic reaction.

The system will oppose a decrease in temperature by giving out thermal energy, favouring the exothermic reaction. The amount of products at equilibrium will increase in the exothermic reaction and decrease in the endothermic reaction.

 Worked example | **Grades 6–7**

1 Ammonia is manufactured from nitrogen and hydrogen (the Haber process). The reaction is exothermic in the forward direction.
Explain how the temperature can be altered to give maximum yield of ammonia. **[2 marks]**

The forward reaction is exothermic, so reducing the temperature will favour this reaction as the equilibrium will oppose the change by giving out more thermal energy.

2 Ammonia and hydrogen chloride are colourless gases; ammonium chloride is a white solid. A student reacts ammonia with hydrogen chloride in the reaction shown below.

ammonia + hydrogen $\rightleftharpoons$ ammonium
chloride   chloride

The reaction is exothermic in the forward direction. Explain how the student could confirm that the reverse reaction is endothermic. **[2 marks]**

The student could heat the products. If the amount of white solid product is reduced, the backward reaction is endothermic.

3 The reaction of NO_2 to N_2O_4 is reversible.
$2NO_2$ (brown gas) $\rightleftharpoons N_2O_4$ (colourless gas)

In a closed system, the reaction reaches equilibrium, producing a pale brown mixture of NO_2 and N_2O_4. When the temperature of the reaction is increased, the mixture becomes darker. Explain this observation, relating your answer to the energy change. **[3 marks]**

When the temperature is increased, the mixture becomes darker which means there must be more NO_2 in the reaction vessel as NO_2 is a brown gas. This suggests that the forward reaction is exothermic as increasing the temperature has driven the reaction to the left.

Exothermic reactions release thermal energy. Excess thermal energy needs to be removed to continue the reaction in the same direction, otherwise the endothermic reaction will be favoured.

 Working scientifically

For industrial processes, such as the **Haber process**, it is important to maximise the yield of the product in a reasonable time for a reasonable cost. Scientists can ensure the optimum yield of product by changing the conditions of the reaction. Scientists have to consider how changing different factors, such as temperature and pressure will interact. They also must consider factors such as cost and energy efficiency, when designing the **optimum conditions** for an industrial process. In the Haber process, the optimum temperature of 450°C is a compromise between yield (low temperature) and speed (high temperature).

 Exam focus

In the exam, you will be told if the forward reaction is exothermic or endothermic. Remember, the reverse reaction is always opposite to the forward reaction, so if the forward reaction is exothermic the reverse reaction will be endothermic.

Thermal energy must be applied to ensure a reversible reaction proceeds in the endothermic direction.

 Exam-style practice | **Grade 5**

Hydrogen is made by the reaction given below.
Use your knowledge of exothermic and endothermic reversible reactions to answer these questions.

$CH_4(g) + H_2O(g) \rightleftharpoons 3H_2(g) + CO(g)$

(a) Explain why a high temperature is used. **[2 marks]**

(b) State what type of reaction the forward reaction is. **[1 mark]**

 Made a start | **Feeling confident** | **Exam ready**

Pressure and equilibrium

In a reversible reaction at equilibrium, if you change the pressure, the system will oppose the change until equilibrium is restored. You need to know how changes in pressure will affect the position of the equilibrium in reactions involving gases.

5 Changing pressure

If a reversible reaction involves a gas, changing the pressure will affect the position of the equilibrium.

If there are different numbers of gaseous molecules on either side of the equation, increasing the pressure will cause the position of the equilibrium to move to the side with fewer molecules. If there are the same number of gaseous molecules on either side of the equation, changing the pressure will not change the position of the equilibrium.

$H_2(g) + I_2(g) \rightleftharpoons 2HI(g)$

2 moles   2 moles

Pressure will not affect the position of the equilibrium.

$2SO_2(g) + O_2(g) \rightleftharpoons 2SO_3(g)$

3 moles   2 moles

Increasing the pressure will drive the position of the equilibrium to the right.

10 Worked example — Grades 6–7

1 Ammonia is manufactured from nitrogen and hydrogen, as shown in the reaction below.

$N_2(g) + 3H_2(g) \rightleftharpoons 2NH_3(g)$

The equation shows that 1 mole of nitrogen reacts with 3 moles of hydrogen, giving a total of 4 moles on the left side of the reaction.

There are 2 moles of ammonia on the right.

(a) Deduce how many moles of reactant and how many moles of product there are in the equation above. **[1 mark]**

There are 4 moles of reactants and 2 moles of product.

(b) Explain how increasing the pressure will affect the amount of ammonia produced. **[2 marks]**

If pressure is increased, the rate at which equilibrium is achieved will speed up as there will be more frequent collisions. However, the rate itself does not affect the position of the equilibrium, although the pressure may do so. Go to page 142 for more about rates of reaction.

More ammonia will be produced because the system moves the position of the equilibrium to the side with fewer molecules in order to reduce the pressure.

When pressure is increased, the system will oppose the pressure by reducing the number of moles present.

2 The following reaction can be used to produce ethanol industrially for use as a solvent or as a fuel.

$C_2H_4 + H_2O \rightleftharpoons CH_3CH_2OH$

Give **one** advantage and **one** disadvantage of increasing the pressure of this reaction. **[2 marks]**

Advantage: increasing pressure drives the reaction to the right so more ethanol is produced.

Disadvantage: increasing pressure is costly as a vessel that can withstand the pressure must be built.

Another disadvantage is the safety issues linked to the high-pressure system used.

5 Exam-style practice — Grades 5–6

(a) Which of the following equilibria are not affected by a change in pressure? **[1 mark]**

- [ ] **A** $CH_4(g) + H_2O(g) \rightleftharpoons CO(g) + 3H_2(g)$
- [ ] **B** $H_2(g) + CO_2(g) \rightleftharpoons H_2O(g) + CO(g)$
- [ ] **C** $CO(g) + 2H_2(g) \rightleftharpoons CH_3OH(g)$

(b) Of the reactions given above, state and explain which one favours the reverse direction if the pressure is increased. **[1 mark]**

(c) Predict how decreasing the pressure in equation **C** will affect the yield of methanol (CH_3OH) produced. **[1 mark]**

Concentration and equilibrium

In a reversible reaction at equilibrium, if you change the concentration of a reactant or product, the system will oppose the change until equilibrium is restored. You need to know how changes in concentration will affect the position of the equilibrium and the concentrations of the reactants and products.

 Changing concentration

If the concentration of the reactants or products is altered, the system is no longer at equilibrium. The concentrations of the reactants and products will change until equilibrium is re-established.

The table shows how changing the concentration of the components in the equation below effects the position of the equilibrium.

$A + B \rightleftharpoons C + D$ This symbol indicates the reaction is reversible.

Change	Shifts the position of equilibrium
increase in the concentration of a reactant (A or B)	right
decrease in the concentration of a product (C or D)	right
decrease in the concentration of a reactant (A or B)	left
increase in the concentration of a products (C or D)	left

Shifting the position of the equilibrium right means that more reactants will react, and so more products will be formed, until equilibrium is reached again.

Worked example Grades 5–7

1 Ammonia is manufactured from nitrogen and hydrogen in the Haber process, as shown in the equation below.
$N_2(g) + 3H_2(g) \rightleftharpoons 2NH_3(g)$

(a) Identify how the equation shows that it is a reversible reaction. **[1 mark]**

The arrow shows that the reaction can go in both directions.

(b) Describe what would happen if the concentration of the reactants was increased. **[2 marks]**

Increasing the concentration of the reactants would shift the position of the equilibrium to the right, so more product would be formed.

(c) During the reaction the position of the equilibrium of the system was found to lie to the left. Describe how the concentration of the reactants compares with the concentration of the products. **[1 mark]**

The concentration of the reactants is higher than the concentration of the products.

2 Methanol (CH_3OH) can be manufactured by reacting carbon monoxide and hydrogen together. The reaction is reversible.
Write a balanced chemical equation to show this reaction.
Explain how altering concentrations can cause the yield of methanol to be increased. **[5 marks]**

$CO + 2H_2 \rightleftharpoons CH_3OH$

To increase the yield of methanol, the concentration of CO and H_2 need to be increased. This will drive the position of the equilibrium to the right-hand side as the system will oppose the change and try to reduce the concentration of reactants by making more of the product.

The yield is the amount of product obtained in the chemical reaction.

If the equilibrium position lies to the left, the reverse reaction is favoured so the concentration of reactants will be higher than the products.

Exam-style practice Grade 6

Hydrogen is produced industrially from reacting methane (CH_4) with water, as shown in the equation below.

$CH_4(g) + H_2O(g) \rightleftharpoons CO(g) + 3H_2(g)$

(a) Predict how the yield of hydrogen would be affected by increasing the concentration of methane in the reaction. Justify your answer. **[2 marks]**

(b) Describe what is meant by 'equilibrium'. **[2 marks]**

Group 1

You need to know the electronic configurations of Group 1 elements, such as sodium and potassium, and the trends in their chemical properties.

⑤ Properties of Group 1 elements

Group 1 elements are known as the **alkali metals** due to the fact that they form alkaline solutions when they react with water. They are soft metals with low melting points.

All Group 1 elements have one outer electron. When they react, they lose this outer-shell electron and form a positively-charged ion.

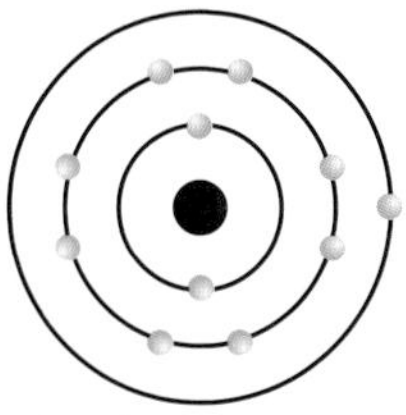

Figure 1 Sodium has the electronic configuration 2.8.1

⑩ Worked example — Grade 6

① Write word and balanced chemical equations to show the reaction of lithium with water. **[3 marks]**

lithium + water → lithium hydroxide + hydrogen

$$2Li + 2H_2O \rightarrow 2LiOH + H_2$$

② Write a word equation and a balanced chemical equation to show the reaction between sodium and water. **[3 marks]**

sodium + water → sodium hydroxide + hydrogen

$$2Na + 2H_2O \rightarrow 2NaOH + H_2$$

Alkali metals react vigorously with water to produce an alkaline solution containing a metal hydroxide that turns universal indicator purple. Hydrogen gas is also produced. You should know the test for hydrogen – a lit splint produces a squeaky pop.

③ The size of the atom increases down Group 1. Explain how this affects the reactivity of the atom. **[3 marks]**

Reactivity increases down the group. The outer electron is further from the positively-charged nucleus and so can be lost more easily.

② Reactions with water

The first three Group 1 metals are lithium, sodium and potassium. The following table shows how these metals react with water.

increasing reactivity

Element	Reaction with water
Li	fizzes
Na	fizzes rapidly, may ignite
K	ignites, may be a small explosion

⑤ Reactivity of Group 1 elements

Group 1 elements react with non-metals to form ionic compounds. The elements become more reactive further down the group, as the outer electron is further from the positive nuclear charge and less attracted to the nucleus. The alkali metals are all soft, not like usual metals which are hard. In fact, they are so soft they can be cut easily with a knife. These elements have relatively low melting points. The melting point of caesium is around 28.5°C and so on a relatively hot day caesium will be in the liquid state. When the first three alkali metals react with water they fizz and move about the surface. They are releasing increasing amounts of energy to the surroundings. Potassium bursts into a lilac flame in the reaction:

potassium + water → potassium hydroxide + hydrogen

Working scientifically

To gain full credit for balancing equations you must first give the correct formulae for the reactants and products.

You should know that Group 1 elements are shown as monoatomic atoms and the formula for water is H_2O.

Exam focus

You need to be able to predict the properties of other alkali metals by extrapolating the trends you have learned for the reactions of lithium, sodium and potassium.

⑩ Exam-style practice — Grades 5–6

① Describe the pattern in reactivity of elements down Group 1. **[1 mark]**

② Lithium reacts with water. Explain why bubbles of gas are seen. **[1 mark]**

③ Look at the table for the reactions of Group 1 metals with water, above. Suggest how rubidium will react with water. **[1 mark]**

Group 7

You need to know the electronic configurations of Group 7 elements, such as chlorine, and their physical properties and reactivity.

(5) Bonding

Group 7 elements, also known as the **halogens**, have seven outer electrons. Removing so many electrons would require a huge amount of energy. Therefore they either gain electrons by reacting with a metal to form an ionic compound, or they share electrons with non-metals to form a covalent bond.

The halogens exist as **diatomic molecules** (pairs of atoms), sharing electrons in a covalent bond (see page 87).

Damp litmus paper will be bleached, turning white, if held in chlorine gas.

If blue litmus paper is used, the paper turns red then white (**Figure 1**).

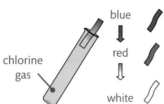

chlorine gas

blue → red → white

Figure 1 Testing for chlorine gas

(10) Worked example — Grades 5–6

1. Explain, in terms of electrons, why fluorine is the most reactive halogen. **[3 marks]**

Fluorine is the most reactive halogen because its outer electron shell is closest to its nucleus. This makes it easier for fluorine to attract electrons. The easier it is to gain an electron, the more reactive the halogen is.

2. Explain why the boiling points of the halogens change down the group from fluorine to iodine. **[3 marks]**

The boiling points increase down Group 7. As the atoms get larger, they have more electrons and so the strength of the intermolecular forces increase. Therefore more energy is needed to overcome the forces of attraction.

3. The size of the atoms increases down Group 7. Explain how this affects the reactivity of Group 7 elements. **[3 marks]**

The reactivity decreases down the group. As the size of the atom increases, the outer electron shell is further from the positively-charged nucleus and so there is less attraction to gain electrons.

Larger molecules have more electrons so more intermolecular forces, which must be overcome to boil the molecule.

(2) Properties

Group 7 elements share similar properties, including:

- non-metals
- low melting and boiling points
- brittle when solid
- poor conductors of heat and electricity
- molecules each contain two atoms (diatomic)
- coloured vapours – at room temperature:
  - Cl_2 is a yellow gas
  - Br_2 is a brown liquid
  - I_2 is a grey solid which sublimes to form a violet gas when warmed.

As you go down Group 7:

- reactivity decreases
- relative molecular mass increases
- melting and boiling points increase.

When a substance sublimes it changes from a solid to a gas without passing through the liquid phase.

(5) Reactions

Halogens react vigorously with metals to form halide ions with a charge of –1. The vigour of these reactions decreases as you go down the group.

$$2Fe(s) + 3Cl_2(g) \rightarrow 2FeCl_3(s)$$

They react with non-metals to form simple molecules (page 88). For example, chlorine, bromine and iodine form hydrogen halides, which dissolve in water to form acidic solutions.

(10) Exam-style practice — Grade 6

1. (a) State the electron configuration of chlorine. **[1 mark]**

   (b) Explain why chlorine readily forms ionic compounds with metals. **[2 marks]**

   (c) Suggest whether fluorine will react with calcium more or less vigorously than chlorine reacts. **[1 mark]**

2. (a) State what you would observe on bubbling hydrogen bromide gas through water. **[1 mark]**

   (b) State and explain what you would observe on touching a piece of blue litmus paper with a drop of the solution from **(a)**. **[2 marks]**

Made a start | Feeling confident | Exam ready

Group 7 reactivity

The trend in reactivity of the halogens can be explained using displacement reactions and their electronic configuration.

 ## Displacement reactions

A more reactive halogen will **displace** (push out) a less reactive halogen from its salt in aqueous solution.

Chlorine is more reactive than iodine, so will displace it from an aqueous solution of its salt.

chlorine + sodium → sodium + iodine
iodide   chloride

Bromine is less reactive than chlorine, so it cannot displace chorine – no reaction takes place.

	Chloride	**Bromide**	**Iodide**
Chlorine	no reaction	bromine forms (turns orange)	iodine forms (turns brown)
Bromine	no reaction	no reaction	iodine forms (turns brown)
Iodine	no reaction	no reaction	no reaction

Table 1 The results of mixing halogens and aqueous solutions of halide salts

Redox reactions

Displacement reactions are always **redox reactions**. In a redox reaction, oxidation and reduction take place. The substance being reduced gains electrons and the substance being oxidised loses electrons.

$$2KBr(aq) + Cl_2(g) \rightarrow 2KCl(aq) + Br_2(l)$$

In the equation above, two bromide ions Br– from KBr are oxidised to Br_2, they have each lost an electron.

In the same reaction the chlorine in Cl_2 picks up those electrons and turns into two chloride ions, Cl^-, it has been reduced.

> Remember: OILRIG: oxidation is loss, reduction is gain.

Electron configuration

The **reactivity** of a halogen depends on its **electron configuration**. All Group 7 elements have seven outer electrons and easily gain one more to make a full outer shell. The closer the outer shell is to the nucleus, the more strongly the nucleus can attract the outer electrons. Therefore, chlorine attracts an extra electron more easily than bromine.

Worked example   Grades 5–6

1 Give the electron configuration of
   (a) a fluorine atom   **[1 mark]**

2.7

   (b) a chlorine atom.   **[1 mark]**

2.8.7

2 Using your understanding of displacement reactions with halide ions, describe the relative reactivity of the halogens down the group. Use this trend to predict the reactions of astatine.   **[3 marks]**

A more reactive halogen (one higher up the group) will displace a less reactive halogen (lower in the group) from its salt in solution, so for example chlorine displaces iodine.

As astatine is at the bottom of Group 7, it is the least reactive of the halogens and so would be displaced from its halide by all of the other halogens. It would be unable to displace any of the other halogen halides due to its lack in reactivity.

> You will be given a copy of the periodic table in the exam. You may be asked to **predict** the properties of elements in Groups 0, 1 and 7 based on trends or patterns seen in the group.

Electron configuration can also be shown as diagrams:

(a) Fluorine atom   **(b)** Chlorine atom

Exam-style practice   Grades 5–7

1 Write a balanced chemical equation for the displacement reaction between potassium iodide and bromine. Identify which of the substances is oxidised and which is reduced.   **[3 marks]**

2 Explain why chlorine displaces iodine from silver iodide.   **[2 marks]**

3 Suggest which halogen produces bromine when it reacts with lithium bromide.   **[1 mark]**

Group 0

You need to know the electronic configurations of Group 0 elements, such as helium and argon, and the trends in their physical and chemical properties.

(10) Electronic configuration

The elements in Group 0 are known as the **noble** or **inert gases** due to their characteristic lack of reactivity. This is due to their stable electron arrangement. They all have a full outer shell – eight electrons in their outermost shell (except helium which has two). They do not easily form molecules but exist as **monatomic** (single) atoms.

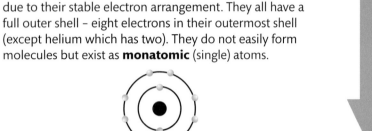

Figure 1 Neon has the electronic configuration 2.8

(10) Worked example   Grade 6

1 Explain why the noble gases are said to be monatomic. **[2 marks]**

Their outer shell is full so they do not need to gain or lose any electrons. Therefore, they do not react with any other atoms.

2 Explain why Group 0 elements are used as the atmosphere for some chemical reactions. **[2 marks]**

Group 0 elements are inert so they do not affect chemical reactions.

3 State and explain how the boiling point of Group 0 elements changes down the group. **[3 marks]**

The boiling point increases down the group. As the size of the atoms increases down the group, there are more electrons leading to increased intermolecular forces between the atoms.

4 The radius of a neon atom is 154 pm. Predict whether the radius of a xenon atom will be larger or smaller than a neon atom. Justify your answer. **[2 marks]**

The radius of a xenon atom will be larger than the radius of a neon atom, because xenon has three more occupied electron shells than neon.

(1) Exam focus

Make sure you know the trends in Group 0, Group 1 and Group 7 of the periodic table. You need to be able to predict the properties of the elements in these groups.

(5) Physical and chemical trends

Trends are observed in the properties of Group 0 elements.

He	The relative atomic mass increases. There are more protons and neutrons in each atom down the group.
Ne	
	The size of the atoms increases due to the number of electron shells increasing.
Ar	
	The boiling points increase. As the atoms get bigger they have more electrons, which leads to increased intermolecular forces between
Kr	
Xe	the atoms.

Go to page 81 to revise electronic configuration.

(2) Uses of noble gases

The inertness of noble gases makes them useful where an unreactive or non-flammable atmosphere is required.

Helium is used to fill balloons and airships, as it has a very low density (so a lot of lifting power) as well as being non-flammable.

Noble gases are often used to exclude air; for example argon, the most readily available noble gas, is used in welding to prevent the hot metal from oxidising and in laboratories to protect highly reactive compounds. Argon and krypton are used in some high-end lighting to prevent lamp filaments oxidising or evaporating.

Noble gases are also used in gas discharge lamps, like car headlamps (xenon) and neon lights (in fact not only neon: all the noble gases, though colourless, produce coloured discharges).

(5) Exam-style practice   Grade 5

1 Explain how electron configuration shows that an atom belongs to Group 0. **[1 mark]**

2 (a) Explain the trend in relative atomic mass down Group 0. **[2 marks]**

(b) Describe how the number of outer electrons affects the reactivity of the noble gases. **[1 mark]**

3 Draw the electronic configuration of an argon atom. **[2 marks]**

Made a start   **Feeling confident**   **Exam ready**

Calculating rate of reaction

You need to be able to find the rate of a reaction using formulae or by drawing a tangent to a graph.

10 Determining a value

The rate of reaction measures how much product is made per second in a particular reaction. It can be calculated using formulae or by drawing tangents to graphs.

The rate of a reaction can be found by measuring the mass of a solid, or volume of a gas, produced over a fixed period of time, during a reaction. Alternatively, it may be found by measuring the quantity of the reactant used over time.

Depending on whether the product or the reactant is being measured, either of the following formulae can be used:

| If mass is measured (in grams) during the reaction, the unit for rate is $g\ s^{-1}$. | $$\text{mean rate of reaction} = \frac{\text{quantity of reactant used}}{\text{time}}$$ | If quantity of reactants is given in moles, the unit for rate is $mol\ s^{-1}$. |

| If volume is measured during the reaction, the unit for rate is $cm^3\ s^{-1}$. | $$\text{mean rate of reaction} = \frac{\text{quantity of product formed}}{\text{time}}$$ | Time is always measured in seconds. |

10 Worked example — Grade 7

A student investigates the reaction between zinc powder and hydrochloric acid. Hydrogen and a solution of zinc chloride are produced.

Consider the reaction being described; it is sometimes worth writing out an equation to see what reaction is taking place.

(a) Describe apparatus suitable for collecting the gas produced in the reaction. **[2 marks]**

A gas syringe could be used to collect the hydrogen gas released.

(b) The table shows the results of the experiment. Calculate the mean rate of the reaction using the data in the table. **[2 marks]**

The rate of reaction is the difference in the *y* values divided by the difference in the *x* values. The steeper the slope, the quicker the rate of reaction.

The rate of reaction changes throughout the course of a reaction. It is usually quickest at the start and it slows down as the reactants are used up.

The results show that the reaction had finished by 50 seconds as no more gas was produced.

Results							
Time (s)	0	10	20	30	40	50	60
Volume of gas (cm^3)	0	20	40	58	72	80	80

$$\text{mean rate} = \frac{\text{volume of gas}}{\text{time}} = \frac{80}{50} = 1.6\ cm^3\ s^{-1}$$

(c) The student plots the results on a graph. Calculate the rate of the reaction at 30 s. **[2 marks]**

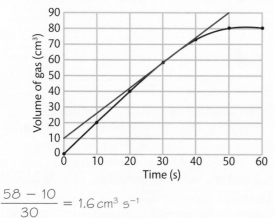

$$\frac{58 - 10}{30} = 1.6\ cm^3\ s^{-1}$$

10 Exam-style practice — Grade 6

Look at **Figure 1**.

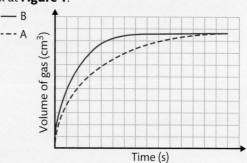

— B
--- A

Figure 1 A graph showing rate of reaction

(a) The student calculated the rate of reaction for the plotted line A. Identify the units needed. **[1 mark]**

(b) The reaction reaches completion after 2 minutes, producing 120 cm^3 of gas. Calculate the mean rate of reaction. **[2 marks]**

(c) Line B shows the same reaction, but with a catalyst. Describe how the catalyst has affected the rate of the reaction. **[2 marks]**

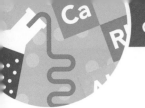

BBC

Factors affecting rate of reaction

For a reaction between two particles to occur, the particles must collide with enough energy to react. If a change causes more collisions, or gives particles more energy, then rates of reaction increase. You need to know about five main factors that can affect the rate of a reaction.

5 Measuring the rate

Depending on the type of reaction taking place, the rate of reaction can be measured by:

- collecting the gas given off during a reaction (with a gas syringe or upturned measuring cylinder)
- mass change (with a balance)
- colour change (disappearing cross).

2 Working scientifically

You need to know how to manipulate the conditions of an experiment to alter the reaction rate. Variables can affect the rate of a reaction. You can control variables to ensure that a reaction occurs efficiently within a reasonable timeframe.

5 Factors affecting rate of reaction

Factors affecting rates of reactions

Pressure of reacting gases
Increasing pressure gives a higher rate of reaction: gas particles are more likely to collide as they are being squashed into a smaller volume, so the rate of collision increases.

Surface area of solid reactants
A larger surface area on a solid gives a higher rate of reaction. Reactions take place on the surface of a solid, so a greater surface area to volume ratio means that there is a greater rate of collision.

Concentration of reactants in solution
The higher the concentration the higher the rate of reaction; there are more particles present in the reaction mixture, so a greater rate of collision.

Temperature
The higher the temperature the higher the rate of reaction; particles gain kinetic energy and so move faster, increasing the rate of collision.

Catalysts
Using catalysts increases the rate of a reaction. They provide an alternative pathway which requires lower activation energy.

5 Worked example — Grade 6

A student investigated the reaction between marble chips and acid by changing the surface area of the marble chips. First, 2 g of marble chips, which were 2 mm × 2 mm × 2 mm, were reacted with 20 cm^3 of hydrochloric acid. Then, the experiment was repeated using 2 g of marble chips which were 1 mm × 1 mm × 1 mm. The student noticed that the smaller the marble chips the faster the reaction occurred.

Calculate the surface area to volume ratio, for each size of marble chip, to show how this affects the rate of reaction. **[4 marks]**

Surface area of first cube = 6 x 2 x 2 = 24; volume = 2 x 2 x 2 = 8 so surface area to volume = 24 : 8 = 3 : 1.

Surface area of smaller cube = 6 x 1 x 1 = 6; volume = 1 x 1 x 1 = 1 so surface area to volume = 6 : 1 (greater SA to vol ratio, therefore faster rate of reaction).

10 Exam-style practice — Grade 6

A student investigated the reaction between marble chips and hydrochloric acid. Their results are shown in the table below.

Time (s)	20	38	52	75	90	110	130	150
Mass of reactant (g)	1.02	0.69	0.46	0.21	0.10	0.10	0.10	0.10

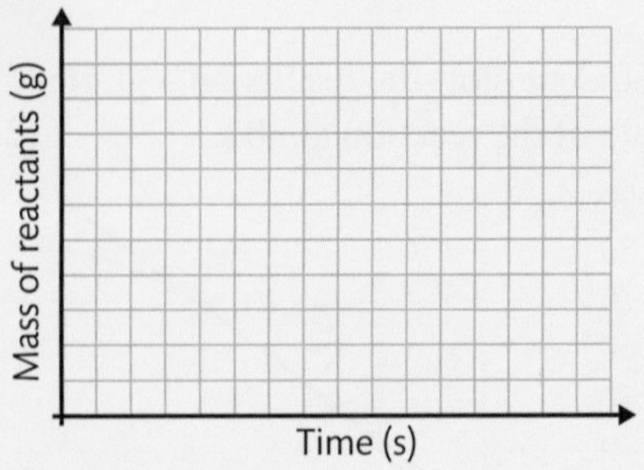

(a) On the axes provided, plot the results of the investigation. Draw a line of best fit. **[4 marks]**

(b) Also on the axes provided, sketch the curve to show the results if the experiment was repeated at a higher temperature. **[2 marks]**

(c) State **two** ways of increasing the rate of the reaction other than changing the temperature. **[2 marks]**

Practical: Monitoring rate of reaction – colour change

You need to know how to investigate the way changes in concentration affect the rates of reactions. This includes measuring the volume of a gas produced and the change in colour.

2 Apparatus

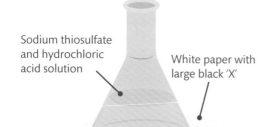

Sodium thiosulfate and hydrochloric acid solution

White paper with large black 'X'

1 Working scientifically

Make sure you use a fume cupboard to avoid breathing in any sulfur dioxide fumes when carrying out this experiment.

10 Method

1. Prepare the sodium thiosulfate solution in a conical flask. Use a measuring cylinder to add water.
2. Place the conical flask on top of the printed black cross.
3. Use a measuring cylinder to measure the dilute hydrochloric acid.
4. Pour this acid into a conical flask. At the same time, swirl the flask gently and start the stop clock.
5. Look down through the top of the flask. Stop the clock when you can no longer see the cross. Record the time in seconds.
6. For reliability, repeat this process three times for each concentration of sodium thiosulfate. Calculate the mean time taken for each concentration.

> Increased concentration means there are more acid particles present so more chance of successful collisions. As a result, the rate of the reaction would increase as the concentration increases.

10 Worked example · Grades 5–6

1. The table shows the effect of changing concentration of sodium thiosulfate on the rate of reaction.

Concentration of sodium thiosulfate (g dm^{-3})	Time taken for cross to disappear (s)			
	1	2	3	Mean
3.95	202	206	206	205
7.91	127	125	128	127
11.86	76	72	74	74

(a) Using the data in the table, state **one** conclusion the student could make about the effect of concentration on the rate of the reaction. **[2 marks]**

Increasing the concentration of sodium thiosulfate caused the rate of reaction to increase.

(b) Describe how you could determine whether the results are reproducible. **[3 marks]**

Compare the results with other groups that have used the same variables. The results are reproducible if the pattern of the results is the same.

2. A student investigates the reaction between magnesium and hydrochloric acid. The student increases the concentration of the hydrochloric acid. Give **three** variables that must be controlled. **[3 marks]**

The temperature of the acid, the surface area of the magnesium and the volume of acid

5 Exam-style practice · Grades 5–6

(a) Give a hypothesis for the rate of reaction between hydrochloric acid and sodium thiosulfate. Think about the effect of the concentration on the time taken for the cross to disappear. **[2 marks]**

(b) Give the independent variable, dependent variable and control variables you would use in this investigation. **[3 marks]**

Made a start | Feeling confident | Exam ready

Practical: Monitoring rate of reaction – gas production

You need to know how to investigate the rate of a reaction by measuring the gas produced over a period of time.

⏱ 5 Investigating the rate of reaction between marble chips and acid ✓

Rate of reaction is affected by several factors, including temperature, concentration of solute, and surface area of solid reactants. In this reaction, you will investigate how the rate is affected by surface area (the size of the marble chips used) and concentration (the concentration of the hydrochloric acid).

⏱ 5 Methods of gas collection ✓

There are two methods you can use to collect a gas produced during a reaction.

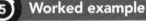

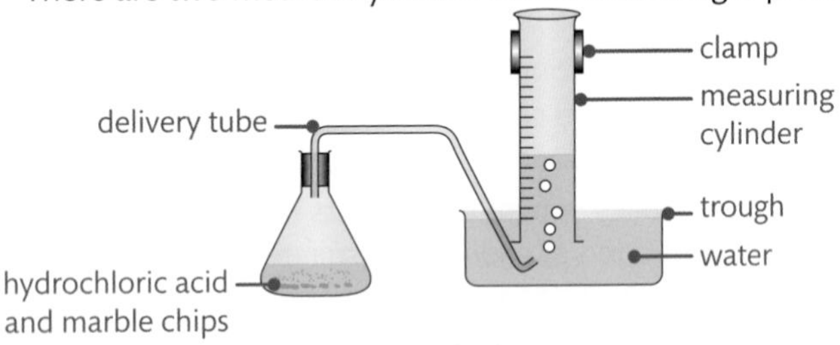

Figure 1 Upturned measuring cylinder over water

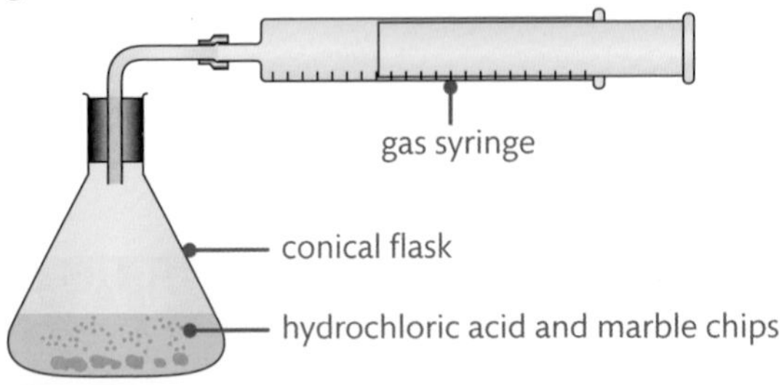

Figure 2 Gas syringe

⏱ 10 Method ✓

1. Measure the volume of acid required and add to the conical flask.

2. Measure the mass of large marble (calcium carbonate) chips and add to the conical flask. Quickly insert the bung to prevent any loss of gas.

3. Measure the total volume of gas produced every 20 seconds and record. Continue until no more gas is produced.

4. Repeat the experiment, first using a different concentration of acid and then using the same mass of smaller marble chips with the same concentration of acid.

> 1 mark is awarded for showing a less steep gradient at the start – as the reaction is slower. The second mark is for recognising that the same total volume of gas would be produced during the reaction.

Exam focus 📌

Size of marble chips and concentration are examples of **independent variables**.

The **dependent variable** is how much gas is produced in a set time.

⏱ 5 Worked example — Grade 5 ✓

A student investigated how concentration of acid affects the rate of reaction with marble chips. The graph below shows the results obtained with **concentrated** hydrochloric acid. **[2 marks]**

(a) Label the axes and give the units for each. **[2 marks]**

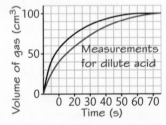

(b) The student repeated the experiment using **dilute** hydrochloric acid. Sketch on the graph to show how the rate of the reaction would change. **[2 marks]**

⏱ 5 Exam-style practice — Grade 6 ✓

1. Explain, in terms of particles and collisions, how decreasing the size of marble chips affects the rate of reaction. **[3 marks]**

2. Use the graph above to calculate the average rate of reaction at:
   - 35 seconds
   - 60 seconds.

   Describe the trend shown by these values. **[4 marks]**

Collision theory and activation energy

You need to know how factors such as temperature, concentration, surface area and pressure (of gases) can be altered to affect the rate of a reaction, using collision theory.

 Collision theory

For a reaction to happen reacting particles must **collide** with **enough energy** to react.

Activation energy is the minimum amount of energy required for a reaction to take place.

Factors affecting rate of reaction

The rate of reaction is directly proportional to the frequency of collisions. This means that increasing factors that make collisions more frequent will increase the rate of reaction.

- Increasing the **temperature** gives the reacting particles more energy, so they are moving faster and more likely to collide and more likely to have at least the activation energy when they do collide.
- Increasing the **concentration** results in more particles in the reaction mixture, so there is a higher chance of collisions.
- Increasing the **pressure** pushes the gas particles closer together, so they are more likely to collide.
- Increasing the **surface area** of solid reactants results in increased frequency of collisions.

Go to page 142 for more about factors that affect rate of reaction.

 Worked example **Grade 7**

A student investigates the volume of gas produced in the reaction between magnesium ribbon and hydrochloric acid. **Figure 1** shows the student's results.

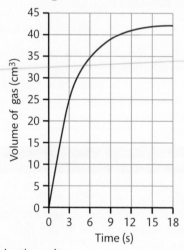

Figure 1 Student's results

The student then repeats the experiment using a more concentrated solution of hydrochloric acid with the same mass of magnesium.

(a) Explain how changing the concentration of hydrochloric acid affects the line on the graph. In your answer, refer to collisions between particles. **[4 marks]**

If the concentration of the acid is increased, the rate of reaction will be faster, as there will be more chance of successful collisions occurring. Therefore, the line will be steeper at the start of the reaction. As there is the same number of magnesium particles in the reaction mixture, the reaction will still produce the same volume of gas, so the curve should plateau at the same volume.

(b) The student repeats the experiment using powdered magnesium, rather than magnesium ribbon.
Explain why the rate of reaction will increase with powdered magnesium. **[2 marks]**

Magnesium powder has a larger surface area than magnesium ribbon. This will facilitate more collisions between the acid and magnesium particles.

 Exam-style practice **Grades 6–7**

1 A student investigated the reaction between zinc powder and sulfuric acid.
State and explain what will happen if the temperature of the reaction mixture is increased. **[3 marks]**

2 The reaction to produce ammonia is given below.
$3H_2 + N_2 \rightarrow 2NH_3$
Explain, in terms of rate of reaction, why increasing the pressure increases the amount of ammonia produced. **[2 marks]**

 Made a start **Feeling confident** **Exam ready**

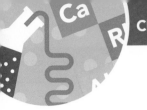

Reaction profiles

You need to know how reaction profiles, also known as energy level diagrams, are used to compare the energy of reactants and products to determine the type of reaction taking place.

5 A reaction profile

A reaction profile provides information on:

- the energy of the reactants
- the energy of the products
- the amount of activation energy needed for the reaction
- whether the reaction is exothermic or endothermic.

Go to page 148 for more information about exothermic and endothermic reactions.

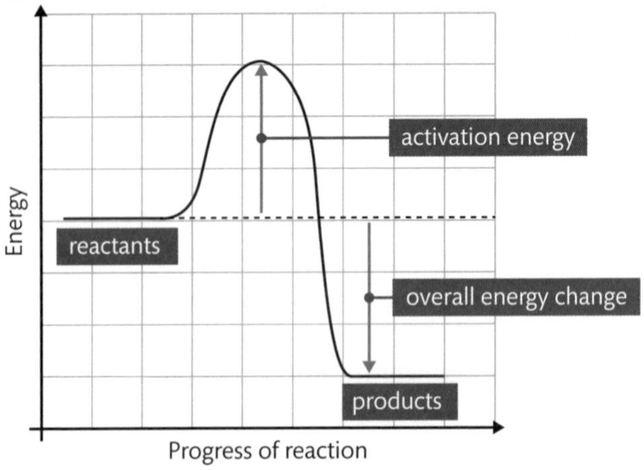

Figure 1 A reaction profile for an exothermic reaction

10 Worked example — Grade 8

The reaction between ammonium chloride and water is endothermic. Draw a reaction profile to show the reaction. Include the following labels on the diagram:

- activation energy
- energy change. **[4 marks]**

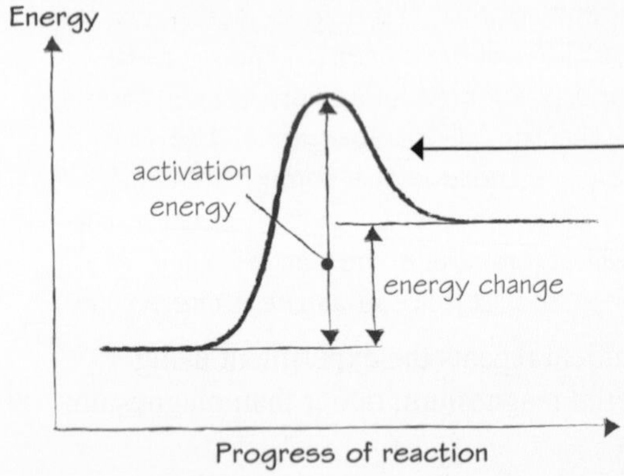

The reaction is endothermic, which means that the products will have more energy than the reactants because energy is being absorbed from the surroundings.

The activation energy is demonstrated by the increase in energy from the energy level of the reactants to the peak of the curve (for both exothermic and endothermic reactions).

The curve is drawn from the reactants to the products. The peak of the curve must be higher than the energy level of the products to show the activation energy required by the reaction (for both exothermic and endothermic reactions).

The energy change is the difference between the energy possessed by the products and the energy possessed by the reactants.

5 Exam focus

In the exam, you could be asked to do the following:

- Draw reaction profiles for exothermic and endothermic reactions.
- Label the activation energy and the overall energy change of a reaction.
- Use reaction profiles provided to identify the type of reaction taking place.

10 Exam-style practice — Grades 6–8

1. Cooling packs used to treat sports injuries involve an endothermic reaction. Draw and label a reaction profile for this type of reaction. **[4 marks]**
2. The diagram below shows the reaction profile for the combustion of methane.

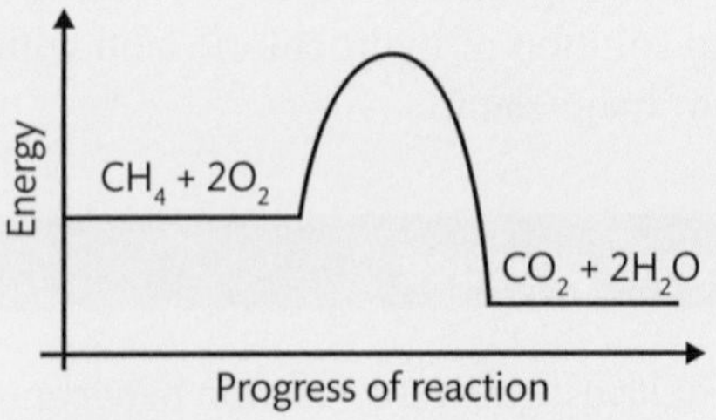

(a) Using the diagram, state and explain what type of reaction is taking place. **[2 marks]**

(b) Label the activation energy of the reaction on the diagram. **[1 mark]**

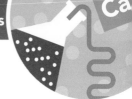

Catalysts

You need to know what a catalyst is and how it affects the rate of a chemical reaction.

5 Reaction pathways

A **catalyst** is a substance that speeds up the rate of a reaction without altering the products of the reaction or being changed chemically or in mass at the end of the reaction. Catalysts increase the rate of reaction by providing a different pathway for the reaction. The pathway provided has a lower activation energy, so more particles will have enough energy to react, and the reaction will be faster. Different catalysts are needed for different reactions. For example, enzymes are biological catalysts.

Go to page 146 to revise reaction profiles.

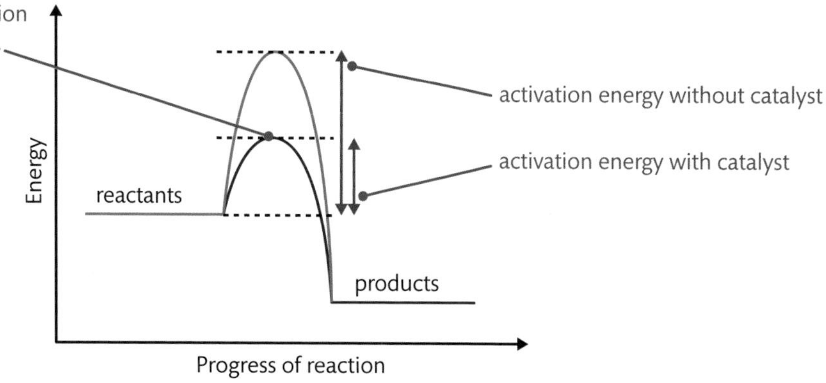
The activation energy is lower for a catalysed reaction so its reaction profile peaks at a lower energy level.
Energy
reactants
products
activation energy without catalyst
activation energy with catalyst
Progress of reaction

Figure 1 A reaction profile diagram showing the effect of a catalyst

10 Worked example — Grade 6

1 Hydrogen peroxide decomposes **slowly** to produce water and oxygen.

$2H_2O_2 \rightarrow 2H_2O + O_2$

(a) Look at **Figure 2**. Does the reaction show an exothermic or endothermic reaction? **[1 mark]**

Exothermic

(b) Draw and label the reaction profile for the reaction with a catalyst added. **[2 marks]**

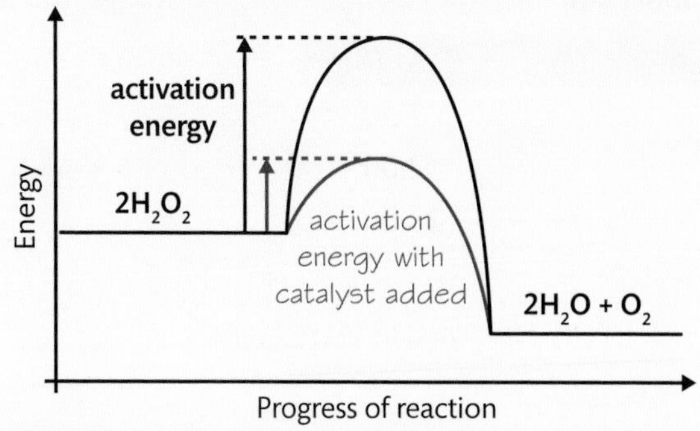
activation energy
Energy
$2H_2O_2$
activation energy with catalyst added
$2H_2O + O_2$
Progress of reaction

Figure 2 Reaction profile for the decomposition of hydrogen peroxide

2 Explain how catalysts work, referring to their effect on the activation energy of a reaction. **[2 marks]**

A catalyst provides an alternative pathway for the reaction, which requires less energy. This makes more of the collisions successful, therefore increasing the rate of reaction.

2 Working scientifically

Enzymes are catalysts in living organisms. For example, yeast uses the enzyme zymase to get energy from sugar, a form of respiration. This reaction can be used to produce alcoholic drinks. Sugars are fermented to ethanol (alcohol) and carbon dioxide, releasing energy. This enzyme-catalysed reaction can be represented by the following word equation:

$$\text{glucose} \xrightarrow{\textit{zymase (yeast)}} \text{ethanol} + \text{carbon dioxide}$$

You can identify a catalyst in a reaction:

- if something is written above the arrow, it is a catalyst
- if a substance is the same on both sides of the reaction, i.e. it's not part of the reaction
- if you are told a reaction speeds up, but the same reaction occurs, when a substance is added.

10 Exam-style practice — Grades 4–6

1 Name the catalyst in the reaction below.

$$\text{hydrogen} + \text{nitrogen} \xrightarrow{\textit{iron}} \text{ammonia}$$ **[1 mark]**

2 Name the catalysts used in biological systems. **[1 mark]**

Exothermic and endothermic reactions

You need to know the difference between endothermic and exothermic reactions and be able to identify the type of reaction when given details about temperature changes.

 Classifying reactions

During a reaction, energy is transferred from the reactants to the surroundings, or from the surroundings to the reactants. **Exothermic** reactions **release** energy (usually as thermal energy) to the surroundings. The temperature of the surroundings **increases**. Examples include: oxidation, metal displacement, neutralisation and combustion.

Endothermic reactions **take in** energy from the surroundings. The temperature of the surroundings **decreases**. Examples include: thermal decomposition, photosynthesis, electrolysis and citric acid reacting with sodium hydrogencarbonate.

Some types of processes always involve an energy change, but may be exothermic or endothermic, depending on the substances involved, for example salts dissolving in water or precipitating out of solution.

 Worked example — **Grade 6**

1 A student investigates the energy change in the reaction between sodium carbonate and ethanoic acid by measuring the temperature at the start and end of the reaction.

Starting temperature: 46 °C   Final temperature: 25 °C

State and explain what type of reaction took place. **[2 marks]**

An endothermic reaction – this is evident because the temperature decreased.

2 Exothermic and endothermic reactions can be used for everyday purposes.

(a) State the type of reaction that hand warmers and self-heating cans use. **[1 mark]**

Exothermic

(b) State the type of reaction that headache cooling pads and sports injury packs use. **[1 mark]**

Endothermic

3 A student measured the energy change that took place in three different chemical reactions.
The student wants to identify which reaction would be best used for the production of hand warmers.
The table shows the results and costs.
Evaluate the use of each reaction and decide which is the most suitable. **[4 marks]**

Reaction	Temperature change (°C)	Cost (£)
A	+6	3.50
B	−3	2.00
C	+17	25.00

A – releases thermal energy and is relatively inexpensive

B – takes in thermal energy so not useful

C – releases a lot of thermal energy but very expensive

A is best used for hand warmers because the reaction releases thermal energy and is comparatively cheap.

 Exam-style practice — **Grade 4**

1 A student reacts two substances and measures the energy change as the reactants become the products during the reaction. The products have less energy than the reactants.
Name this type of reaction. **[1 mark]**

2 Thermal decomposition is an example of an endothermic reaction.
Describe how the temperature of the reaction mixture will change during the reaction. **[1 mark]**

 Made a start   **Feeling confident**   **Exam ready**

Temperature changes

You need to know how to investigate variables that affect temperature changes in reacting solutions, including acid with metals or carbonates, salts dissolving in water, precipitation reactions, neutralisation reactions and displacement of metals. When these reactions occur in solution, the temperature change can be measured to reflect the energy change that has occurred.

(2) Apparatus

- ☑ $2 \, mol \, dm^{-3}$ dilute hydrochloric acid
- ☑ $2 \, mol \, dm^{-3}$ sodium hydroxide solution
- ☑ expanded polystyrene cup and lid
- ☑ $250 \, cm^3$ beaker
- ☑ measuring cylinder
- ☑ thermometer

(5) Maths skills

You may need to plot a graph of your results.

You will need to draw a line of best fit. This is a line that is produced to show the trend or correlation in the points plotted on a graph. The line should be drawn so that the points the line does not pass through are evenly distributed either side of the line.

(2) Working scientifically

Control variables are the things you need to keep the same during the experiment, to ensure the results are valid. In this reaction, the concentration and volume of hydrochloric acid must be kept the same.

(10) Method

1. Using a measuring cylinder add $20 \, cm^3$ dilute hydrochloric acid into a polystyrene cup.

2. Stand the cup inside a beaker. This will make it more stable and will insulate it.

3. Use a thermometer to measure the temperature of the acid. Record the temperature.

4. Measure $10 \, cm^3$ of sodium hydroxide.

5. Pour the sodium hydroxide into the cup. Loosely fit the lid and gently stir the solution with the thermometer through the hole. When the reading on the thermometer remains constant record the temperature in your table.

6. Repeat steps **4** and **5** two more times, adding $5 \, cm^3$ more of sodium hydroxide solution each time.

7. Repeat this experiment two more times and record the findings.

Total volume of NaOH added (cm^3)	Increase in temperature (°C)			
	1	2	3	Mean
10	8	6	5	6.3
15	17	19	19	18.3
20	24	25	26	25.0

(5) Worked example Grade 6

A student uses the apparatus in **Figure 1** to measure the temperature change when sulfuric acid reacts with calcium carbonate.

(a) Describe how the apparatus can be altered to reduce heat loss to the surroundings. **[2 marks]**

Use a polystyrene cup instead of the beaker and loosely place a lid on top of the cup.

(b) When observing the reaction, describe how the student would know if it is exothermic. **[2 marks]**

The reading on the thermometer would increase.

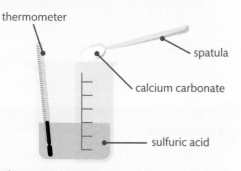

Figure 1 Adding calcium carbonate to sulfuric acid

(5) Exam-style practice Grade 6

A student measures the temperature change when water is added to anhydrous cobalt chloride and hydrated cobalt chloride is formed. Calculate the mean temperature change and identify the type of reaction that took place. **[3 marks]**

	Trial 1	Trial 2	Trial 3	Mean
Temperature change (°C)	−6	−8	−5	

Energy change in reactions

You should be able to describe chemical reactions in terms of the breaking and making of bonds.

(5) **Bond energy**

Energy is **required** to **break** bonds, so bond breaking is endothermic. Energy is **released** when bonds are **formed**, so bond making is exothermic. Bond energies can be used to work out if the overall reaction is exothermic or endothermic.

In an exothermic reaction, the energy released from forming bonds is greater than the energy needed to break bonds. Exothermic reactions always have **negative** energy values.

In an endothermic reaction, the energy released from forming bonds is less than the energy needed to break bonds. Endothermic reactions always have **positive** energy values.

(1) **Maths skills**

You can calculate the overall energy change for a reaction with the following calculation.

overall energy change = energy used to break the bonds in the reactants − energy used to form the bonds in the products

Bond energy is measured in kilojoules per mole (kJ mol^{-1}).

(10) **Worked example** — **Grade 7**

Figure 1 shows the balanced equation for the combustion of methane using structural formulae.

Figure 1 Combustion of methane

The bond energies for the reactants and products are given in **Table 1**.

Table 1

Bond	Bond energy (kJ mol^{-1})
C–H	413
O=O	498
C=O	805
O–H	464

(a) Calculate the energy change for the reaction. **[3 marks]**

energy change = bond breaking − bond making

bond breaking: (4 × 413) + (2 × 498) = 2648

bond making: (4 × 464) + (2 × 805) = 3466

energy change = 2648 − 3466

= −818 kJ mol^{-1}

(b) State the type of reaction that has taken place. **[1 mark]**

An exothermic reaction

You will need to use the bond energy values provided. These values are per bond. In methane, the bond energy is 413 kJ mol^{-1} per C–H bond, so the total energy to break all four bonds in methane is 4 × 413 = 1652 kJ mol^{-1}.

(5) **Exam-style practice** — **Grades 8–9**

The bond energies for the reactants and products are given in **Table 2**. **Figure 2** shows ethene reacting with fluorine.

Table 2

Bond	Bond energy (kJ mol^{-1})
C–H	413
C=C	614
F–F	155
C–C	348
C–F	485

Figure 2 Reaction of ethene and fluorine

(a) Using the bond energy values, calculate the energy change for the reaction. **[3 marks]**

(b) In terms of energy change, what type of reaction is taking place. **[1 mark]**

 Made a start   **Feeling confident**   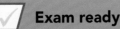 **Exam ready**

Crude oil and hydrocarbons

Organic chemistry is the study of the structure, properties and reactions of the large variety of compounds that contain carbon. The main sources of these organic compounds are living or once-living organisms. You need to know the general formula for alkanes, as well as their physical and chemical properties.

Crude oil

Crude oil is a mixture of a very large number of compounds. It formed millions of years ago from the remains of biomass (mainly plankton) buried in mud. Crude oil can be found in rocks and trapped under the seabed of oceans. Due to the time it takes to create crude oil, it is a finite resource.

Crude oil is an important source of useful substances. It is used for a variety of fuels, including petrol and diesel, and as a feedstock for the production of many substances, including plastics, soaps and detergents, healthcare products such as aspirin, synthetic fibres for clothes and furniture, rubbers and paints.

Exam focus

You need to know that carbon atoms can form rings or chains but you do not need to know the names or structures of any ring molecules.

Alkanes

Alkanes share the general formula C_nH_{2n+2} where n is equal to the number of carbon atoms in the compound. Each alkane differs by CH_2 in its molecular formulae from its neighbouring compound. Alkanes are saturated; this means they have no double bonds between carbon atoms.

Name	Molecular formula
methane	CH_4
ethane	C_2H_6
propane	C_3H_8
butane	C_4H_{10}

Worked example — Grade 6

1 Give the molecular formula for an alkane with eight carbons. **[2 marks]**

C_8H_{18}

2 Explain why hydrocarbons of different chain lengths have different boiling points. **[2 marks]**

The larger molecules have stronger forces of attraction between molecules so require more energy to overcome those forces.

3 State what is meant by the term 'hydrocarbon'. **[2 marks]**

A compound that contains only hydrogen and carbon.

Hydrocarbons

Most of the compounds in crude oil are hydrocarbons – compounds consisting of hydrogen and carbon only. Most of these hydrocarbons belong to a homologous series called the alkanes, these are formed from chains of carbon atoms. Some molecules may be found as rings of carbon atoms (**Figure 1**).

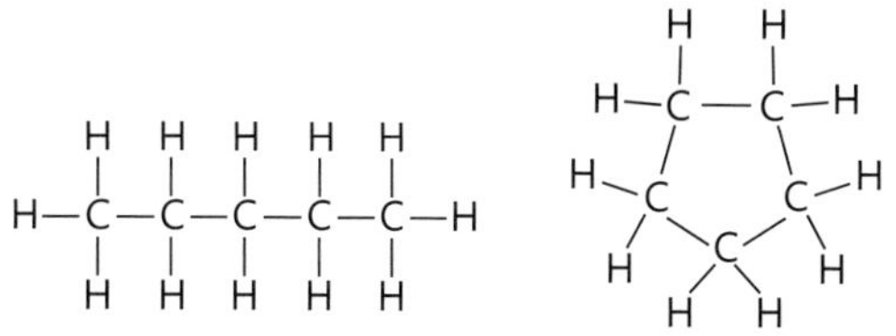

straight-chain hydrocarbon   ring formation

Figure 1 Hydrocarbon molecules contain carbon atoms joined together in straight chains or in rings.

Properties of hydrocarbons

In a homologous series, such as the alkanes, a gradual change in physical properties, such as their boiling points, can be seen as the chain length increases.

Alkane	Boiling point (°C)
methane	–164
ethane	–89
propane	–42
butane	–0.5
pentane	36
hexane	39

Compounds in a homologous series have similar chemical properties.

See page 153 for further properties of hydrocarbons.

Using the general formula C_nH_{2n+2}
if C = 8 then H = (8 × 2) + 2 = 16 + 2 = 18

Exam-style practice — Grade 5

1 Crude oil is a finite resource. State what is meant by the term '**finite**'. **[1 mark]**

2 State what is meant by the term 'homologous series'. Give an example. **[3 marks]**

3 Using the general formula for alkanes, show that the molecular formula of hexane is C_6H_{14}. **[1 mark]**

Fractional distillation

You need to know how fractional distillation is used to separate mixtures of several liquids, such as crude oil.

⑩ Fractions

Crude oil is a mixture of substances, which can be separated into fractions. Each fraction contains hydrocarbon molecules with a similar number of carbon atoms.

The fractions are then processed to produce fuels such as petrol, diesel oil, kerosene, fuel oil and gases.

The fractions are also processed to be used as the raw materials for the petrochemical industry to produce an array of products, such as lubricants, solvents, detergents and polymers.

See page 151 for more about crude oil.

The fractionating column has a **temperature gradient**. The temperature is controlled so that the hottest part of the column is actually at the bottom, not the top as you might expect.

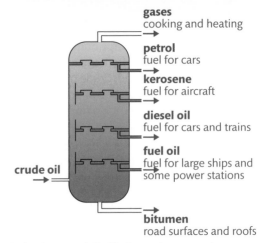

gases
cooking and heating

petrol
fuel for cars

kerosene
fuel for aircraft

diesel oil
fuel for cars and trains

fuel oil
fuel for large ships and some power stations

crude oil

bitumen
road surfaces and roofs

Figure 1 The fractional distillation column used to separate crude oil, the fractions and their uses.

⑩ Worked example — Grades 5–6

1 Crude oil can be separated into fractions. State the property of the fractions that makes this possible. **[1 mark]**

They have different boiling points.

2 Crude oil is a mixture of hydrocarbons. Explain how fractional distillation is used to separate crude oil into useful fractions. **[4 marks]**

Crude oil is heated to evaporate the hydrocarbons. The column is cooler at the top and hotter at the bottom. The gaseous fractions travel up the column until they reach their boiling point, where they condense and can be collected.

3 Describe how the molecules in a fraction are similar to each other. **[1 mark]**

They all contain a similar number of carbon atoms.

4 Give **one** use for the diesel oil produced during fractional distillation. **[1 mark]**

Diesel oil can be used in engines (of cars, buses, tractors, etc).

Key words to include in your answer when writing about the process of fractional distillation are 'evaporate' and 'condense'.

② Exam focus 📌

You should be able to explain how crude oil is separated into simpler, more useful substances. Learn the steps involved in fractional distillation and the uses of the fractions produced.

⑩ Exam-style practice — Grade 5

1 Fuel oil has many uses. It is separated from crude oil by fractional distillation.

Using **Figure 1** to help you, describe the steps involved in the fractional distillation of crude oil. **[4 marks]**

2 **Figure 2** shows a laboratory experiment used to separate crude oil.

Describe what processes are taking place at **X** and **Z**. **[2 marks]**

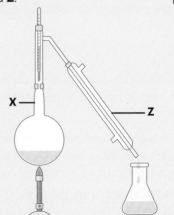

Figure 2 Laboratory-scale fractional distillation

✓ **Made a start** ✓ **Feeling confident** ✓ **Exam ready**

Properties of hydrocarbons

You need to know how the size of hydrocarbon molecules affects their properties.

Properties of hydrocarbons

As the hydrocarbon chain increases in length, hydrocarbons become less flammable (i.e. ignite less easily), more viscous and their boiling points increase.

Members of a homologous series have similar chemical properties, for example, when a hydrocarbon burns in plenty of oxygen, **complete combustion** takes place. The hydrocarbon fuel is oxidised. This process releases thermal energy.

When complete combustion of hydrocarbon fuel occurs, the same products are always produced.

hydrocarbon fuel + oxygen → carbon dioxide + water

Worked example Grade 5

1 Petrol is a fuel produced from crude oil.
Write a word equation to show the complete combustion of petrol. **[2 marks]**

petrol + oxygen → water + carbon dioxide

2 Describe how the following properties of methane and decane differ. **[3 marks]**

(a) flammability – methane is more flammable than decane

(b) viscosity – methane is less viscous than decane

(c) boiling point – methane has a lower boiling point than decane

3 Suggest a reason why the bitumen fraction, rather than the kerosene fraction, is used for road surfaces. **[2 marks]**

At outdoor temperatures the kerosene fraction is in the liquid state, and it is easily flammable. Bitumen has a much higher melting point and so is in the solid state at room temperature, and it does not burn so easily. This makes it better for road surfaces, as it will not drain away but can be heated enough to bind gravel and spread on the road without catching fire.

Incomplete combustion

When there is only a limited amount of oxygen available, fuel cannot burn completely, and instead **incomplete combustion** occurs. This reaction produces water, carbon monoxide and carbon (soot).

butane (fuel) + oxygen → carbon monoxide + carbon + water

$$C_4H_{10}(l) + 4O_2(g) → 3CO(g) + C(s) + 5H_2O(g)$$

This reaction releases less energy than complete combustion, and the products can cause health and environmental issues (carbon monoxide is toxic and carbon (or soot) can cause breathing problems).

> The term **complete combustion** means there is enough oxygen available for the fuel to completely react.

> The type of hydrocarbon given is not important. If complete combustion of a hydrocarbon is taking place, the products will always be **water** and **carbon dioxide**.

> You need to consider the length of the hydrocarbon chain to determine how the properties will change from one hydrocarbon to another. Decane is longer than methane.

Exam focus

Remember to read the question carefully. For **in**complete combustion, there is not enough oxygen for the fuel to burn completely and the products formed are more harmful.

 Exam-style practice Grades 5–6

1 Name the products of the complete combustion of a hydrocarbon. **[1 mark]**

2 Write the word equation for the incomplete combustion of the hydrocarbon propane. **[1 mark]**

3 Describe how the viscosity of hydrocarbons changes with increasing molecular size. **[1 mark]**

4 Give a reason why combustion is classified as an oxidation reaction. **[1 mark]**

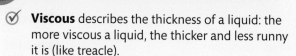 Key terms

- ☑ **Viscous** describes the thickness of a liquid: the more viscous a liquid, the thicker and less runny it is (like treacle).

- ☑ **Flammable** is used to describe materials that will catch fire more easily.

 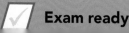

Atmospheric pollutants

You need to know about the different ways in which atmospheric pollutants can be formed when fuels burn.

5 Pollution from combustion of fuels

Hydrocarbons, or carbon-containing compounds, are widely used as fuels. When they burn in plenty of oxygen, carbon dioxide and water only are produced. This is **complete combustion**.

If there is not enough oxygen present, then **incomplete combustion** occurs, producing carbon monoxide (CO), water and soot (carbon, C). These products can cause health issues and atmospheric pollution.

Hydrocarbon fuels contain impurities, such as sulfur, which can cause atmospheric pollution when burned.

Burning fuels in car engines can cause nitrogen to react with oxygen to produce oxides of nitrogen; these are also pollutants.

5 Oxides of nitrogen

When fuels are burned in engines, the temperature is so high that it can enable atmospheric oxygen and nitrogen to react together, producing **oxides of nitrogen**.

Effects of oxides of nitrogen:

- Cause a photochemical smog.
- Increase the acidity of rain.
- Irritate eyes, nose, throat and lungs.

10 Worked example — Grades 5–7

1 State what is meant by 'incomplete combustion'. **[1 mark]**

When a fuel burns in a limited supply of oxygen, not all the carbon in it is converted to carbon dioxide.

2 Incomplete combustion of carbon-containing fuels causes harmful products to be released. Explain the problems caused by these products. **[4 marks]**

Carbon monoxide is produced. It is a toxic gas which is colourless and odourless and so cannot be detected easily.

Carbon or soot is produced, which causes breathing problems. It also blackens buildings and settles in chimneys, presenting a fire hazard.

5 Acid rain

Sulfur in some hydrocarbon fuels gives sulfur dioxide gas when the fuel is burned. When sulfur dioxide enters the atmosphere, it dissolves in rainwater, forming sulfurous acid. This then reacts with oxygen to form sulfuric acid – **acid rain**.

Effects of acid rain:

- Acidifies lakes and rivers, which may harm or kill aquatic life.
- Damages carbonate statues and buildings.
- Corrodes metals.
- Acidifies soil, preventing healthy crops from growing and killing trees.

Carbon monoxide binds to haemoglobin in the blood preferentially over oxygen, preventing the blood from carrying enough oxygen.

People may feel drowsy and have headaches if they are breathing high levels of carbon monoxide. At very high levels it can be fatal.

Inhalation of carbon particulates has been linked to respiratory problems including asthma and cardiovascular issues.

5 Exam-style practice — Grade 5

1 Write a balanced chemical equation for the formation of sulfur dioxide from sulfur. **[1 mark]**

2 State what is meant by the term 'pollutant'. **[1 mark]**

3 Name **three** types of pollutants that may be produced when a fuel is burned. **[3 marks]**

Comparing fuels

You need to be able to evaluate the advantages and disadvantages of using different fuels for cars.

(5) Renewable and non-renewable fuels

A **non-renewable fuel** is one that is being used faster than it is being formed, so will run out eventually. Petrol, kerosene and diesel oil are non-renewable fossil fuels obtained from crude oil, and methane is a non-renewable fossil fuel found in natural gas.

Hydrogen is a fuel that can be used in cars, and can be obtained from both renewable and non-renewable sources:

- The reaction of natural gas with steam (non-renewable).
- Cracking of crude oil (non-renewable).
- Electrolysis of water (renewable).

(10) Worked example — Grade 7

Evaluate the advantages and disadvantages of using hydrogen, rather than petrol, as a fuel in cars.   **[6 marks]**

Advantages of hydrogen as a fuel for cars:

When hydrogen is burned as a fuel the only product is water: $2H_2(g) + O_2(g) \rightarrow 2H_2O(g)$. If the hydrogen was originally obtained from water, then hydrogen does not contribute to global warming or any other form of pollution.

When petrol is burned in plenty of oxygen it produces carbon dioxide and water. Carbon dioxide is a greenhouse gas responsible for global warming. Petrol may also contain impurities including sulfur, which contributes to acid rain when burned.

Hydrogen releases more energy per gram of fuel burned compared with petrol.

Petrol is produced from crude oil, a finite resource, whereas there is an unlimited supply of hydrogen from water.

Disadvantages of hydrogen as a fuel for cars:

Hydrogen is a flammable gas and therefore difficult to store safely in a form that can be fitted into a vehicle. Petrol is easier to store as it is a liquid at room temperature.

Energy has to be used to obtain hydrogen from water, so unless this energy comes from renewable sources itself, the use of hydrogen indirectly contributes to greenhouse gas emissions.

There are problems with designing cars that can carry hydrogen safely, but hydrogen produced from renewable energy sources is better for the environment than hydrogen produced using fossil fuels. This does not contribute to the greenhouse effect or acid rain. Overall then, hydrogen is a far better fuel for the environment than petrol.

Exam focus

If you are asked to **evaluate**, you need to discuss **both** the advantages and disadvantages and then give a statement to conclude as to whether or not the advantages outweigh the disadvantages.

To gain 6 marks you need to give at least two advantages and two disadvantages.

(2) Exam-style practice — Grade 4

Using hydrogen as a fuel does not create pollution. Suggest **two** issues with using hydrogen as a fuel.   **[3 marks]**

Cracking and alkenes

You need to understand how hydrocarbons can be cracked to produce smaller, more useful alkane and alkene molecules.

(10) Cracking

The demand for the lighter fractions distilled from crude oil is much greater than demand for the heavy fractions. Cracking is a method used to break down long hydrocarbons into shorter, more useful ones.

Cracking produces shorter alkane molecules and alkenes. Shorter alkanes can be used for fuels, such as petrol. Alkenes can be used to make polymers. For example, poly(ethene), the plastic used in carrier bags, is formed from ethene.

Cracking can be carried out with vaporised hydrocarbons and a catalyst such as aluminium oxide, or else steam and heating to about 800 °C.

(1) Alkenes

Alkenes are unsaturated hydrocarbons – they have a double bond between two carbon atoms, shown as C=C. Alkenes share the general formula C_nH_{2n}.

The total number of C and H atoms in the products must equal the total number of C and H in the hydrocarbon (on the left) being cracked.

(2) Demand for hydrocarbons

Fractions	Approximate %	
	Typical supply from crude oil	Global demand
LPG	2	4
Petrol	16	27
Kerosene	13	8
Diesel	19	23
Fuel oil and bitumen	50	38

Table 1 Global supply and demand for the fractions of crude oil

(5) Worked example — Grades 5–6

1 Hydrocarbons can be cracked to produce shorter hydrocarbons. Complete the equation to show the cracking of dodecane ($C_{12}H_{26}$). **[1 mark]**

$$C_{12}H_{26} \rightarrow C_5H_{12} + C_4H_8 + C_3H_6$$

2 **Figure 1** shows how cracking can be performed in the laboratory.

(a) Explain why aluminium oxide is used. **[1 mark]**

To speed up the reaction (it is a catalyst).

(b) Explain why cracking is classed as a thermal decomposition reaction. **[2 marks]**

It uses thermal energy to break something down.

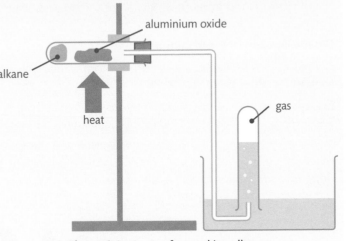

Figure 1 Apparatus for cracking alkanes

(5) Exam-style practice — Grades 5–6

Look at **Table 1**.

(a) Name the fractions that are in greater demand than can be supplied. **[1 mark]**

(b) State the difference in percentage of fuel oil and bitumen produced and percentage demanded by the global market. **[1 mark]**

(c) Excess hydrocarbons from one fraction may be cracked to produce more useful fractions. Suggest and explain which fraction is most likely to be produced by cracking. **[2 marks]**

Earth's early atmosphere

You need to know how Earth's atmosphere has developed over time.

(15) Evolution of Earth's atmosphere

Scientists think that Earth formed about 4.6 billion years ago. To begin with, Earth was a ball of molten rock. Many scientists believe that Earth's early atmosphere was formed from the gases given out by volcanoes.

Although Earth was a volatile place with a lot of volcanic activity, significant changes occurred within its first billion years that changed the make-up of the atmosphere, allowing life to begin and thrive.

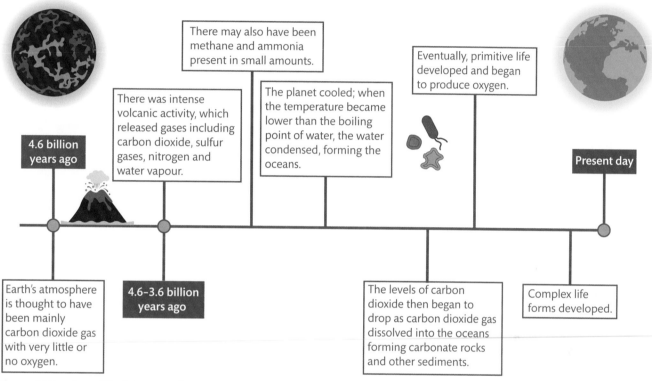

4.6 billion years ago

There was intense volcanic activity, which released gases including carbon dioxide, sulfur gases, nitrogen and water vapour.

There may also have been methane and ammonia present in small amounts.

The planet cooled; when the temperature became lower than the boiling point of water, the water condensed, forming the oceans.

Eventually, primitive life developed and began to produce oxygen.

Present day

Earth's atmosphere is thought to have been mainly carbon dioxide gas with very little or no oxygen.

4.6–3.6 billion years ago

The levels of carbon dioxide then began to drop as carbon dioxide gas dissolved into the oceans forming carbonate rocks and other sediments.

Complex life forms developed.

Figure 1 Timeline of Earth's atmosphere

(2) Working scientifically

There are many different theories about the composition of Earth's early atmosphere and the events that occurred in its evolution. However, there is very limited evidence to support these theories because Earth formed such a long time ago.

(5) Worked example — Grade 6

1 Describe what happened to most of the water vapour in Earth's early atmosphere. **[2 marks]**

The water vapour condensed and formed the oceans.

2 Name the activity thought to have contributed to the high levels of carbon dioxide. **[1 mark]**

Volcanic activity

(5) Exam-style practice — Grades 5–7

The current atmospheres of Mars and Venus are very similar to Earth's early atmosphere.

The approximate proportions of the gases in the atmosphere of Mars are given below.

Gas	Percentage composition
carbon dioxide	95
nitrogen	X
oxygen	0.5
argon	1

(a) Give the approximate value of X. **[1 mark]**

(b) Suggest a reason why there is only a small percentage of oxygen on Mars. **[2 marks]**

(c) The percentage of argon in Earth's atmosphere has remained the same since its formation. Give a reason why the percentage of argon on Mars is unlikely to change if the atmosphere changes. **[1 mark]**

Oxygen and carbon dioxide levels

Earth's early atmosphere is thought to have been mainly carbon dioxide with little or no oxygen. You need to know how the oxygen and carbon dioxide levels have changed over time.

Increasing O₂ levels

Over billions of years, numerous events have caused dramatic changes to the carbon dioxide and oxygen levels on Earth. About 2.7 billion years ago, cyanobacteria, also known as blue-green algae, started to produce oxygen, increasing the levels present in the atmosphere.

Over the next billion years, plants evolved, causing the levels of oxygen to increase further (to about 20 per cent). This increase in oxygen enabled animals to evolve.

The process by which plants and algae produce oxygen is called **photosynthesis**. It can be represented by the following equation:

$$\text{carbon dioxide} + \text{water} \xrightarrow{\text{light}} \text{glucose} + \text{oxygen}$$

Decreasing CO₂ levels

Atmospheric carbon dioxide levels were decreased by:

- algae and primitive plants photosynthesising
- dissolving in the oceans.

Additional processes further reduced the amount of atmospheric carbon dioxide, for example the production of shells by marine life and the formation of sedimentary rocks containing calcium carbonate, or the formation of fossil fuels from the remains of dead organisms.

> Carbon dioxide gas is readily soluble in water.

> When plants and animals die, the carbon inside them became trapped. Under specific conditions of temperature and pressure their remains become fossil fuels.

Worked example   Grades 5–7

1 **(a)** Describe **two** processes that caused atmospheric levels of carbon dioxide to change from around 95% to around 0.04%.   **[2 marks]**

CO₂ was absorbed by plants and algae for photosynthesis. It also dissolved in the oceans.

(b) Determine the ratio of carbon dioxide in Earth's early atmosphere to carbon dioxide in Earth's current atmosphere.   **[2 marks]**

early : current

2375 : 1

2 **(a)** Name the process carried out by plants and algae that increases the levels of oxygen in the atmosphere.   **[1 mark]**

Photosynthesis

(b) Complete the chemical equation for this process by balancing it.   **[1 mark]**

$$6CO_2 + 6H_2O \rightarrow C_6H_{12}O_6 + 6O_2$$

> The equation for photosynthesis is the reverse of the equation for respiration. Remember there are six of each substance in the reaction (except glucose).

Exam focus

If you know the chemical formula of a substance, you can write it in your answer to save time. Make sure that you write it correctly: you will not get a mark for CO2 or CO².

Maths skills

To work out the ratio of the gas levels divide both values by the lowest value.

$95 \div 0.04 = 2375$

$0.04 \div 0.04 = 1$

Exam-style practice   Grade 6

1 State the approximate percentage of Earth's atmosphere today that is oxygen.   **[1 mark]**

2 Explain why the evolution of algae and primitive plants caused a decrease in carbon dioxide levels and an increase in oxygen levels in the atmosphere.   **[3 marks]**

 Made a start   **Feeling confident**   **Exam ready**

Gases in the atmosphere

You need to know the proportions of the most abundant gases in the atmosphere today.

 5 Earth's atmosphere

The composition of Earth's atmosphere has stayed mostly the same for the past 200 million years, but the exact proportions of each gas varies constantly. Scientists can use software to measure the effects humans are having on the atmosphere to develop solutions to reduce the impact.

- nitrogen (approximately 80%)
- oxygen (approximately 20%)
- all others, including carbon dioxide, water vapour and noble gases (less than 1%)

Figure 1 The proportions of gases in the atmosphere today

Oxygen
A glowing splint will relight if it comes into contact with a test tube of oxygen.

Maths skills

To convert from a percentage to a fraction you must divide the percentage of oxygen by the total percentage of the atmosphere: $20 \div 100 = \frac{1}{5}$.

 2 Maths skills

You are expected to be able to convert data provided as percentages, ratios and fractions. For example, the ratio of nitrogen to oxygen in the atmosphere is:

divide by 20 $\quad 80:20$
$\quad\quad\quad\quad\quad 4:1$

Ratios are a comparison of values. They are shown in their simplest form. This is done by dividing both values by the same factor.

Exam focus
You will need to draw graphs in the exam.

- Choose a sensible scale to work with.
- Ensure the graph covers more than half of the grid provided.
- Label the axes to identify what they are showing and give units if applicable.

 10 Worked example **Grade 7**

The table shows the approximate proportions of gases in the atmosphere today.

Gas	Percentage composition
nitrogen	80
oxygen	20
other gases	< 1

(a) Using the data in the table, determine approximately what fraction of gas in Earth's atmosphere is oxygen. **[1 mark]**

$\frac{1}{5}$

(b) Using the grid below, draw a graph to represent the data in the table. **[3 marks]**

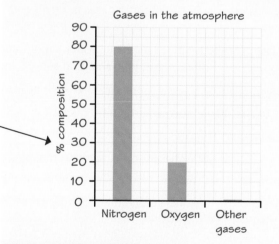

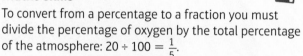

 5 Exam-style practice **Grade 5**

1 Give the proportion of Earth's atmosphere that is nitrogen gas. **[1 mark]**

2 Show that the fraction of oxygen in the atmosphere is approximately one fifth. **[1 mark]**

Greenhouse gases

You need to know about the effects greenhouse gases have on the temperature of the Earth.

(10) Production of greenhouse gases

Greenhouse gases in the atmosphere, such as carbon dioxide, water vapour and methane, maintain the temperature of Earth by trapping solar energy from the Sun. Theories suggest that greenhouse gases were originally produced by volcanic activity as Earth formed. Today, greenhouse gases are mainly produced by burning fossil fuels, such as coal, oil and gas.

Trapping solar energy

Greenhouse gases trap solar energy from the Sun in Earth's atmosphere, keeping it warm enough to support life.

Solar energy from the Sun reaches us as radiation, such as ultraviolet (UV) and light waves.

Some of the solar energy is absorbed by rocks and Earth's crust, causing the planet to warm up.

Some of the solar energy is reflected away from Earth's surface. The warm Earth emits infrared (IR) radiation. Some of this radiation is absorbed by the greenhouse gases in the atmosphere and re-emitted back towards Earth. This heats up the surface of the planet, including the oceans.

Go to page 161 to revise how human activity is increasing the amount of greenhouse gases in Earth's atmosphere.

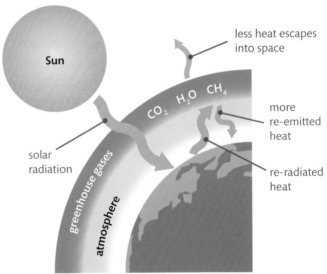

Figure 1 Trapping solar energy

(10) Worked example   Grades 5–7

1 State what is meant by the term 'greenhouse gas'.   **[2 marks]**

It is a gas that traps solar energy in the atmosphere, thus maintaining the temperature of Earth's surface.

2 Water vapour is a greenhouse gas found in Earth's atmosphere.
Explain how the greenhouse effect increases the amount of water vapour in the atmosphere.   **[2 marks]**

Water vapour traps the radiation that is being reflected from Earth's surface, causing Earth to warm up.
As Earth warms up more water will evaporate, which will result in the formation of more water vapour.

3 The greenhouse gases methane, water vapour and carbon dioxide are all produced by natural and artificial processes. For each gas, give a natural source and an artificial source.   **[6 marks]**

Methane: Natural source – produced when organic material such as plants rot

      Artificial source – rotting of waste in landfill and agriculture, e.g. cattle and rice fields

Water vapour: Natural source – evaporation from water bodies, e.g. lakes and rivers

      Artificial source – burning fossil fuels

Carbon dioxide: Natural source – respiration of plants and animals, forest fires

      Artificial source – combustion of fossil fuels

(10) Exam-style practice   Grades 5–7

1 Name **three** greenhouse gases.   **[1 mark]**

2 Explain how the greenhouse effect contributes to maintaining temperatures on Earth.   **[4 marks]**

3 Describe how greenhouse gases were produced in Earth's early atmosphere.   **[1 mark]**

Made a start   **Feeling confident**   **Exam ready**

Human contribution to greenhouse gases

You need to be able to evaluate how some human activities are causing climate change.

(10) Carbon dioxide and climate change

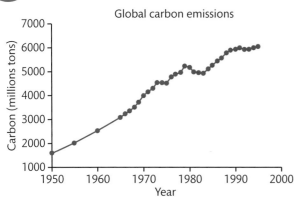

Global carbon emissions

Atmospheric carbon dioxide concentration

Temperature variation from mean
- □ Annual mean
- ■ Lowess smoothing

Figure 1 Average global temperature, carbon dioxide concentration and fossil fuel emissions

Figure 1 seems to show a close correlation between the variables. Still, some questions remain. The carbon dioxide concentrations were measured in Hawaii, near an active volcano. Many of the temperatures used to calculate global averages are measured in towns, which are warmer than rural areas. Temperatures from previous centuries rely on less accurate instruments and records from fewer places. Carbon dioxide concentrations or temperatures over thousands of years are estimated from other measurements, such as concentrations in ice cores from the poles.

(2) Working scientifically

Scientists think that human activity is causing global temperatures to rise and resulting in global climate change. This idea is based on peer-reviewed evidence.

Peer review is a process where scientists evaluate the reliability of other scientists' investigations and results in order to help validate the research.

(2) Greenhouse gases

Burning fossil fuels and dumping waste in landfills releases carbon dioxide and methane. Deforestation and rising human population also increase CO_2 emissions, and livestock farming produces CH_4.

(5) Worked example — Grade 6

Explain why many scientists are concerned about the use of fossil fuels in cars. **[2 marks]**

Fossil fuels release carbon dioxide, which contributes to climate change.

(10) Exam-style practice — Grade 6

1. Give **two** human activities that are causing carbon dioxide levels to increase. **[2 marks]**

2. Explain why many scientists are concerned about the increasing levels of greenhouse gases. **[1 mark]**

 Made a start **Feeling confident** **Exam ready**   **161**

Global climate change

Increased levels of carbon dioxide and methane generated by human activity, including burning fossil fuels and livestock farming, are likely to affect the climate. You need to be able to describe the effects of climate change on Earth and the environment.

 Impacts of climate change

Changes in the climate can be observed across the globe. If climate change continues at its current rate, scientists predict that its effects will continue to intensify.

Global warming is the overall warming of the planet, based on average temperature over the entire surface.

Climate change refers to changes in regional climate characteristics, including temperature, humidity, rainfall and wind.

The effects of global climate change can already be observed across the world:

- Natural habitats are changing, making them inhospitable for some plants and animals.
- Unpredictable weather patterns are making it increasingly difficult for farmers to grow crops.
- Flooding and other extreme weather events destroy buildings and cause deaths.

Agriculture

Crop yields are expected to decrease for all major world crops. Agricultural land on the edge of deserts will become unusable, through the process of desertification. Crops could be wiped out in low-lying areas that suffer from flooding. With fewer crops available on the world market, prices are likely to increase. The growing season in some areas will increase. This would be a benefit to places such as the UK as more crops could be grown.

Water and ice

Sudden shifts of landmass, such as avalanches and rockfalls, can occur as glaciers melt. Habitats will be destroyed or flooded, which may displace or destroy entire species. Communities that use the melt water from glaciers may see this supply decrease, increasing the number of water-stressed areas. This is especially the case in Asia. Less fresh water will be available in coastal areas as it will mix with sea water. Economically, areas that rely on winter tourism may suffer from a lack of snow.

Sea level increases

Coastal land is at risk, especially land on deltas. Sea defences are under more stress. Low-lying land is threatened so the lives of 80 million people across the globe will be threatened.

Population

People will migrate from areas suffering drought. Any that remain will be in danger of dying from starvation and lack of water. 17 million people in Bangladesh alone will be threatened by flooding. As the world population increases, more people will be living in cities located on the coast. More people will be affected by coastal flooding as a result.

 Worked example — **Grade 6**

Evidence suggests that global climate change is melting the polar ice caps, changing precipitation patterns, causing more intense heatwaves and droughts, and increasing the intensity of storms.
Describe the problems caused by these environmental issues. **[5 marks]**

Melting of the polar ice caps is causing sea levels to rise, increasing flooding and eroding rocks and beaches. Rising temperatures cause more water to evaporate, which will lead to an increased amount of rain and snow. This may also lead to flooding. In some areas, there may be too little rainfall leading to drought and starvation. Heatwaves also will lead to droughts. This will result in countries not having enough water to sustain the growth of crops for food, which in the long term could lead to starvation. Increased storm intensity is leading to millions of pounds worth of damage, which can have significant effects on a country's economy.

 Working scientifically

You need to know how scientists collect data that gives them an insight into the composition of Earth's atmosphere in the past. When ice forms it traps bubbles of air. This sample of the atmosphere can then be tested to measure the concentration of greenhouse gases and evaluate how they have changed over time, providing evidence about climate change.

 Exam-style practice — **Grade 5**

1 Name **two** impacts of climate change. **[2 marks]**

2 Describe how a change in the amount of rainfall could have a negative impact on the population. **[2 marks]**

3 Give the major cause of climate change. **[1 mark]**

 Made a start **Feeling confident** **Exam ready**

Reducing the use of resources

Using resources more efficiently by **reusing** and **recycling** them or **reducing** their use is vital because it leads to less waste, minimises climate change and other damage to the environment and is more cost-effective. You need to know how resources can be preserved using these methods.

Mitigating the effects of climate change

Climate change mitigation includes reducing the human contribution to greenhouse gases. Most countries are now working to limit global warming, by increasing energy efficiency, reducing the use of fossil fuels and using alternative low-carbon energy sources.

Carbon dioxide could be removed from Earth's atmosphere using carbon capture and storage or planting more trees.

Improved building materials such as insulation reduce the usage of fuels for heating.

Worked example   Grade 6

1 Building materials, such as clay, glass and metal, are produced from limited raw materials. Much of the energy for the processes also comes from limited resources. Extracting these raw materials by quarrying and mining has significant environmental impacts. Evaluate ways in which the level of raw materials being used can be reduced.

[4 marks]

The materials used for buildings are in limited supply, so these valuable resources could be saved by recycling or reusing them. The processes of recycling and reusing are usually better for the environment than the extraction processes, as less energy is required, so fewer fossil fuels are burned. This also means there would be less pollution released. Quarrying damages the landscape and creates dust and noise pollution. Waste materials are sent to landfill if not recycled or reused.

2 Scientists believe global effort is needed to significantly reduce the human effect on climate change. Suggested methods include reflecting CO_2 back into the atmosphere or carbon capture and storage (CCS). Suggest why these may not be successful in mitigating the effects of the human contribution to global warming.

[2 marks]

These methods would involve large-scale engineering, which would be costly. Some countries may refuse to cooperate therefore lessening the effort to reduce climate change.

Reusing and recycling

Reusing a resource creates no waste or pollution, for example refilling a drinks bottle or reusing a plastic bag. Although this will have some effect in reducing greenhouse emissions it is unlikely that it will be significant enough to mitigate (lessen) the effects of climate change.

Exam-style practice   Grade 6

1 Use **Figure 1** to answer the following questions.

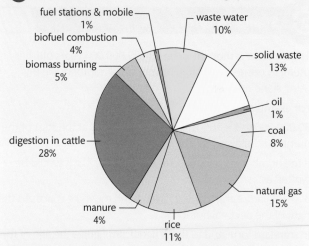

Figure 1 The relative amounts of methane produced (in 2000) by human activities, including livestock farming, burning fossil fuels and crop farming.

(a) Which of these **three** human activities produced the most methane?   **[1 mark]**

     A livestock farming

     B burning fossil fuels

     C crop farming

(b) Give the total proportion produced by your answer to (**a**).   **[1 mark]**

(c) Give the main environmental issue related to the production of methane by human activity.

Describe **two** ways in which human activity could be controlled to reduce this effect.   **[3 marks]**

2 The oceans are natural 'carbon sinks'. As levels of carbon dioxide increase in the atmosphere, the ocean acts as a buffer to try to reduce these atmospheric levels. As carbon dioxide dissolves into the oceans some may react to form carbonic acid. Suggest the impact this will have on the oceans.   **[2 marks]**

Key concepts in physics

You need to be able to recall and use SI units for quantities, as well as using multiples of these units.

2 Quantities and their units

Physics relies on measuring things. For everything that we measure, there is an agreed unit that we measure in.

The following are units you should know:

length	metre, m
mass	kilogram, kg
time	second, s
current	ampere, A
temperature	kelvin, K
amount of substance	mole, mol

5 Multiples and sub-multiples of units

Measurements in physics very often involve either very large or very small numbers. Multiples or sub-multiples of units are used for these.

You should know the following conversions:

giga (G) $= \times 10^9$	centi $= \times 10^{-2}$
mega (M) $= \times 10^6$	milli $= \times 10^{-3}$
kilo (k) $= \times 10^3$	micro (μ) $= \times 10^{-6}$
	nano (n) $= \times 10^{-9}$

2 Standard form

The universe is thought to be 13 799 000 000 years old. It is useful to express very large or very small numbers like this using standard form.

For example:

30 000 000 $= 3 \times 10^7$. This means that the '3' at the start of the number is followed by 7 zeros.

If the number is very small, for example 0.0003, it would be written as:

3×10^{-4}, indicating that the '3' has been moved 4 spaces to the right of the decimal point.

In standard form and to three significant figures the age of the universe is 1.38×10^{10} years.

2 Significant figures

It is often not sensible to write an answer to many decimal places. For example, a calculation may give an answer to many more decimal places than you could realistically measure.

It is more useful to quote to a certain number of significant figures. 0.0342 is 0.03 to one significant figure. 5.975 is 6.0 to two significant figures.

2 Worked example — Grade 4

A journey from home to school takes quarter of an hour.

Lizzie wants to calculate the speed of the car in metres per second.

Calculate the number of seconds the journey took. **[2 marks]**

quarter of an hour = 0.25 hours

1 hour = 60 minutes; 1 minute = 60 seconds

1 hour = 60 × 60 seconds

0.25 hours = 0.25 × (60 × 60) = 900 seconds

Start by converting one hour into seconds. Then you can multiply your answer by the number of hours in the question, in this case 0.25.

10 Exam-style practice — Grade 6

1 The average radius of an atom can be measured indirectly and is about 0.000 000 000 1 m.

(a) Write this measurement in standard form. **[1 mark]**

(b) Convert this measurement into nanometres, nm. **[1 mark]**

2 The radius of a particular atom is 5.0×10^{-10} m. The radius of the atom's nucleus is 8.2×10^{-15} m. How many times larger is the radius of the atom than the radius of the nucleus? Give your answer to two significant figures. **[2 marks]**

When dividing values in standard form, remember that you need to:

- divide the numbers at the front
- subtract the powers.

i.e. $A \times 10^x \div B \times 10^y = (A/B) \times 10^{(x-y)}$

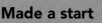

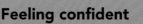

Scalar and vector quantities

You need to know the difference between a scalar quantity and a vector quantity.

 Definitions

Scalars are quantities that have only a **magnitude** (a size).

Vectors are quantities with both a magnitude and a direction.

You can add scalar quantities like numerical values. When adding vectors, you need to consider the direction.

 **Vector quantities**

- ✓ velocity (m/s)
- ✓ displacement (m)
- ✓ acceleration (m/s²)
- ✓ force (N)
- ✓ weight (N)
- ✓ momentum (kg m/s)
- ✓ gravitational field strength (N/kg)

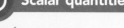 **Scalar quantities**

- ✓ distance (m)
- ✓ speed (m/s)
- ✓ charge (C)
- ✓ density (kg/m³)
- ✓ efficiency ← | Efficiency does not have a unit. It is usually given as a decimal or percentage.
- ✓ energy (all types) (J)
- ✓ frequency (Hz)
- ✓ mass (kg)
- ✓ power (W)
- ✓ pressure (Pa)
- ✓ temperature (°C)
- ✓ time (s)
- ✓ wavelength (m)
- ✓ volume (m³)
- ✓ area (m²)

⑩ Adding vectors

Vector quantities can be represented by arrows. The length of the arrow represents the magnitude. The direction of the arrow represents the direction of the vector quantity.

If two vectors act in a straight line, they can be added (same direction) or subtracted (opposite direction).

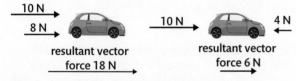

Figure 1 Finding the resultant vector

Vectors that are at right angles can also be added to find the resultant vector. Draw the arrows end to end to make a right-angled triangle. The resultant vector is the hypotenuse of the triangle and can be found using a scale drawing.

You need to know how to add vectors when you calculate resultant forces. See page 207 for more on this.

Choose a suitable scale, such as 10 N = 1 cm. Draw the diagram to scale (use a protractor or set square, or use squared paper to make sure the right angle is exactly 90°).

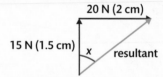

Figure 2 A scale drawing showing the resultant vector

Measure the length of the resultant vector. This should be 2.5 cm at this scale.

Convert this to the correct unit. 2.5 × 10 = 25 N

Use a protractor to measure the angle x. This is 53° when drawn to scale. You can also use Pythagoras' theorem to calculate resultant vectors.

 Worked example | **Grade 5**

Write down **one** similarity and **one** difference between speed and velocity. **[2 marks]**

Similarity: they both measure how fast something is moving.

Difference: only velocity gives its direction.

⑤ **Exam-style practice** | **Grades 5–7**

1 When there is no wind blowing, a plane travels at 65 m/s. The plane enters an area where the wind is blowing at 12 m/s due north. The output of the engines remains the same. Calculate the plane's velocity if it:

(a) flies due north **[1 mark]**

(b) flies due south. **[1 mark]**

2 A bird flies north at 12 m/s. The wind blows it east at 9 m/s. Use a scale drawing to find the resultant velocity. **[3 marks]**

Distance and speed

Distance and displacement mean different things in Physics. You need to understand the difference between them.

Distance, displacement, speed and velocity

Distance is how far an object has travelled. Distance only has a magnitude. It is a scalar quantity (page 165).

Displacement is the distance travelled in a straight line, in a particular direction. Displacement has direction as well as magnitude, so it is a vector quantity (page 165). The displacement at the end of a journey is usually less than the total distance travelled because of turns or bends in the journey.

Speed is how fast an object is travelling.

Velocity is how fast an object is travelling in a given direction. So if you run in a circle at a constant speed, your velocity is constantly changing, since your direction of travel is constantly changing.

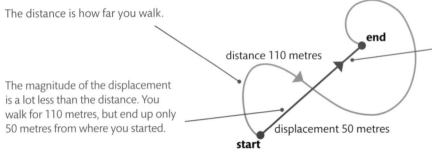

The distance is how far you walk.

distance 110 metres

The magnitude of the displacement is a lot less than the distance. You walk for 110 metres, but end up only 50 metres from where you started.

end

The arrow shows the direction of the displacement.

Directions can be given as compass bearings or simple descriptions like 'to the right' or 'up'.

displacement 50 metres

start

Figure 1 Going for a walk

 Worked example Grade 5

1 Mahad walks from home to the shop, then to school. The diagram shows the route he takes. Give Mahad's final displacement from his starting position. **[3 marks]**

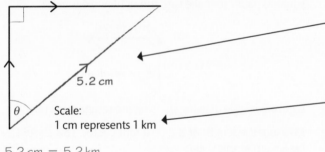

5.2 cm

Scale:
1 cm represents 1 km

5.2 cm = 5.2 km

bearing = 050°

Exam focus

You need to give a length and a distance. Make sure you apply the scale to your measurement.

Use a ruler to draw a diagonal line from the start point to the finish point. Measure this and apply the scale. You also need to measure the angle from the vertical to the diagonal.

Bearings should be written as a three figure number, giving the angle going clockwise from north.

2 A cyclist travels east at a constant speed of 5 m/s. Write down the velocity of the cyclist. **[1 mark]**

Velocity = 5 m/s due east

 Exam-style practice Grade 5

For each of the journeys given below, find:
- the total distance travelled
- the displacement.

Exam focus

You need to use the equation for the circumference of a circle. Check your formulae sheet on page 244.

(a) travel 200 km north, 200 km east and 200 km south **[2 marks]**

(b) go up 180 m in a lift, then walk 50 m along the corridor **[2 marks]**

(c) run 350 m to the shops, then the same distance back to your home **[2 marks]**

(d) run once around a circle with a diameter of 10 m. **[2 marks]**

 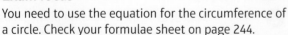

Speed and velocity

You need to know the difference between speed and velocity, and how to calculate them. Speed only has magnitude so is a scalar quantity. Velocity has magnitude and direction so is a vector quantity.

5 Speed

Speed is a measure of the distance an object has moved in a specific amount of time.

distance travelled (m) = average speed (m/s) × time (s) $s = v \times t$

As most moving objects do not have a constant speed, this equation gives the average speed over a time.

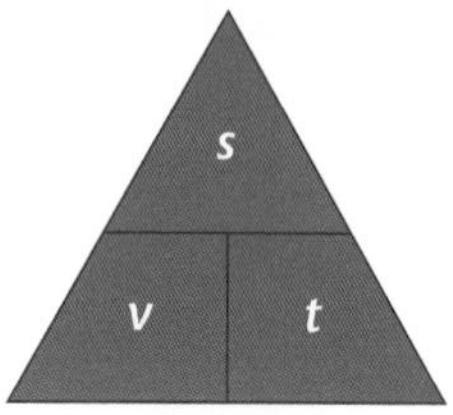

Figure 1 You can use this formula triangle to help you to rearrange the equation and calculate an unknown value.

You need to know typical examples of everyday speeds.

	walking	running	cycling	wind	cars on a motorway	sound waves
Approximate speed in m/s	1.5	3	6	5–20	20–30	330

The speed of sound can vary.

5 Velocity

Velocity is speed in a particular direction.

Unlike speed, velocity has a direction. This can be shown as:

- a word, such as 'north' or 'left'
- a positive (+) or negative (−)
- an arrow.

Even at constant speed, the velocity changes if an object changes direction. A car driving around a roundabout at 20 km/h will have constant speed but its velocity changes as it changes direction. If the car drives in one full circle, the displacement is zero, which means the car's average velocity will be zero but the average speed will be 20 km/h.

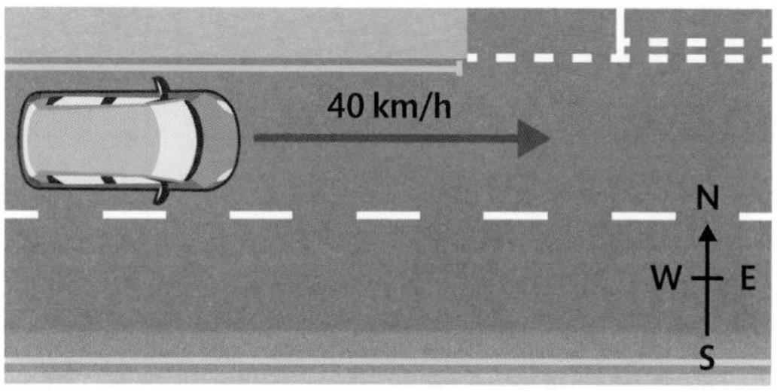

Figure 2 A car has a velocity of 40 km/h east

Maths skills
Convert km to m by multiplying by 1000;
hours to minutes by multiplying by 60;
minutes to seconds by multiplying by 60.

10 Worked example — Grades 5–6

Train A travels in a straight line due east and covers 4.5 km in 2 minutes.

(a) Calculate its average speed. **[2 marks]**

$v = \frac{s}{t} = \frac{4500}{120} = 37.5$ m/s

Write down the equation and check the units as you put the numbers in.

(b) Write down its velocity. **[1 mark]**

37.5 m/s east

The questions give a compass direction (due east), so you should include a direction in your answer.

Train B travels at twice the speed of train A.

(c) Calculate the distance travelled by train B in 4 minutes. **[2 marks]**

Train B speed = 37.5 × 2 = 75 m/s

$v \times t = s$

75 × 240 = 18 000 m = 18 km

10 Exam-style practice — Grades 5–6

1 A runner travels 22 km at an average speed of 3 m/s. Calculate the time he takes. Give your answer in minutes. **[2 marks]**

2 The table shows the distances travelled in certain amounts of time by four cars. Which car has the fastest average speed? **[5 marks]**

Car	A	B	C	D
Distance	600 m	200 km	20 m	3000 km
Time	24 s	1.5 hours	0.5 s	1 day

Distance–time relationships

Distance–time graphs show the distance an object travels over a period of time. You need to be able to interpret these types of graph to work out the speed of an object moving in a straight line.

Distance–time graphs

A **distance–time graph** shows how far an object moves over time.

The gradient of a distance–time graph represents the speed of an object.

- When the line on the graph becomes steeper, the gradient increases. This means the object is **accelerating**.
- When the line on the graph becomes less steep, the gradient decreases. This means the object is **decelerating**.
- When the line on the graph is horizontal, it has a gradient of zero. This means the object is **stationary**.

Worked example   Grade 7

1 Look at **Figure 1**.

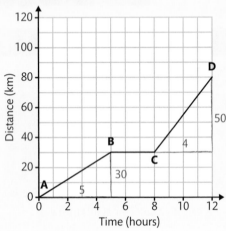

Figure 1 The journey of a horse rider

Describe the journey in as much detail as possible.

[4 marks]

A–B the horse travels 30 km in 5 hours

The speed (gradient) = 30 ÷ 5 = 6 km/h

B–C the horse is stationary for 3 hours

C–D the horse moves a further 50 km in 4 hours

Its speed is 50 ÷ 4 = 12.5 km/h

> When asked to describe a graph in detail, you should describe the different sections of the graph, giving the times for each section, the distance travelled and the speed.

2 Look at **Figure 2**.

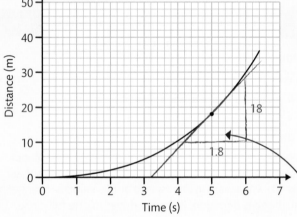

Figure 2 The journey of a cyclist

    (a) Describe the motion of the cyclist. **[1 mark]**

The cyclist is accelerating.

    (b) Estimate the speed at 5 s. **[4 marks]**

18 ÷ 1.8 = 10 m/s

Maths skills

Draw a tangent to the curve at the time where you want to know the speed.

Exam-style practice   Grade 5

1 Look at **Figure 2**. Without performing any calculations, explain how the graph shows that the cyclist is accelerating. **[2 marks]**

2 A new Mars exploration vehicle is tested in the lab for the first time. For the first 8 seconds it moves 4 metres then stops for 2 seconds. It then moves at full speed covering a further 12 metres in the next 6 seconds. Draw a distance–time graph to show this motion. **[3 marks]**

    ✓ **Made a start**   ✓ **Feeling confident**   ✓ **Exam ready**

Uniform acceleration

Acceleration is the measure of how quickly an object's velocity changes. Acceleration is a vector quantity. **Uniform** means the acceleration is constant. You need to know how to calculate acceleration for the exam.

(5) Calculating acceleration

The **average acceleration** of an object can be worked out using this equation:

$$\text{acceleration (m/s}^2) = \frac{\text{change in velocity (m/s)}}{\text{time taken (s)}}$$

$$a = \frac{(v - u)}{t}$$

For uniform acceleration:

s is the distance

$$v^2 - u^2 = 2a \times s$$

v is the end velocity in m/s   u is the start velocity in m/s

(10) Worked example   Grades 5–6

1 A train travelling at 50 m/s must slow down to 20 m/s before it reaches a bend.

(a) It takes 90 s to slow down. Find the acceleration of the train. **[2 marks]**

$$a = \frac{(v - u)}{t} = \frac{20 - 50}{90} = -0.33 \text{m/s}^2$$

(b) Assuming the deceleration is constant, calculate the distance it takes the train to slow down to 20 m/s. **[3 marks]**

$$s = \frac{v^2 - u^2}{2a} = \frac{20^2 - 50^2}{2 \times (-0.33)} = 3182 \text{ m}$$

2 A ball is dropped and hits the floor at 6 m/s. Calculate how long it takes to fall. **[2 marks]**

$$t = \frac{(v - u)}{a} = \frac{6 - 0}{10} = 0.6 \text{ m}$$

3 Each lorry in **Figure 1** is accelerating at a constant rate of -2 m/s². The initial velocity of each lorry is shown. Calculate the velocity of each lorry after 5 seconds. **[2 marks]**

 20 m/s   stationary   −20 m/s

Figure 1 Three lorries accelerating at a constant rate

$$v - u = a \times t$$
$$= -2 \times 5 = -10 \text{m/s}$$

A: $20 + -10 = 10 \text{m/s}$

B: $0 + -10 = -10 \text{m/s}$

C: $-20 + -10 = -30 \text{m/s}$

(2) Acceleration examples

You need to know some typical accelerations and the forces needed to achieve them.

Action	Acceleration (m/s²)	Force needed (N)
Train pulling off	0.5	50 000
Person	1	70
Car	1–5	1000–5000
Object in free fall	10	equal to the weight of the object

Exam focus

This equation appears on your formula sheet. You need to be able to rearrange it.

Write s, u, v, a and t in the margin and make a note of what numbers you know as you read the question.

It is decelerating, so the answer will be negative.

Ensure you get the start and end velocities the right way around. This gives a negative answer, indicating deceleration.

Negative acceleration can cause an object to speed up if the object is moving in the negative direction. Calculate the end velocity first. Then add it to the initial velocity.

(10) Exam-style practice   Grades 5–6

1 An apple falls from a branch onto the ground. The time taken for the apple to fall is 1.5 s. Calculate the speed of the apple when it hits the ground. $(g = 10 \text{ m/s}^2)$ **[2 marks]**

2 (a) A jet lands at 65 m/s and has a constant acceleration of -5 m/s². Calculate how long it takes to stop. **[2 marks]**

(b) Calculate the minimum length of runway needed for the jet in part **(a)**. **[2 marks]**

3 A car is travelling at 30 m/s. The driver brakes suddenly and the speed decreases to 20 m/s. The car travels 100 m during this time. Calculate the acceleration of the car. **[2 marks]**

4 Describe how the speed of an object travelling at 40 m/s is changing if its acceleration is:

(a) 2 m/s² **[1 mark]**

(b) -2 m/s². **[1 mark]**

Velocity–time graphs

Velocity–time graphs show how the velocity of an object changes over time. You need to know how to calculate acceleration from the gradient of a velocity–time graph and distance travelled from the area under the velocity–time graph.

[5] Distance and acceleration

- The acceleration for a given section is equal to the gradient of the line. If the line is straight, the acceleration is constant.
- The distance travelled is the area under the line.

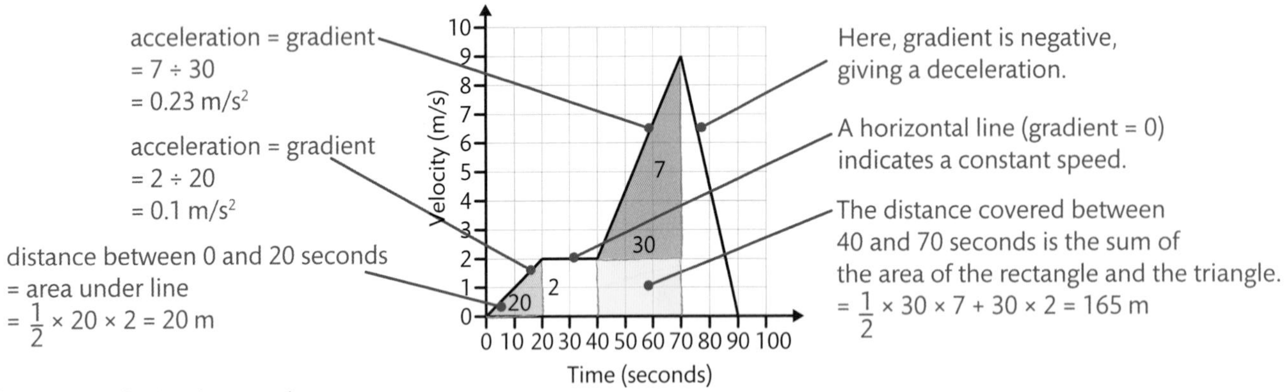
acceleration = gradient
= 7 ÷ 30
= 0.23 m/s²
acceleration = gradient
= 2 ÷ 20
= 0.1 m/s²
distance between 0 and 20 seconds
= area under line
= 1/2 × 20 × 2 = 20 m
Velocity (m/s)
Time (seconds)
7
30
20
2
Here, gradient is negative, giving a deceleration.
A horizontal line (gradient = 0) indicates a constant speed.
The distance covered between 40 and 70 seconds is the sum of the area of the rectangle and the triangle.
= 1/2 × 30 × 7 + 30 × 2 = 165 m

Figure 1 A velocity–time graph

[10] Worked example — Grade 6

1 The graph opposite shows the velocity of a bus.
Calculate:

(a) the acceleration of the bus between:

(i) 0 and 8 s **[2 marks]**

$$\text{acceleration} = \frac{v - u}{t} = \frac{16 - 0}{8} = 2 \text{ m/s}^2$$

(ii) 14 and 24 s **[2 marks]**

$$\text{acceleration} = \frac{0 - 16}{10} = -1.6 \text{ m/s}^2$$

(b) the total distance travelled by the bus. **[2 marks]**

Total distance = area under graph

$= 0.5 \times 8 \times 16 + 6 \times 16 + 0.5 \times 10 \times 16$

$= 64 + 96 + 80 = 240$ m

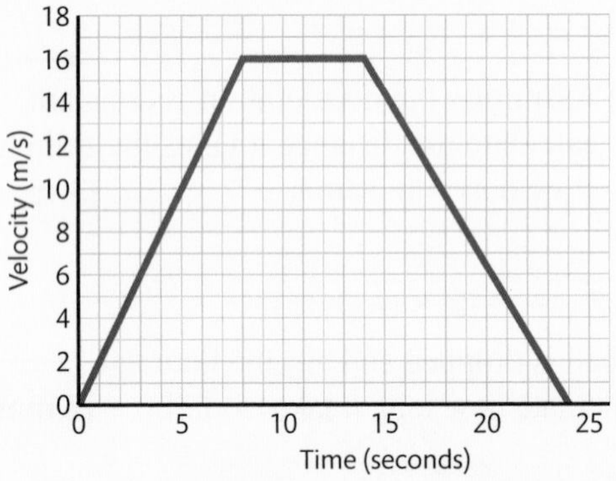
Velocity (m/s)
Time (seconds)

[5] Worked example — Grade 5

2 The diagram shows the velocity–time graphs for the motion of three different objects.

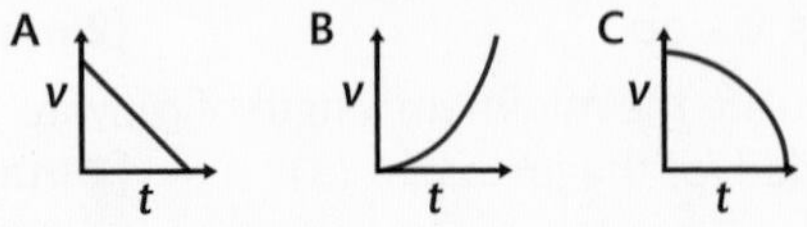
A
B
C
v
t

Describe the motion of each object. **[3 marks]**

A is decelerating at a constant rate (or accelerating at a constant negative rate).

B is increasing in velocity with non-uniform acceleration.

C is decelerating at a non-uniform rate.

[10] Exam-style practice — Grades 5–6

The graph shows the velocity of a golf cart over 45 seconds.

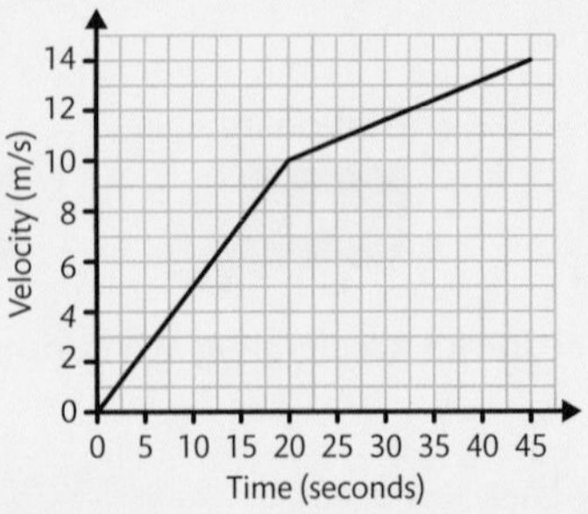
Velocity (m/s)
Time (seconds)

(a) Describe the motion of the golf cart without any calculations. **[2 marks]**

(b) Calculate the acceleration of the golf cart at 10 s and at 35 s. **[4 marks]**

Gravity

You need to know the relationship between gravity, weight and mass.

 Mass, weight and gravity

The weight of an object is dependent on its mass and the strength of gravity. The weight of an object may change but its mass remains constant.

Mass (m)
- the amount of matter in an object
- measured in kilograms, kg

Weight (W)
- the force of gravity acting on a mass; the force acts downwards, towards the centre of the planet
- measured in newtons, N
- measured using a calibrated spring-balance (newtonmeter)

Gravitational field strength (g)
- the strength of gravity at any one point
- measured in N/kg or m/s^2
- also called acceleration due to gravity

You need to know the equation:
weight (N) = mass (kg) × gravitational field strength (N/kg)
$W = m \times g$

 Worked example | **Grades 4–5**

A Mars rover weighs 670 N on Earth.
Gravitational field strength = 10 N/kg

(a) Find the mass of the rover. **[2 marks]**

$$m = \frac{W}{g}$$
$$\frac{670}{10} = 67 \text{ kg}$$

(b) On Mars, $g = 3.7$ N/kg.
Find the mass and, hence, the weight of the rover on Mars. **[2 marks]**

Mass does not change so on Mars it is still 67 kg.
$W = m \times g$
$67 \times 3.7 = 253$ N

(c) A second rover is tested for use on a planet where the gravity is exactly half the strength it is on Earth. Explain how the rover's mass and weight on this new planet would compare to when it is on Earth? **[2 marks]**

Its mass would be the same on the new planet, but its weight would be half what it is on Earth.

 Point mass

When forces are studied (page 206) or added together to find the resultant force (page 207), weight is usually one of the forces included in the calculation. The calculations are often aided by diagrams, such as free-body diagrams (page 206). In this case, the weight of an object can be treated as though it is all acting from one point at the centre of the object.

skydiver mass = 75 kg
individual forces ↓   resultant force ↓

drag = 400 N

weight = 735 N

$F = 735 - 400 = 335$ N
$a = \frac{F}{m}$
$= \frac{335 \text{ N}}{75 \text{ kg}}$
$= 4.5$ m/s^2

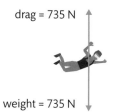

drag = 735 N

weight = 735 N

$F = 335$ N
$a = \frac{F}{m}$
$= 0$ m/s^2

Figure 1 The weight of this skydiver is a force acting downwards through his centre.

 Weight and mass

Weight and mass are directly proportional.
weight ∝ mass

If one object has twice the mass of another, it will also have twice the weight for the same gravitational field strength. Mass is constant. Weight depends on the gravitational field strength at the point where the object is.

 Exam-style practice | **Grades 4–6**

1 State the equipment used to measure the weight of an object. **[1 mark]**

2 State the relationship between weight and gravitational field strength. **[1 mark]**

3 A student says that an astronaut on the Moon will have difficulty walking because of the lack of atmosphere. Part of their statement is true. Give a more correct version and explain your statement. **[3 marks]**

4 A spacecraft has a weight of 12 000 N on Earth. Calculate its weight on the Moon. The gravitational field strength on the Moon is 1.6 N/kg. **[2 marks]**

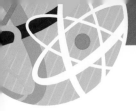

Newton's laws of motion

Newton's three laws of motion explain how forces affect the motion of objects. You need to consider resultant forces when using Newton's laws. There is more about calculating resultant forces on page 207.

5 Newton's first law

If all the forces acting on an object are balanced (the resultant force = 0), the object will remain at a constant velocity or at rest.

What does it mean?

This means that once an object is moving, it keeps moving at the same velocity as long as no overall (resultant) force acts upon it.

To make the object speed up, slow down, or change direction, you need to apply a resultant force.

If an object has no resultant force, then all the forces are balanced. It will continue to move with constant velocity, or remain stationary.

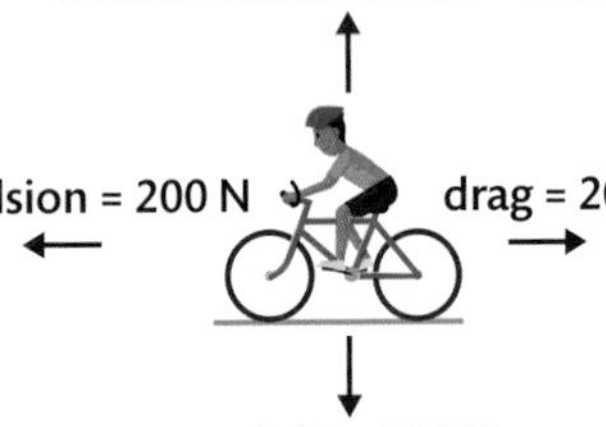
normal contact force = 900 N
propulsion = 200 N
drag = 200 N
weight = 900 N

Figure 1 Balanced forces acting on a cyclist

The vertical and horizontal forces add up to zero. We cannot say all the forces are equal, we say they are balanced or in equilibrium.

The cyclist will continue at a constant speed because the resistive force (drag) balances the driving force (propulsion). If the cyclist stops pedalling, the forces become unbalanced and the cyclist slows down.

Most moving objects that are not being moved by another force will eventually stop because of the force of friction.

5 Newton's third law

When two objects interact they exert an equal and opposite force on each other.

What does it mean?

When one object applies a force to another, it experiences the same force itself but in the opposite direction. Note that the two forces:

- are the same size
- act in exactly opposite directions
- act on different objects, so they do not cancel out.

A bat hits a ball with a force of 200 N. The ball exerts a force of 200 N on the bat in the opposite direction.

The force has a greater effect on the ball's speed because the ball has a smaller mass.

5 Newton's second law

If the forces acting on an object are unbalanced, the object's acceleration will be:

- in the direction of the resultant force
- directly proportional to the resultant force.

The acceleration is inversely proportionate to the mass of the object: acceleration $\propto \frac{1}{\text{mass}}$

What does it mean?

An unbalanced force makes an object accelerate. It might speed up, slow down or change direction.

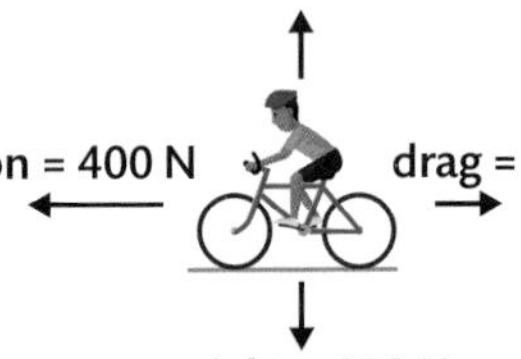
normal contact force = 900 N
propulsion = 400 N
drag = 200 N
weight = 900 N

Figure 2 Unbalanced forces acting on a cyclist. There is a resultant force in the forwards direction so the cyclist will accelerate.

If you double the resultant force, the acceleration will also double. If the mass being accelerated doubles, then the acceleration will halve for the same force. If something slows down and stops, it is decelerating. This means there must be a resultant force acting in the opposite direction to its motion.

2 Worked example — Grade 5

Explain why a vehicle has a lower acceleration when it is heavily loaded than when it is empty. **[2 marks]**

Acceleration is inversely proportional to an object's mass. So for the same force, if its mass increases, its acceleration will decrease by the same amount (so if the mass doubled, the acceleration would halve).

10 Exam-style practice — Grades 5–6

1. Explain why it is necessary to keep a foot on the accelerator to keep a car moving at uniform speed. **[2 marks]**
2. A student pushes on a desk with a force of 30 N.
   (a) Give the force the student experiences as a result. **[1 mark]**
   (b) Explain, in terms of forces, how the desk could remain in equilibrium. **[2 marks]**

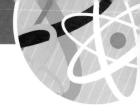

Newton's second law

Newton's second law shows the relationship between force, mass and acceleration. This relationship can be shown in two ways: $F = m \times a$ and $F = \frac{(mv - mu)}{t}$. You will need to be able to use both of these equations.

5 $F = m \times a$

Newton's second law tells you how much force you need to accelerate a mass.

force (N) = mass (kg) × acceleration (m/s²)

The force that causes the acceleration must be the resultant (overall) force.

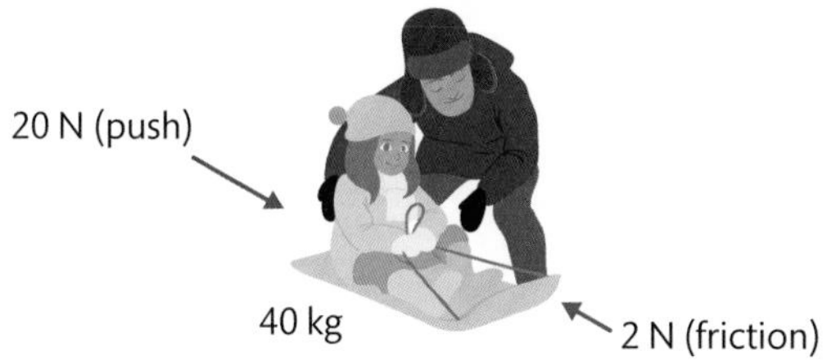
20 N (push)
40 kg
2 N (friction)

Figure 1 The sledge and passenger have a combined mass of 40 kg. The resultant force is 20 N forward – 2 N friction = 18 N.

$$a = \frac{F}{m} = \frac{18}{40} = 0.45 \text{ m/s}^2$$

Newton's second law can also be expressed in terms of the rate of change of momentum of an object (page 178). The force is the change in momentum of an object divided by time.

$$F = \frac{(mv - mu)}{t}$$

5 Inertial mass

An object will tend to remain at rest or carry on with uniform motion. This is called **inertia**. Inertial mass is a measure of how difficult it is to accelerate an object, or how hard it is to stop it moving once it has started. It is defined as the ratio of force over acceleration.

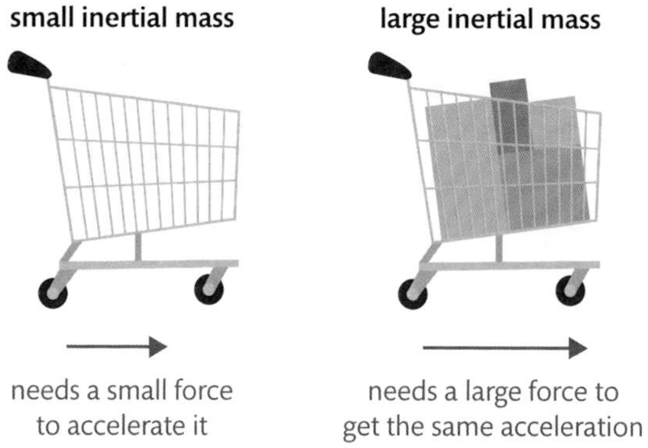
small inertial mass
large inertial mass
needs a small force to accelerate it
needs a large force to get the same acceleration

Figure 2 The trolley with the larger inertial mass requires a greater force to stop or change its direction once it has started moving.

5 Worked example — Grade 5

A firework has an initial mass of 400 g. It is launched vertically upwards with a thrust of 45 N.

(a) Calculate its initial acceleration. **[2 marks]**

Resultant upwards force, F = thrust – weight:

$45 - (0.4 \times 10) = 41$

$$a = \frac{F}{m} = \frac{41}{0.4} = 102.5 \text{ m/s}^2$$

> All masses need to be in kilograms not grams.
> $400 \div 1000 = 0.4$ kg

b) Other than losing mass, explain how the acceleration is affected in the seconds after the firework has launched. **[2 marks]**

Air resistance would lower the resultant force. $F \propto a$ so acceleration would also decrease.

> Air resistance acts in the opposite direction to the way the object is moving. Drag increases with speed.

5 Exam-style practice — Grade 5

(a) A scooter accelerates at 1.67 m/s². The forward force is 300 N and there is 50 N of drag. Calculate the total mass of the scooter and its rider. **[3 marks]**

(b) Carrying a passenger and luggage doubles the scooter's mass. Calculate its acceleration if the forces remain the same. **[2 marks]**

Centripetal force

For an object in orbit to stay in orbit, there must be a resultant force acting on the object.

 Centripetal force

Any object that is moving in a circle, like a hammer whirled by a hammer thrower, is changing direction and therefore changing velocity. That means it must be experiencing a resultant force to keep it in motion.

> Go to page 172 for more about resultant forces keeping objects in motion.

Figure 1 The hammer is whirled in a circle by the athlete holding on to the cable. It is always changing direction so it is being accelerated.

This force acts towards the centre of the circle and is known as the **centripetal force**.

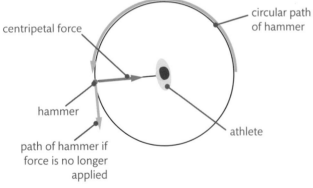

Figure 2 The athlete is holding on to the hammer – she is exerting a pull (a force) on the cable. When she lets go, the centripetal force stops, so the hammer is no longer being accelerated in a circle. It will travel in a straight line.

Figure 3 These cars are going round a roundabout. The centripetal force comes from the friction between the tyres and the road.

 Worked example   **Grade 5**

A satellite orbits the Earth at constant speed in a circular orbit.

(a) Explain how you know that the satellite is accelerating. **[1 mark]**

Something moving at constant velocity moves at the same speed in the same direction so, if it is going in a circle, its velocity is not constant. A change in velocity over time is acceleration.

(b) State the name of the type of force that is acting on the satellite. **[1 mark]**

A force that accelerates an object in a circle is called a centripetal force.

(c) Give the source of the force acting on the satellite. **[1 mark]**

The force is due to gravity.

 Exam-style practice   **Grade 6**

A car accelerates around a corner.

(a) State the direction of the force causing the acceleration. **[1 mark]**

(b) The car has a mass of 1000 kg and the acceleration is 3 m/s^2. Calculate the force that is making the car turn. **[2 marks]**

 **Made a start**   **Feeling confident**   **Exam ready**

Practical: Investigating acceleration

You need to know how to investigate the effect of force and mass on acceleration.

 Two experiments

Experiment 1

1 Increase the force on the trolley (**Figure 1**) by moving masses from the trolley to the hanging masses.

2 The interrupt card passes through the light gate. A data logger calculates the acceleration.

Experiment 2

1 Increase the mass of the trolley by fixing masses to it.

2 Measure the acceleration. Keep the force (hanging mass) the same.

The masses accelerate as well as the trolley, so this keeps the total mass the same.

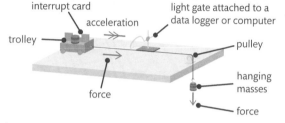

interrupt card
acceleration
trolley
light gate attached to a data logger or computer
pulley
hanging masses
force
force

Figure 1 Apparatus for measuring acceleration

 Worked example | Grades 5–7

(a) Give the expected findings of Experiment 1. **[2 marks]**

Increasing the force on the trolley would increase its acceleration. Force and acceleration are proportional.

(b) State **one** other force acting on the trolley. Explain what could be done to minimise its impact on your results. **[2 marks]**

Friction – lift the ramp so the trolley runs slightly downhill to counteract friction.

(c) A graph is plotted using the results from Experiment 1. **[3 marks]**

(i) State what should be plotted on each axis.

Force on the x-axis and acceleration on the y-axis

(ii) State the value of the gradient of the graph.

The gradient gives $\frac{1}{\text{mass of trolley}}$.

(d) For Experiment 2, give **one** variable you would need to control and explain why. **[2 marks]**

The force used to accelerate the trolley would need to be the same. If a different force was used when the trolley mass was increased, you would not be able to tell what caused the change in acceleration.

 **Interrupt card**

The two sections of card break the light beam for a period of time. The data logger calculates the speed for each side:

$$\text{speed} = \frac{\text{card length}}{\text{time}}$$

It also measures the time between interruptions:

$$\text{acceleration} = \frac{\text{difference in speeds}}{\text{time between interruptions}}$$

They are proportional (written $F \propto a$) because if you double the force, the acceleration doubles.

Doing the experiment on an air track would be ideal, but there will still be friction in the pulley. Drag is another force that acts on the trolley. You could make the trolley more streamlined to minimise its effects.

Maths skills

The gradient is acceleration ÷ force. Rearrange the equation $F = m \times a$, to give $\frac{a}{F} = \frac{1}{m}$. This is the gradient.

If you reverse the axes (plot force on the y-axis), the gradient would be the trolley mass.

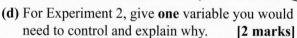

 Exam-style practice | Grades 5–6

1 In Experiment 1, explain how you would find the magnitude of the force accelerating the trolley and what the size of this force depends on. **[3 marks]**

2 A student says it does not matter where the light gate is placed as long as the trolley is accelerating when it passes through. While the student is correct, explain why the light gate should not be moved during the experiment. **[3 marks]**

3 Describe in detail the relationship between the mass of the trolley and its acceleration, and the force acting on the trolley and its acceleration. **[3 marks]**

Momentum

You need to know how to calculate an object's momentum from its velocity and mass.

 (5) Calculating momentum

momentum (kg m/s) = mass (kg) × velocity (m/s)

$p = m \times v$

The unit for momentum is kg m/s, a combination of the units for mass and velocity. Make sure you learn the unit but if you forget, use the equation to remind you.

As momentum depends on velocity, momentum is also a vector. This means it can have a negative value, to indicate a different direction.

> Remember that no matter how much mass something has, if its velocity is zero then it has no momentum.

Figure 1 This train does not go very fast, but it has a huge mass which gives it a high momentum even at low speeds.

 (10) Worked example   Grades 6–7

1 (a) A ferry of mass 125 000 kg is travelling at 12 m/s. Calculate its momentum. **[1 mark]**

$p = m \times v$

125 000 kg × 12 m/s = 1 500 000 kg m/s
             (1.5 × 10⁶ kg m/s)

(b) A second ferry has a higher momentum. Choose the incorrect statement from the following. Tick **one** box. **[1 mark]**

☐ **A** The ferry might have a higher mass.

☐ **B** The ferry might be moving more quickly.

☑ **C** The ferry might be stationary.

☐ **D** The ferry might have a lower mass.

☐ **E** The ferry might be moving more slowly.

(c) As a firework flies upwards, its mass changes as it burns fuel. Its speed doubles at the same time as its mass halves. Explain what has happened to its momentum. **[2 marks]**

It has the same momentum. Doubling the speed would double the momentum, but halving the mass would halve the momentum.

  **(10) Worked example**   Grade 7

2 A 2500 kg car accelerates from 5 m/s in 10 seconds. The car's engine provides a force of 5000 N. Calculate the final speed of the car. **[2 marks]**

$F = \dfrac{(m \times v) - (m \times u)}{t}$

$5000 \text{ N} = \dfrac{(2500 \text{ kg} \times v) - (2500 \text{ kg} \times 5 \text{m/s})}{10 \text{ s}}$

$5000 = (250 \times v) - 1250$

Rearranging the equation:

$v = \dfrac{6250}{250} = 25 \text{ m/s}$

> Keep track of all the zeroes in long numbers, or write your answer in standard form.

> If it was stationary, the momentum would be zero, so it could not possibly have more momentum.

> D and E are true. An object with lower mass could still have more momentum if it moves fast enough. An object moving more slowly could have more momentum if it has a much higher mass.

> Momentum is proportional to velocity and to mass.

 (10) Exam-style practice   Grade 7

1 (a) A horse and rider have a momentum of 5400 kg m/s. If the velocity is 12 m/s, find the mass of the horse and rider. **[2 marks]**

(b) Give the horse and rider's momentum if they are travelling in the opposite direction. **[1 mark]**

2 Find the momentum of a snail with mass 22 g travelling at 1.5 mm/s. **[2 marks]**

3 A firework of mass 850 g is travelling at 20 m/s. After a few seconds, it has accelerated to 35 m/s and has burned 300 g of fuel. Calculate its change in momentum. **[3 marks]**

 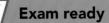

Conservation of momentum

You need to know that the total momentum, p, is constant if there are no external forces acting on the system.

⏱ 15 Conserving total momentum

Newton's third law of motion states: If body A exerts a force on body B then body B exerts an equal and opposite force on body A. This means that momentum in a collision must be conserved. In a closed system, the total momentum before any interaction must equal the total momentum after the interaction. This is the vector addition of momentum, not just the arithmetic sum. When solving problems, work out the momentum of every moving object. Add them all together to get the total momentum.

One moving object

A lorry crashes into a stationary car, and they stick together. The momentum must be conserved. This means that the momentum of the lorry and car must be the same after the collision as the momentum of the lorry before. Therefore, the velocity after the collision must be slightly lower than it was before, as the mass now includes the mass of the car.

Go to page 165 for more about vector addition.

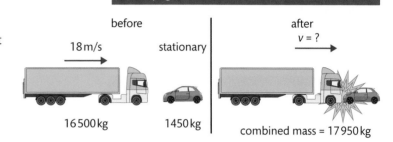

Two moving objects

When two objects travelling in opposite directions collide, the total momentum still has to be conserved. Momentum is a vector, so choose one direction to be positive and one to be negative. As a convention, objects travelling towards the left of the page have a negative velocity.

After the collision, the objects may bounce off each other or stick together. Their total momentum after the collision will be equal to their total momentum before. Positive and negative velocities indicate the direction of motion.

If the two objects had equal momentum in opposite directions, their momentum would be zero before and after the collision. They could either stick together and become stationary, or bounce off each other in opposite directions with equal momentum.

⏱ 5 Worked example — Grade 7

A car with a mass of 1100 kg is travelling at 3 m/s. It collides with a car with a mass of 1000 kg travelling at 5 m/s in the opposite direction. After the collison, the two cars move together.

Calculate the velocity and direction of travel of the cars after the collision. **[3 marks]**

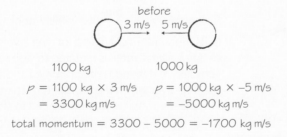

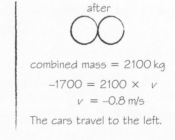

$p = 1100 \text{ kg} \times 3 \text{ m/s}$
$= 3300 \text{ kg m/s}$

$p = 1000 \text{ kg} \times -5 \text{ m/s}$
$= -5000 \text{ kg m/s}$

total momentum $= 3300 - 5000 = -1700 \text{ kg m/s}$

combined mass $= 2100 \text{ kg}$
$-1700 = 2100 \times v$
$v = -0.8 \text{ m/s}$

The cars travel to the left.

⏱ 2 Explosions

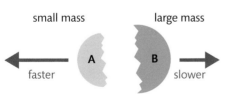

Figure 3 A stationary object explodes

The momentum before the explosion is zero, so the momentum after the explosion must also be zero.
Momentum of A = −(momentum of B).
The larger mass (B) will have a lower velocity.

⏱ 10 Exam-style practice — Grade 7

1. When a cannon fires a cannonball, the cannon recoils. Compare the motion of the cannon and cannonball just after it is fired and explain the differences. **[3 marks]**

2. In a rugby match, a player running at 8 m/s tackles another player who is standing still. Immediately after the tackle, the two of them move together.

   Explain why the velocity of the pair just after the tackle is around 4 m/s. **[3 marks]**

Stopping distance

Stopping distance refers to the distance over which a vehicle stops. It is the total of the thinking distance and the braking distance. You need to know about factors that affect the stopping distance of a vehicle.

(15) Calculating stopping distance

To calculate the stopping distance of a car, you need to account for the driver's **reaction time** (thinking distance) and the braking distance.

stopping distance = thinking distance + braking distance

- **Thinking distance** – the distance travelled while the driver is reacting. This occurs before they start to brake.
- **Braking distance** – the distance it takes the car to stop once the brakes have been applied.

Revise the factors affecting braking on page 179.

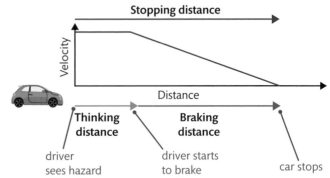

Figure 1 A graph showing the stopping distance of a car

(2) Factors affecting thinking distance

Thinking distance increases at higher speeds and when reaction time is slowed. Typical reaction times vary from 0.2 s to 0.9 s. Factors that can slow reaction time include:

- drinking alcohol
- taking drugs/medicine
- being tired
- poor visibility, e.g. due to fog
- distraction, e.g. using a mobile phone.

(5) Measuring reactions

Method 1
Reaction times can be measured using a stop clock. One person presses start and the other has to hit the stop button as quickly as possible.

Method 2
One person holds a ruler vertically while the other holds their finger and thumb at the bottom of the ruler. When the ruler is dropped they have to catch it. The slower their reactions, the more of the ruler passes through their fingers.

(5) Worked example — Grade 6

Explain why modern cars are built with crumple zones. **[3 marks]**

Force = change in momentum / time.
Crumple zones increase the time it takes
for a car to stop completely in an accident.
An increase in time reduces the force felt
by the passengers in the car.

(2) Momentum change

Because $F = \dfrac{(mv - mu)}{t}$, if a vehicle stops suddenly (that is, its momentum changes a lot over a very short period of time), a large force is required to stop the vehicle. Most vehicles are designed with crumple zones, which increase the time over which the momentum change takes place. This means a smaller force is needed to stop the vehicle.

Reducing the forces on passengers in the vehicle helps to reduce injuries to passengers.

(10) Exam-style practice — Grades 5–6

1. A driver's reaction time is 0.6 s. Calculate their thinking distance at 31 m/s (70 mph). **[1 mark]**

2. Using the table, compare and evaluate the two methods used for determining the reaction time of the student. **[3 marks]**

You need to use the equation that relates speed, distance and time. Go to page 169 to revise how to use this equation.

	Result 1	Result 2
Method 1 concentrating	0.31 s	0.35 s
Method 1 distracted	0.60 s	0.64 s
Method 2 concentrating	10 cm	15 cm
Method 2 distracted	24 cm	28 cm

Factors affecting braking distance

You need to know how to calculate braking distance and the factors that affect it.

 Factors affecting braking distance

Factors such as greater speed and greater mass increase the kinetic energy, which means there is more work for the brakes to do. The vehicle therefore travels further before it stops.

The following factors reduce friction and brake force:

- mass of the vehicle
- speed of the vehicle
- condition of the vehicle's brakes
- condition of the road (loose, wet, icy, rough)
- the condition of the tyres on the vehicle.

The energy of braking

Brakes use friction to do work and stop the vehicle. This energy is transferred to thermal energy in the brakes. If the brakes overheat, they may not function as well.

Go to page 178 to revise stopping distances.

Braking distances vary from 6 m at a lower speed of 9 m/s up to 96 m at a higher speed of 31 m/s. That is why when travelling faster or in conditions that make the braking distance longer, drivers need to leave larger gaps between them and the vehicle in front. Cars decelerate in emergencies at ~ 3–5 m/s². Rapid deceleration can cause the car to skid and the driver to lose control.

Worked example | **Grade 5**

Look at **Figure 1**.

1 **(a)** Calculate the stopping distance when the car is travelling at a speed of 25 m/s. **[2 marks]**

thinking + braking = stopping
distance   distance   distance

17 + 46 = 63 m

(b) The car accelerates so it is now travelling at 30 m/s. Will the stopping distance be higher or lower than that calculated in part **(a)**? Give a reason for your answer. **[2 marks]**

Higher because the thinking distance and braking distance increase with speed.

2 A driver brakes over a long period of time while driving down a hill. Explain why this could be dangerous. **[2 marks]**

Friction causes brakes to heat up as they are used. As the brakes get hotter they apply less friction so the brakes are not as effective.

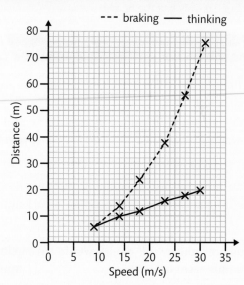

Figure 1 A graph showing the effect of speed on stopping distance for a car

As the speed increases, the thinking distance increases in direct proportion to speed.

The braking distance depends on speed squared, because the kinetic energy of the vehicle depends on speed squared.

Exam-style practice | **Grades 5–6**

1 A car has a mass of 1200 kg and is travelling at 25 m/s. It takes 40 m to stop. Calculate the braking force. **[2 marks]**

2 Explain the effect that doubling the speed of a vehicle has on braking and thinking distances. **[2 marks]**

Gravitational potential energy

You need to be able to calculate the change in gravitational potential energy of an object when it is raised or lowered in the Earth's gravitational field.

② Calculating GPE

The gravitational potential energy (GPE) of an object, measured in joules (J), depends on its mass, its height and the **gravitational field strength**.

It can be calculated using the equation:

change in = mass × gravitational field × change in
GPE (J)   (kg)   strength (N/kg)   vertical height (m)

$\Delta GPE = mg\Delta h$

The gravitational field strength of Earth is 10 N/kg.

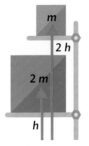

Figure 1 Both of these boxes have the same gravitational potential energy. The bottom box has twice the mass of the top box, but has only half the height.

② Kinetic energy

work done = change in GPE   GPE ⟶ kinetic energy

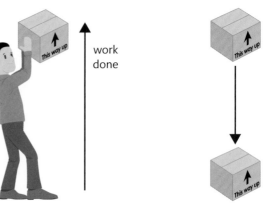

Figure 2 Lifting and dropping a box

To lift the box, the GPE is equal to the work done in lifting it. When dropped, the GPE is transferred to kinetic energy as it falls. The kinetic energy upon hitting the ground is equal to the GPE it had at the top.

⑩ Worked example   Grades 5–6

A lift full of people has a mass of 550 kg.
($g = 10$ N/kg).

(a) Calculate the GPE gained by the lift if it moves upwards 20 m.   **[2 marks]**

$\Delta GPE = mg\Delta h = 550 \times 10 \times 20 = 110\,000$ J

(b) State how the answer would be different if the lift had carried fewer people.   **[1 mark]**

GPE would have been smaller.

(c) Find how much GPE the lift would have gained if it only went up 10 m.   **[1 mark]**

$110\,000 \div 2 = 55\,000$ J

(d) Some passengers get off, and the lift moves up another 10 m. It gains 40 000 J of GPE. Calculate the new mass of the lift and its passengers.   **[3 marks]**

$m = \dfrac{\Delta GPE}{g\Delta h} = \dfrac{40\,000}{10 \times 10} = 400$ kg

g = 10 N/kg from the question stem.

Maths skills

When putting this into your calculator remember to use brackets on the (10 × 10) on the bottom of the fraction.

The GPE depends on mass. If there are fewer people, there will be less mass so the change in GPE will be smaller.

Notice that the height is half, therefore the GPE will be half.

⑮ Exam-style practice   Grades 5–6

1 Calculate the energy in the gravitational potential energy store for a 70 kg rock climber 100 m up a cliff. ($g = 10$ N/kg)   **[2 marks]**

2 If the same rock climber only has 50 000 J of GPE, calculate their height.   **[2 marks]**

3 Use the idea of energy transfer to explain:
   (a) why the speed of a ball increases as it falls   **[2 marks]**
   (b) why something dropped from a greater height will hit the ground faster.   **[2 marks]**

4 (a) A crane lifts a crate 20 m and the crate gains 1000 J of GPE. Calculate how much more GPE it will gain if it is lifted a further 40 m.   **[2 marks]**
   (b) State how much work the crane has done in each case.   **[2 marks]**

 Made a start   Feeling confident   Exam ready

Kinetic energy

All moving objects have kinetic energy. You should be able to work out the kinetic energy of a moving object.

 ② Calculating *KE*

kinetic energy (J) = 0.5 × mass (kg) × (speed)^2 (m/s)^2

$$KE = \frac{1}{2} \times m \times v^2$$

Doubling the mass will double the kinetic energy.

As the speed is squared, doubling the speed will make the kinetic energy four times larger.

② Key equations

Finding mass

$$m = \frac{KE}{\frac{1}{2}v^2}$$

Finding speed

Rearrange for v^2 first: $v^2 = \dfrac{KE}{\frac{1}{2}m}$

then square root both sides: $v = \sqrt{\dfrac{KE}{\frac{1}{2}m}}$

Maths skills

40 m/s is two times the speed. The kinetic energy will be $2^2 = 4$ times larger.

60 m/s is three times the speed. The kinetic energy will be $3^2 = 9$ times larger.

When putting the numbers in your calculator, make sure you use brackets for the numbers on the bottom of the fraction and that only the speed is squared:

200 000 ÷ (0.5 × 20^2)

Remember to square root the whole answer.

⑮ Worked example **Grades 5–6**

When travelling at 20 m/s a vehicle has 200 000 J of kinetic energy.

(a) Calculate the kinetic energy at 40 m/s and 60 m/s. **[3 marks]**

At 40 m/s: 200 000 × 4 = 800 000 J

At 60 m/s: 200 000 × 9 = 1 800 000 J

(b) Calculate the mass of the vehicle. **[3 marks]**

$$m = \frac{KE}{\frac{1}{2}v^2} = \frac{200\,000}{0.5 \times 20^2} = 1000 \text{ kg}$$

(c) Calculate how fast the vehicle is moving if it stores 12 500 J of kinetic energy. **[3 marks]**

$$v = \sqrt{\frac{KE}{\frac{1}{2}m}} = \sqrt{\frac{12\,500}{0.5 \times 1000}} = \sqrt{25} = 5 \text{ m/s}$$

(d) A car requires more fuel to do the same journey when fully loaded with passengers than with no passengers. Explain why. **[3 marks]**

It will have greater mass, so a higher kinetic energy (for the same speeds). At higher masses, the engine has to do more work to reach the same speed. Chemical energy stored in the fuel is transferred to the kinetic energy store of the car, so the increase in energy stored means more fuel used.

 ② Energy transfers

If you do 500 J of work to move something, you transfer 500 J of kinetic energy. It will also take 500 J of work to stop it from moving. If it stops due to friction, then it has done 500 J of work against friction.

500 J work done → 500 J kinetic energy

Figure 1 Moving a trolley

 ⑩ Exam-style practice **Grades 5–6**

1 (a) Calculate the kinetic energy of a 1200 kg car travelling at 20 m/s. **[2 marks]**

(b) Determine how much work the brakes will have to do to stop the car. **[1 mark]**

2 A car and a van are driving on a straight road. The van has twice the mass of the car, but the car travels at twice the speed. Compare their kinetic energies. **[2 marks]**

3 (a) Calculate the mass of a horse with 12 000 J of kinetic energy travelling at 8 m/s. **[2 marks]**

(b) Determine how fast the horse is travelling if it has 17 000 J of kinetic energy. **[2 marks]**

 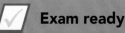

Conservation of energy

A system is an object or group of objects. When there are energy changes in a closed system there is no net change to the total energy in that system.

 Principle of conservation of energy

Energy is either transferred usefully, stored or dissipated. Energy cannot be created or destroyed.

This means the total amount of energy in any closed system remains constant. Where energy appears to be 'lost', it is usually being wasted. Energy can be transferred by heating, forces and an electric current.

Catching a ball
kinetic → thermal
A moving object hitting an obstacle transfers kinetic energy to thermal energy.

Archer shooting an arrow into the air
chemical (from muscles) → strain potential (stored in the bow) → kinetic (as arrow flies) → gravitational potential energy (as arrow goes up) → kinetic (as arrow falls back down) → thermal
Some energy would be wasted as thermal energy due to work done against air resistance as the arrow moves.

A boat constantly accelerating
chemical → kinetic and thermal
The boat gains kinetic energy as it accelerates, and thermal energy due to more work being done against the resistance of water on the boat.

Energy transfers
(Wasted forms of energy are underlined.)

Vehicle braking
kinetic → thermal
The friction in the brakes transfers thermal energy.

Electric kettle
electrical → thermal
Energy is transferred by heating to boil the water.

 Reducing energy losses

Energy is transferred to thermal energy when work is done against friction in moving parts. Friction can be reduced by lubricating moving parts, reducing the amount of energy wasted.

Thermal energy is often a wasted energy in electrical circuits. The wasted energy can be reduced by using low currents or decreasing the resistance of the circuit.

Thermal energy is wasted in many buildings as it can be conducted through the walls. The lower the thermal conductivity and the thicker the walls, the less energy wasted. Many types of building insulation are thick and contain trapped air. Air has poor thermal conductivity, which reduces the rate of wasted thermal energy being transferred from the building.

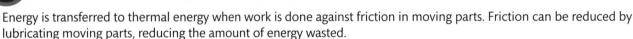

 Exam-style practice — Grades 4–5

1 Describe the energy transfers for:
  (a) a horse galloping at constant speed   **[1 mark]**
  (b) a firework launching upwards at constant speed   **[1 mark]**
  (c) a car moving at constant speed.   **[1 mark]**

2 Identify how energy is wasted in a coal power station and suggest how it can be reduced.   **[2 marks]**

3 Explain how thick woolly jumpers reduce the amount of thermal energy being transferred to the surroundings.   **[3 marks]**

Efficiency

Efficiency is a measure of how much of an energy transfer is used usefully. The more efficient something is, the less energy it wastes. You need to be able to calculate efficiency and comment on how efficient something is.

② Calculating efficiency

You can calculate efficiency using the equation:

$$\text{efficiency} = \frac{\text{useful energy transferred by device (J)}}{\text{total energy supplied to device (J)}}$$

Efficiency can also be calculated as a percentage:

$$\text{efficiency (\%)} = \frac{\text{useful energy transferred by device}}{\text{total energy supplied to device}} \times 100$$

Energy is normally measured in joules. As long as the units for both output and input are the same the calculation will work, for example, if both output and input energy are in MJ.

② Efficiency: key facts

- ✓ Efficiency does not have any units.
- ✓ The first equation will give you a result between 0 and 1.
- ✓ The closer to 1 (or 100%), the more efficient the process and the less energy is wasted.
- ✓ If something is 65% efficient, 65% of the energy is used usefully and 35% is wasted.

> If your answer is higher than 100% or 1, you have substituted the numbers into the equation the wrong way round.

⑩ Worked example — Grade 5

A power station produces 150 000 kJ of electrical energy per second and uses chemical energy in coal at a rate of 380 000 000 J per second.

(a) Assuming all other energy is wasted as thermal energy, state how much energy is wasted. **[2 marks]**

380 000 kJ − 150 000 kJ = 230 000 kJ

> Remember, watts are joules per second (page 205), so the rate of use of chemical energy in coal can be given in watts. Convert this to kJ so the units match.
> 380 000 000 J ÷ 1000 = 380 000 kJ

> All of the 380 000 kJ that is taken in must be given out. 150 000 kJ comes out as electrical energy every second, so whatever is left must be the thermal energy.

(b) Calculate the efficiency of the power station. **[2 marks]**

$$\text{efficiency} = \frac{150\,000}{380\,000} = 0.39$$

> The calculation uses the values for useful energy transferred in one second divided by total energy supplied in one second, so the time values cancel.

(c) In a load of coal, there is 250 kJ of energy. Calculate how much electrical energy this will produce. **[2 marks]**

useful energy transferred by the device =
efficiency × total energy supplied to the device
= 0.39 × 250 kJ = 97.5 kJ

> You need to use the efficiency from the previous answer and rearrange the equation for useful energy output.

(d) The power station recycles some of the lost heat to provide heating in the buildings. State why this improves its efficiency. **[1 mark]**

It increases the useful output of energy.

> Efficiency measures the proportion of energy that is used usefully. Efficiency is improved by reducing wasted energy or by making waste energy useful. You can review ways of reducing wasted energy on page 182.

⑩ Exam-style practice — Grades 4–6

1 A TV uses 400 J of energy and wastes 150 J. Calculate its efficiency. **[1 mark]**

2 A house's central heating is 85% efficient. State what **85% efficient** means. **[1 mark]**

3 Appliance A has an input of 100 J per second. Appliance B has an input of 50 J per second.
Explain which is more efficient if they both give out thermal energy at a rate of 35 J per second. **[2 marks]**

4 A heater transfers 2000 J of thermal energy. Find the input energy if it is 60% efficient. **[2 marks]**

5 Clockwork watches transfer elastic potential energy to kinetic energy. Some is lost heating the surroundings.
Suggest how a watchmaker reduces the energy lost. **[1 mark]**

Renewable energy resources

Renewable energy resources provide alternative sources of energy that will not run out or are easy to replace. They are used for heating, transport, or to generate electricity. You need to know the advantages and disadvantages of renewable energy resources.

One advantage of all renewable resources is that none of them produce carbon dioxide when generating electricity and so do not contribute to global warming. They help to reduce overall emissions of carbon dioxide.

 Comparison of renewable resources

Renewable resource	Advantages	Disadvantages
Sun – can directly warm buildings and water supplies, or sunlight can be used to generate electricity using solar panels	👍 free energy once installed 👍 low maintenance costs (no moving parts) 👍 works anywhere	👎 only works when the sun shines 👎 low power output
Biofuels – fuel for transport or electricity is made from vegetable oil, alcohol, wood, methane or waste	👍 reliable 👍 high power output	👎 fuel crops can drive up the cost of food 👎 environmental impact if forests cleared to make room for crops
Wind – wind turbines generate electricity	👍 can be placed in isolated locations 👍 free energy once installed, but some maintenance costs	👎 danger to birds if badly placed 👎 noisy 👎 spoil landscape 👎 only work when it is windy 👎 cannot be used in storms
Hydroelectricity – water movement rotates turbines to generate electricity	👍 reliable 👍 high power output 👍 small waterwheels work in some isolated locations 👍 free energy once installed, but some maintenance costs	👎 building dams can flood valleys, which destroys habitats
Tides – the daily movement of the ocean is used to generate electricity	👍 reliable 👍 high power output 👍 free energy once installed, but has maintenance costs	👎 flooding river estuaries can destroy habitats

 Worked example   Grade 5

An Arctic scientific base wants to power their camp using only solar cells. Give the advantages and disadvantages of this idea.   **[5 marks]**

It is a good idea in summer because solar cells are portable so they are easily moved and can be set up anywhere. It will not work in winter as it does not get light and so no electricity would be produced through the winter. The power outputs are quite low.

 Exam-style practice   Grade 5

1 Sugar cane is worth more as ethanol for fuel than as food. Explain why this could cause problems.   **[2 marks]**

2 Wind and hydroelectricity are renewable energy sources. Discuss the reliability of each power source.   **[2 marks]**

3 Biofuels can be used to generate electricity. State one advantage and one disadvantage of using biofuels to generate electricity.   **[4 marks]**

Non-renewable energy resources

Non-renewable energy resources, such as fossil fuels and nuclear power (nuclear energy from atoms), are used to generate electricity. You need to be able to compare the ways in which renewable and non-renewable resources are used.

② Non-renewable resources

People use fossil fuels directly by:

- burning coal, oil or natural gas to heat their homes or cook food
- using petrol or diesel in their cars.

People use fossil fuels or nuclear power indirectly when using electricity. The majority of electricity in the UK is generated from non-renewable resources, mainly natural gas.

② Three issues around supply

1. If non-renewable energy resources run out, people will have to find other ways to produce energy.

2. Oil has many other uses, such as producing plastics. If oil runs out, people would have to find alternatives for these other uses.

3. Burning fossil fuels produces carbon dioxide that is released into the atmosphere. Increased levels of carbon dioxide in the atmosphere contribute to global warming.

⑤ Comparing nuclear and fossil fuels

	Nuclear power	Fossil fuels
Advantages	👍 Other than steam, no gases are emitted. There is no effect on global warming or health. 👍 Small amounts of fuel produce large amounts of energy. 👍 Nuclear fuel will last much longer than fossil fuels and nuclear power stations do not release carbon dioxide.	👍 The fuels are relatively low cost. 👍 Fossil fuel power stations can be started up very quickly (especially gas). It is easy to adapt to changing power demands.
Disadvantages	👎 The nuclear waste stays radioactive for thousands of years and has to be safely stored. 👎 Transport of radioactive fuel and waste is dangerous and costly. 👎 Nuclear power plants are costly to decommission. 👎 Accidents can release radioactive substances into the environment. 👎 Nuclear power stations take a very long time to start up and shut down.	👎 Carbon dioxide, a greenhouse gas, is produced, which contributes to global warming. 👎 Burning fossil fuels produces more pollution, not just carbon dioxide but sulfur dioxide, carbon soot and smoke. 👎 Sulfur dioxide and smoke can cause breathing problems. 👎 A large amount of fuel needs to be transported with coal. Coal is much less efficient.

② Worked example — Grade 5

Suggest whether using an electric car is more environmentally friendly than using a petrol car.

[2 marks]

The electricity for electric cars is generated from either renewable or non-renewable sources. If the source is non-renewable, greenhouse gases and smoke are still produced, but at a power plant, so pollution around busy roads is reduced.

⑩ Exam-style practice — Grade 5

1. Compare the advantages and disadvantages of nuclear and coal-fired power stations.

[4 marks]

2. The UK is moving to using more renewable rather than non-renewable resources.
Suggest **four** reasons for this trend. **[4 marks]**

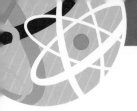

Types of wave

All waves are either transverse or longitudinal. You need to know the differences between these two types of wave.

[5] Longitudinal waves

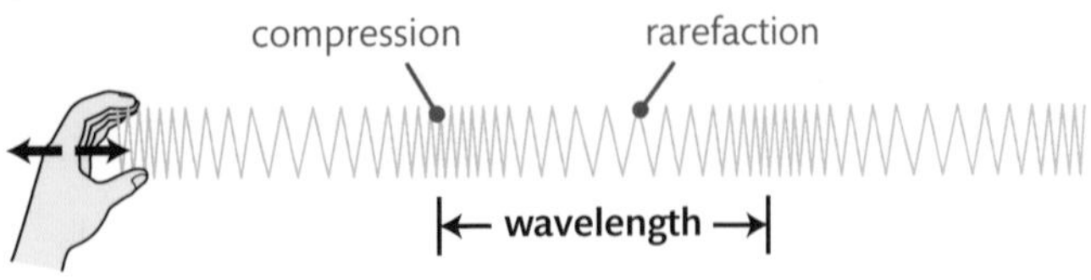

Figure 1 Longitudinal waves

A **wavelength** is measured from the centre of one compression to the next.

For **longitudinal waves**, vibrations of the particles in the wave are parallel to the direction of movement of the wave (or energy transfer).

There are no **peaks** or **troughs**. Instead, the wave has **compressions** (for sound, this means regions of high pressure), where particles are close together and **rarefactions** (regions of low pressure), where the particles are more spread out.

Examples:

- sound (in any medium)
- seismic P waves in earthquakes
- a slinky being pushed and pulled.

Measuring the speed of sound in air

Measure the distance to a large wall that reflects sound.

Clap and use a stop watch to time how long it takes for the echo to be heard. The wave has travelled the distance to the wall twice so:

$$\text{wave speed (m/s)} = \frac{\text{distance to wall (m)} \times 2}{\text{times (s)}}$$

[5] Transverse waves

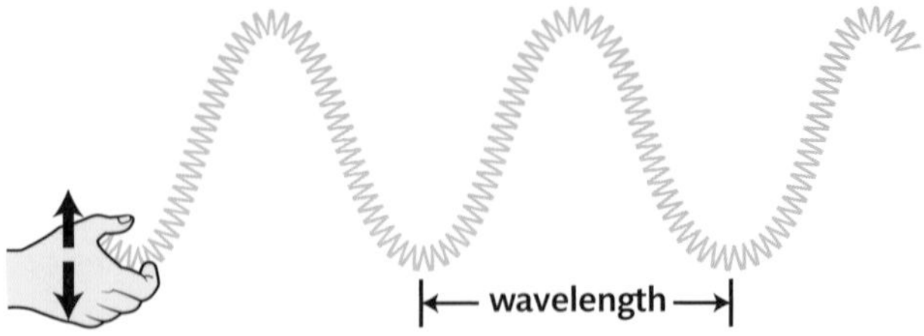

Figure 2 Transverse waves

For **transverse waves**, the vibrations of the particles are perpendicular to the direction of the wave (or energy transfer).

Examples:

- ripples on water
- a slinky being shaken
- seismic S waves in earthquakes
- light (and all electromagnetic waves).

Measuring the speed of ripples on water

Lay a ruler flat on the bottom of a ripple tank so the ripples pass over it.

Measure the time it takes for a ripple to travel the length of the ruler.

$$\text{wave speed} = \frac{\text{distance}}{\text{time}}$$

Alternatively, set the frequency of the ripples using a signal generator attached to the motor and measure the distance between the ripples.

wave speed = frequency × wavelength

[2] Waves transfer energy

Place a piece of paper on a slinky and create the two types of wave. Notice that the paper moves back and forth or up and down, but it does not move along the wave. This shows that waves do not transport material from one place to another. They only transfer energy by vibrations in the material.

[2] Worked example — Grade 5

A seagull floats on the sea. As waves pass, the gull bobs up and down but not forwards. Explain what this shows about ocean waves. **[2 marks]**

Ocean waves are transverse as they transfer mass perpendicular to the direction of the wave. It also demonstrates that the water itself is not travelling as the wave travels.

[15] Exam-style practice — Grades 4–5

1. A student wants to investigate the speed of sound. They stand 50 m away from a large building. The student claps their hands and uses a stop watch to time how long it takes for an echo to be heard. Explain how they could use their results to determine the speed of sound. **[3 marks]**
2. A student is trying to measure the speed of sound in air, using the method described in question 1. They stand in the playground and measure the time it takes for the echo to reach them from the side of the sports hall. Give the most significant source of error in this experiment and suggest how it could be improved. **[2 marks]**
3. Explain why sound cannot pass through a vacuum. **[2 marks]**

Properties of waves

A wave transfers energy without transferring matter. You need to understand the properties of waves.

(10) Parts of a wave

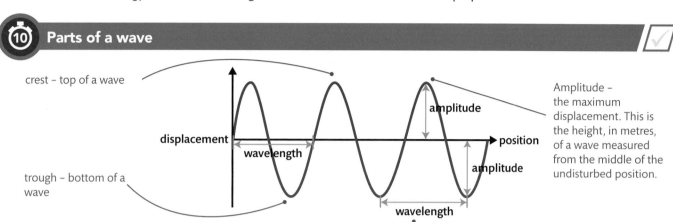

crest – top of a wave

amplitude

displacement

wavelength

position

Amplitude – the maximum displacement. This is the height, in metres, of a wave measured from the middle of the undisturbed position.

trough – bottom of a wave

amplitude

wavelength

Wavelength, λ – the length of one complete wave. It can be measured from anywhere on the wave to the next equivalent point, but crest to crest or trough to trough are the easiest to find and measure.

Figure 1 A wave

- **Wavelength**, λ, is measured in metres, but may be given in centimetres depending on the type and size of wave.
- Time period, or just **period**, T, is the time to complete one full cycle or wave, measured in seconds, s.
- **Wave velocity**, v, is the speed that energy is transferred (or the wave moves) through the medium, measured in m/s.
- **Frequency**, f, is the number of waves passing a point per second, measured in hertz, Hz.
- **Wave front** is a line on which the vibration of all points on it are in phase and at the same distance from the source.

(2) Wave behaviour

All waves exhibit certain behaviours. For example, all waves can be:

- absorbed
- transmitted
- refracted
- reflected.

Refraction happens when a wave passes through a boundary between different materials. If a wave passes from air into glass, it will slow down as waves travel at different speeds in different media. The greater the difference in speed, the greater the refraction.

The wavelength of a wave will determine how it is reflected, refracted, transmitted or absorbed by different substances.

(5) Key equations

- $\checkmark$ wave speed (m/s) = frequency (Hz) × wavelength (m)
  $$v = f\lambda$$
- $\checkmark$ speed (m/s) = $\dfrac{\text{distance (m)}}{\text{time (s)}}$
  $$v = \frac{s}{t}$$

(2) Worked example Grades 6–7

(a) It takes 1.51 s for a sound to travel 500 m.
Calculate the speed of sound. **[2 marks]**

$$speed = \frac{distance}{time} = \frac{500}{1.51} = 331\,m/s$$

(b) The sound has a frequency of 100 Hz.
Calculate its wavelength. **[2 marks]**

wave speed = frequency × wavelength
331 m/s = 100 Hz × wavelength
wavelength = 331 ÷ 100 = 3.31 m

(15) Exam-style practice Grade 7

1 It takes 0.03 s for a sound to travel 174 m in steel. Calculate the speed of sound in steel. **[2 marks]**

2 The speed of sound in water is 1500 m/s. Calculate how long it will take the sound made by a fish to reach a shark that is 2 km away. **[2 marks]**

3 20 ripples on a pond are measured to be 15 cm long in total and take 5 s to pass a point. Calculate the frequency, period and wave speed of these ripples. **[3 marks]**

Practical: Investigating waves

These practicals investigate the speed, frequency and wavelength of waves in a ripple tank and in solids.

(10) Waves in a ripple tank

1 Time how long it takes for one wave to travel from the paddle to the edge of the ripple tank.

2 Measure the distance.

3 Calculate the wave speed.

$$\text{wave speed (m/s)} = \frac{\text{distance (m)}}{\text{time (s)}}$$

4 Time 10 rotations of the motor and divide by 10 to get the period. Calculate the frequency.

$$\text{frequency (Hz)} = \frac{1}{\text{period (s)}}$$

5 Calculate the wavelength.

$$\text{wavelength (m)} = \frac{\text{wave speed (m/s)}}{\text{frequency (Hz)}}$$

6 Alternatively, hold a ruler next to the water and try to estimate the distance from one ripple to the next.

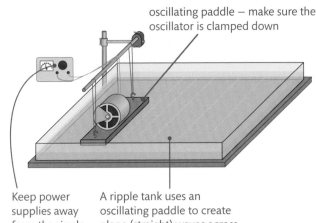

oscillating paddle — make sure the oscillator is clamped down

Keep power supplies away from the ripple tank.

A ripple tank uses an oscillating paddle to create plane (straight) waves across shallow water.

Figure 1 Using a ripple tank to measure the speed of waves

(10) Waves on a string

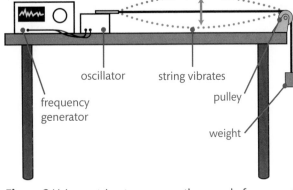

frequency generator

oscillator   string vibrates

pulley

weight

Figure 2 Using a string to measure the speed of waves

1 Using the frequency generator attached to the oscillator, adjust the frequency until you get a wave on the string as shown.

2 Read the frequency from the frequency generator.

3 Measure the length, L, of the string from oscillator to pulley. This is half a wavelength, so $\lambda = 2L$.

4 Calculate wave speed using:

$$\text{wave speed (m/s)} = \text{frequency (Hz)} \times \text{wavelength (m)}$$

You could use a wire instead of string.

(2) Worked example   Grade 6

A student uses a camera to help them to carry out Step 6 in the 'ripple tank' practical described above. Explain how this will affect the accuracy of their results.   **[2 marks]**

The accuracy should improve. It is difficult to measure a distance when the object is moving. If they take a photograph of a ruler next to the waves, they will obtain a more accurate wavelength.

(1) Working scientifically

- Wear goggles if you use wire.
- Keep clear of hanging weights.

(5) Exam-style practice   Grade 7

Explain the advantages of using a datalogger rather than a stopwatch in measuring time in the experiment at the top of this page.   **[2 marks]**

  Made a start   **Feeling confident** **Exam ready**

Types of electromagnetic waves

Waves on the electromagnetic spectrum are continuous but are grouped according to their wavelength and frequency. You need to know the properties of electromagnetic waves.

(10) Properties of electromagnetic waves

Electromagnetic (EM) waves have properties that depend on their wavelength. All waves on the electromagnetic spectrum are transverse and transfer energy from the source to an absorber. All electromagnetic waves travel at the same speed through a vacuum or air.

Radio waves are produced by vibrations of electrons in electrical circuits. They have low energy so are harmless.

Microwaves have slightly higher energy than radio waves. They can cause a heating effect in water and internal heating of body cells.

Infrared radiation is thermal energy travelling as a wave. It is emitted from hot objects. It can burn skin.

Visible light is seen as different colours by the human eye depending on its wavelength.

Ultraviolet (UV) light is present in sunlight. It is linked to premature ageing and skin cancer.

X-rays pass through soft tissue but are absorbed by denser bones.

Gamma rays are produced by changes to the nucleus of an atom.

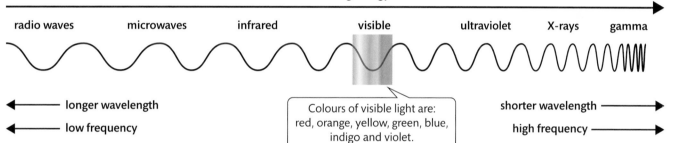

Colours of visible light are: red, orange, yellow, green, blue, indigo and violet.

Figure 1 Electromagnetic waves

The harmful effects of radiation depend on the type of radiation. X-rays and gamma rays are ionising radiation. Ionising radiation can change genes, which can cause cancers and kill cells.

EM waves are often produced over a large range of frequencies by changes to atoms, such as nuclear processes or electrons moving. When EM waves are absorbed, they can cause changes; for example, they can cause electrons to move, or even be lost from an atom. When radio waves are absorbed they can create an alternating current with the same frequency as the radio wave. They can induce oscillations in an electrical circuit.

The speed of light is 3×10^8 m/s (300 000 000 m/s)
You can use the wave equation $v = f\lambda$.
wave speed (m/s) = frequency (Hz) $\times$ wavelength (m)

(2) Worked example — Grade 5

The wavelength of visible light ranges from 4×10^{-7} m to 7×10^{-7} m. Calculate the frequencies of visible light. **[2 marks]**

$f = \dfrac{v}{\lambda} = \dfrac{3 \times 10^8}{4 \times 10^{-7}} = 7.5 \times 10^{14}$ Hz

$f = \dfrac{v}{\lambda} = \dfrac{3 \times 10^8}{7 \times 10^{-7}} = 4.3 \times 10^{14}$ Hz

(15) Exam-style practice — Grades 4–5

1. Give **two** examples that show that electromagnetic waves transfer energy. **[2 marks]**

2. Give some risks posed by sunbathing. **[2 marks]**

3. Explain why hospitals use X-rays despite the risk of cell damage. **[2 marks]**

4. The maximum yearly dose for people working with radiation is 50 millisieverts (mSv). A patient having an X-ray receives a 0.1 mSv dose.

   (a) Calculate the maximum number of X-rays a patient would be allowed to have in one year. **[2 marks]**

   (b) Explain why a patient would be advised to have far fewer than this. **[1 mark]**

Made a start | Feeling confident | Exam ready | 189

Properties of electromagnetic waves

When electromagnetic waves are incident on a surface they can be reflected, refracted, absorbed or transmitted. You need to be able to predict the effect depending on the substance and the wavelength of the electromagnetic wave.

 Properties of electromagnetic radiation ✓

We know that there are sound waves that we can't hear, for example ultrasound. The same is true for light waves. Our eyes are only able to detect a limited range of frequencies of electromagnetic radiation: visible light.

Electromagnetic radiation travels freely in a vacuum, but when it hits materials, it can be absorbed, transmitted, reflected or refracted.

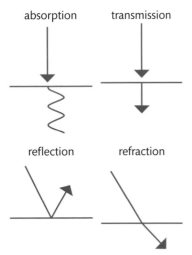

Figure 1 Absorption, transmission, reflection and refraction

Table 1 Properties of electromagnetic radiation

Absorption	When an electromagnetic wave passes into a medium, specific wavelengths of the wave are not transmitted through the material
Transmission	When an electromagnetic wave passes through a medium
Reflection	The 'bouncing back' of an electromagnetic wave from a surface
Refraction	The bending of a wave when it enters a medium and it changes speed

 Worked example Grade 5 ✓

Explain what happens to a ray of light shone at an angle into a glass block. **[2 marks]**

At the boundary between air and glass, the light wave would slow down as glass is more dense than air. This would cause the ray to bend towards the normal as a result of the change in speed.

 Wavefronts ✓

Wavefront diagrams are used to represent all types of waves in the way you might draw a diagram of ripples on water. When light waves hit glass, they slow down. The waves 'bunch up', making the wavelength smaller, but the frequency stays the same. When the wave hits at an angle, one side slows down first, so the wavefront bends and the wave changes direction.

The experiments you will do will most likely use only light waves, but remember that all waves in the electromagnetic spectrum will behave in this way.

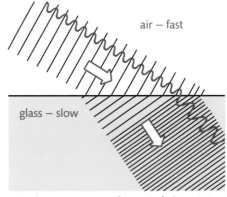
air – fast

glass – slow

Figure 2 As the wave passes from air (where it is travelling fast) into glass (where it travels more slowly), the wavelength decreases and the lines are closer together

 Exam-style practice Grades 5–6 ✓

1. Suggest what type of energy light is transferred to when it is absorbed by a surface. **[1 mark]**

2. Visible light is electromagnetic radiation that our eyes can detect.
   (a) State which colour of visible light has the longest wavelength. **[1 mark]**
   (b) State a part of the electromagnetic spectrum that has a higher frequency than that of visible light. **[1 mark]**

3. Window glass is transparent – it allows light to pass through it. The glass in windows transmits about 90% of the light that hits it. Explain what happens to the remaining 10% of the light. **[3 marks]**

4. A student says that when light hits a glass block with an incident angle of 0° it does not slow down, because it does not change direction. Explain whether or not the student is correct. **[2 marks]**

Practical: Investigating refraction

When light passes from one material to another, the velocity of the light wave changes. You need to know how to investigate refraction of a light wave when it interacts with an air-to-glass boundary.

⑮ Experiment to investigate refraction

1 Produce a narrow ray of light using a ray box and a slit.

2 In the centre of a sheet of paper, draw around a rectangular glass block using a pencil.

3 Draw a straight line perpendicular to the longer side of the block and label this 'N' for 'normal'.

4 Use the ray box to shine a ray of light at the point where the normal line meets the longer side of the glass block. Label this as the incident ray.

5 Measure the angle of incidence between the normal line and the incident ray. Record this in a suitable table.

6 Mark the path of the ray as it emerges from the block.

7 Remove the block and draw a line joining where the ray enters and leaves the glass block. Draw a new normal line where the light ray leaves the block.

8 Use this line to measure the angle of refraction. This is given by the angle between the joining line and the normal line.

9 Repeat the procedure for different angles of incidence.

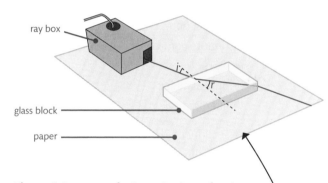

Figure 1 Apparatus for investigating refraction

⑤ Worked example Grade 5

When a light ray enters a glass block at an angle, it is refracted towards the normal.

Explain what this tells you about the speed of the wave the moment it enters the block. **[2 marks]**

The light ray has changed direction towards the normal as it enters the glass block, which means it has slowed down. This shows that light travels more slowly in glass than in air.

Working scientifically
Be careful: the ray box will get very hot. Disconnect it between experiments and allow it to cool down before you handle it.

⑤ Exam-style practice Grade 6

Refraction of waves can be investigated using a light ray and a rectangular glass block. In this investigation, different angles of incidence are used and the path of the light ray plotted through the block.

1 (a) Name the independent variable in this investigation. **[1 mark]**

(b) State one way in which the accuracy of the investigation could be improved. **[2 marks]**

2 Light travels at 300 000 000 m/s in air and approximately 200 000 000 m/s in glass. Use this information to explain why the light ray bends towards the normal when it passes through the air-to-glass boundary. **[3 marks]**

 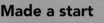

Applications of EM waves

Electromagnetic waves have many different uses. You should be able to explain why each type of electromagnetic wave is suited to its applications.

(15) Electromagnetic wave applications

Type of wave	Applications	Further details
radio waves	• broadcasting • communications • satellite transmissions	The frequency of radio waves allows them to be transformed into electrical signals when received by aerials, and allows aerials to emit radio waves using electrical signals.
microwaves	• cooking • communications • satellite transmissions	Microwaves are absorbed by water, so can be used to heat most food. They penetrate food up to about 1 cm, which means that they cook food faster than infrared.
infrared	• cooking • thermal imaging • short-range communications • optical fibres • remote controls and security systems	The frequency of infrared waves means that when an object absorbs them, its temperature increases.
visible light	• vision • photography • illumination	Visible light waves have a frequency that interacts with the rods and cones in the eyes, causing the retina to detect light. Fibre optic cables transmit information through internal refraction.
ultraviolet (UV)	• security marking • tanning • fluorescent lamps • detecting forged bank notes • disinfecting water	UV can penetrate skin cells and interact with pigments to cause tanning. UV can be absorbed by some substances, such as invisible ink, which then re-emit the energy as visible light. In strip lights, an electrified gas emits UV, which is absorbed by a powder that glows emitting visible light.
X-ray	• observing the internal structure of objects • airport security scanners • medical scans	X-rays can penetrate through soft materials like skin and suitcases. They are absorbed by dense materials like bones and metal. This makes them ideal for seeing inside bodies and luggage.
gamma	• sterilising food and medical equipment • detection of cancer • treatment of cancer	Gamma radiation is very high energy and can kill cells and bacteria easily. As it can penetrate through most materials, a weak source can be used for medical scans and large doses can target cancer cells deep within the body.

(1) Walkie-talkies

radio wave emitted ──────➤ radio wave absorbed

electrical signal causes electrons to vibrate

electrons vibrate, creating an electrical signal

Figure 1 Radio waves

> Notice how the potential danger of electromagnetic waves increases with increasing frequency.

(2) Worked example — Grade 6

Suggest why the police might use a thermal-imaging camera to find a person. **[2 marks]**

It can pick up infrared radiation from a person's body, even if it is night time or they are hidden.

(10) Exam-style practice — Grades 5–6

1. Give an example of each type of wave used for communication. **[3 marks]**

2. Explain why any electrical equipment might cause interference with a radio. **[2 marks]**

Made a start | Feeling confident | Exam ready

The structure of an atom

You need to know the structure of an atom, in terms of electrons, protons and neutrons.

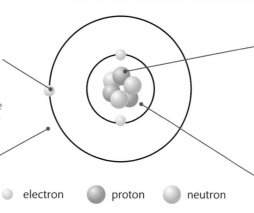

Electrons have a negative charge and occupy energy levels (electron shells) around the nucleus. Electrons orbit the nucleus in shells at set distances from the nucleus. Electrons are very small and have a tiny mass, but occupy most of the volume of the atom. This means the atom is mostly empty space.

Atoms contain equal numbers of electrons and protons. The charges balance, so atoms are neutral.

The number of protons in an atom determines what element it is. An atom is carbon if it has six protons. If it had seven, it would be nitrogen.

The **nucleus** contains positive protons and neutral neutrons. It contains most of the mass, but its radius is one ten-thousandth of the radius of the atom. Protons and neutrons have similar masses.

⚪ electron ⚪ proton ⚪ neutron

Figure 1 Atoms are around 1×10^{-10} m in radius. Small molecules are usually 2 or 3 atoms big, so approximately 3×10^{-10} m in diameter.

Table 1 Mass and charges of particles

	Particle			
	proton	neutron	electron	positron
Relative mass	1	1	negligible	negligible
Relative charge	+1	0	−1	+1

An atom is 1×10^{-10} m in diameter. Calculate how many atoms would fit across a needle point that is 0.1 mm wide. **[2 marks]**

$0.1 \div 1000 = 1 \times 10^{-4}$ m

Number of atoms $= 1 \times 10^{-4}$ m $\div 1 \times 10^{-10}$ m
$= 1\,000\,000$

When electrons absorb electromagnetic radiation, they absorb the energy and move to a higher energy level further away from the nucleus.

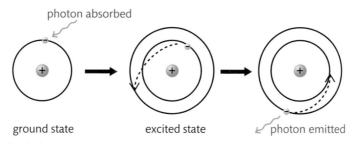

photon absorbed

ground state   excited state   photon emitted

Figure 2 As the electron drops back down to its ground state, its original energy level, it emits electromagnetic radiation.

1 A magnesium atom has 12 protons. How many electrons does it have? Explain your answer. **[2 marks]**

2 A student says that if you break a magnesium atom in half, you get two smaller magnesium atoms. Is this statement true? Explain your answer. **[3 marks]**

3 State **two** differences between electrons and protons. **[2 marks]**

4 State **two** similarities between protons and neutrons. **[2 marks]**

Mass number, atomic number and isotopes

Every element has a mass number and an atomic number. You can use these numbers to work out how many protons and neutrons are in an element's nucleus.

Particles in an atom

number of neutrons = mass number − atomic number

$^{14}_{7}N$ has 7 protons and 7 neutrons (14 − 7). A nitrogen atom has 7 electrons.

$^{7}_{3}Li$ has 3 protons, 3 electrons and 4 neutrons (7 − 3).

$^{19}_{9}F$ has 9 protons, 9 electrons and 10 neutrons (19 − 9).

The mass number is equal to the total number of protons and neutrons.

$$^{14}_{7}N$$

The atomic number is equal to the number of protons.

Figure 1 An atomic symbol

Isotopes

Isotopes are atoms with the same atomic number (number of protons) but different mass numbers (protons + neutrons). As the number of protons is the same, this means there is a different number of neutrons.

Carbon $^{12}_{6}C$ has six protons and six neutrons. An atom is carbon only if it has six protons. Carbon $^{14}_{6}C$ is an isotope of carbon. It has six protons and eight neutrons. As $^{14}_{6}C$ has six protons, it is still carbon, but it is heavier because of the extra neutrons. The protons in the nucleus give the element its characteristic positive charge.

Ionisation

If an atom loses or gains electrons, it becomes charged. Charged atoms are called **ions**.

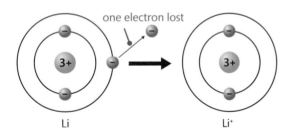

Li atom with 3 electrons   Li⁺ ion with only 2 electrons

Figure 2 If an atom loses one or more electrons, it becomes a positive ion.

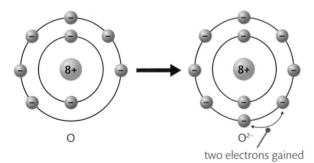

Figure 3 When an atom gains electrons, it becomes a negative ion.

Worked example — Grade 5

An ion has 14 protons, 14 neutrons and 12 electrons. State the atomic number, the mass number and the charge on the ion. **[2 marks]**

Atomic number 14, mass number 28. The neutral atom would have 14 electrons, so it has lost two, resulting in charge 2+.

Exam-style practice — Grade 5

1 State the number of particles in:
   (a) $^{9}_{4}Be$ **[1 mark]**
   (b) $^{7}_{3}Li$ **[1 mark]**
   (c) $^{56}_{26}Fe$ **[1 mark]**

2 State the number of electrons in:
   (a) Be^{2+} **[1 mark]**
   (b) Li^{+} **[1 mark]**
   (c) Fe^{3+} **[1 mark]**

3 The most common form of carbon has six protons, six neutrons and six electrons. State an example of how these numbers can change but the atom can remain a carbon atom. **[2 marks]**

Development of the atomic model

Scientists' theories about the atom changed as new experimental evidence was discovered. You need to know how the model of the atom has developed over time.

 Developing the model of the atom

1. Before electrons were discovered, it was thought that atoms were tiny spheres that could not be divided into anything else.

2. The **plum pudding model** was proposed by scientists who thought that the atom was like a positively-charged 'pudding', with electrons like 'plums' embedded in it.

3. Rutherford, Geiger and Marsden tested the plum pudding model by aiming a beam of positively-charged alpha particles at a very thin sheet of gold foil (scattering experiment). Some of the alpha particles were repelled by positively-charged particles that were concentrated in the centre of the atom (the nucleus). Most alpha particles passed through unaffected, showing that the nucleus was only a very small part of the atom. This evidence gave rise to the **nuclear model**.

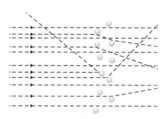

Rutherford's scattering experiment

4. Niels Bohr adapted the nuclear model. Using theoretical calculations alongside experimental observations, Bohr suggested that electrons travel in circular orbits around the nucleus. Further research showed that the nucleus was actually composed of smaller particles with equal amounts of positive charge. These became known as protons.

Approximately 20 years after the nuclear model became accepted, neutrons were discovered in the nucleus.

 Worked example　　**Grade 5**

Explain how the alpha particle scattering experiment showed that the mass of an atom is concentrated at the centre and that atoms are mostly empty space. **[2 marks]**

Most of the alpha particles passed straight through without hitting anything, showing that atoms are mostly empty space. Occasionally they were deflected or bounced back, showing they were repelled by the positive nucleus.

 Exam-style practice　　**Grades 5–6**

1 Describe the plum pudding model of the atom. **[3 marks]**

2 Give the differences between the plum pudding model and the nuclear model. **[2 marks]**

3 Describe how the results of the alpha scattering experiment would have been different if:

(a) the plum pudding model was correct **[2 marks]**

(b) the nuclear model was correct, but the nucleus was negatively charged. **[2 marks]**

4 A student suggests that the plum pudding model of the atom was wrong and that the nuclear model is correct. Do you agree? Explain your answer. **[3 marks]**

 Made a start　　 **Feeling confident**　　 **Exam ready**

Ionising radiation

In radioactive decay, atoms with unstable nuclei can emit alpha or beta particles, neutrons or gamma rays.

(5) Radioactive decay

Radioisotopes are atoms with unstable nuclei. An unstable nucleus will decay by emitting radiation. Decay is random; there is no way to tell which atom will decay next or when an atom will decay.

All radiation is emitted from the nucleus of the atom, not the outer part.

This radiation is known as **ionising radiation**. Ionising radiation can cause damage to cells that it comes into contact with. The bigger and more highly charged the particles, the more they can ionise and damage molecules in cells.

(5) Types of radiation

1 An alpha particle is the same as a helium nucleus. It contains 2 protons and 2 neutrons.

2 A beta particle is a fast-moving electron.

3 A gamma wave is a high frequency, short wavelength electromagnetic wave.

(10) Properties of radiation

Radiation	Particle	Charge	Ionisation power	Penetrative power
alpha	two protons, two neutrons (a helium nucleus)	+2	high	low
beta-minus	fast-moving electron (from the nucleus)	−1	medium	medium
beta-plus	positron	+1	medium	medium
gamma	electromagnetic wave	0	low	high
neutron	neutron	0	zero	very high

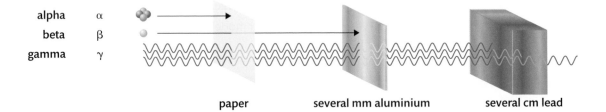

alpha	α
beta	β
gamma	γ

paper — several mm aluminium — several cm lead

(2) Worked example — Grade 5

Alpha particles cannot pass through the skin, but if a source of alpha particles is ingested, it can cause very serious health problems. Explain why alpha particles pose such a risk inside the body. **[2 marks]**

Alpha particles are the largest and most highly charged form of ionising radiation. This means that the ionising power of alpha particles is very high. If they are emitted inside the body, they can cause damage to cells within the body.

(10) Exam-style practice — Grade 7

1 Explain why alpha particles have a higher ionising power than beta particles or gamma rays. **[2 marks]**

2 Give a reason why alpha particles or gamma rays cannot be used to monitor the thickness of paper. **[2 marks]**

3 A tracer is a radioactive source injected into the blood. It can be detected outside the body and used in diagnosis. Suggest which type of radioactive source would be most suitable. **[2 marks]**

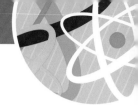

Background radiation

You need to know how ionising radiation can be detected, its units of measurement, and how background radiation affects measurements.

5 Detecting radiation

A **Geiger-Müller** (G-M) tube is used to detect ionising radiation by counting the ions formed in a chamber of low-pressure gas when radiation passes through it.

Radioactivity can also be measured using photographic film. For example, health workers who carry out X-ray scans wear a film badge dosimeter to measure the radiation they are exposed to when carrying out their job.

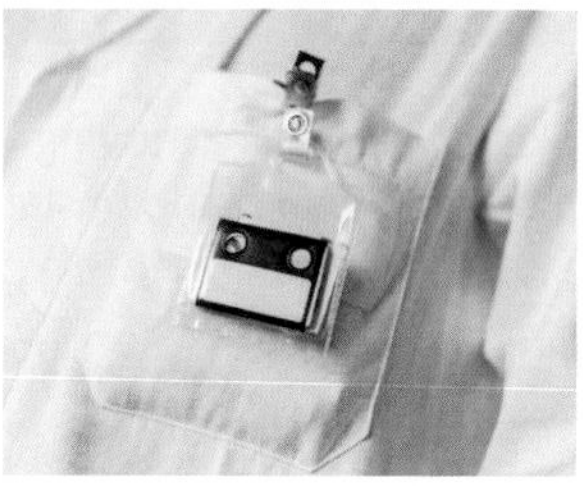

Figure 1 A film badge dosimeter measures radiation.

5 Measuring radiation

The **activity** is the rate at which atoms in a radioactive source decay. Activity is measured in becquerels (Bq). 1 Bq means 1 decay per second.

The **count rate** is the number of decays recorded per second by a detector such as a G-M tube.

5 Background radiation

Background radiation is radiation that is not due to a specific radioactive source. It comes from many sources, both from Earth and space, including food and drink, the air and the ground.

Radon is a gas given out by some rocks, such as granite. It emits alpha particles, and humans can inhale it. There are also cosmic rays from space that contribute to background radiation. Nuclear power stations and medical procedures also contribute to background radiation. In most places, the level of background radiation is low and so does not pose a serious risk to health.

There is always some background radiation present, so when you are measuring a count for a radioactive source, you must first measure the background count and then subtract it from your final measurement.

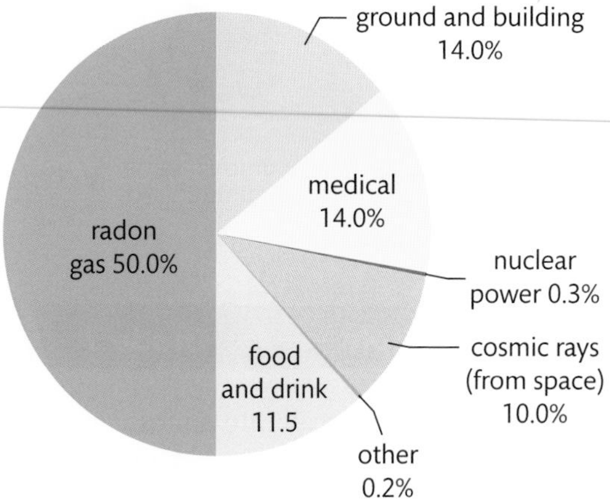
ground and building 14.0%
medical 14.0%
nuclear power 0.3%
cosmic rays (from space) 10.0%
other 0.2%
food and drink 11.5
radon gas 50.0%

Figure 2 Sources of background radiation

2 Worked example — Grade 7

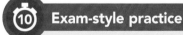

Suggest why the count rate measured by a G-M tube may be different from the activity of the source. **[2 marks]**

The activity is the number of decays per second in a sample but the count rate is the number of decays detected. The radiation goes in all directions so does not all hit the detector, and the radiation that does reach the detector might not all be detected, so the count rate will be less than the activity.

10 Exam-style practice — Grade 7

1. A student wishes to investigate the radioactivity of a source. She measures the background radiation using a G-M tube, which gives a reading of 2 Bq. When she places the source near to the G-M tube, the count rate increases to 50 Bq. Determine the activity of the source. **[2 marks]**

2. Radioactive sources need to be kept securely in a lead-lined box. Explain the potential dangers of leaving a gamma source out in the school laboratory. **[2 marks]**

Detecting and measuring radioactivity

Beta decay is one type of radioactive emission from an unstable nucleus.

β– decay

β– particles are electrons that are moving very fast. They are emitted from the nuclei of some unstable atoms when one of the neutrons changes into a proton and an electron.

Changes as a result of β– decay

The β– particle has a relative charge of –1. When it is emitted from the nucleus of an atom, the atomic number of the remaining atom increases by one because a new proton has formed.

However, the β– particle has negligible mass, so the mass number of the atom after emission of the β– particle remains the same.

Figure 1 β– decay

β+ decay

β+ particles are positrons. They have the same mass as an electron but a relative charge of +1. They are emitted from the nucleus of some unstable atoms when a proton changes into a neutron and a β+ particle.

Changes as a result of β+ decay

The β+ particle has a relative charge of +1. When it is emitted from the nucleus of an atom, the atomic number of the remaining atom decreases by one.

The β+ particle, just like the electron, has negligible mass, so the mass number of the atom after β+ emission remains the same.

Figure 2 β+ decay

$$\substack{\text{mass number} \\ \text{atomic number}} X \rightarrow \substack{\text{mass number} \\ \text{atomic number}} \substack{\text{same} \\ +1} Y + {}^{0}_{-1}\beta$$

Figure 3 β– decay

After the decay, the nucleus still has the same total number of protons and neutrons, so the mass number does not change. As there is an extra proton, the atomic number increases by one. This means that the nucleus is a new element.

Worked example Grade 7

A carbon-14 atom can decay into a nitrogen atom through beta decay. Write a balanced nuclear equation to show this decay. **[2 marks]**

$${}^{14}_{6}C \rightarrow {}^{14}_{7}N + {}^{0}_{-1}e$$

Notice how the atomic number of the nitrogen has increased by one and the mass number has remained the same.

The mass numbers and atomic numbers balance on each side of the equation:

$14 = 14 + 0$

$6 = 7 - 1$

Exam-style practice Grade 7

Carbon-11 is an isotope of carbon. It has 6 protons, 6 electrons and 5 neutrons.

Carbon-11 can decay into boron by β+ decay.

1 State the change in:

(a) atomic number **[1 mark]**

(b) mass number **[1 mark]**

when a ${}^{11}C$ nucleus undergoes β+ decay.

2 Write a balanced nuclear equation to show this decay. **[2 marks]**

Nuclear decay

When a nucleus undergoes radioactive decay, there may be changes to the atomic and/or mass number of the atom.

(5) Changes to the atomic and mass numbers

Type of decay		Change to atomic number	Change to mass number
alpha	α or $^{4}_{2}He$	decreases by 2	decreases by 4
beta-minus	$\beta-$ or $^{0}_{-1}e$	increases by 1	no change
beta-plus	$\beta+$ or $^{0}_{+1}e$	decreases by 1	no change
gamma	γ	no change	no change
neutron	$^{1}_{0}n$	no change	decreases by 1

(5) Alpha decay

When a nucleus undergoes **alpha decay**, it loses two protons and two neutrons. The mass number of the nucleus decreases by four and the atomic number and the charge on the nucleus decrease by two. The nucleus becomes a new element.

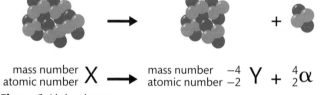

$$\begin{array}{c}\text{mass number} \\ \text{atomic number}\end{array} X \longrightarrow \begin{array}{c}\text{mass number} \quad -4 \\ \text{atomic number} \quad -2\end{array} Y + ^{4}_{2}\alpha$$

Figure 1 Alpha decay

Remember that these decays happen randomly. The products, or daughter nuclei, created may be radioactive isotopes that decay again.

(2) Gamma decay

Nuclei that have undergone alpha, $\beta-$ or $\beta+$ decay are often left in a high-energy unstable state and undergo nuclear rearrangement in order to make the remaining nucleus more stable. In this rearrangement, some energy is lost from the nucleus in the form of gamma radiation.

(2) Neutron decay

In **neutron decay**, a neutron is emitted from the nucleus. The mass decreases by 1 and another isotope of the same element is formed. For example, beryllium-13 decays to form beryllium-12 by emitting a neutron.

$$^{13}_{4}Be \rightarrow ^{12}_{4}Be + ^{1}_{0}n$$

In all nuclear decays, mass and charge are conserved.

(2) Worked example — Grade 8

Thorium-232 has 90 protons. It decays into radium-228, which has 88 protons.

State the type of nuclear decay and write a balanced nuclear equation for the process.

[3 marks]

The atomic number has decreased by 2 (90 to 88).

The mass number has decreased by 4 (232 to 228).

Therefore, the decay is alpha decay.

$$^{232}_{90}Th \rightarrow ^{228}_{88}Ra + ^{4}_{2}He$$

(10) Exam-style practice — Grade 7

1 Fill in the gaps.

(a) $^{239}_{94}Pu \rightarrow ^{\square}_{\square}U + ^{4}_{2}\_\_$ **[2 marks]**

(b) $^{16}_{5}B \rightarrow ^{\square}_{5}B + ^{1}_{0}\_\_$ **[2 marks]**

2 Uranium-238 ($^{238}_{92}U$) decays into thorium-234 ($^{234}_{90}Th$).

Write a balanced nuclear equation for the process. **[3 marks]**

3 Lead-212 ($^{212}_{82}Pb$) decays into bismuth-212 ($^{212}_{83}Bi$).

Write a balanced nuclear equation for the process. **[3 marks]**

4 Radon-222 ($^{222}_{86}Rn$) decays to polonium-218 ($^{218}_{84}Po$) and then to lead-214 ($^{214}_{82}Pb$) and finally to bismuth-214 ($^{214}_{83}Bi$). Write a balanced nuclear equation for each decay. **[6 marks]**

Half-lives

Half-life is a measure of how radioactive a source is. It can be anything from a fraction of a second to many thousands of years. You need to be able to determine a substance's half-life from a graph or table of data.

⏱ 5 Half-life

The half-life of a radioactive source is the time taken for either:

- the **count rate** (activity) to fall to **half** its initial value *or*
- half the radioactive nuclei in a sample to decay.

Half-life is an average time, resulting from the random nature of radioactive decay. Looking at the half-life of a radioactive source allows us to predict the activity of a large number of nuclei during radioactive decay.

Table 1 Half-life can be estimated from data

Time (minutes)	Number of radioactive nuclei
0	1000
2	842
4	681
6	540
8	428
10	353

⏱ 5 Worked example   Grade 7

The activity after a nuclear accident is 600 Bq. The area is considered safe when the activity drops under 75 Bq. If the radioactive source has a half-life of 20 years, calculate how long this will take.   **[4 marks]**

1 half-life ➔ $\frac{1}{2}$ initial value = 300 Bq

2 half-lives ➔ $\frac{1}{4}$ initial value = 150 Bq

3 half-lives ➔ $\frac{1}{8}$ initial value = 75 Bq

3 half-lives is $3 \times 20 = 60$ years

The number of nuclei halves to 500 between 6 and 8 minutes. This means the half-life is between 6 and 8 minutes. You can use a graph to find a more accurate answer.

⏱ 5 Half-life graphs

Drawing a line from half the start count down to the time will give the half-life.

If possible, halve the count rate again to get the time for two half-lives.

One half-life on the graph is 13.5 days.

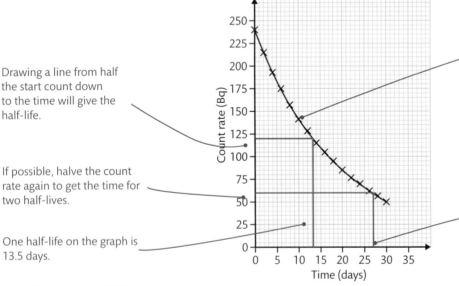

The activity of a radioactive sample decreases over time. It gets closer and closer to zero until all the nuclei have decayed.

Using two half-lives gives 27 days. $27 \div 2 = 13.5$ days.

Using two half-lives can be more accurate as it gives an average over a longer period of time.

Figure 1 Finding a half-life from a graph

⏱ 10 Exam-style practice   Grade 7

1 Calculate the fraction of a radioactive isotope left in a sample after four half-lives.   **[2 marks]**

2 A sample with a half-life of 10 mins has an activity of 45 Bq. If the sample started at 1440 Bq, calculate how old it is.   **[2 marks]**

3 The activity of a sample drops from 640 Bq to 160 Bq in 12 years. Calculate its half-life.   **[2 marks]**

4 If the half-life of a sample is 3 hours, calculate how long it will take for the activity to drop to a quarter of the original activity.   **[2 marks]**

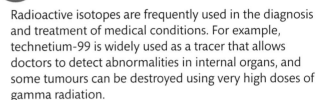

Dangers of radioactivity

Ionising radiation can be useful to us, but it also poses some dangers. It is important to be aware of the precautions needed in order to minimise the risks and to ensure the safety of people exposed to radiation.

5 Dangers of ionising radiation

Ionising radiation has both direct and indirect dangers for humans. Direct damage can be caused to body tissues if particles of radiation collide with the cells. Indirect damage can occur if the radiation causes ions to be produced. These ions can destroy cells in our body or they can mutate the genes within our cells.

During the Fukushima nuclear disaster in Japan in 2011, both caesium-137 and iodine-131 were emitted. Caesium-137 has a half-life of about 30 years, so the ground and the water surrounding the plant site will remain contaminated for many decades to come. Iodine-131 has a half-life of 8 days, so the dangers posed by iodine are severe, but short-lived.

Figure 1 A major earthquake in March 2011 caused a tsunami that affected the power supply and cooling to the Fukushima nuclear power station and caused a nuclear accident.

5 Precautions to ensure safety

Radioactive isotopes are frequently used in the diagnosis and treatment of medical conditions. For example, technetium-99 is widely used as a tracer that allows doctors to detect abnormalities in internal organs, and some tumours can be destroyed using very high doses of gamma radiation.

It is important that the dose a patient receives is as small and targeted as possible, to limit unnecessary exposure. Doctors and nurses who regularly administer such treatments are required to wear badges that record the amount of radiation they are exposed to. They also limit their exposure, for example by sheltering behind a lead screen or wearing protective clothing such as lead-lined aprons.

5 Radiation dose

The amount of radiation an object is exposed to is called the **dose**. For small doses, such as radiation treatment in hospitals, the risks are much less than the benefit from the treatment.

A dose can be reduced by:

- reducing the exposure time
- lower activity of the radioactive source
- wearing protective clothing and/or staying behind a screen
- keeping your distance from sources, for example, using long tweezers, tongs or robotic arms.

Ultraviolet rays and X-rays can have a similar hazardous effect on the body as gamma rays, although they are less powerful and less penetrating. UV can cause premature ageing of the skin and increase the risk of skin cancer.

5 Worked example — Grade 6

The half-life of technetium-99 is 6 hours. Suggest why this makes it suitable to use as a medical tracer. **[2 marks]**

For the period of scanning, the doctors will be able to detect high activity from the radioisotope. However, the radioisotope soon decays and once this has happened, there is no further activity, making it safe.

5 Exam-style practice — Grades 6–7

Using a radioisotope inside the body to diagnose a medical condition involves a level of risk to the patient.

(a) Explain why radioisotopes are used despite this risk. **[2 marks]**

(b) Outline some of the precautions taken by medical professionals when carrying out such procedures. **[2 marks]**

Radioactive contamination and irradiation

Contamination and irradiation are both harmful to living organisms. You need to know about the measures taken to avoid radioactive contamination and also understand the difference between contamination and irradiation.

5 Irradiation

To be **irradiated** means to be exposed to a source of radiation, be it alpha, beta or gamma radiation. The irradiated object does not become radioactive. Irradiation can cause damage to cells, alter genes and cause mutations that can lead to cancer. When you move away from the source of radiation, irradiation stops.

5 Contamination

Touching a source can leave traces of radioactive material on you or an object. If this radioactive material is unwanted, it is called **contamination**. Contamination is dangerous, especially for living things, as you continue to be irradiated by the radioative material that is in contact with you. The level of hazard depends on the type of radiation. Contamination should be cleaned off immediately. Removing contaminated materials from skin can be difficult.

Avoid contamination by avoiding direct contact with sources. Precautions for reducing irradiation will reduce the risk of contamination. Liquid and powdery sources are particularly risky and need to be kept in sealed containers.

There is more about reducing radiation doses on page 201.

5 Worked example — Grade 8

1. When not in use, a radioactive source in a hospital is stored in a box. Suggest a material for the box and explain the role of scientific research in coming to your decision. **[3 marks]**

It depends on the type of radiation being given off, but lead would stop all three types. Research informs this decision as it would tell us what type of radiation is being emitted, depending on the source, and also what material would stop this source. If it was beta, then a box made of a few mm thick pieces of aluminum could be used.

2. Compare and contrast irradiation and contamination. **[4 marks]**

Irradiation is when radiation from a source is absorbed by something. Contamination is when something gets the radioactive material on it. They can both damage cells, change genes and possibly cause cancer. If you are being irradiated, you can stop or reduce this by moving away from the source or moving behind a screen. If you are contaminated, the source is already on you so you cannot move away from it, and are being irradiated constantly until it is cleaned off.

5 Peer review and scientific research

Before a scientist publishes their research, their work is checked and evaluated by other scientists. This process is known as **peer review**. During this process, scientists check the findings, improve the methods and repeat the published experiments to check the results. This process makes scientists more confident about each other's findings.

It is important to understand the effects of radiation on human beings, in order to protect and treat anyone exposed to high levels of radiation. This means that people who work with radiation are better able to protect themselves and treat anyone who may have been contaminated or received a high dose of radiation.

10 Exam-style practice — Grade 8

1. A science teacher is using radioactive rocks. Explain why the teacher is at risk from both contamination and irradiation and what they can do to reduce the risk. **[4 marks]**
2. Workers in a nuclear power station wear dosimeters to measure their exposure to ionising radiation. A total dose of less than 100 mSv per year is considered to have a low risk of cancer. After one year, two workers' doses are:

   person A: 28 mSv   person B: 56 mSv

   (a) Suggest why the dose for person B might be higher. **[2 marks]**

   (b) Is person A at risk of cancer? Give a reason for your answer. **[2 marks]**

Revising energy transfers

Appliances transfer energy from one store to another. Some energy transfers are useful, others are not. The law of conservation of energy states that energy can neither be created nor destroyed, but moved from one form into another. This means that there is no overall (net) change to the total energy in a system.

Changes in energy stores

When an object is raised, its kinetic energy is transferred into gravitational potential energy:

$$\triangle GPE = mg\triangle h = \triangle KE = \frac{1}{2} m\triangle v^2$$

Energy is always conserved, but it is not always transferred in a useful form.

For example, when a driver brakes to slow a car, the kinetic energy is transferred into thermal energy in the brakes, which dissipates into the surroundings.

A television usefully transfers energy to the surroundings by light and sound. It also transfers energy by heating, which is not useful.

Energy is transferred to an electric kettle by electricity. The kettle transfers energy to the kettle and water by heating. Useful energy is transferred to the water. Wasted energy is transferred to the body of the kettle by heating. A little energy is transferred by sound. An efficient kettle maximises the fraction of energy transferred usefully into the water.

> Look at pages 180 and 181 where GPE and KE are explained in more detail.

Sankey diagrams

Sankey diagrams can be used to represent energy transfers.

Figure 1 shows that 80% of the energy transferred by the television is transferred by light and sound. The remaining 20% of the energy is wasted as thermal energy.

The width of the arrow represents the amount of energy.

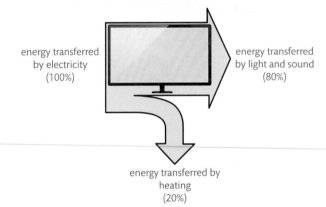

energy transferred by electricity (100%)

energy transferred by light and sound (80%)

energy transferred by heating (20%)

Figure 1 A Sankey diagram for energy transfers by a television

Worked example | Grade 6

1500 J is transferred to a kettle by electricity. 1000 J is stored as thermal energy in the water in the kettle.

(a) Calculate the amount of energy transferred to the kettle body and its surroundings. **[1 mark]**

1500 – 1000 = 500 joules

(b) Draw a Sankey diagram to represent this energy transfer. **[3 marks]**

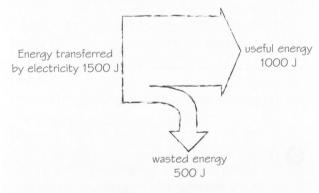

Energy transferred by electricity 1500 J

useful energy 1000 J

wasted energy 500 J

(c) Calculate the efficiency of the kettle. **[2 marks]**

$$efficiency = \frac{useful\ energy\ transferred}{total\ energy\ supplied}$$
$$= \frac{1000}{1500} = 0.67$$

Exam-style practice | Grade 6

1 A light bulb has 40 J of energy transferred to it by electricity every second. 15 J are transferred to the surroundings by light.

(a) Draw a Sankey diagram to show the energy transfers. **[3 marks]**

(b) Explain how you calculated the amount of energy transferred to the surroundings by heating. **[2 marks]**

2 A television transfers 100 J by electricity every second. 85 J are transferred to the surroundings by light and sound every second.

(a) State the final energy transfer when the television is switched on. **[1 mark]**

(b) Draw a Sankey diagram to represent the energy transfers in the television. **[3 marks]**

Work done and energy transfer

Work done is energy transferred when a force moves an object through a distance. You need to be able to calculate work done, given the force and distance.

Calculating W

work done (J) = force (N) × distance moved in the direction of the force (m)

$W = Fd$

One joul of work is done when a force of one newton is applied over a distance of one metre.

> Distance is measured along the line of action of the force.

When calculating work done, the force is measured along the same line of action as the distance. You may need to resolve forces to calculate work done.

As work done = force × distance, you can give the unit for work done as newton metres (Nm) instead of joules.

Worked example | Grades 5–6

1 **Figure 1** shows a person carrying a box that weighs 20 N. How much work does the person do against gravity in carrying the box 10 m forwards? Explain your answer. **[2 marks]**

force

distance

Figure 1 A person carrying a box

None. The force applied to hold the box is up against its weight and the distance travelled is forwards, at 90° to the force.

2 **Figure 2** shows a person who weighs 650 N. How much work do they have to do against gravity to climb the stairs? **[2 marks]**

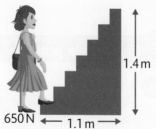

1.4 m

650 N ← 1.1 m →

Figure 2 A person climbing stairs

$W = F \times d = 650 \times 1.4 = 910\,J$

3 A car has 20 000 J of kinetic energy when it starts to brake.

(a) How much work will the brakes need to do to stop the car? **[1 mark]**

20 000 J

(b) If the braking force of the car is 2 kN, find its stopping distance. **[2 marks]**

$d = \dfrac{W}{F} = \dfrac{20\,000}{2000} = 10\,m$

Energy transfer

If you do work pushing an object, it will gain **kinetic energy**. If you do work lifting an object, it gains **gravitational potential energy**.

Force × distance would have the unit newton metres, Nm, which is equal to work done measured in joules. So one newton metre is equal to one joule.

When a potential difference makes a current flow by 'pushing' charge around a circuit, it is doing work. Work done against friction heats up the moving object. When surfaces rub together, there is friction between the two surfaces, which causes the objects to heat up. This unwanted energy transfer can be reduced by lubricating the surfaces.

> The person will use energy and their arms will get tired from holding the box, but we do not call this energy *work*.
> Work would only be done when they lift or put down the box as it is moving in the line of action of the force (up or down).

> The person has weight 650 N, so the force they must use to climb the stairs must match their weight: 650 N.
> As they are applying an upward force, you are only interested in the upwards motion; the 1.1 m is not used in the calculation.

Exam-style practice | Grades 5–6

1 Calculate how much work is done against or by gravity by:

(a) a person of weight 500 N walking 12 m along a flat floor **[1 mark]**

(b) a person of weight 500 N walking up a hill 35 m high **[1 mark]**

(c) a ball of weight 20 N falling 1.5 m **[1 mark]**

(d) a person pushing a shopping trolley along a flat floor 120 m with a force of 25 N. **[1 mark]**

2 (a) An ice skater slides across ice and slowly comes to a stop. Explain if work has been done and what the energy change would be. **[3 marks]**

(b) The ice skater starts with 400 J of kinetic energy. The frictional force is 80 N. Calculate the distance they travel before coming to a stop. **[2 marks]**

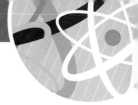

Power

Power is a measure of the rate of energy transfer. It tells you how much energy is transferred per second. You need to know how to calculate power using two different equations.

2 Calculating power

You can calculate power with the equation:

$$\text{power (W)} = \frac{\text{work done (J)}}{\text{time (s)}} \qquad \text{power} = \frac{\text{energy transferred}}{\text{time}}$$

$$P = \frac{E}{t}$$

Power is the **rate** of energy transfer. It measures how quickly work is done, or energy is transferred. A power of 1 watt means 1 joule is being transferred every second. A 1000 W heater will transfer 1000 J of electrical energy into heat and waste energy every second.

5 Worked example — Grade 6

An electric heater has a power of 2 kW.

(a) It takes 20 minutes to heat a room from 5 °C to 20 °C. How much energy is required to heat the room? **[2 marks]**

$E = P \times t$

$2000 \times 1200 = 2\,400\,000$ J

(b) Give your answer in standard form. **[1 mark]**

2.4×10^6 J

(c) A back-up heater has a power of 500 W. How many times longer would it take this heater to heat the same room from 5 °C to 20 °C, assuming no heat is lost? **[1 mark]**

4 times longer

Watch the units. Electrical appliances will often have powers measured in kW. Remember 1 kW = 1000 W.

The time needs to be in seconds; 1 min = 60 s.

Energies can get very large so you must be prepared to use standard form. Make sure you know how to put standard form into your calculator and how read it.

Exam focus

Notice that the question did not ask for the *time*, it asked 'how many *times longer*'.

If it had asked for time, the answer would be 80 minutes. Make sure you read questions carefully.

As the power is four times smaller, it will take four times longer to heat the room.

5 Units

$$\text{power (W)} = \frac{\text{energy transferred (J)}}{\text{time (s)}} = \frac{\text{work done (J)}}{\text{time (s)}}$$

so the unit for power, watts, is the same as joules per second or 1 W = 1 J/s

Many appliances have large powers which are measured in kilowatts. 1 kW = 1000 W

Likewise for energy: 1 kJ = 1000 J

If you use kilojoules in the equation, the power will be in kilowatts. The time must still be in seconds.

10 Exam-style practice — Grades 5–6

1 **(a)** A motor transfers 4800 J of electrical energy in one minute. Calculate its power. **[2 marks]**

(b) The motor only transfers 2160 J of the electrical energy into kinetic energy. Calculate the rate of kinetic energy production. **[2 marks]**

2 **(a)** An athlete lifts herself 40 times in 90 s. If each lift takes 30 J of work, calculate her useful power output. **[2 marks]**

(b) Assuming she keeps a constant rate, calculate how much work the athlete would do if she did lifts for 10 minutes. **[2 marks]**

3 As a cup of coffee cools down, the rate of energy loss decreases. If the heat loss was measured as power, describe the relationship between power output and temperature. **[2 marks]**

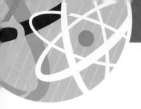

Forces

A force is a push or pull that acts on an object due to its interactions with another object. You need to know about forces that require contact to exert the force and forces that can act at a distance (non-contact).

2 Contact forces

- friction
- normal contact force
- air resistance
- water resistance
- tension
- drag
- lift
- upthrust

1 Non-contact forces

- gravitational force (weight)
- electrostatic force
- magnetic force

10 Free body diagrams

Free body diagrams show a simplified version of the forces acting on an object, usually just shown as a dot or a box. The forces can be labelled with their name or the magnitude of the force.

Remember, forces are vectors so the direction of the arrow shows the direction of the force and the length of the arrow shows the magnitude. Larger forces have longer arrows.

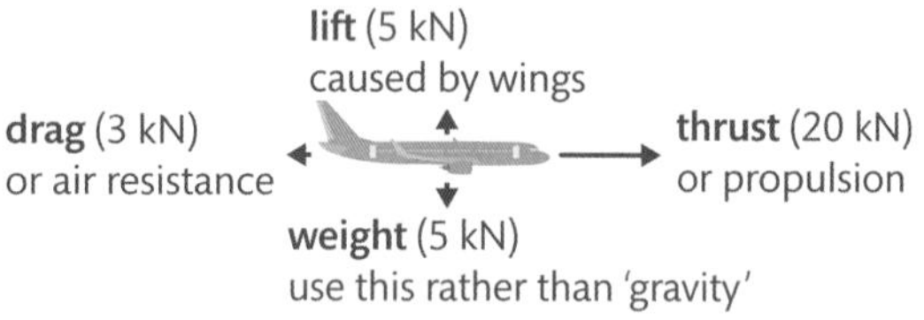
lift (5 kN)
caused by wings
drag (3 kN)
or air resistance
thrust (20 kN)
or propulsion
weight (5 kN)
use this rather than 'gravity'

Figure 1 Forces on an aeroplane

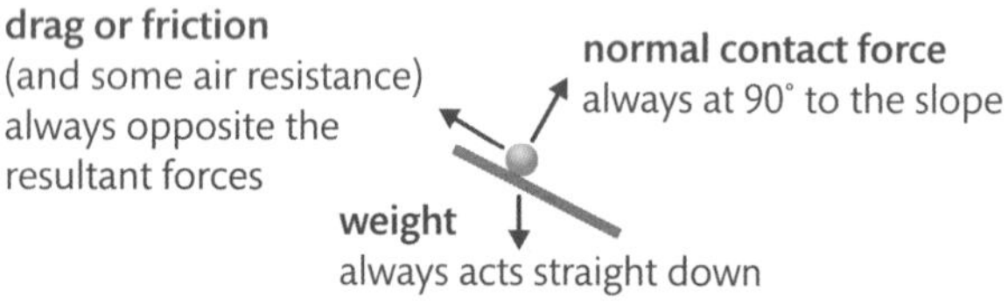
drag or friction
(and some air resistance)
always opposite the
resultant forces
normal contact force
always at 90° to the slope
weight
always acts straight down

Figure 2 Forces on a ball rolling down a slope

The aeroplane has four forces acting on it. You can draw these forces as a free body diagram. Draw a dot to represent the aeroplane, then draw an arrow from the dot in the direction of each force. You should draw the arrows to scale. The thrust arrow should be four times as long as the weight arrow.

You can then rearrange the arrows to find out whether there is a resultant force. Draw the dot and any one arrow first, then draw the next arrow from where the first ends. Continue until you have drawn all four arrows end to end.

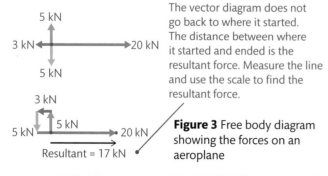

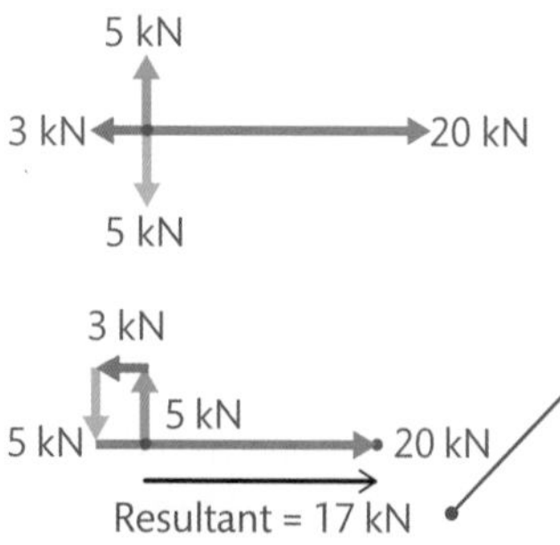
5 kN
3 kN
20 kN
5 kN
3 kN
5 kN
5 kN
20 kN
Resultant = 17 kN

The vector diagram does not go back to where it started. The distance between where it started and ended is the resultant force. Measure the line and use the scale to find the resultant force.

Figure 3 Free body diagram showing the forces on an aeroplane

2 Exam focus

When talking about forces, use 'weight' or 'gravitational force' instead of 'gravity'.

When drawing a force diagram, make sure the arrows point in exactly the right direction. The weight arrow should always point straight down, never at an angle. Check the direction an object is moving in before drawing a drag force.

5 Worked example — Grade 5

(a) Draw and label a free body diagram to show the forces acting on a magnet stuck to a fridge. **[2 marks]**

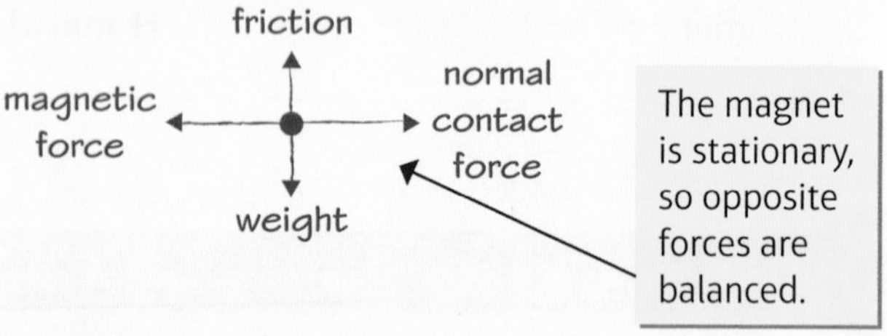
friction
magnetic force
normal contact force
weight
The magnet is stationary, so opposite forces are balanced.

(b) Describe the features of your diagram that show that the magnet is stationary. **[2 marks]**

The arrows acting in opposite directions to each other are equal in length, so the forces are balanced.

10 Exam-style practice — Grade 5

1. A maglev train uses magnets to float above the track. Draw a free body diagram to show the forces acting on the train if it is travelling at a constant velocity and a constant height. **[2 marks]**
2. If Amy is statically charged, her hair stands on end. Give the name of the force that is making her hair repel. **[1 mark]**
3. A student suggests that air resistance is a non-contact force. Explain why the student is incorrect. **[1 mark]**

Resultant forces

If multiple forces are acting on an object, they can be represented as one **resultant force**, which has the same effect as all the original forces acting together. You should be able to find the resultant force of a given object.

⑩ Forces on a skydiver

As a skydiver falls, their weight stays constant, but the drag will increase with speed. This changes the resultant force and the acceleration.

skydiver mass = 75 kg

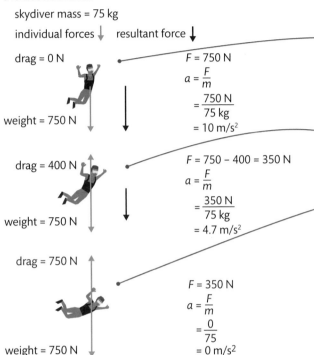

individual forces ↓   resultant force ↓

drag = 0 N

weight = 750 N

$F = 750$ N
$a = \dfrac{F}{m}$
$= \dfrac{750 \text{ N}}{75 \text{ kg}}$
$= 10$ m/s²

drag = 400 N

weight = 750 N

$F = 750 - 400 = 350$ N
$a = \dfrac{F}{m}$
$= \dfrac{350 \text{ N}}{75 \text{ kg}}$
$= 4.7$ m/s²

drag = 750 N

weight = 750 N

$F = 350$ N
$a = \dfrac{F}{m}$
$= \dfrac{0}{75}$
$= 0$ m/s²

Figure 1 The forces change as a skydiver falls.

As the skydiver jumps, they are not yet moving. They have no air resistance (drag). The resultant force is just the weight, so they accelerate at 10 m/s². This is the acceleration due to gravity.

As speed increases, drag increases. This cancels part of the weight. The resultant force, which causes the acceleration, is a lot smaller. The skydiver is still increasing in speed, but at a reduced acceleration.

When weight and drag are equal, the resultant force and the acceleration are zero. The skydiver has reached maximum speed. This is called terminal velocity.

⑤ Worked example   Grade 5

Figure 3 shows two forces acting on a plane: thrust of 600 N and wind of 400 N.

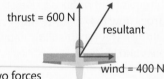
thrust = 600 N
resultant
wind = 400 N

Figure 3 Two forces acting on a plane

Draw a scale diagram to find the resultant force of these two forces.   **[4 marks]**

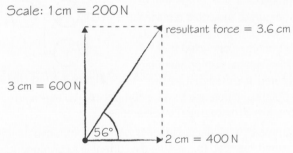
Scale: 1 cm = 200 N
resultant force = 3.6 cm
3 cm = 600 N
56°
2 cm = 400 N

Resultant force = 3.6 × 200 = 720 N
Angle = 34° to the right of the aeroplane's thrust

⑤ Resolving forces   🖩 ✓

When you have a force at an angle it can be resolved into two forces at right angles to each other, one horizontal and one vertical. These two forces have the same effect as the original force, but can be more useful when solving problems.

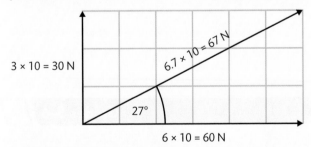
3 × 10 = 30 N
6.7 × 10 = 67 N
27°
6 × 10 = 60 N

Figure 2 A diagonal force can be resolved into vertical and horizontal forces using a diagram.

Draw the arrow at the correct angle using an appropriate scale (such as 1 cm = 10 N so 67 N = 6.7 cm).

This line is the diagonal of a rectangle. Draw in the sides of the rectangle and measure their lengths.

A force of 67 N at 27° has the same effect as a horizontal force of 60 N and a vertical force of 30 N.

⑩ Exam-style practice   Grades 5–6

1 A car is travelling at a constant speed. Explain what the resultant force on it is.   **[2 marks]**

2 A car of mass 1200 kg is accelerating at 1.4 m/s². The drag force is 800 N. Calculate the force from the engine.   **[2 marks]**

Circuit diagrams

You need to be able to recognise and draw the universal symbols used to represent the components of a circuit.

⑤ Circuit symbols

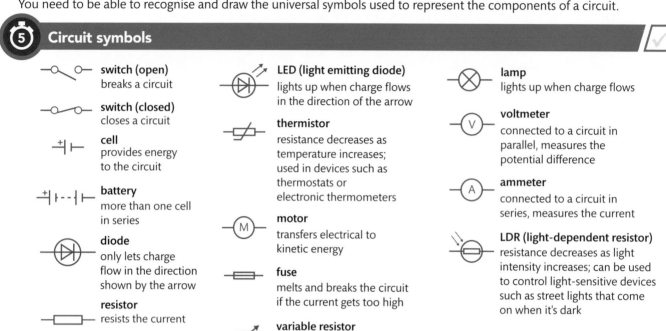

switch (open) breaks a circuit

switch (closed) closes a circuit

cell provides energy to the circuit

battery more than one cell in series

diode only lets charge flow in the direction shown by the arrow

resistor resists the current

LED (light emitting diode) lights up when charge flows in the direction of the arrow

thermistor resistance decreases as temperature increases; used in devices such as thermostats or electronic thermometers

motor transfers electrical to kinetic energy

fuse melts and breaks the circuit if the current gets too high

variable resistor a resistor you can change

lamp lights up when charge flows

voltmeter connected to a circuit in parallel, measures the potential difference

ammeter connected to a circuit in series, measures the current

LDR (light-dependent resistor) resistance decreases as light intensity increases; can be used to control light-sensitive devices such as street lights that come on when it's dark

⑤ Circuits

For charge to flow, there must be a complete circuit. Conventional current is from positive to negative (even though the electrons flow the opposite way – see page 193 for electrons in atoms). This is particularly important when dealing with diodes and LEDs.

Test circuits

Circuits powered by a cell carry direct current (d.c.). A **test circuit** allows the current and potential difference across a component to be measured. You could replace the lamp with any other component. A voltmeter is connected in parallel with the component being measured. It is used to measure the potential difference across a component. Voltage is an alternative term for potential difference.

An ammeter is connected in series with the component being measured. It is used to measure the current in a component.

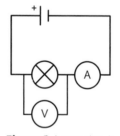

Figure 1 A test circuit

⑤ Worked example — Grade 5

Look at **Figure 2**.

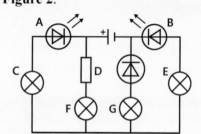

Figure 2 A circuit diagram

Which of the components **A–G** will receive a flow of charge? Explain your answer. **[3 marks]**

D, F, G, E and B, as the current can pass through all the LEDs and diodes in the right direction.

LED A is the wrong way around and would conduct no current so charge cannot flow to lamp C.

⑮ Exam-style practice — Grades 5–6

1 Look at **Figure 3**. When the switch is closed, state if the bulbs **A**, **B**, **C** or the LED (**D**) would light up. Explain your answer. **[4 marks]**

2 Draw a circuit diagram for a circuit containing a cell and
  (a) a bulb in parallel with an LDR **[2 marks]**
  (b) a resistor in series with a variable resistor. **[2 marks]**

3 Suggest a device that might use:
  (a) a variable resistor **(b)** an LDR **(c)** a thermistor. **[3 marks]**

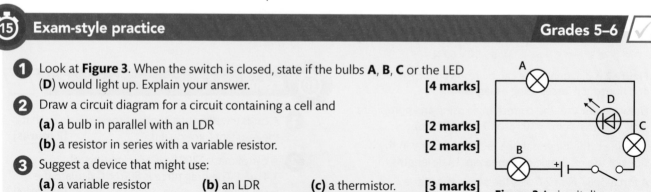

Figure 3 A circuit diagram

Current, resistance and potential difference

You need to understand current, resistance and potential difference to understand the basics of electrical circuits.

Key definitions

Current is the rate of flow of charge (page 210). In metal wires, this is carried by electrons. The greater the current, the greater the rate of flow of electrical charge. Electrical current is always conserved at a junction in a circuit. In other words, no current is 'lost' through components.

Potential difference (pd), measured in volts, is the energy transferred per unit charge passed and therefore the volt is a joule per coulomb (the unit of charge; see page 210). You will sometimes hear pd referred to as *voltage*.

Resistance opposes the current. It is measured in ohms or Ω (for example, 10 ohms or 10 Ω). Resistance is caused by electrons colliding with the metal ions inside a wire.

V = IR

The current in a circuit depends on the resistance and the potential difference. When there is a pd in a closed circuit there will be a current.

potential difference (V) = current (A) × resistance (Ω)

$V = I \times R$

When the potential difference is increased, more energy is given to the charge, increasing the current.

If you increase the resistance, it becomes harder for charge to flow. If the pd is kept the same, the current decreases.

Maths skills

Potential difference is proportional to current.

$V \propto I$ (for ohmic conductors where R is constant)

If you double V, you also double I for the same resistance.

Current is inversely proportional to resistance.

$I \propto \dfrac{1}{R}$

If you double the resistance, you halve the current.

Worked example — Grades 4–6

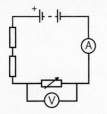

Figure 1 A circuit diagram

The fixed resistors and variable resistors in **Figure 1** have resistance 15 Ω. The battery has a potential difference of 3 V.

(a) Give the reading on the voltmeter. **[1 mark]**

1 V

You will need to understand resistances in series circuits for these questions. Go to page 211 to revise resistance. Remember, the potential difference is split across components. If they are identical, they will take an equal share, so 1 V each.

(b) Calculate the reading on the ammeter. **[2 marks]**

$I = \dfrac{V}{R} = \dfrac{3}{(15+15+15)} = 0.0667\,A$

(c) What happens to the current when the variable resistor in the circuit is used to double the total resistance of the circuit? **[1 mark]**

The current would halve. 0.0667 ÷ 2 = 0.033 A

(d) What happens to the current if the potential difference of the battery is doubled? **[1 mark]**

The current would double. 0.0667 × 2 = 0.13 A

You need to use the equation here, so work out the total resistance first. Add the three resistors that are in series together.

Exam-style practice — Grade 5–6

1 Calculate the resistance of the bulb in **Figure 2**. **[2 marks]**

2 A second identical bulb is added in series with the first. Explain whether this would change the potential difference of the battery and give the potential difference that would be measured across each bulb. **[2 marks]**

3 (a) The second bulb is removed and the original bulb replaced with an 80 Ω resistor. Calculate the new current. **[2 marks]**

(b) The battery pd is doubled to 12 V. State how this will change the current in the circuit. **[1 mark]**

Figure 2 A circuit diagram

6 V, I = 0.1 A

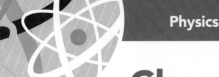

Charge, current and energy

Electrical current is rate of flow of charge, usually carried by electrons in wires. You need to be able to calculate charge, given the current and time the charge has been flowing.

5 Charge and current

The size of the electrical current (I) is the rate of flow of the electrical charge (Q). Charge is measured in coulombs (C) and current is measured in amps (A), which is the number of coulombs of charge per second.

The equation to work these quantities out is

charge (C) = current (A) × time (s)

$Q = I \times t$

An ammeter can be used to measure the current over a period of time, and this equation can be used to work out the electrical charge.

Using the charge and the potential difference in a circuit, you can use the equation $E = Q \times V$ to find out how much energy is transferred. This can then be used to work out the work done or the power of an electrical circuit.

5 Charge and potential difference

The energy transferred to a component (E) is given by the charge moving through the component (Q) multiplied by the potential difference across the component (V).

energy transferred (J) = charge moved (C) × potential difference (V)

$E = Q \times V$

You can also calculate the energy if you know the power.

Go to page 205 to revise this.

Make sure the five minutes is converted to 300 s before you use the equation.

Remember that the current is the same in all places in a series circuit. This also means that the amount of charge flowing through each bulb is the same.

1 Exam focus

The equations on this page won't be on your exam sheet, so you need to be able to remember them. Make sure you know how to rearrange the equations as well.

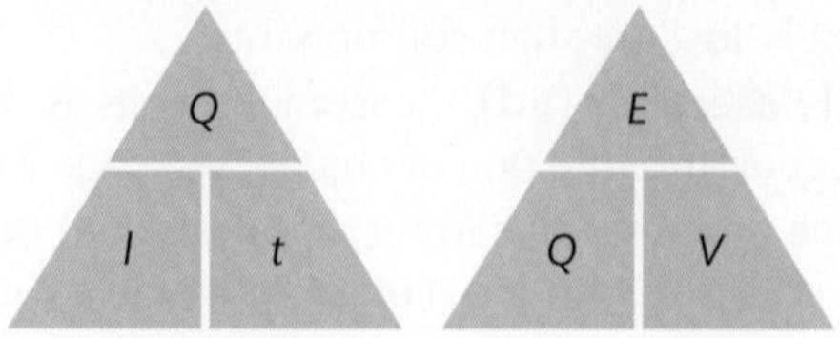

5 Worked example — Grade 5

Figure 1 shows two bulbs in series.

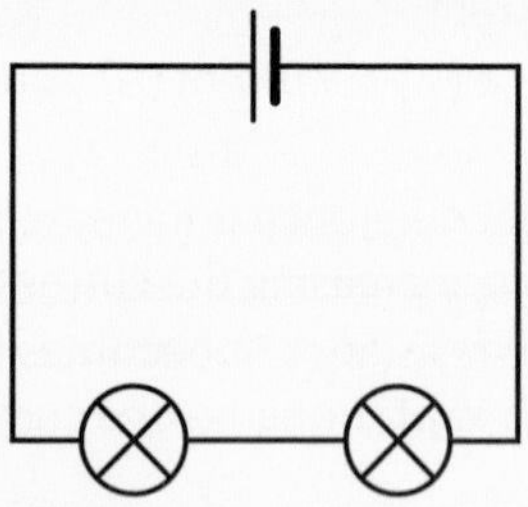

Figure 1 A circuit diagram

(a) A current of 0.6 A flows for five minutes. Calculate the amount of charge transferred. **[2 marks]**

$Q = I \times t = 0.6 \times 300 = 180\,C$

(b) How much charge will pass through each bulb in this time? **[1 mark]**

180 C

(c) The potential difference of the cell is 1.5 V. Calculate the amount of energy transferred by the cell. **[2 marks]**

$E = Q \times V = 180 \times 1.5 = 270\,J$

(d) Calculate the current if 30 C of charge flows in 20 s. **[1 mark]**

$I = \frac{Q}{t} = \frac{30}{20} = 1.5A$

10 Exam-style practice — Grade 5

1. The current in a car starter motor needs to be 60 A to start the car. If it needs to transfer 30 C of charge, calculate how long it needs to be switched on. **[2 marks]**
2. An ammeter is connected on the positive side of two bulbs connected in series. It reads 0.6 A.
   (a) What does the ammeter read when placed between the bulbs? **[1 mark]**
   (b) Calculate the charge transferred in 15 s. **[2 marks]**

Series and parallel circuits

Electrical components can be joined either in series or in parallel. You need to know the differences between series and parallel circuits.

 Series and parallel circuits

Potential difference and current behave differently in series and parallel circuits.

	Series circuit	Parallel circuit
Current	same through all components	sum of the current through each component
Potential difference (pd)	split across components	same across each component
Total resistance	sum of all resistances (equivalent to a single resistor with the same value)	less than the smallest resistance

 Resistors in series

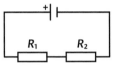

Any components connected in the same loop are in series. The resistances can be added together to give a total resistance equivalent to using just one resistor of that size. $R_{total} = R_1 + R_2$

In series, each added component increases the resistance and decreases the current. This is because every additional component makes it more difficult for charge to flow. The potential difference is divided evenly when the resistances are the same.

 **Resistors in parallel**

Components connected in different loops are in parallel. In parallel circuits, every new loop gives the current a new route to get around the circuit. Even though each route contains a component, it is easier overall for the charge to flow, decreasing the overall resistance. The total resistance of two resistors in parallel is always less than the resistance of the smaller of the two resistors. The current through the cell is the sum of the currents in the different loops.

 Worked example **Grade 5**

Two identical bulbs are connected **(i)** in series and **(ii)** in parallel.

(i)

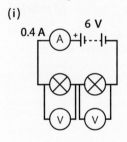

(ii)

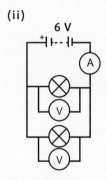

(a) State the reading on each voltmeter in each circuit. **[2 marks]**

(i) Each voltmeter reads 3 V. The pd splits up evenly as the bulbs are identical.

(ii) Each voltmeter reads 6 V as they get the same pd.

(b) State and explain what the current is in each bulb in circuit **(i)**. **[2 marks]**

0.4 A, current is the same in every component.

(c) Each bulb in circuit **(ii)** conducts 0.3 A of current. State the reading on the ammeter. **[1 mark]**

0.6 A, the two currents are combined.

 Exam-style practice **Grades 5–6**

1 A series circuit has two resistors, $R_1 = 12\,\Omega$ and $R_2 = 4\,\Omega$. Calculate the total resistance. **[1 mark]**

2 Two bulbs are connected in series.

(a) Explain what happens to the brightness of the bulbs when additional bulbs are connected in series. **[1 mark]**

(b) Explain what happens when they are connected in parallel. **[2 marks]**

3 A heater has five heating elements connected in parallel. One of the elements breaks. Explain what happens to the total current in the circuit of the heater. **[2 marks]**

 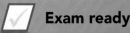

Practical: Resistance

This practical investigates the factors affecting the resistance of electrical circuits. You need to be familiar with the method and results.

⑤ Potential difference, current and resistance

❶ Set up a circuit with a power supply, ammeter, voltmeter, variable resistor and a fixed resistor.

❷ Use the variable resistor to change the potential difference across the resistor. Record the current in the resistor for five different potential differences across the resistor.

❸ Change the fixed resistor to a filament lamp. Repeat step 2 to find the current in the filament lamp for five different potential differences.

❹ Draw a graph of your results.

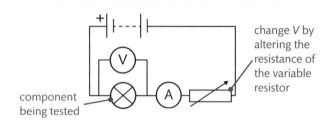

Figure 1 Circuit for investigating the potential difference and current in a filament lamp

⑤ Resistors in series and parallel

❶ Set up a circuit with a power supply, ammeter, voltmeter and a single resistor (or filament lamp, which acts as a resistor).

❷ Note the readings from the ammeter and voltmeter. Use them to calculate the resistance of the resistor using $R = \frac{V}{I}$.

❸ Change the resistor and repeat step 2 to determine the resistance of the second resistor.

❹ Arrange the two resistors in series and repeat step 2 to determine the total resistance of the resistors in series.

❺ Arrange the two resistors in parallel and repeat step 2 to determine the total resistance of the resistors in parallel.

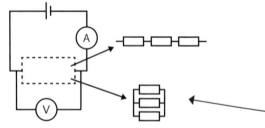

Figure 2 You can find the total resistance of the combination of resistors using the equation above.

⑤ Worked example   Grades 5–6

A student measures the current through a resistor for eight different values of potential difference across the resistor. The results are plotted as a graph of current against potential difference.

(a) State **two** advantages of plotting a graph to show the results.   **[2 marks]**

It is easier to identify a pattern from a graph than from a table, and it is easier to spot any results that may be errors or that do not follow the pattern.

(b) Describe the graph the student should obtain, and the conclusion she should draw from this.   **[2 marks]**

The line on the graph should be a straight line through the origin, showing that current is directly proportional to the potential difference across the resistor.

For resistors in parallel, the total resistance is less than the resistance of the smallest resistor.

⑩ Exam-style practice   Grade 7

Describe how you could use a test circuit to perform an experiment to test the effect of light intensity on an LDR and of temperature on a thermistor. State what you would find in each case.   **[6 marks]**

Resistors

Some components have constant resistance. The resistance of other components, such as lamps, diodes, thermistors and LDRs, changes. The resistance of a thermistor changes with temperature and the resistance of an LDR changes with light intensity. You need to be able to interpret an *I–V* graph to study the resistance of a component.

 Fixed resistor

I–V graphs for resistors at constant temperature

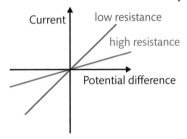

Figure 1 An *I–V* graph

The gradient of the *I–V* graph indicates the resistance. The **higher** the gradient, the **lower** the resistance.

If the resistance is constant, then the graph will be a straight line.

Review the effect of temperature on resistance on page 214.

 Diodes

Diodes are like electrical valves. They only let current flow one way. Above the threshold pd the diode conducts. If the current is reversed, the graph is flat and shows a very high resistance, so no current can flow.

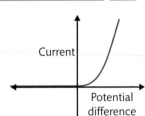

Figure 2 An *I–V* graph for a diode

The *I–V* graph for a diode is non-linear. The *I–V* graphs for ohmic conductors are linear.

LDRs and thermistors

The resistance of a **light-dependent resistor (LDR)** is high in the dark. The resistance gets less if light shines on it. The brighter the light, the lower the resistance.

The resistance of a **thermistor** depends on its temperature. The higher the temperature, the lower the resistance.

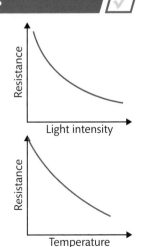

 Worked example **Grades 5–6**

1 Sketch the *I–V* graph for a filament lamp and describe how the resistance changes as the pd increases. **[4 marks]**

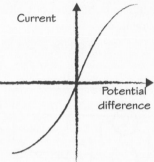

The gradient decreases as the potential difference increases or decreases from 0. As resistance is indicated by $\frac{1}{\text{gradient}}$, the resistance gets higher as pd increases.

2 As potential difference is increased across a filament bulb, it causes an increase in current. Explain how this affects the resistance. **[5 marks]**

Any electrical current flowing through a component causes heating. The increased current at higher potential differences increases the temperature of the filament, and so increases its resistance. Higher currents cause heating in the filament, which increases the resistance.

Increasing the resistance does not make the current decrease, but it does reduce the rate at which it increases when the pd is increased.

 Exam-style practice **Grade 6**

1 Sketch the shape of a graph for a wire that is allowed to heat up as potential difference increases. **[2 marks]**

2 Describe how you can tell that pd is proportional to current for a resistor but not for a filament bulb. **[3 marks]**

Practical: *I–V* characteristics

You need to be able to plot an *I–V* graph for a filament bulb, a diode, a thermistor and a resistor.

(5) Plotting an *I–V* graph

To plot a graph for current against pd:
- Change the potential difference across the component and measure the current passing through it.
- Switch the direction by changing the pd from positive to negative. The current and potential difference will be negative values in this direction. Diodes do not behave the same in both directions, although most other components do.
- Plot potential difference on the *x*-axis and current on the *y*-axis.

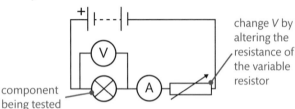

change *V* by altering the resistance of the variable resistor

component being tested

Figure 1 This circuit is a bit more complex than the circuit used to find the resistance of components as you need to be able to change the potential difference across the component.

(2) Resistor and diode

Resistor
Allow the resistor to cool between readings in order to keep the temperature constant.
It should give a straight line showing constant resistance.

Diode
In one direction the resistance will be tiny, meaning a high current can flow. A high current will damage the diode. Use an extra resistor in series to keep the current low and protect the diode.

(2) Gradient and resistance

A general straight line equation is $y = mx + c$, where:
- *m* is the gradient
- *c* is the *y*-intercept.

Rearrange the equation $V = IR$ to give:

$$\left(\begin{array}{c} I \\ y \end{array}\right) = \left(\begin{array}{c} \frac{1}{R} \\ m \end{array}\right)\left(\begin{array}{c} V \\ x \end{array}\right) + c$$

The gradient is $\dfrac{1}{\text{resistance}}$ so resistance is $\dfrac{1}{\text{gradient}}$.

Even for curves, the gradient still **indicates** the resistance. Where the gradient is lower at larger potential differences, the current increases more slowly as potential difference increases, showing that the resistance increases.

(5) Thermistors and LDRs

You can investigate how the resistance of a thermistor varies with temperature. Replace the variable resistor in **Figure 1** with a fixed resistor. Measure the potential difference across the thermistor and the current at different temperatures. Use these results to calculate the resistance at different temperatures. You can also use this circuit to investigate how the resistance of an LDR varies with light intensity.

(2) Reducing errors

- If doing repeat readings, make sure the component has a chance to cool down between tests. Do this by switching the circuit off between readings.
- For wires and resistors, keep the potential difference low to reduce heating from large currents.

Exam focus
- Make sure you know what the shape of the graph would be for each component and what this tells you about the resistance.
- A constant gradient means constant resistance.
- For curves, link the change in resistance to the pd.

(3) Worked example — Grade 7

A student produces an *I–V* graph for a diode. Their conclusion is 'a diode only works in one direction'. Write a better conclusion. **[3 marks]**

In one direction the graph's gradient is very high. This shows that the resistance is very low, so high currents can flow. In the other direction, the graph's gradient is zero. This shows that the resistance is very high, so no current can flow. Therefore, the diode only lets current flow in one direction.

(10) Exam-style practice — Grade 7

1. A student produces an *I–V* graph for a length of wire, shown in **Figure 2**. The graph should have produced a straight line. Suggest what could have caused the line to be curved and give **one** way to improve the experiment in order to avoid this. **[4 marks]**

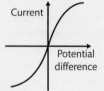

Current

Potential difference

Figure 2 An *I–V* graph for a wire

2. A student plots an *I–V* graph for a resistor. The points have a lot of scatter; this suggests random error. Suggest how the student could reduce the effect of random error. **[2 marks]**

 Made a start **Feeling confident** **Exam ready**

Energy transfer in circuits

In any electrical circuit, there are wanted and unwanted energy transfers.

Energy transfers in resistors

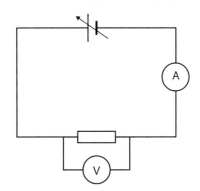

Figure 1 A circuit containing a resistor

When there is an electric current in a resistor, there is an energy transfer that causes the resistor to heat up. This is due to collisions between the moving electrons (the electric current) and the ions in the metal lattice of the resistor.

Energy dissipation

Electrical energy is dissipated into the surroundings in the form of thermal energy when an electrical current does work against electrical resistance.

This waste is usually undesirable, particularly when trying to transmit lots of power, such as through the National Grid. Using low-resistance (high-voltage) cables reduces the energy loss.

In an electric heater or a hairdryer, you do want energy transferred to the surroundings as thermal energy.

For more about the National Grid go to page 223.

Advantages and disadvantages of heating effect

Advantages:

- 👍 Tungsten light bulbs: the tungsten filament glows white-hot when a current flows and the temperature rises, emitting light.
- 👍 Heaters, kettles: electrical current is transferred into thermal energy.
- 👍 Fuses: heating effect of the current increases the temperature of the wire, melting the fuse wire above a certain current, breaking the circuit for safety.

Disadvantages:

- 👎 Component lifespan: the heating effect of the electric current can shorten the life of components in a circuit, meaning they have to be replaced more regularly.
- 👎 Wastage: energy is wasted in power transmission because of the heating effect of an electric current.
- 👎 Cooling systems and heat sinks: if these have to be added to circuits to stop overheating, the cost of manufacture is increased.

Calculating energy transferred

The energy transferred in a circuit can be calculated using the equation:

energy transferred (joule, J) = current (ampere, A) × potential difference (volt, V) × time (second, s)

$E = I \times V \times t$

Worked example — Grade 6

An electric kettle is connected to the mains electricity supply with a potential difference of 230 V. It takes three minutes for the kettle to boil the water inside it. The current flowing through the kettle is 12 A.

Calculate the total energy transferred by the kettle. **[3 marks]**

$E = I \times V \times t$

$t = 3 \times 60 = 180$ seconds

$E = 12 \times 230 \times 180 = 496\ 800$ J or 496.8 kJ

Exam-style practice — Grades 6–7

1. A microwave oven is connected to the mains electricity supply with a potential difference of 230 V. If it draws a current of 4.5 A and is used for five minutes, calculate the energy transferred. **[3 marks]**

2. A dishwasher takes 45 minutes to complete a cycle. It is connected to the mains supply, with a potential difference of 230 V. The dishwasher transfers 7750 kJ of energy. Calculate the current passing through the dishwasher. Give your answer to three significant figures. **[4 marks]**

Electrical power

Electricity transfers energy from a source to its components via an electrical circuit. Power is a measure of how quickly the energy is transferred. You need to be able to calculate power from several different equations. Some domestic devices transfer energy from batteries to motors. Others transfer energy from the a.c. mains supply instead.

2 Power

$$\text{power (W)} = \frac{\text{energy transferred (J)}}{\text{time (s)}}$$

$$P = \frac{E}{t}$$

1 W = 1 J/s; 1 joule of energy is transferred per second.

Many electrical appliances have power ratings measured in kilowatts. 1 kW = 1000 W.

5 Electrical power equations

electrical power (W) = current (A) × potential difference (V)

$P = I \times V$

electrical power (W) = current^2 (A) × resistance (Ω)

$P = I^2 \times R$

The larger the potential difference across a component, or the higher the current through it, the more power it uses. The power of a circuit tells us how quickly it transfers energy.

This shows why using high-voltage cables reduces energy loss in the National Grid: for a given amount of energy over a given time, a higher voltage means a lower current, so less heating effect.

10 Worked example — Grade 6

Two kettles boil 1 litre of water each.

Kettle	Power	Time to boil
A	2.4 kW	3 min 50 s
B	6.0 kW	70 s

Note the units are kW. You may need to convert these to W.

This must be changed to seconds. 3 × 60 s = 180 s
180 s + 50 s = 230 s

(a) Which kettle is more efficient? **[2 marks]**

A: $E = P \times t = 2.4 \times 230 = 552\text{ kJ}$

B: $E = P \times t = 6 \times 70 = 420\text{ kJ}$

Kettle A uses more energy for the same task, so kettle B is more efficient.

You need to work out how much energy is transferred by kettle A and by kettle B in order to make this comparison.

You can leave the power in kW if you give the answer in kJ. Read the question to check if you need to give specific units with your answer.

(b) How long does it take kettle B to boil 2.5 litres of water? Ignore losses to the surroundings. **[2 marks]**

2.5 times longer.
2.5 × 70 = 175 s

If there is 2.5 times more water, 2.5 times more energy will be required to boil it. If the power is the same, this means it will take 2.5 times longer to boil.

(c) Kettle A uses mains pd (230 V). Calculate the current passing through it. **[2 marks]**

$$I = \frac{P}{V} = \frac{2400}{230} = 10.4\text{ A}$$

(d) Kettle B uses 13 A of current. Find the resistance of the heating element. **[2 marks]**

$$R = \frac{P}{I^2} = \frac{6000}{13^2} = 35.5\,\Omega$$

You need to convert to standard units before putting the numbers in.

10 Exam-style practice — Grades 5–6

1. A TV uses 230 V and 0.5 A. Calculate its power rating. **[3 marks]**
2. A heater has power 2.2 kW and resistance 140 Ω. Calculate the current it uses. **[2 marks]**
3. A battery gives out an average current of 0.4 A and has potential difference 1.5 V.
   (a) Calculate its average power output. **[1 mark]**
   (b) The battery stores 13 kJ of energy. Calculate how long it will last. **[1 mark]**

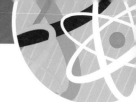

Mains electricity

A direct voltage can vary, but it does not change direction. A direct current is one which is always in the same direction. An alternating voltage causes an alternating current, which continually changes direction. The UK mains supply is an alternating (a.c.) supply.

2 Alternating and direct currents

- **Alternating current (a.c.)**: movement of charge changes constantly from one direction to the opposite direction and back.
- **Direct current (d.c.)**: charge moves in one direction.

Mains electricity in the UK uses a.c. with a frequency of 50 Hz. The current changes direction between +230 V and −230 V and back 50 times a second.

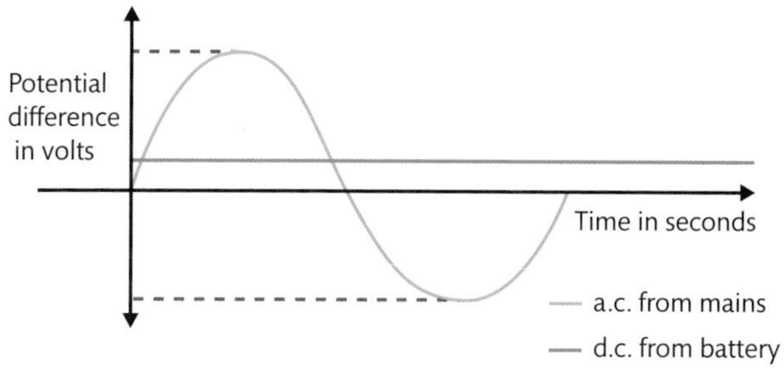

Figure 1 Batteries provide d.c. while mains electricity uses a.c.

5 Three wires in a plug

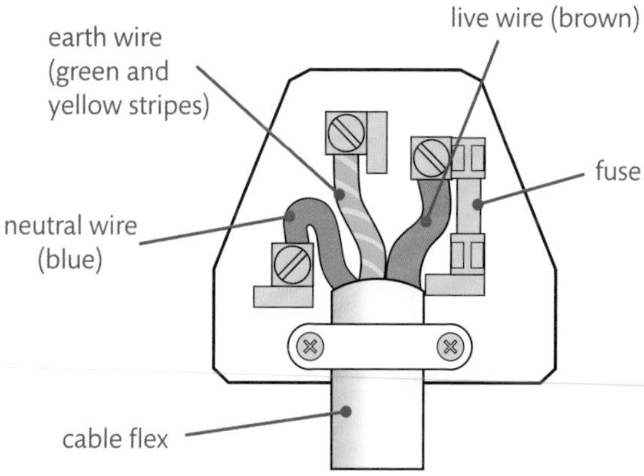

Figure 2 Appliances are connected to the mains using a three-core cable and a plug.

The **live wire** carries the a.c. pd at +/−230 V.

The **neutral wire** has a pd of 0 V. It completes the circuit.

The **earth wire** is at 0 V. It only carries a current if there is a fault. It 'earths' a casing that has accidentally become live, reducing the risk of an electric shock. The earth wire is only required to earth a metal casing.

The earth wire connects the outer case to the ground. If the case becomes live, the current is conducted by the earth wire rather than shocking a person who touches it.

5 Electrical safety

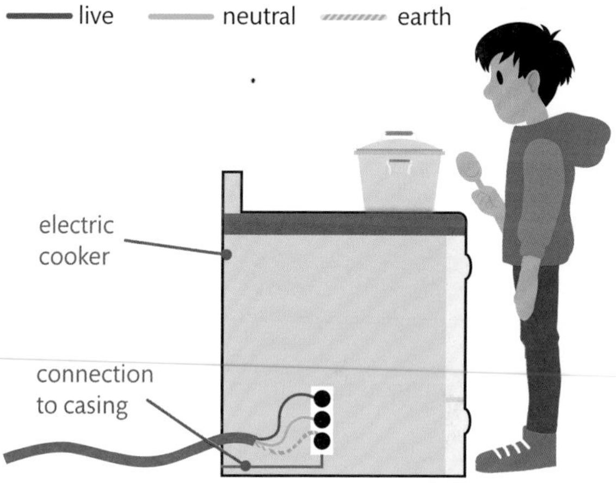

Figure 3 Take care when handling electrical equipment.

If you touch a live wire while the appliance is on, you can get an electric shock. This is because you are completing a new circuit between the live wire and the ground. If there is a fault, the metal outer casing might become live. If someone touches the casing, they would receive an electric shock as the charge flows through them to the ground.

When an appliance is earthed, the live wire touches the earth wire and causes a short circuit. A short circuit can carry very large currents. This breaks the fuse and disconnects the appliance. It can also cause a fire. This is why switches and fuses must be connected to the live wire.

2 Worked example — Grade 4

Metal parts of appliances are connected to the earth wire. A fuse is connected in the live wire.

Explain why this is done. **[2 marks]**

If there is a fault and the live wire touches the metal casing, a very large current flows to the earth. This heats up the earth wire and blows the fuse, cutting off the mains supply.

10 Exam-style practice — Grades 4–5

1. Explain why a plastic appliance does not need an earth wire. **[2 marks]**
2. Potential difference in a circuit increases and decreases repeatedly from 0 V to 120 V. Explain if the current is a.c. or d.c. **[2 marks]**

Energy transfers in appliances

All electrical appliances transfer electrical energy into other useful forms; however, some energy is always wasted.

 Energy stores

Energy cannot be created or destroyed, only transferred. All the energy going into an appliance has to go somewhere.

- Mains appliances transfer electrical energy into other **energy stores**.
- Battery-powered appliances transfer chemical energy to electrical energy, then into other energy stores.

Work is done when charge flows in a circuit.

 Energy transfers

The appliances shown below transfer electrical energy into other useful types of energy. The amount of energy transferred depends on the power of the appliance and how long it is switched on for.

The useful energy outputs are in blue, and wasted energy outputs are in red.

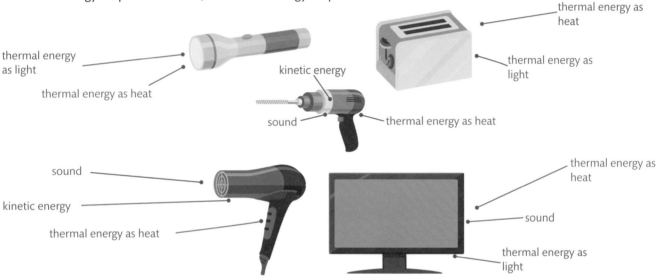

thermal energy as light

thermal energy as heat

kinetic energy

sound

thermal energy as heat

thermal energy as heat

thermal energy as light

sound

kinetic energy

thermal energy as heat

thermal energy as heat

sound

thermal energy as light

Wasted energy

It is important to always identify all the types of energy that are transferred, whether or not they are useful. Energy is often wasted when friction between moving parts causes heating, increasing the temperature of the appliance and the surroundings. A small amount of energy may be wasted as sound.

 Worked example — **Grade 5**

1 Explain why thermal energy is such a common form of wasted energy in devices. **[2 marks]**

Any machine with moving parts will have some friction that converts kinetic energy into heat. Electrical appliances convert electrical energy into thermal energy in the wires.

2 The greater the power rating of an appliance, the more energy it transfers per second. What is the relationship between the power rating and the changes in stored energy when an appliance is switched on? **[1 mark]**

The greater the power rating the greater the change in stored energy.

Exam-style practice — **Grades 4–5**

1 Give the energy transfers and state the wasted energy for:

(a) a radio **[1 mark]**

(b) an electric fan **[1 mark]**

(c) an electric car motor **[1 mark]**

(d) a mobile phone. **[1 mark]**

2 If an electric room heater does not glow or make noise, the only type of energy it produces is thermal. Explain why the heater may still waste some energy. **[2 marks]**

3 A torch uses 1000 J of chemical energy and 800 J is transferred as light. State how much is transferred to other forms of energy. **[1 mark]**

Magnetic fields

A magnetic field is the region around a magnet where forces are exerted on another magnet or on materials with magnetic properties. A magnet can attract or repel another magnet, but always attracts magnetic materials.

Magnetic fields and forces

Magnets do not have to touch to exert forces. Magnetism is a non-contact force. The closer the magnets, the stronger the force. The magnetism gets weaker as the magnets get further apart. Compasses point in the direction of a **magnetic field**. Like poles repel and unlike poles attract.

The field is strongest at the poles.

The direction of magnetic field lines is from north to south. This is the direction of the force on another north pole near the magnet.

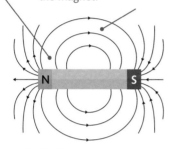

Figure 1 A magnetic field

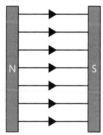

Figure 2 A uniform magnetic field

Because compasses point in the direction of magnetic fields, they can be used as evidence of Earth's magnetic field.

Figure 3 Earth's magnetic field is the same shape as the field around a bar magnet. It is produced by the rotating iron core.

Permanent magnets (like bar magnets) produce their own magnetic field. They can cause objects made from magnetic materials such as cobalt, iron, nickel and steel (remember CoINS) to become **induced magnets**.

Figure 4 An induced magnet

Induced magnets do not stay magnetic like permanent magnets. The magnetic force is always attractive. Uses of permanent magnets include: motors, generators, loudspeakers, compasses, door closers on fridges and fridge magnets. Uses of temporary magnets include: electromagnets, circuit breakers, magnetic relays and electric bells.

Mapping field lines

plotting compass

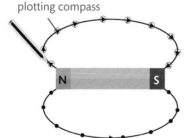

Figure 5 Drawing field lines around a magnet

1 Place a plotting compass at the north pole of a magnet. It will point away in the direction of the field. Draw a dot where it points.

2 Move the compass so the back of the needle is on the dot and draw another dot.

3 Repeat until the compass reaches the other side of the magnet.

4 Join all the dots together. Don't forget to put an arrow showing the direction of the field, north to south. This shows the direction the compass is pointing.

Worked example — Grade 6

Describe how **Figure 1** shows that the magnetic force is stronger at the poles. **[2 marks]**

The closer together the lines are, the stronger the field. At the poles, the lines are closer together, so the force must be stronger.

Exam-style practice — Grade 6

1 Describe how you could find the north pole of an unmarked bar magnet. **[2 marks]**

2 Describe how you could demonstrate that the magnetic force of attraction is non-contact. **[2 marks]**

3 State the difference between a permanent magnet and an induced magnet and give an example of each. **[2 marks]**

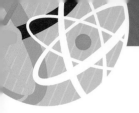

Electromagnetism

Electromagnets are made from coils of wire. You need to know the shape of a magnetic field around a straight wire and a coil of wire.

5 Electrical wires

Wires carrying an electrical current produce a magnetic field. The strength of the magnetic field depends on the current through the wire and the distance from the wire. Conventional current is from the positive to the negative terminal of a cell.

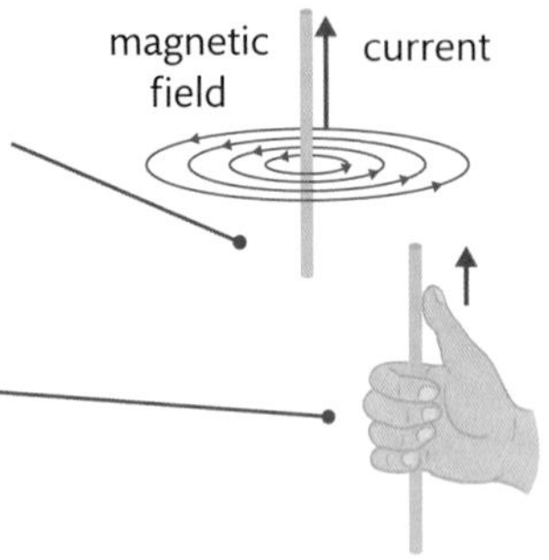

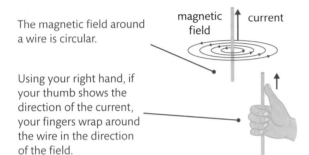

The magnetic field around a wire is circular.
magnetic field
current
Using your right hand, if your thumb shows the direction of the current, your fingers wrap around the wire in the direction of the field.

Figure 1 A magnetic field around a wire

You can show the magnetic effect of a wire carrying current by holding a compass near the wire and turning the current on and off.

2 Electromagnets

- Electromagnets can be switched off.
- Their strength can be altered easily by controlling the current.
- Increasing the number of coils increases the strength of the field.

5 Electromagnetic fields

You can test the strength of an electromagnet by seeing how many paperclips it picks up as you change factors like current and number of coils.

Direction

The current is positive to negative. Curl the fingers of your right hand as shown in **Figure 1**, with your fingers pointing in the direction of the current. Your thumb will point in the direction of the north pole of the magnet.

You could also use a compass, which will point towards the south pole.

5 Solenoids

A **solenoid** is a coil of wire carrying a current that produces a magnetic field like the field around a bar magnet. When you add an iron core, the field is strengthened and the solenoid becomes an electromagnet.

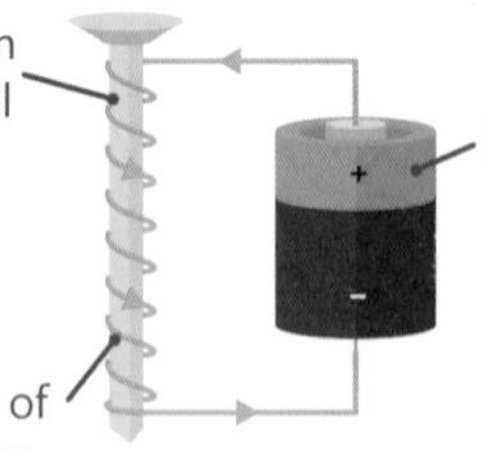

iron nail
battery
+
-
coil of wire

Figure 2 You can make an electromagnet by coiling wire around an iron nail and passing an electrical current through the wire.

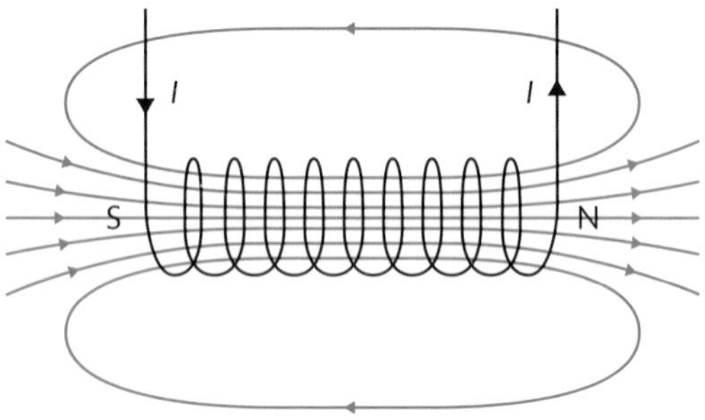

I
I
S
N

Figure 3 Coiling the wire into a solenoid increases the strength of the magnetic field. The magnetic field inside a solenoid is strong and uniform.

Inside a solenoid the fields from individual coils add together to form a very strong almost uniform field along the centre of the solenoid.

Outside the solenoid the fields cancel to give a weaker field.

2 Worked example — Grade 4

Describe how you would find the direction of the magnetic field on an electromagnet. **[2 marks]**

Hold a compass over the magnet. The arrow will point in the direction of the magnetic field from north to south.

10 Exam-style practice — Grade 4

1. A scrapyard uses an electromagnet rather than a permanent magnet. Explain why. **[2 marks]**
2. Sketch the magnetic field of the electromagnet in **Figure 2**. **[3 marks]**
3. Suggest how you would change the direction of the magnetic field in an electromagnet. **[1 mark]**

The motor effect

If a current-carrying conductor is placed near a magnet, it experiences a force. An equal and opposite force acts on the magnet. These magnetic forces are due to interactions between the different magnetic fields. This is called the motor effect.

5 Force on a wire

The force acting on the wire is at right angles to the magnetic field and to the direction of the current. The direction of the current refers to conventional current (from + to −), not the direction of electron travel. This force is called the **motor effect**.

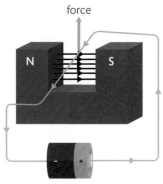

Figure 1 The motor effect

5 Magnetic flux density

The **magnetic flux density** is the strength of the magnetic field, measured in teslas (T).

You can increase the force by:

- increasing the current
- increasing the length of wire in the magnetic field (in an electric motor this is done by making it into a coil)
- increasing the magnetic flux density by using stronger magnets.

The size of the force can be found using the equation:

force = magnetic flux density × current × length
(N)   (T or N/Am)   (A)   (m)

$F = B \times I \times l$

> You are given this equation in the exam but you need to be able to rearrange it.

2 Left-hand rule

thuMb = Motion (direction of force)

First Finger = magnetic Field

seCond finger = Current

Figure 2 Fleming's left-hand rule

Use your left hand. Line up your fingers and thumb with two of the directions of: magnetic field, motion (force) or current. You can now work out the direction of the third.

> Only one thing has changed direction, so the force direction will switch to down. You can check this using the left-hand rule.

5 Worked example   Grades 5–6

1 The current in **Figure 1** is reversed. What is the direction of the force on the wire? **[1 mark]**

Down

2 What magnetic flux density would be needed to make a 10 cm length of wire carrying 0.2 A experience a force of 0.0025 N? **[1 mark]**

$$\text{magnetic flux density} = \frac{\text{force}}{\text{current} \times \text{length}}$$

$$= \frac{0.0025}{0.2 \times 0.1}$$

$$= 0.125\,\text{T}$$

> Most lengths of wire will be small, and might be measured in cm. Make sure you convert them to metres.

10 Exam-style practice   Grades 5–6

field

current

force

Figure 3

1 Give the direction that the current is flowing in **Figure 3**. **[1 mark]**

2 The current changes direction and the north and south poles are swapped. Describe what happens to the direction of the force. **[2 marks]**

3 The flux density in **Figure 3** is 0.1 T and the current 3 A. Calculate the force on 5 cm of wire. **[3 marks]**

4 Give **three** ways that the size of the force could be increased. **[3 marks]**

Transformers

Transformers are used to change the size of the potential difference of an alternating current.

 Transformers

Transformers are used to increase or decrease the potential difference of an alternating current electricity supply.

Most transformers contain two separate coils of wire around an iron core, known as the primary and the secondary coil. When an alternating current is supplied to the primary coil, a changing magnetic field is induced. This causes the iron core to become magnetised, which in turn induces a changing magnetic field around the secondary coil. This magnetic field induces an alternating potential difference around the secondary coil. The magnetic field produced opposes the original change.

 Changing the size

You can change the direction of the current by:
- changing the direction of motion of the wire
- changing the direction of the magnetic field.

You can increase the size of the current by:
- moving the wire faster
- using stronger magnets
- using more loops of wire, so there is more wire moving through the magnetic field.

 The power equation

Assuming that the transformer is 100% efficient, we can say that the power supplied to the primary coil is equal to the power provided by the secondary coil.

We also know that power = potential difference × current, so we are able to calculate the pd of the secondary coil provided we know the pd of the primary coil and the current flowing through the coils.

The power equation is:

potential difference across primary coil × current in primary coil = potential difference across secondary coil × current in secondary coil:

$$V_p \times I_p = V_s \times I_s$$

 Worked example **Grades 5–6**

An alternating current supply with a potential difference of 230 V is supplied to a transformer. The current in the primary coil is 10 A, and the current in the secondary coil is 5 A.

(a) Calculate the potential difference in the secondary coil. **[2 marks]**

$$V_p \times I_p = V_s \times I_s$$

$$so\ V_s = \frac{[V_p \times I_p]}{I_s}$$

$$V_s = \frac{(230 \times 10)}{5} = 460\ V$$

(b) State, with a reason, whether the transformer is a step-up or a step-down transformer. **[2 marks]**

This is a step-up transformer, as the potential difference in the secondary coil is greater than the potential difference in the primary coil.

 Exam-style practice **Grades 5–6**

1 A transformer is used to increase or decrease the potential difference of an alternating current supply. With reference to the structure of a transformer, explain how the potential difference of an alternating current can be changed. **[4 marks]**

2 A power station supplies an alternating current with a potential difference of 30 000 V. The current in the primary coil of the transformer is 1500 A. The current in the secondary coil is 150 A.

(a) Calculate the potential difference in the secondary coil. **[2 marks]**

(b) State, with a reason, whether the transformer is a step-up or a step-down transformer. **[2 marks]**

 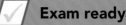

Transformers and the National Grid

You need to know how the National Grid transfers electrical energy around the country.

 The National Grid

The National Grid uses a system of cables and transformers to transfer electrical energy from power stations to consumers. When a current flows through a wire some energy is lost by heating. The National Grid transmits electricity at a low current to minimise heat loss. This requires a high voltage.

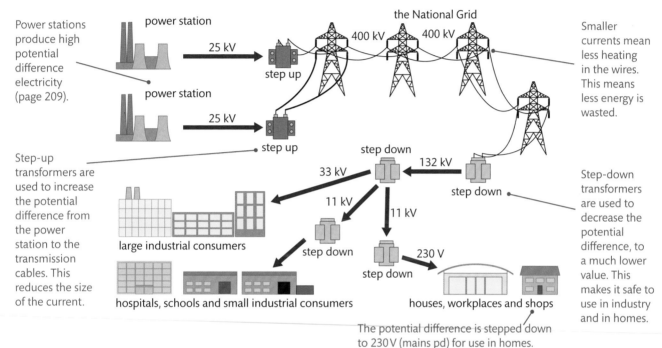

Power stations produce high potential difference electricity (page 209).

Step-up transformers are used to increase the potential difference from the power station to the transmission cables. This reduces the size of the current.

Smaller currents mean less heating in the wires. This means less energy is wasted.

Step-down transformers are used to decrease the potential difference, to a much lower value. This makes it safe to use in industry and in homes.

The potential difference is stepped down to 230 V (mains pd) for use in homes.

Figure 1 The National Grid transports electrical energy around the country. Energy is wasted when high currents cause the cables to heat up.

 Primary and secondary coils

A transformer can change the potential difference between the primary coil (input) and secondary coil (output). The power transfer must be constant.

Power out of the secondary coil = power into the primary coil

Primary potential difference × primary current = secondary potential difference × secondary current

$V_s \times I_s = V_p \times I_p$

 **Worked example** Grade 5

Explain the effects of not using transformers in the National Grid. **[4 marks]**

The current would be very high, wasting lots of energy as thermal energy in the wires. Electricity would become very expensive. More fuel would need to be burned in order to produce enough electricity to meet demand, releasing more greenhouse gases into the atmosphere and increasing global warming.

 Exam-style practice Grade 5

1 Heating in wires is caused by the current and resistance in the wire. Other than reducing the current to very small values, suggest how the energy lost to heating might be reduced. **[2 marks]**

2 A transformer is used in a mobile phone charger to turn 230 V mains pd into 12 V to charge a battery. Give the name of this type of transformer. **[1 mark]**

 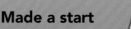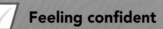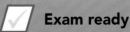

Changes of state

You need to know about the three states of matter: solid, liquid and gas.

(5) States and state changes

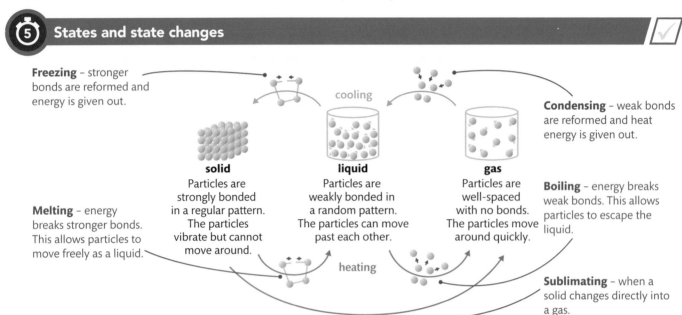

Freezing – stronger bonds are reformed and energy is given out.

Melting – energy breaks stronger bonds. This allows particles to move freely as a liquid.

cooling

heating

solid
Particles are strongly bonded in a regular pattern. The particles vibrate but cannot move around.

liquid
Particles are weakly bonded in a random pattern. The particles can move past each other.

gas
Particles are well-spaced with no bonds. The particles move around quickly.

Condensing – weak bonds are reformed and heat energy is given out.

Boiling – energy breaks weak bonds. This allows particles to escape the liquid.

Sublimating – when a solid changes directly into a gas.

Figure 1 The particle model

(2) State changes: key facts

☑ The temperature a substance both melts and freezes at is called the **melting point**.

☑ The temperature a substance both condenses and boils at is called the **boiling point**.

☑ Changes of state are physical and reversible. The material recovers its original properties.

☑ Particles in a solid are arranged more closely than in a liquid, so solids tend to have higher density.

☑ Particles in gases are very far apart, so gases have very low densities.

☑ The properties of a substance may change when it changes state. Its density and volume may alter, but the mass will stay the same. This is because the number of particles does not change. Mass is conserved.

(5) Heating and cooling curves

Thermal energy is transferred to kinetic energy in the particles, raising the temperature.

At the melting and boiling points, the particle bonds break. The temperature remains constant and the state changes.

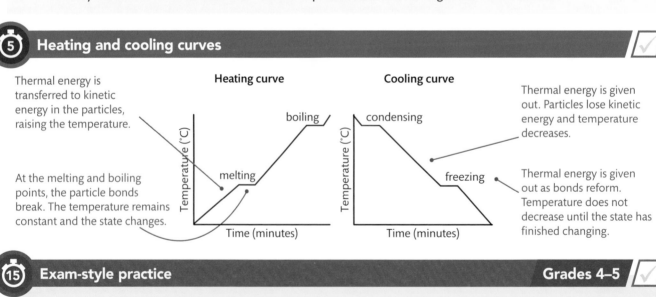

Heating curve

boiling

melting

Temperature (°C)

Time (minutes)

Cooling curve

condensing

freezing

Temperature (°C)

Time (minutes)

Thermal energy is given out. Particles lose kinetic energy and temperature decreases.

Thermal energy is given out as bonds reform. Temperature does not decrease until the state has finished changing.

(15) Exam-style practice — Grades 4–5

1 Water is heated to its boiling point of 100 °C. The water is heated further but the temperature stays constant. Explain what is happening to the energy. **[2 marks]**

2 Describe the motion of particles in a solid, a liquid and a gas. **[5 marks]**

3 An ice cube is placed in a glass of water. Describe the change in the arrangement of particles in both the ice and the water. **[4 marks]**

Made a start | Feeling confident | Exam ready

Density

You need to know how to calculate density, the amount of mass per unit volume.

2 Calculating density

Density is a property of a substance. You can work out the density of a substance using the equation:

$$\text{density (kg/m}^3) = \frac{\text{mass (kg)}}{\text{volume (m}^3)} \qquad \rho = \frac{m}{V}$$

Having a higher density does not mean something will be heavier or have a larger mass. The density also depends on the volume. Gases have a lower density than solids because the particles in a gas are spread further apart, increasing the volume and so decreasing the density.

5 Worked example — Grade 5

> Convert the lengths to metres before working out the volume; it is more complicated to do so later.

Figure 1 shows a copper cube with sides 25 cm. The mass of the cube is 140 kg.

Figure 1 A copper cube

> The volume of a cube is the (length of a side)^3.

Maths skills
You can calculate the volume of a cuboid using $V = abc$

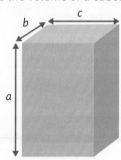

Figure 2 Cuboid with sides a, b and c

(a) Calculate the volume of the cube in m^3. **[2 marks]**

$25\,cm = 0.25\,m$
$V = 0.25\,m \times 0.25\,m \times 0.25\,m = 0.0156\,m^3$

(b) Calculate the density of copper. **[2 marks]**

$P = \frac{m}{V} = \frac{140}{0.0156} = 8974\,kg/m^3$

(c) Calculate the volume of a copper cube of mass 2.2 kg. **[2 marks]**

$V = \frac{m}{\rho} = \frac{2.2}{8794} = 2.5 \times 10^{-4}\,m^3\ (=0.00025\,m^3)$

> As the density is a property of the material, any size piece of copper will have the same density.

> Small volumes measured in m^3 will be very small numbers and are best expressed in standard form. Make sure you can enter standard form into your calculator and read it off.

10 Exam-style practice — Grades 4–5

1. A bucket contains twice as much water as a bottle. Compare the density, volume and mass of the water in the bucket with the water in the bottle. **[2 marks]**

2. **(a)** The density of water is 1000 kg/m^3. An object will float in water if its density is lower than water.
   State which of these objects will float in water. **[5 marks]**

Object	apple	steel box	plastic	human
Mass (kg)	0.074	1.3	0.5	70
Volume (m³)	1.04×10^{-4}	2×10^{-3}	4.1×10^{-4}	0.071

   (b) Find the mass of an apple with volume 1.5×10^{-4} m^3. **[3 marks]**

Practical: Density of materials

You need to know how to accurately measure the mass and volume of an object so that you can calculate its density.

② Measuring density

$$\text{density (kg/m}^3) = \frac{\text{mass (kg)}}{\text{volume (m}^3)}$$

Go to page 225 to practise calculating density.

The mass of the object can be found using a top pan balance. Using a top pan balance with a higher level of precision will improve the precision of the answer.

Measuring the volume of an object depends on the size and shape of the object.

② Density of irregular shapes

You can find the volume by measuring the volume of water that the shape will displace.

displacement can

1 Fill the displacement can to the spout.

2 Place the object in the can.

3 Collect the water that runs off in a measuring cylinder.

Figure 1 Apparatus

4 If the object floats, push it down until it is all below the surface, but without putting your finger into the water.

② Density of liquid

1 Find the mass of the liquid by measuring the mass of the empty measuring cylinder on a digital balance. Make sure the measuring cylinder is completely dry.

2 Measure the mass of the measuring cylinder again with the liquid inside. The mass of the liquid will be the difference between the two measurements.

3 Measure the volume of liquid using a measuring cylinder.

② Worked example   Grade 6

A student finds the mass of a liquid. They measure the mass of the measuring cylinder full of liquid. They then empty the measuring cylinder and measure the mass again to find the difference. Suggest a problem with this method.   **[2 marks]**

There may be some liquid left over in the measuring cylinder when they weigh it 'empty'. It would be better to weigh the cylinder first while it is dry, or make sure it is thoroughly dry once emptied.

⑤ Measuring objects

To get an accurate volume, you need to measure the dimensions of a regular object to as high a precision as possible.

The size of a large object can be measured using a ruler or tape measure. Smaller objects can be measured using vernier calipers. They will measure to 0.01 mm.

volume of a cuboid = length × width × depth

Remember to convert the lengths to metres to get the volume in m³.

② Reducing errors

- Suspend the object from a piece of string so it can be lowered carefully into the water to avoid making a splash.
- Stand the measuring cylinder on a flat surface.
- Make sure your eyes are at the same level as the water.
- Read the level of the water, ignoring the meniscus created at the edge.

water level

Figure 2 Taking a reading from a measuring cylinder

⑩ Exam-style practice   Grades 5–6

(a) Give the methods you would use to find the most accurate density of a rock, a metal cube and a sample of oil.   **[3 marks]**

(b) For each method in **(a)**, suggest **one** thing you could do to reduce the errors in the method.   **[3 marks]**

☑ **Made a start**   ☑ **Feeling confident**   ☑ **Exam ready**

Specific heat capacity

The specific heat capacity, c, is the energy needed to raise the temperature of 1 kg of a substance by 1 °C. It is measured in joules per kilogram per degree Celsius.

⑤ Calculating specific heat capacity

change in thermal energy (J) = mass (kg) × specific heat capacity (J/kg°C) × temperature change (°C)

$\Delta Q = mc\Delta\theta$

Δ (delta) means 'change in' and θ (theta) means temperature. The greater the specific heat capacity, the more energy it takes to raise the temperature of a given mass through a given temperature rise. Energy is stored in a system as internal energy, which is the total of all the kinetic and potential energy of the particles.

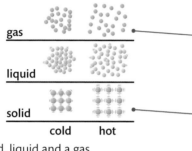

A higher temperature means the particles in a substance have greater kinetic energy. The particles will move around faster, or vibrate faster.

Heat energy added to a system is either used to break bonds and change the state or increase the energy of the particles and raise the temperature.

Figure 1 Particles in a solid, liquid and a gas

⑩ Worked example — Grades 5–6

Liquid	Melting point (°C)	Boiling point (°C)	Specific heat capacity as a liquid (J/kg°C)
A	15	80	200
B	0	100	4200
C	−12	15	2150

(a) The three liquids in the table are heated by a 1 kW heater. Identify which liquid's temperature would rise most quickly. Explain why. **[3 marks]**

Liquid A, it has the lowest specific heat capacity so it takes the least energy to warm up.

(b) 3 kg of liquid A is heated from 20 °C to boiling point. Calculate how much energy it would take. **[2 marks]**

$\Delta Q = mc\Delta\theta = 3 \times 200 \times 60 = 36\,000\,J$

(c) Suggest which liquid would be best used in a central heating system. Give **two** reasons for your choice. **[2 marks]**

Liquid B. It has the highest specific heat capacity and is unlikely to reach its boiling point.

② Exam focus

Use this equation to help you remember the unit for specific heat capacity:

$c = \dfrac{\Delta Q}{m\Delta\theta} \rightarrow \dfrac{J}{kg\,°C} = J/kg°C$

Look carefully at the headings in a table of data so you are familiar with all the information it gives before you read the question.

Liquid A has the lowest specific heat capacity. This means it takes very little energy to increase the temperature, so it would warm up the fastest.

Work out the temperature change 20–80 °C first. Use the equation.

The one with the highest specific heat capacity would be best, as it will hold (and therefore give out) more energy. However, it also needs to still be a liquid at temperatures up to approximately 60 °C.

⑤ Exam-style practice — Grades 5–6

1 2 kg of liquid B was given 84 000 J of energy. Calculate the final temperature if it was heated from:
(a) 20 °C **(b)** 80 °C. **[3 marks]**

2 Give **two** reasons why liquid A would be unsuitable as coolant liquid in a freezer. **[2 marks]**

Made a start | Feeling confident | Exam ready

Specific latent heat

Specific latent heat, L, is the energy required to change the state of 1 kg of a substance with no change in temperature.

Calculating L

energy for a change of state = mass × specific latent heat
(J)   (kg)   (J/kg)

$Q = m \times L$

The **specific latent heat of fusion** is the energy required to melt or freeze a substance.

The **specific latent heat of vaporisation** is the energy required to condense or evaporate a substance.

Worked example   Grade 6

120 kg of metal is heated to its melting point.

(a) The melting point of the metal is 1500 °C. Explain why the temperature will not increase until all of the metal has melted. **[3 marks]**

The heat energy is used to break bonds between metal atoms and change their state. The temperature will increase when the energy is used to increase the kinetic energy of the metal atoms. This will not happen until all the bonds have broken and all the metal is liquid.

(b) If it takes 54 000 J of energy to melt the metal, find the specific latent heat. **[2 marks]**

$L = \dfrac{Q}{m} = \dfrac{54\,000}{120} = 450\,\text{J/kg}$

(c) Explain why much more energy than this would actually be transferred while melting the metal. **[2 marks]**

At such a high temperature, a lot of heat energy would be transferred to the surroundings and not all would be used to break bonds in the metal.

(d) How much energy would be given out as 120 kg of molten metal turned solid? **[1 mark]**

54 000 J

Latent heat and particles

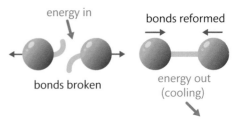

Figure 1 When a substance changes state, energy is used to break bonds or is given out as the bonds reform.

As something cools down, energy is released from it. When it condenses or freezes, the temperature stays constant because energy is transferred when the bonds form between the particles.

> The temperature of any substance will stay constant while it changes state, whether it is being heated or cooled.

Exam focus

The units for specific latent heat are J/kg.

You can use the equation to help you remember the unit:

$L = \dfrac{Q\,(J)}{m\,(kg)} \rightarrow \text{J/kg}$

> This unwanted energy transfer is reduced in industry by using furnaces with thick walls and other forms of insulation (page 182).

> Latent heat works in both directions. You have to put 54 000 J in to melt 120 kg of metal. When you freeze 120 kg of molten metal you will get 54 000 J of energy back out.

Exam-style practice   Grade 6

1 Copper has a specific latent heat of 200 J/kg and gold has a specific latent heat of 64 J/kg.

   (a) Compare the energies required to melt each metal. **[2 marks]**

   (b) Calculate the masses of gold and copper that could be melted with 2500 J of heat energy. **[3 marks]**

2 Water has specific latent heat of fusion of 336 000 J/kg. Calculate how much heat energy will be removed from a drink in order to melt a 50 g ice cube. **[2 marks]**

Practical: Properties of water

You need to know how to determine the specific heat capacity and latent heat of water. This practical investigates a method for each.

(5) Experiment 1: Specific latent heat

1. Into a calorimeter, place 50 g of crushed ice.
2. Place the immersion heater into the central hole in the lid of the calorimeter.
3. Clamp the thermometer so that its bulb is in the ice but near to the top.
4. Record the temperature of the ice.
5. Connect the heater to the power supply and joulemeter, turn it on and record the temperature every 20 seconds. If no joulemeter is available, connect an ammeter and a voltmeter instead.
6. Continue until no more ice is present.
7. Plot a graph of temperature against time and identify where the ice melted.
8. Use the reading on the joulemeter to determine the energy supplied to the ice.
9. Calculate latent heat using the equation:

$$\text{latent heat} = \frac{\text{energy supplied to ice}}{\text{mass of ice}}$$

(5) Experiment 2: Specific heat capacity

1. Into a calorimeter, place 1 kg (1 litre) of water.
2. Place the immersion heater into the central hole in the lid of the calorimeter.
3. Clamp the thermometer into the smaller hole with a stirrer next to it.
4. Wrap the calorimeter completely in an insulating material.
5. Record the initial temperature of the water.
6. Connect the heater to the power supply and a joulemeter and turn it on for 10 minutes. If no joulemeter is available, connect an ammeter and a voltmeter instead. Stir the water regularly.
7. After 10 minutes, switch the heater off. The temperature of the water will rise further before it begins to cool. Record the highest temperature it reaches. Use this value to calculate the temperature rise during the experiment.
8. Calculate the specific heat capacity using the equation: $c = \frac{\Delta Q}{m} \times \text{temperature change}$

(10) Worked example — Grade 6

1. Describe the safety factors you must consider in each method described above. **[4 marks]**

- Do not touch the heating element directly.
- Do not overfill the container; wait until cooled before moving it, and keep the temperature low.
- Mop up any spills immediately and keep the water away from electrical equipment (apart from the heater).
- Do not lean the thermometer in a beaker of water in case it pulls it over.

2. A 1.0 kg copper block is heated from 25 to 60°C. If 13.50 kJ of energy was supplied to the block, calculate the specific heat capacity of copper. **[4 marks]**

$$c = \frac{\Delta Q}{(m \times \text{temperature change})} = \frac{13500}{(1.0 \times 35)}$$

$$c = 386 \, J/kg°C$$

(5) Reducing errors

- Measure the temperature of water in the middle, as hot water rises to the top. Make sure not to touch the heater.
- Insulate the water. A lid on the water also reduces energy and mass loss by evaporation.
- Take the mass of ice or water before and after and calculate an average.
- Limit heat loss to the environment by keeping heating time short.
- Reduce the initial temperature of the water to allow a greater increase in temperature. A temperature change of only a few degrees makes the result very inaccurate.
- The hotter the water gets, the more energy it will lose to the environment.

Some of these points work against each other, but it is acceptable to mention them all if asked in the exam.

(10) Exam-style practice — Grade 6

1. Suggest why you do not take the end temperature of Experiment 2 at 10 minutes. **[2 marks]**
2. Identify actions that could be taken to minimise the errors in Experiment 2 above. **[3 marks]**

Particle motion in gases

Gas molecules are in constant random motion. You need to be able to explain the effect of temperature and type of container on particle motion in gases.

When a gas is heated, the particles gain kinetic energy. They move faster than in liquids and solids. As there are no forces between the particles, they spread out and expand as much as they can.

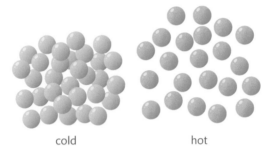

cold   hot

Figure 1 Heating a gas

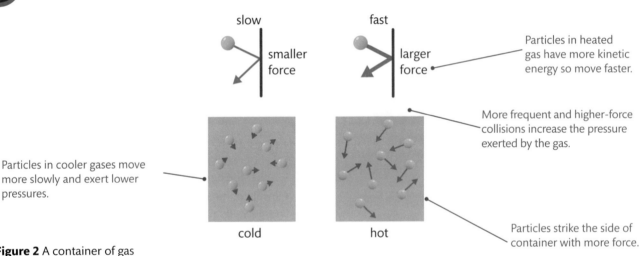

slow   fast

smaller force   larger force

Particles in heated gas have more kinetic energy so move faster.

More frequent and higher-force collisions increase the pressure exerted by the gas.

Particles in cooler gases move more slowly and exert lower pressures.

cold   hot

Particles strike the side of container with more force.

Figure 2 A container of gas

Explain why heating a gas in a rigid container results in an increase in pressure of the gas.

[2 marks]

Gas particles will have greater kinetic energy so they exert more force when colliding with the walls of the container.

The kelvin scale starts at absolute zero. There is no movement of particles at absolute zero, so it is not possible to get any colder. Absolute zero is –273 °C, or 0 K. To convert from degrees celsius to kelvins, you need to add 273. For example, 25 °C is 298 K.

1   A container of air is heated and then sealed. When it has cooled it is difficult to remove the lid. Explain why this might be. **[3 marks]**

2   A student heats up the air in a gas syringe. State and explain what happens to the air inside the syringe. **[3 marks]**

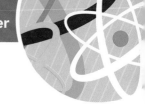

Forces and elasticity

Forces can cause objects to change shape permanently or temporarily, by bending, stretching or compressing them. You need to know the effects of forces on elastic objects like springs.

2 Types of distortion

Distortion is the term used to describe an object changing shape. Distortion can be elastic or inelastic:

- **Elastic distortion** – an object changes shape when a force is applied but returns to its original shape when the force is removed.
- **Inelastic distortion** – an object changes shape when a force is applied but does not return to its original shape when the force is removed.

The amount an object changes shape is the **extension** or **compression**. To cause an object to compress, stretch or bend, you usually need two forces working against each other. If you try to squash a rubber ball, you have to push from both sides or the ball will simply move.

2 Linear elastic distortion

The extension of an elastic object is directly proportional to the force applied to it:

force applied (N) = spring constant (N/m) × extension (m)

$F = k \times x$

- The force, F, is the load or weight applied to the object being deformed.
- The spring constant, k, is a measure of how stiff the spring or object is.
- Extension, x, is the amount the object changes shape. It is the stretched length – original length.

This equation works for the straight-line part of a force-extension graph.

5 Springs

Force against extension of a spring

An object that obeys the equation for linear elastic distortion has a straight line on a force–extension graph. If the object is stretched too far, it is permanently distorted.

The gradient gives you the spring constant, but be careful to only use the straight line section.

Energy in a spring

Anything that stretches, compresses or bends stores elastic potential energy.

energy transferred in stretching (J) = 0.5 × spring constant (N/m) × extension^2 (m)

$E = \frac{1}{2}kx^2$

When released, the stored energy is usually transferred into kinetic energy.

This is true for the linear part of the graph. In the non-linear part, work is being done in permanently distorting the object.

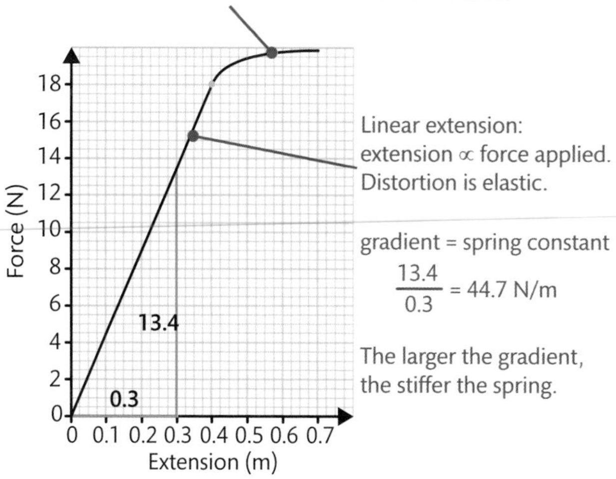

Non-linear extension: there is a large increase in extension for a small increase in force. Distortion is inelastic.
Linear extension: extension ∝ force applied. Distortion is elastic.
gradient = spring constant
$\frac{13.4}{0.3}$ = 44.7 N/m
The larger the gradient, the stiffer the spring.
13.4
0.3
Force (N)
0
2
4
6
8
10
12
14
16
18
Extension (m)
0
0.1
0.2
0.3
0.4
0.5
0.6
0.7

Figure 1 A graph showing how the extension of a spring changes when different force is applied

5 Worked example — Grade 7

A force is applied to a spring so that it is distorted elastically. 18 N of weight is added to make the spring 36 cm longer.

(a) Calculate the spring constant of the spring. **[3 marks]**

$k = \frac{F}{x} = \frac{18}{0.36} = 50\,\text{N/m}$

(b) Calculate the total elastic potential energy stored in the spring. **[4 marks]**

$E = \frac{1}{2}kx^2$

$= 0.5 \times 50 \times 0.36^2 = 3.24\,\text{J}$

10 Exam-style practice — Grade 7

Look at **Figure 1**.

(a) Give the maximum force that the spring can take before being damaged. **[1 mark]**

(b) Explain how the graph shows that the spring will not return to its original length when the force is removed. **[1 mark]**

(c) Calculate the energy stored in the spring when the extension is 0.3 m. **[3 marks]**

(d) The original length of the spring is 9 cm. Calculate its length when it supports a 10 N weight. **[3 marks]**

Practical: Force and extension

You need to know how to investigate the relationship between force and extension with a spring.

 Method

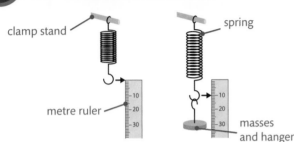

Figure 1 Apparatus

1 Clamp a ruler so that the zero mark is next to the end of the spring.

2 Hang a range of masses from the spring.

3 Record the force, which is the weight of each mass.

4 Record the extension of the spring for each force.

5 Plot a graph of force (*y*-axis) against extension (*x*-axis).

6 You can then use the graph to estimate the weight of another object that is hung from the spring by measuring the extension.

Maths skills

The force is in newtons and the extension (*x*) in m, so the gradient is N/m. The gradient is also the spring constant, calculated from $F = kx$. If the graph is plotted with the axes reversed, remember that the

$$\text{spring constant} = \frac{1}{\text{gradient}}.$$

If the plotted points are not close to the line of best fit, it might mean that errors need reducing in the experiment.

 Reducing errors

- Measure the spring length from the same point on the spring each time.
- Make sure the spring is at eye level when measuring it.
- Repeat each extension by removing and rehanging the mass in case larger masses deform the spring inelastically.

 Worked example **Grade 7**

Look at **Figure 2**.

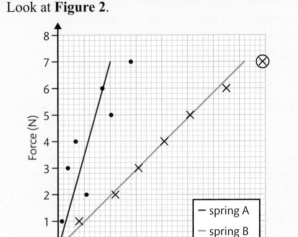

Figure 2 A graph showing the force and extension of springs A and B

(a) An outlier in the results of spring B has been circled. Suggest why this point may not fit the pattern. **[2 marks]**

The point may be in the non-linear part of the graph, so force is no longer proportional to extension. Therefore, the line would start to curve and the gradient decrease.

(b) The gradient of the line for spring A is 70. Give the unit for the gradient. **[1 mark]**

N/m

(c) Looking at the graph, a student suggests that the spring constant calculated for spring B is more accurate than the spring constant calculated for spring A. Do you agree with this? Explain your answer. **[2 marks]**

The points in spring B are closer to the line of best fit. This means that there is less uncertainty in its position and gradient compared to line A so you can be more confident about the value of the gradient and spring constant for spring B.

 Exam-style practice **Grade 7**

Look at **Figure 2**.

(a) Determine the spring constant of spring B. **[2 marks]**

(b) A student wants to determine if the outlier in spring B is part of a change in the pattern. State how this might be achieved. **[1 mark]**

(c) Suggest **two** possible reasons for the increased scatter in the results for spring A. Give some ways this could be reduced. **[3 marks]**

Made a start   Feeling confident   Exam ready

Equations

You need to know which equations to use and how to rearrange them to answer questions in the exam. You will be given a formulae sheet with some equations on.

(2) Three rules for rearranging

1. Decide what you want to work out. Get this on one side of the equation and everything else on the other.
2. Make sure the value you want to find is not on the bottom of a fraction.
3. When you move something across the equals sign, the operation needs to be reversed.

(2) Exam focus

In the exam, you can save time by using symbols rather than words. For example, use:

$F = ma$ rather than *force = mass × acceleration* as it is quicker to write and rearrange.

Take your time when rearranging equations and allow time to check your calculations to ensure you have written the correct answer.

(10) Maths skills

Equations with three quantities
If you needed to calculate the mass, m:

$$F = ma \rightarrow \frac{F}{a} = m \rightarrow m = \frac{F}{a}$$

Equations with four or more quantities

$$\Delta GPE = mgh \rightarrow \frac{\Delta GPE}{mg} = h \rightarrow h = \frac{\Delta GPE}{mg}$$

Divide both sides of the equation by mg.

Equations with squares

$$KE = \frac{1}{2}mv^2 \rightarrow v^2 = \frac{KE}{\frac{1}{2}m} \rightarrow v = \sqrt{\frac{KE}{\frac{1}{2}m}}$$

First rearrange for v^2, you can move the $\frac{1}{2}$ and m as normal, then square root both sides.

$$v^2 = u^2 + 2as$$

To find u, first rearrange so that u^2 is on its own:

$$u^2 = v^2 - 2as \rightarrow u = \sqrt{v^2 - 2as}$$

To find a, first rearrange so that $2as$ is on its own:

$$v^2 - u^2 = 2as \rightarrow \frac{v^2 - u^2}{2s} = a \rightarrow a = \frac{v^2 - u^2}{2s}$$

1. Find out what you are being asked to find (current).
2. Identify which values you have been given in the question and what their units are: a potential difference (V), a resistance (Ω) and a power (W).
3. Think of the equation that includes the thing you want to find and the numbers that you have.
4. Rearrange the equation isolating the unknown value on one side and replace the symbols with the known values.
5. Check whether you need to convert the unit.

(5) Worked example — Grade 7

A 12 V motor has resistance 4.8 Ω. Find its current if it has power 30 W. **[2 marks]**

power = potential difference × current

$$P = IV \rightarrow I = \frac{P}{V} = \frac{30}{12} = 2.5A$$

Alternatively, put the numbers in first then rearrange the equation.

$$P = IV \rightarrow 30 = I \times 12 \rightarrow I = \frac{30}{12} = 2.5\ A$$

(10) Exam-style practice — Grade 5

1. Rearrange the following for each of the other quantities in the equation:

(a) $\rho = \frac{m}{V}$ **[1 mark]**

(b) $E = \frac{1}{2}kx^2$ **[1 mark]**

(c) $\Delta Q = mc\Delta\theta$ **[1 mark]**

(d) $a = \frac{\Delta v}{t}$ **[1 mark]**

2. Give the name and units for each of the quantities in question 1. **[6 marks]**

Converting units

BBC

Pages 76, 164, 205 LINKS

You need to know how to convert quantities to the standard unit.

5 Prefixes

Prefix	nano	micro	milli	centi	kilo	mega	giga
Example unit	nm	μm	mm	cm	km	M	G
Standard form	1×10^{-9}	1×10^{-6}	1×10^{-3}	1×10^{-2}	1×10^{3}	1×10^{6}	1×10^{9}
Factor	0.000 000 001	0.000 001	0.001	0.01	1000	1 000 000	1 000 000 000
Example	atom 0.1 nm	cells 1–100 μm	ball bearing few mm	pencil 15 cm	Mount Everest 9 km	Earth 13 M	Moon orbit 0.4 G

Standard form is written in terms of powers of 10. Negative numbers mean you divide by 10 that many times and positive numbers mean you multiply by 10 that many times. This value is equal to: $1 \times 10^9 = 1\,000\,000\,000$.

5 Converting units

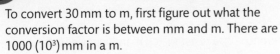

To convert 30 mm to m, first figure out what the conversion factor is between mm and m. There are 1000 (10^3) mm in a m.

Then decide if you need to multiply or divide.

30 mm is much smaller than a metre so should be a very small number:

30 mm ÷ 1000 = 0.03 m

Complex units

To convert spring constant 4.5 N/cm to N/m, first figure out what the conversion factor is between cm and m (100).

4.5 N/cm × 100 = 450 N/m

Now, check logically: if it takes 4.5 N to stretch the spring 1 cm, you would expect a lot more force to stretch it 1 m, so 450 N makes sense.

Time

Remember, that when dealing with time you need to multiply or divide by 60, not 100.

1 hour = 60 minutes, 1 minute = 60 seconds

Areas

When converting areas, take the normal conversion factor and square it.

Convert cm^2 to m^2

$250\ cm^2 \div 100^2 = 0.025\ m^2$

For volumes, cube the usual factor:

Convert m^3 to mm^3

$1.2\ m^3 \times 1000^3 = 1\,200\,000\,000\ mm^3$

or $1.2 \times 10^9\ mm^3$

2 Worked example — Grade 6

Convert:

(a) 0.56 kg to g **[1 mark]**

0.56 kg × 1000 = 560 g

(b) 12 mm to cm **[1 mark]**

12 mm ÷ 10 = 1.2 cm

(c) 25 MJ to J **[1 mark]**

$25\ MJ \times 10^6 = 25\,000\,000\ J$ or $2.5\times10^7\ J$

(d) 0.037 mm to μm **[1 mark]**

$0.037 \div 10^3 = 3.37\ \mu m$

2 Matching units

$$\text{velocity} = \frac{\text{displacement}}{\text{time}}$$

Normally, the velocity is in m/s, so the displacement and time need to be converted into metres and seconds to match.

However, if the displacement is in kilometres and the time in hours, the velocity will be in km/h.

Check which units you should use in your calculation and answer.

5 Exam-style practice — Grade 6

1 Convert:

(a) 200 μg to g **[1 mark]**

(b) 10 N/kg to N/g **[1 mark]**

(c) 330 J/minute to J/s. **[1 mark]**

2 Calculate how many orders of magnitude larger 10 kg is than 1 g. **[1 mark]**

Making estimations

You need to know how to estimate the results of simple calculations.

⑤ **Estimating speeds and masses**

Speeds

You need to have an idea of how fast some objects move.

- Cars move at around 10 m/s up to 30 m/s at motorway speeds.
- People walk at around 1–2 m/s and sprint at up to around 10 m/s.
- Jet planes can fly up to around 250 m/s.

> Try and picture an object moving and estimate how far you think it would get in 1 second. Use this to estimate its speed.

Masses

You need to have an idea of the masses of certain objects. The following are rough estimates and vary with size:

- a person: 50–70 kg
- a car: 1000 kg
- 1 litre of water: 1 kg
- a dog: 5–25 kg
- a mobile phone: 100–200 g.

> You can estimate the mass of an object by comparing it with objects of a similar mass.

⑩ **Worked example** | Grade 4

❶ Estimate the kinetic energy of a person sprinting in a race. **[3 marks]**

kinetic energy = ½ × mass × speed²

mass ~ 60 kg and speed ~ 10 m/s

kinetic energy = ½ × 60 kg × (10 m/s)² = 3000 J

❷ Calculate the increase in potential energy of a 1.45 kg mass lifted 9.5 m ($g = 9.8$ N/kg). **[3 marks]**

ΔGPE = mgh = 1.45 × 9.8 × 9.5 = 135 J

> Check the answer is correct by rounding the numbers and working out an approximate answer.
> 1.5 × 10 × 10 = 150, so this answer is about right.

① **Exam focus**

If a question instructs you to 'calculate', you should work out the answer exactly using a calculator. It is good practice to then estimate the answer to check it is correct.

① **Maths skills**

If you are asked to estimate the area under a curve, you do not need to try and calculate the area. First, work out the value of each square, then count roughly how many squares there are on the graph and then multiply these two numbers together.

⑤ **Worked example** | Grade 6

The time it takes an insulated beaker of hot water to cool by 5 °C is recorded.

Thickness of insulation (mm)	2	4	6	8
Time to cool (s)	250	569	603	798

(a) Using the table, estimate the time taken for 3 mm to cool. **[1 mark]**

400 seconds

(b) Using **Figure 1**, estimate the time taken for 7 mm to cool. **[1 mark]**

700 seconds

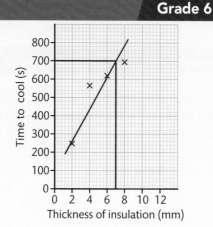

Figure 1 Time taken for hot water to cool

⑩ **Exam-style practice** | Grade 7

❶ Estimate the speed of a snail in mm/s. **[1 mark]**

❷ Estimate the mass of a person riding a bicycle. **[1 mark]**

 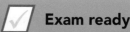

Pages
13, 31,
141
LINKS

Interpreting data

In the exam, you will need to demonstrate that you can interpret data from a range of equipment, tables, charts and graphs.

② Correlations

Scatter graphs show patterns, **outliers** and **anomalies** in numerical data. Anomalies do not fit the pattern at all, and outliers fit poorly. You may need to discount these results when finding an average for your data.

A **correlation** is a relationship between two variables that can easily be seen by drawing a line of best fit on a scatter graph. If the line is straight, then the relationship is linear. If it also goes through the origin (0,0), you can say that the measurements are proportional. A lot of scatter can indicate random error affecting your experiment. Think about how you can reduce this.

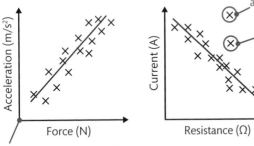

Positive correlation

Negative correlation

anomaly

outlier

If the line of best fit should go through (0,0) and does not, this indicates a systematic error. All of your readings are likely to be too high or too low by the same amount.

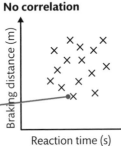

No correlation

The closer together the results are, the more precise they are.

Reaction time (s)

⑩ Worked example | Grade 7

A student is investigating the reaction between an acid and a metal. Give the volume of acid in the measuring cylinder. **[1 mark]**

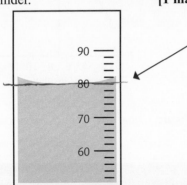

80 cm³

Make sure that you include the correct units. For area, this will be the unit squared. For volume, this will be the unit cubed.

⑤ Data in tables

If you are given data in a table, it is helpful to first of all look for a pattern to work out the relationship between the variables. In the table below, as speed increases, braking distance increases.

Speed (m/s)	5	10	15	20	25	30
Braking distance (m)	4	16	36	64	100	144

Now, look for further patterns. What happens when one of the quantities is doubled? As you double any speed the distance gets four times bigger.

You can make estimates for other speeds based on the values in the table. For example, the braking distance at a speed of 12 m/s would be between 16 m and 36 m.

As one measurement doubles, if the other:

- doubles, they are **directly proportional**
- halves, they are **inversely proportional**.

② Averages

$$\text{mean} = \frac{\text{sum of numbers}}{\text{amount of numbers}}$$

Use the **mean** for repeat readings. This is the most commonly used average in science. However, it should not be used where the range includes extremely large or small numbers that would affect the mean.

The **mode** is the number or measurement that occurs most often. It could be used with measurements that are not numbers, like average eye colour.

The **median** is the middle number when values are placed in order of increasing size.

When measuring a volume of liquid, make sure you take your reading from the **bottom** of the meniscus (the curved line that the skin of the water makes). If this comes up in an exam, draw a line across the bottom of the meniscus to help you find the right value.

⑩ Exam-style practice | Grade 7

1. Puppies in a litter weigh 1.1 kg, 1.2 kg, 1.2 kg, 1.3 kg, 3.3 kg. Calculate the mean, mode and median. Comment on how suitably each number represents the average mass of puppies in the litter. **[4 marks]**

2. Calculate the stopping distance from a speed of 40 m/s. **[3 marks]**

Using charts and graphs

Graphs are commonly used in science, particularly line and scatter graphs. You need to know how to interpret and draw a graph.

(5) Types of graphs and charts

Pie charts
Pie charts show the proportional measurements that make up a total. For example, percentage use of energy resource.

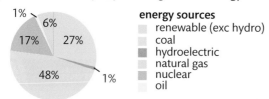

energy sources
- renewable (exc hydro)
- coal
- hydroelectric
- natural gas
- nuclear
- oil

Bar charts
Bar charts should only be used to show information about discrete data. For example, the strength of the gravitational field on different planets. They are not to be confused with histograms, which show continuous data.

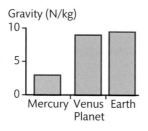
Gravity (N/kg)

Graphs
Graphs, such as scatter graphs, show the relationship between two variables. For example, length of wire and resistance, weight and mass.

(5) Worked example — Grade 7

The table shows a student's results for an investigation.

Time (s)	0	10	20	30	40	50	60
Temperature (°C)	5	6	11	17	35	72	180

(a) Use these results to draw a line graph. **[3 marks]**

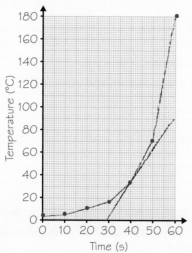

(b) Draw a tangent to work out the rate of reaction at 45 seconds. **[2 marks]**

$$80 - \frac{20}{54} - 36 = \frac{60}{18} = 3.33$$

(10) Interpreting graphs

Straight line graphs
The general equation of a straight line is $y = mx + c$, where:
- x and y are values on the x and y axes
- m is the gradient
- c is where the line meets the y-axis.

A straight line represents a linear relationship. The equation for the line in the graph in **Figure 1** is $y = 0.5x + 2.5$. You can replace x and y with the quantities you have plotted.

The meaning of the gradient depends on the quantities being divided. For example, with speed on the y-axis and time on the x-axis the gradient is speed ÷ time = acceleration.

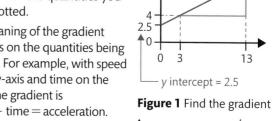
$$\text{gradient} = \frac{\text{rise}}{\text{run}} = \frac{5}{10} = 0.5$$
y intercept = 2.5

Figure 1 Find the gradient

Tangents
You can find the gradient of a curve at any point by drawing a tangent at that point. Find the gradient of the tangent but remember that the gradient is different at every point on the curve.

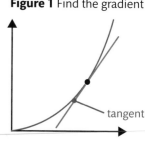
tangent

Figure 2 Drawing a tangent

Areas under the line
You can figure out what the area under the line represents by looking at the quantities that are being multiplied together. If the axes are speed and time, speed × time = distance. The area represents distance.

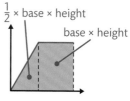
$\frac{1}{2}$ × base × height
base × height

Figure 3 Finding the area under a line

(10) Exam-style practice — Grade 8

1 State a suitable type of graph to show:
  (a) the stopping distances of different cars **[1 mark]**
  (b) the mass of salt that dissolves in water at different temperatures **[1 mark]**
  (c) the percentage of energy lost from the windows, doors, walls and floors in a house. **[1 mark]**

2 A straight line graph has force on the y-axis and extension on the x-axis. It has a gradient of 120 and goes through the origin. Give the equation of the line and the significance of the gradient. **[3 marks]**

Page
6, 24, 113, 159
LINKS

Using diagrams

You could be asked to draw or label a diagram in the exam. Diagrams can also help you to organise information to answer a question.

② Key questions

- ✓ Do you need to use a ruler?
- ✓ Do you need to label any parts?
- ✓ Should you add arrows to show direction?

- ✓ Should you draw anything to scale?
- ✓ Do you need to use symbols (like circuit symbols)?
- ✓ Do you need to use a particular shape or position?

⑮ Worked example — Grade 5

① Draw a diagram of an animal cell and label the following features:

- nucleus
- ribosomes
- mitochondria
- cell membrane.

Include a scale bar. **[4 marks]**

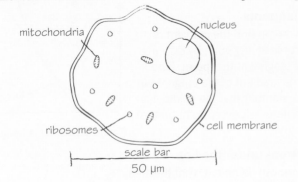

Exam focus

When asked to add a label to a diagram, make sure you think carefully about the position and draw your labels in exactly the right place. Consider using arrows or lines to clearly show the position.

The crest is just one position, but amplitude and wavelength must indicate between two positions.

The wavelength needs to be indicated exactly from the crest of one wave to the crest of the next and the amplitude from the centre line to the very highest point.

② Find the acceleration of a car of mass 1200 kg if the engine force is 1000 N and it experiences 350 N of air resistance and 200 N of friction. **[3 marks]**

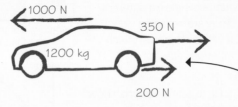

Resultant force = 1000 − 350 − 200 = 450 N

$$\text{acceleration} = \frac{\text{force}}{\text{mass}} = \frac{450}{1200} = 0.375 \text{ m/s}^2$$

③ Look at **Figure 1**.

Figure 1 A wave

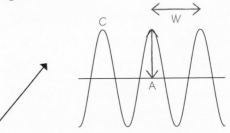

(a) Label the crest of a wave with **C**. **[1 mark]**
(b) Indicate the amplitude and label it **A**. **[1 mark]**
(c) Indicate a wavelength and label it **W**. **[1 mark]**

This sketch isn't part of the answer but it helps to organise all the numbers in the question.

⑩ Exam-style practice — Grade 5

① Sketch a skydiver of weight 600 N experiencing 300 N air resistance upward and a 200 N side wind. **[3 marks]**

② Draw a circuit diagram that could be used to find the resistance of a lightbulb. **[3 marks]**

Made a start ☑ | Feeling confident ☑ | Exam ready ☑

Planning practicals

You need to know how to write a plan for a practical, including an equipment list, a method and details about control and safety measures.

(15) Worked example — Grade 8

A student makes the hypothesis that the average speed of a trolley rolling down a ramp increases with the height of the ramp.

(a) Identify the variables that would need to be measured and calculated. **[3 marks]**

Change the height of the ramp and measure the distance the trolley moves and the time it takes to reach the bottom.

$$average\ speed = \frac{distance\ down\ ramp}{time}$$

> The variables are speed and height. You either have to measure speed directly or measure distance and time for it to be calculated.

(b) Draw a diagram to show the equipment needed. List any other items not shown. **[3 marks]**

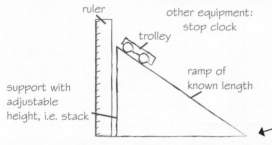

ruler

other equipment: stop clock

trolley

ramp of known length

support with adjustable height, i.e. stack

> Your equipment needs to reflect the variables you are going to measure.
>
> You could suggest using two light gates and a data logger set up for timing here instead. A sonic distance sensor and data logger could measure the speed of the trolley directly so no need to measure time and distance individually. This would also be a way to remove the reaction time uncertainty mentioned in **(c)**.

> The diagram is meant to save you wasting space in a method describing the layout of equipment. Not every single piece needs to be shown, but every piece needs mentioning in an equipment list.
>
> It can be useful to label some of the variables on your diagram like height of ramp and distance.

(c) Explain why there is an uncertainty involved in using a stop clock in this experiment. **[1 mark]**

The reaction time of the person who judges when the trolley reaches the bottom will affect the measurement of time.

> There would also be an issue starting the stop clock at the same time as the trolley is released.

(d) Suggest how the uncertainty in (c) could be reduced. **[2 marks]**

Use two light gates at a set distance and a data logger set to measure.

> Using a longer ramp and small heights would increase the time. This would make the uncertainty in reaction time less significant.

(e) Give **one** hazard the student should consider when writing their method and what steps could be taken to reduce it. **[2 marks]**

The trolley may roll onto the floor and become a trip hazard. Someone should catch it at the end of the ramp.

> Even experiments without acid or fire have a small hazard. Keep your hazards and solutions simple, avoid getting too inventive.

(10) Exam-style practice — Grade 8

A student conducts two experiments:

Experiment 1: The first experiment is conducted to find out if a radioactive source emits alpha, beta or gamma radiation by seeing what materials it will pass through.

Experiment 2: The second experiment tests the hypothesis 'the higher the temperature of a length of wire, the higher its resistance'. For each experiment:

(a) identify the variables that need measuring and controlling **[2 marks]**

(b) list the equipment needed to take the measurements **[2 marks]**

 Made a start   Feeling confident   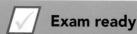 Exam ready

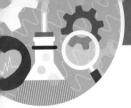

Page 113, 229, 232 LINKS

Improving results

It is important to be able to suggest improvements to practical methods.

5 Types of error

Systematic errors are consistent throughout a practical investigation and are caused by the measuring equipment, for example calibration errors. They lead to all measured values being either greater than or lower than the true value.

Random errors are those that are unpredictable. The effect of random errors can be reduced by taking repeat readings and then calculating a mean.

Zero errors occur when a piece of measuring equipment gives a reading when the true value is zero.

10 Worked example — Grade 6

1 The specific heat capacity of an aluminium block can be measured using the equipment shown in **Figure 1**.

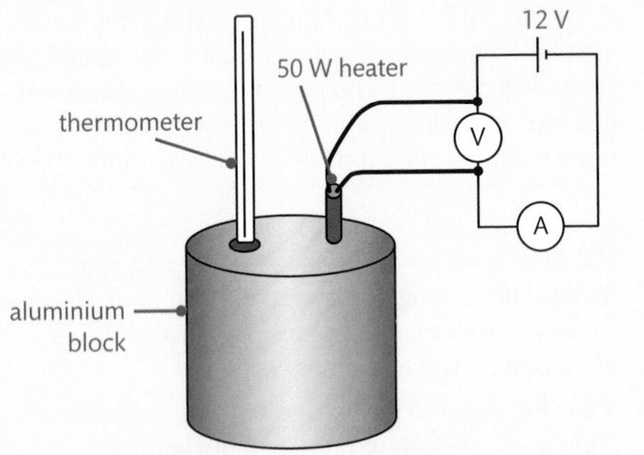

Figure 1 Apparatus for measuring the specific heat capacity of a solid

Suggest **one** change that could be made to the equipment that would allow more accurate measurements to be taken. Explain your choice. **[2 marks]**

Some of the heat from the heater will be lost to the surroundings as opposed to heating up the aluminium block. In order to minimise this heat loss, the block could be wrapped in some insulating material.

2 A student investigates the relationship between the force on a spring and the extension of the spring using the equipment in **Figure 2**.

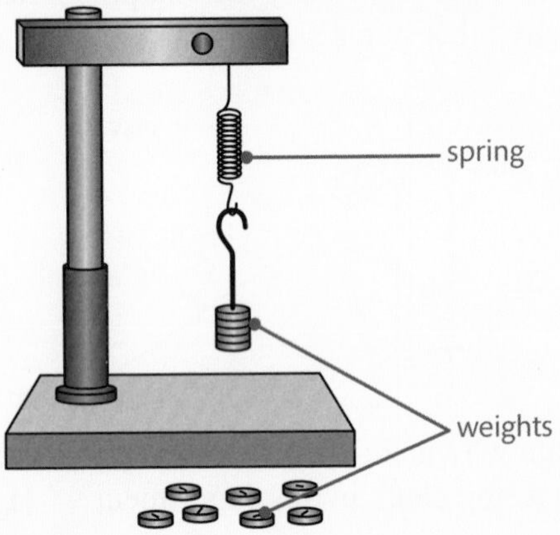

Figure 2 Apparatus for testing the extension of a spring

Suggest a change to the equipment shown that would allow the student to measure the length of the spring consistently and so calculate the extension. Explain your suggestion. **[2 marks]**

The student should clamp a ruler behind the spring. This would mean that they are always measuring from the same point each time.

10 Exam-style practice — Grade 6

A student investigates the behaviour of light shining through a clear plastic block using the equipment in **Figure 3**.

(a) Add a label to the diagram to show the normal. **[1 mark]**

(b) Outline a method the student could follow in order to investigate the relationship between the angle of incidence and the angle of refraction. **[4 marks]**

(c) State **one** way the student could improve the accuracy of the results they obtain from the experiment. **[2 marks]**

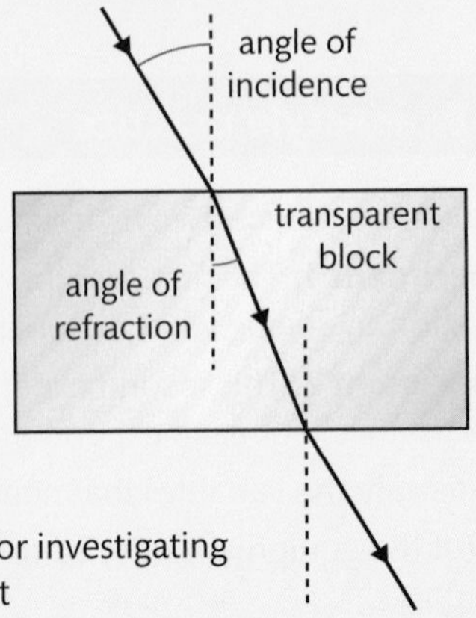

Figure 3 Apparatus for investigating the behaviour of light

Comparing data

You need to know how to compare data and be able to discuss the advantages and disadvantages of different ideas.

 Worked example — **Grade 8**

The table shows the estimated figures for the percentage of electricity produced from different resources in Spain and the UK.

Resource	Electricity production	
	UK	Spain
wind turbine	2.3%	26.4%
solar	0.2%	2.6%
hydroelectric	0.6%	23.9%
biomass	1.7%	0.2%
fossil fuel	87.4%	17.9%
nuclear	7.8%	29.0%

(a) Compare usage of renewable to non-renewable resources in each country. **[2 marks]**

4.8 per cent of electricity in UK comes from renewable resources compared to 53.1 per cent in Spain, which is over ten times higher.

(b) Suggest a reason for the difference in solar electricity production by each country. **[2 marks]**

Spain may have more hours of sunshine, or less clouds, making solar power a more useful resource.

(c) Compare wind turbines with nuclear power as sources of electricity production. **[4 marks]**

Neither of the sources give out chemical pollution or carbon dioxide so they do not contribute to global warming. Nuclear power has a much higher and more reliable power output. You need a lot of wind turbines to match the output of a nuclear power plant, and turbines only produce electricity when it is windy. After the initial costs, wind turbines have free energy and low maintenance costs, while nuclear power plants are costly to run and to decommission at the end of their life-cycle.

Compare the similarities, then say what is different about each one. It can be a good idea to work through some factors and compare each one in turn. For instance, power output, reliability, costs and effects on the environment. Make sure to mention some advantages and disadvantages of each one.

For every statement you make, you must compare it to the other resource, for instance wind turbines having low reliability must be compared to the higher consistency of nuclear power. If you only give facts about one, then they are not being compared.

 2 Comparing data

- Look for patterns in the data.
- Identify any similarities or differences, and what they mean.
- Consider the advantages and disadvantages of different variables.

Exam focus
When comparing data, look at the table's headings. Make sure you know exactly what the data is before answering the question.

When comparing, make sure you refer to both values and clearly state which is greater. Look for any patterns, e.g. if something is approximately ten times larger.

First, look at what the difference is, then apply what you know about solar power to try and explain it.

 Exam-style practice — **Grade 8**

1 A tyre manufacturer wants to compare the performance of two tyres. Using the same car and driver, they perform emergency stops at different speeds with each set of tyres, A and B.

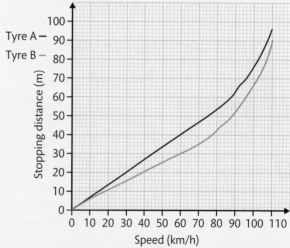

(a) Compare how the stopping distances of the two sets of tyres are affected by speed. **[3 marks]**

(b) Compare the stopping distances shown on the graph with what you might expect if the same test were performed on a wet road. **[2 marks]**

2 Compare emitters of alpha, beta and gamma radiation for use in hospitals, where they are fired as a beam to destroy cancerous cells in the body. **[3 marks]**

 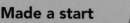

Working scientifically

Pages 43, 113, 157 LINKS

You need to demonstrate the ability to work scientifically through your experimental skills, analysis and evaluation of data.

 Experimental skills and strategies

Experiments are designed to test hypotheses (ideas or explanations).

Scientists use experiments to find data, such as the specific heat capacity of a material. They also test how one measured quantity affects another: one variable (the independent variable) is changed and another variable (the dependent variable) is measured.

Planning

Being able to choose the correct equipment and method to carry out a practical is an important skill for scientists. A plan should include an equipment list and a step-by-step method, as well as details about any control or safety measures.

Analysis and evaluation

After making and recording their observations, scientists process and present data in a way that enables them to evaluate the validity of a hypothesis.

It is important to use scientific theories and explanations to explain data and reflect on whether patterns and observations support the original hypothesis. The evaluation should also include suggestions on how the practical could be improved.

Development of scientific ideas

As new evidence comes to light, scientists change and develop their theories and knowledge. These changes may have ethical, social, environmental or economic implications.

Experimental results are published for peer review. This means other scientists can check the findings and carry out further experiments based on the original results.

 Worked example Grades 7–8

1 A student makes a hypothesis that the higher the light intensity, the taller a plant will grow.

(a) Identify the dependent and independent variables. **[2 marks]**

The independent variable is the level of light intensity, which needs changing. The height of the plant needs to be measured. This is the dependent variable.

> The variables need to come from the hypothesis. In this case light intensity and height can be measured directly. However, for variables like speed, you might need to measure distance and time and then calculate the variable you are investigating.

(b) Give **three** factors that need to be controlled. **[3 marks]**

Type of plant, time and growing conditions (water and carbon dioxide)

> There are lots of other factors, but these three are the most important and you should always choose the most obvious first. Others could include: temperature or soil pH.

(c) Suggest how the collected data would be best presented. **[3 marks]**

A scatter graph of light intensity on the x-axis and height of plant on the y-axis with a line of best fit.

> A scatter or line graph is best for any experiment that tests the relationship between two numerical variables.

2 Scientists are researching a cure for Parkinson's disease using embryonic stem cells. Compare the advantages and disadvantages of this method of stem cell treatment. **[4 marks]**

> Consider the ethical, social, environmental and economic aspects. They may not all be relevant.

The advantages are that it will replace the patient's damaged cells with healthy cells, which may help them to recover. It is also easier to extract cells from an embryo, which saves time and money. One disadvantage is that some people have ethical issues with the use of embryos in stem cell research, as embryos cannot consent to being used. Another disadvantage is that stem cell treatment can cause viral infections.

 Exam-style practice Grade 8

1 A student wants to find out which metal is the best conductor of electricity. Identify the variables that can be changed and controlled, what equipment would be needed and how the data would best be presented. **[6 marks]**

2 Describe the social implications of the development of uses for alpha, beta and gamma radiation. **[6 marks]**

  Made a start **Feeling confident** **Exam ready**

Extended-response questions

You will be expected to answer questions worth 4–6 marks as part of your biology, chemistry and physics exams.

⏱ Worked example   Grade 5 ☑

1 Explain, in terms of structure and bonding, why sodium chloride, NaCl, is a solid at room temperature but chlorine, Cl_2, is a gas at room temperature. **[6 marks]**

Sodium chloride is an ionic substance. It is made up of positive sodium ions and negative chloride ions. In the solid, the ions form a giant lattice. As the ions are oppositely charged, there are strong forces of attraction between the ions, meaning that large amounts of energy are needed to overcome these forces and melt the substance. This means that, at room temperature, NaCl will be a solid.

Chlorine is a small covalent molecule. It has a strong covalent bond between the two atoms of chlorine, but much weaker intermolecular forces between the separate molecules of chlorine. It is these intermolecular forces that need to be overcome in order to melt and boil chlorine. As the forces are weak, it does not take very much energy to do this. This means that, at room temperature, Cl_2 will be a gas.

> Be sure to answer the question fully: the student has stated the type of structure and bonding of each substance and has then explained the difference in melting and boiling points in terms of the bonding in these structures.

> Break your answer down to give it a logical order: the student writes about sodium chloride first, and then chlorine. Each paragraph states the structure and the bonding and then explains the effect on melting and boiling point.

2 Compare alpha, beta and gamma radiation in terms of their penetrating and ionising powers. **[6 marks]**

Alpha radiation can be stopped by skin or paper. It is the most ionising type of radiation as it is the largest and has the highest charge.

Beta radiation can be stopped by a few mm of aluminium. It is moderately ionising as, although it is small, it has a charge.

Gamma radiation is the most penetrating. It takes a few centimetres of lead or a few metres of concrete to stop it. It is the least ionising as it is very small and has no charge.

> It is often useful to include a diagram in extended-response questions, such as **Figure 1**:

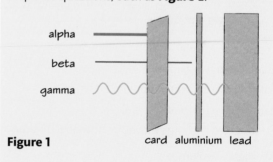

Figure 1

3 Gases can be compressed but solids cannot. Use ideas about particles to explain why. **[4 marks]**

The particles in a gas are spread out, with a lot of space between them. This means that gas particles can be pushed closer together. Solid particles are tightly packed together: there is no space between them, which means that they cannot be pushed closer together.

4 Explain why reactivity decreases going down Group 7. **[4 marks]**

Group 7 elements all have 7 electrons in their outer shell. When they react, they will gain an electron. The reactivity decreases down the group because the size of the atoms increases as you go down the group. This increase in size means that the outer-electron shell is further away from the nucleus. This means that the 'incoming' electron feels less pull from the nucleus.

⏱ Exam-style practice   Grade 5 ☑

Describe the levels of organisation within the human circulatory system. **[4 marks]**

Equations for physics

In the exam, you could be asked about any of the equations on this page. Make sure you know how to rearrange each of the equations and learn the units that match each quantity.

10 Equations to learn

Word equation	Symbol equation
weight = mass × gravitational field strength	$W = m \times g$
work done = force × distance moved in the direction of the force	$E = F \times d$
force exerted on a spring = spring constant × extension	$F = k \times x$
distance travelled = average speed × time	
acceleration = change in velocity ÷ time taken	$a = \dfrac{(v - u)}{t}$
force = mass × acceleration	$F = m \times a$
momentum = mass × velocity	$p = m \times v$
kinetic energy = $\frac{1}{2}$ × mass × (speed)^2	$KE = \dfrac{1}{2} \times m \times v^2$
change in gravitational potential energy = mass × gravitational field strength × change in vertical height	$\Delta GPE = m \times g \times \Delta h$
power = energy transferred (J) ÷ time taken	$P = \dfrac{E}{t}$
power = work done ÷ time taken	$P = \dfrac{E}{t}$
efficiency = $\dfrac{\text{(useful energy transferred by the device)}}{\text{(total energy supplied to the device)}}$	
wave speed = frequency × wavelength	$v = f \times \lambda$
wave speed = distance ÷ time	$v = \dfrac{x}{t}$
charge = current × time	$Q = I \times t$
potential difference = current × resistance	$V = I \times R$
electrical power = current × potential difference	$P = I \times V$
electrical power = (current)^2 × resistance	$P = I^2 \times R$
energy transferred = charge moved × potential difference	$E = Q \times V$
density = mass ÷ volume	$\rho = \dfrac{m}{v}$

5 Physics equation sheet

You will be given a list of some of the more complicated equations in the exam.

Word equation	Symbol equation
(final velocity)^2 – (initial velocity)^2 = 2 × acceleration × distance	$v^2 - u^2 = 2 \times a \times x$
change in thermal energy = mass × specific heat capacity × change in temperature	$\Delta Q = m \times c \times \Delta\theta$
thermal energy for a change of state = mass × specific latent heat	$Q = m \times L$
force = change in momentum ÷ time	$F = \dfrac{(mv - mu)}{t}$
energy transferred = current × potential difference × time	$E = I \times V \times t$
force on a conductor (at right angles to a magnetic field) carrying a current = magnetic flux density × current × length	$F = B \times I \times l$
For transformers with 100% efficiency, potential difference across primary coil × current in primary coil = potential difference across secondary coil × current in secondary coil	$V_p \times I_p = V_s \times I_s$
energy transferred in stretching = 0.5 × spring constant × (extension)^2	$E = \dfrac{1}{2} \times k \times x^2$

 Made a start   Feeling confident   Exam ready

The Periodic Table of the Elements

1	2											3	4	5	6	7	0
						1 H Hydrogen 1											4 He Helium 2
7 Li Lithium 3	9 Be Beryllium 4											11 B Boron 5	12 C Carbon 6	14 N Nitrogen 7	16 O Oxygen 8	19 F Fluorine 9	20 Ne Neon 10
23 Na Sodium 11	24 Mg Magnesium 12											27 Al Aluminium 13	28 Si Silicon 14	31 P Phosphorus 15	32 S Sulfur 16	35.5 Cl Chlorine 17	40 Ar Argon 18
39 K Potassium 19	40 Ca Calcium 20	45 Sc Scandium 21	48 Ti Titanium 22	51 V Vanadium 23	52 Cr Chromium 24	55 Mn Manganese 25	56 Fe Iron 26	59 Co Cobalt 27	59 Ni Nickel 28	63.5 Cu Copper 29	65 Zn Zinc 30	70 Ga Gallium 31	73 Ge Germanium 32	75 As Arsenic 33	79 Se Selenium 34	80 Br Bromine 35	84 Kr Krypton 36
85 Rb Rubidium 37	88 Sr Strontium 38	89 Y Yttrium 39	91 Zr Zirconium 40	93 Nb Niobium 41	96 Mo Molybdenum 42	[98] Tc Technetium 43	101 Ru Ruthenium 44	103 Rh Rhodium 45	106 Pd Palladium 46	108 Ag Silver 47	112 Cd Cadmium 48	115 In Indium 49	119 Sn Tin 50	122 Sb Antimony 51	128 Te Tellurium 52	127 I Iodine 53	131 Xe Xenon 54
133 Cs Caesium 55	137 Ba Barium 56	139 La Lanthanum 57	178 Hf Hafnium 72	181 Ta Tantalum 73	184 W Tungsten 74	186 Re Rhenium 75	190 Os Osmium 76	192 Ir Iridium 77	195 Pt Platinum 78	197 Au Gold 79	201 Hg Mercury 80	204 Tl Thallium 81	207 Pb Lead 82	209 Bi Bismuth 83	[209] Po Polonium 84	[210] At Astatine 85	[222] Rn Radon 86
[223] Fr Francium 87	[226] Ra Radium 88	[227] Ac Actinium 89	[261] Rf Rutherfordium 104	[262] Db Dubnium 105	[266] Sg Seaborgium 106	[264] Bh Bohrium 107	[277] Hs Hassium 108	[268] Mt Meitnerium 109	[271] Ds Darmstadtium 110	[272] Rg Roentgenium 111							

Answers

Page 1 Levels of organisation

1. A group of organs that collectively perform specific functions within a system, such as the respiratory system

2. The circulatory system is an organ system made up of several organs, including the heart and blood vessels, working together. The organs consist of different types of tissues: epithelial, muscle, nervous or connective tissues. The tissues are made up of cells, such as red blood cells.

Page 2 Eukaryotic and prokaryotic cells

1. Differences:
   - All prokaryotic cells have a cell wall; many eukaryotic cells do not.
   - Eukaryotic cells have their DNA inside a nucleus; prokaryotic cells do not.
   - Prokaryotic cells have loops of DNA; eukaryotic cells do not.
   - Eukaryotic cells contain mitochondria; prokaryotic cells do not.

   Similarities:
   - Both types of cell contain ribosomes, cytoplasm and a cell membrane.

2. Ribosomes, mitochondria, nucleus

Page 3 Animal and plant cells

1. (a) The nucleus is shown by A.

   (b) Approximately five to six times wider

2. Unlike animal cells, plant cells have a cell wall. Plant cells also contain chloroplasts and a permanent vacuole, whereas animal cells do not.

Page 4 Specialised animal cells

(a) Any two from: egg cells contain: cytoplasm containing nutrients needed for growth; a cell membrane that changes after fertilisation so that only one sperm cell can enter; a haploid nucleus to combine with the sperm cell nucleus during fertilisation.

(b) Any two from: sperm cells have: an acrosome containing enzymes needed to digest the outer layers of the egg cell; a tail for movement; mitochondria to provide energy for movement; a haploid nucleus to combine with the egg cell nucleus during fertilisation.

(c) Ciliated epithelial cells have cilia to move mucus containing dirt and bacteria away from the lungs.

Page 5 Microscopy

1. $\dfrac{200\,000}{100} = 2000$

   2×10^3

2. $15 \times 50 = \times 750$

Page 6 Practical: Using microscopes

1. To produce an image that the eye can see, light needs to be able to pass through the tissue. If the tissue is made of many layers of overlapping cells it is difficult to see individual cells clearly.

2. To make the cells, or parts of the cells, easier to see.

Page 7 Enzyme action

The enzyme and substrate molecule collide. The substrate binds to the enzyme's active site, because they have complementary shapes. The enzyme catalyses the reaction and the products are released.

Page 8 Practical: Enzymes

1. Changes in temperature affect the activity of the enzyme, amylase. Higher temperatures will cause the amylase to break down the starch more quickly than lower temperatures. If the temperature is too high, the enzymes will become denatured and no more starch will be broken down.

2. Take the drops more frequently, e.g. every 15 seconds, or have a colour reference to compare the samples to.

Page 9 Digestion and enzymes

Enzymes in the small intestine need alkaline conditions, so the stomach acid must be neutralised, otherwise the enzymes in the small intestine could be denatured.

Page 10 Diffusion

1. Oxygen diffuses from the lungs into the blood. A good blood supply carries the oxygen away very quickly, maintaining the maximum concentration gradient.

2. The larger the surface area, the more space there is for oxygen to diffuse from the lungs into the blood, and for carbon dioxide to diffuse from the blood into the lungs, so gas exchange will happen more quickly.

Page 11 Osmosis

1. As the concentration of glucose increases, the concentration of water molecules decreases. This results in a greater difference in water concentration on either side of the membrane. This means water will pass through the membrane from the left to the right more quickly.

2. As the molecules get warmer they move across the membrane more quickly, increasing the rate of osmosis.

Page 12 Practical: Osmosis

1. Different-sized potato chips would have different surface areas, which would affect the rate of osmosis. It is the effect of concentration that is being investigated so all other variables should be kept the same (controlled).

2. The hypothesis was only partly correct. The change in mass only increased in sugar concentrations above 68 gdm^{-3}.

Page 13 Active transport

1. Diffusion is the movement of molecules from a high concentration to a low concentration, whereas active transport is the movement of molecules against the concentration gradient, from a low concentration to a high concentration. Active transport requires energy, whereas diffusion does not.

2. Answers may vary, e.g.
   - plants absorbing mineral ions through their root hair cells
   - animals absorbing glucose through the cells of the intestine.

Page 14 Mitosis and the cell cycle

1. The cell needs to grow and increase its sub-cellular structures, such as ribosomes and mitochondria. The genetic material needs to replicate.

2. Interphase is when the cell is growing and preparing to divide. Mitosis is when the nucleus and chromosomes divide. Mitosis is made of four stages: prophase, metaphase, anaphase and telophase. Cytokinesis is when the rest of the cell divides in two.

3. 46 (23 pairs)

Page 15 Importance of mitosis

1. Mitosis is the type of cell division that occurs in growth and repair, and asexual reproduction, producing new cells that are genetically identical to the original cells.

2. Uncontrollable cell division caused by changes (mutations) to the genes. The likelihood of these changes is increased by various risk factors, such as smoking.

Page 16 Cell differentiation and growth

1. Answers may vary, e.g.
   - hair growing
   - fingernails growing.

2. When a particular type of tissue is damaged, it can be replaced or repaired.

3. 140 cm.

Page 17 Stem cells

1. Answers may vary e.g.
   - farmers can grow a whole field of disease-resistant crops
   - farmers can grow crops with a large yield.

2. Ethical considerations include:
   - the embryo's right to life
   - the sufferer's right to a better quality of life.

Page 18 The human nervous system

Any two from: long length, to carry impulses a long distance; myelin sheath, to carry impulses quickly; many nerve endings/dendrites, to connect with muscles/other neurones.

Page 19 Meiosis

1. Gametes from the same parent show variation. This is because they all contain different combinations of chromosomes (and therefore alleles). Sexual reproduction involves the random combination of gametes at fertilisation.

2. **(a)** A sex cell has half the number of chromosomes (haploid) as a body cell.

   (b) 23 chromosomes (unpaired)

Page 20 The structure of DNA

DNA is a double helix-shaped polymer, made of two strands of nucleotides. Each nucleotide is made of a sugar, phosphate and one of four different bases. The strands are held together by hydrogen bonds between complementary base pairs.

Page 21 DNA and the genome

1. A sample of DNA can be taken from the foetus and compared with the genome of a cystic fibrosis sufferer to identify if the gene for cystic fibrosis is present.

2. By identifying the mutated gene and knowing what the healthy gene should be and what it should do, scientists can develop methods of treating genetic mutations.

3. It can be used to identify genetic diseases, trace human migration and identify disease-causing genes.

Page 22 Genetic inheritance

(a)

	Mother	
	D	D
d	Dd	Dd
d	Dd	Dd

(Father)

(b) 100 %

Page 23 Inherited disorders

(a) FF

(b) They will be homozygous (ff) because the condition is recessive (represented by a lower case f). This means that to have the condition, the person must inherit both alleles for it.

(c)

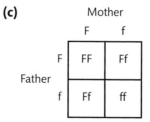

	Mother	
	F	f
F	FF	Ff
f	Ff	ff

(Father)

Therefore the probability is 0.25 or $\frac{1}{4}$.

(d) 1:1

Page 24 Sex determination

1. **(a)** XX

   (b) One chromosome (always an X)

   (c) 0.5 / ½ / 50% / 1 : 1 / 50 : 50 / 1 in 2

   Half of the sperm contains a Y chromosome, so half of the offspring will be male.

Page 25 Variation and mutation

1. Answers will vary, e.g.
   - genetic – tongue rolling, Down's syndrome, blood group, eye colour, natural hair colour
   - environmental – hair style, language spoken, scars.

2. A mutation is a change in the genetic material. Mutations usually occur when DNA replicates, and are caused by environmental factors such as smoking cigarettes or exposure to high levels of radiation.

3. Mutation could improve chances of survival. For example, a crop plant could become more resistant to a disease.

Page 26 Evolution by natural selection

1. All species have evolved from simpler organisms over billions of years.

2. Birds and other predators will assume the scarlet king snake is harmful and not attempt to eat it. This means that the snake is left to reproduce.

3. Variation occurs between organisms within a species. Those most suited to their environment ('the fittest') are better able to survive, and pass on their genes (alleles) to their offspring. Over many generations the species changes to become better adapted to its environment.

Page 27 Evidence for human evolution

As tools became better designed, they showed more skill in their construction; this demonstrates that early humans were becoming more intelligent and had more dexterity in their hands.

Page 28 Classification

1. It is an easily understandable system to use.

   You can tell from the genus name which species are closely related.

2. Any two from:
   - improvements to microscopes
   - DNA analysis and sequencing
   - improved understanding of biological processes.

Page 29 Selective breeding

1. Selective breeding involves humans choosing and enhancing desired characteristics in a species, by selecting which individuals breed. Natural selection is where a feature is passed down through generations because it gives an organism a better chance of survival, making it more likely to reproduce.

2. Inbreeding, which can lead to genetic disease.

   There is a reduction in genetic variation, making the species more susceptible to disease.

3. Answers will vary, e.g.
   - improved disease resistance
   - improved pest resistance
   - improved drought resistance
   - increased fruit size
   - improved taste.

Page 30 Genetic engineering

Farmers may use more herbicide and the herbicide may harm people who eat the crops. It may also cause a herbicide-resistant weed to develop.

Page 31 Health issues

1. Communicable diseases can be passed on by, or caught from, another person, non-communicable diseases cannot. Communicable disease are caused by pathogens; non-communicable diseases have other causes.

2. Pathogens are microorganisms that cause disease.

Page 32 Communicable diseases

1. A disease that can be passed from one person to another.

2. Infectious microorganisms can be breathed in without coming into contact with the infected person.

Page 33 Viral diseases

Viruses are much smaller than bacteria. They consist of small packets of DNA surrounded by protein. When a virus invades a cell, the DNA in the virus instructs the cell to make more copies of the virus.

Page 34 Bacterial diseases

1. Some bacteria produce toxins, which kill cells. The destruction of cells and tissue causes symptoms of the disease to appear.

2. The spread of *Chlamydia* can be prevented by abstaining from sex, using a condom and regular screening followed by treatment if necessary.

Page 35 Fungal diseases

1. Fungi reproduce through spores, which means they are not an animal. Fungal cells have a cell wall, like plants, but do not contain any chlorophyll. This means that, unlike plants, they cannot make their own food.

2. The leaves should be burned or buried so that the spores cannot spread through the air and infect healthy ash trees.

Page 36 Protist diseases

1. Mosquitoes

2. Because it is the protist, the parasite which is carried by the mosquito, that causes the disease.

Page 37 Human defence systems

1. Some white blood cells engulf bacteria and kill them (phagocytosis); other white blood cells produce antibodies (also some produce antitoxins).

2. The person's immune system responds to the first infection by producing white blood cells, which kill the pathogen. The white blood cells produce antibodies that stay in the blood for a short while to kill the pathogen if it returns. Memory lymphocytes that remember how to produce the antibodies stay in the blood system for much longer.

Page 38 Immunisation

1. They immunise their children so that they will not get the disease, and so they cannot pass the disease onto others.

2. Different diseases are caused by different pathogens, each with their own unique antigens. Each immunisation causes the production of a different type of antibody specific to those antigens.

3. So they cannot reproduce, causing the disease and its symptoms.

4. Memory lymphocytes recognise reinvading antigens and produce specific antibodies to destroy them.

Page 39 Antibiotics

1. Antibiotics work by inhibiting cell processes in bacteria. Viruses are not living things and are not made of cells.

2. Bacteria develop resistance to antibiotics by natural selection. Some bacteria have mutations which make them resistant to a particular antibiotic. These resistant bacteria will survive and reproduce rapidly. The bacteria that are susceptible to the antibiotic will be destroyed. Eventually, only bacteria that are resistant to the antibiotic will exist.

3. So that the doctor can prescribe an antibiotic that will work specifically just against that type of bacteria. This avoids prescribing antibiotics that work against many different types of bacteria, as it is the overuse of this type of antibiotic that is the main cause of the spread of antibiotic resistance in bacteria.

Page 40 Development of drugs

1. The work of a scientist, or a group of scientists, is checked by others to make sure that it is correct.

2. 9 to 16 years

3. Clinical trials involve testing on human volunteers or patients, to check a new drug's safety, its effectiveness and the optimum dose. Pre-clinical trials involve testing on cells, tissues or animals to make sure the new drug has the wanted effect and that it's safe to start testing on humans.

Page 41 Non-communicable diseases

(a) People aged less than 30

(b) People who have never smoked can still get lung cancer.

The older you are when you stop smoking, the more likely you are to get lung cancer (or the reverse).

(c) (i) 0.4 per cent

(ii) 5.6 per cent

Page 42 Effects of lifestyle

1. Teenagers are still growing, so their heights and BMI may be changing quite dramatically. This is quite normal.

2. Poor diet affects both physical health, by causing obesity or nutritional deficiencies, and mental health.

Page 43 Cardiovascular disease

1. All surgery carries some risk. It may be very small, but it means that any surgery is not 100 % safe.

2. A stent or drugs such as statins or warfarin.

Page 44 Photosynthesis

1. Photosynthesis provides food for plants and algae and therefore indirectly all the organisms in the food chains that begin with them. Photosynthesis also provides oxygen for all the organisms that respire aerobically.

2. Plants make their own food by photosynthesis, using carbon dioxide, water and light which can all be available in one place. Animals need to eat other organisms for food and so have to move to find them.

Page 45 Rate of photosynthesis

(a) Light intensity

Carbon dioxide concentration

Temperature

(b) Light intensity – if the light intensity is increased from this point, then the rate of photosynthesis increases, which shows that light intensity was the limiting factor.

(c) Temperature – if the temperature is increased from this point (to 25 °C), then the rate of photosynthesis increases, which shows that temperature was the limiting factor.

(d) Light intensity

Page 46 Practical: Photosynthesis

Use a gas syringe. This measures the actual volume of gas produced. This is more accurate than counting bubbles because the bubbles will not be all the same size.

Page 47 Specialised plant cells

1. A root hair cell contains many mitochondria to provide the energy needed for the absorption of mineral ions by active transport. It also has a large surface area to increase the rate of water and mineral ion absorption.

2. Translocation is the movement of sucrose through the phloem up and down a plant. Transpiration is the movement of water (and minerals) through the xylem up the plant.

Page 48 Transport in plants

Water enters the root hair cells by osmosis. It moves up through the roots, then through the stem, to the leaves. It evaporates and diffuses out through the stomata.

Page 49 Water uptake in plants

1. On a hot, sunny, windy day.

2. Rate of uptake

   $= 27$ mm in 10 minutes

   $= 2.7$ cm in 10 minutes

   $= 2.7 \times 6$ cm in 1 hour

   $= 16.2$ cm/hour

Page 50 Human endocrine system

1. The pancreas.

2. A hormone is a substance secreted by an endocrine gland, that travels through the blood to its target organ(s), and helps regulate processes in the body.

Page 51 Adrenalin and thyroxine

1. Thyroxine controls metabolic rate and helps growth and development.

2. Negative feedback happens where an output of a process, such as a hormone, feeds back into the system to reverse any changes and bring them back to a set level.

Page 52 Hormones in reproduction

1. During the 28-day menstrual cycle, the level of luteinising hormone increases and stimulates the release of an egg. The hormone level then falls before the cycle is repeated the following month.

2. Follicle stimulating hormone (FSH) stimulates oestrogen production. Oestrogen inhibits FSH production.

3. Progesterone, because during the menstrual cycle this is the hormone that maintains the lining.

Page 53 Contraception

1. Scientific evidence and data can provide reliable information about the different types of contraception, such as how they work, their effectiveness and any side effects, which helps people to make an informed decision.

2. Is it morally right to use contraception?

   How much will it cost?

Page 54 Hormones to treat infertility

1. To ensure that there are enough eggs to give a realistic chance of at least some of them successfully developing into embryos and babies.

2. Two hormones often used in fertility drugs are follicle stimulating hormone (FSH) and luteinising hormone (LH). These are used to stimulate egg production and release (ovulation).

Page 55 Control of blood glucose

If the blood glucose concentration changes from the normal level, the pancreas acts to return it to normal. If the blood glucose concentration rises above normal, the pancreas releases insulin to reduce the concentration. If the blood glucose concentration falls below normal, the pancreas releases glucagon to increase the concentration.

Page 56 Diabetes

Type 1 diabetes is where the pancreas does not produce sufficient insulin. Type 2 is where the cells in the body no longer respond to insulin.

Type 1 diabetes is controlled by injections of insulin. Whereas, Type 2 is controlled by diet.

Obesity is a risk factor for Type 2 diabetes but not for Type 1.

Page 57 Transport in animals

1. Surface area : volume $= (6 \times 4 \times 4):(4 \times 4 \times 4)$

   $= 96:64$

   $= 3:2$

   $= 1.5:1$

2. They increase the surface area (: volume ratio) for the absorption of (digested) food.

Page 58 Alveoli

1. Alveoli have a large surface area to absorb oxygen and remove carbon dioxide. They also have thin, moist membranes to allow gases to diffuse easily. They have a good blood supply to transport oxygen to the rest of the body and to transport carbon dioxide to the lungs to be breathed out.

2. Rapid breathing maintains a high concentration of oxygen and a low concentration of carbon dioxide inside the alveoli. This maintains high concentration gradients between the alveoli and the blood, ensuring diffusion occurs quickly.

Page 59 The blood

1. Red blood cells have no nucleus, which increases the space available for haemoglobin. They are a biconcave disc shape, which increases the surface area for oxygen to diffuse in and out of the cell. They have a large surface area to volume ratio which increases the rate of diffusion of oxygen in and out of the cell. They are small/flexible, which allows them to pass easily through capillaries.

2. Phagocytes are white blood cells which ingest and destroy pathogens.

Page 60 Blood vessels

1. Blood entering the arteries has only just been pumped by the heart (unlike the blood in veins which is returning to the heart). The thick elastic and muscular walls of the arteries then maintain the pressure. The high pressure is necessary to make sure the blood circulates around the whole body.

2. Veins carry blood at low pressure, usually upwards back to the heart against the force of gravity. Valves are needed to ensure blood will not flow backwards. The pressure in the other vessels is high enough to keep the blood flowing in the correct direction, so they do not need valves.

Page 61 The heart

1. left ventricle ➔ aorta ➔ body ➔ vena cava ➔ right atrium ➔ right ventricle ➔ pulmonary artery ➔ lungs ➔ pulmonary vein ➔ left atrium

2. Having two ventricles and two atria means that the blood is pumped twice on each complete circulation of the body. This maintains a high blood pressure and ensures more efficient circulation of the blood. This means oxygen can be transported more quickly around the body, releasing more energy in respiration.

Page 62 Aerobic and anaerobic respiration

Both aerobic and anaerobic respiration break down glucose to release energy. Both types of respiration are exothermic reactions. Aerobic respiration produces carbon dioxide and water, whereas anaerobic respiration produces lactic acid. Aerobic respiration releases more energy and uses oxygen.

Page 63 Practical: Rate of respiration

1. As the organisms respire, they take up oxygen from the air inside the apparatus. Although they give out carbon dioxide, this is absorbed by the soda lime. So overall there is a decrease in the number of molecules in the air inside the apparatus; so the air pressure inside the apparatus decreases, causing the drop of liquid to move along the glass tube, decreasing the air volume inside the apparatus.

2. The drop would not move. This is because the number of oxygen molecules taken up by the organisms during respiration would be replaced by the same number of carbon dioxide molecules given out. So, there would be no overall change in air pressure and air volume inside the apparatus.

Page 64 Response to exercise

1. Compared with before exercise, cardiac output will rise during exercise and then fall after exercise. This is because heart rate, and stroke volume, increase during exercise. This is to deliver oxygen and glucose to muscles more quickly, and to remove the extra carbon dioxide.

2. Stroke volume = $\dfrac{\text{cardiac output}}{\text{heart rate}} = \dfrac{4}{60} = 0.0667 \, \text{l} = 66.7 \, \text{ml}$

Page 65 Communities

1. **(a)** When the population of algae increases, the population of snails increases shortly after. This is because there is more food for the snails, which makes them more likely to reproduce. As the population of snails increases, the amount of food (algae) available per individual decreases, causing them to compete for it. Some snails die, decreasing the population. The cycle then begins again.

   (b) The snail population would decrease as more are being eaten. With fewer snails to feed on it, the algal population would then increase.

Page 66 Abiotic factors

1. Three from the following for 1 mark each: temperature, pH and mineral content of soil, wind intensity and direction, light intensity, carbon dioxide levels, oxygen levels, moisture levels.

2. A change in temperature could cause the ice to melt, which could damage or destroy animal or plant habitats. It could also lead to a lack of food, causing starvation of certain species and possible extinction.

Page 67 Biotic factors

1. Predators (e.g. polar bears) and food (e.g. fish for seals and polar bears).

2. Abiotic factors: temperature, carbon dioxide levels, wind intensity.

   Biotic factors: new pathogens, food availability, predators.

3. Grey squirrels compete with red squirrels for food and territory, causing a great decrease in the population of red squirrels.

Page 68 Practical: Population studies

1. To avoid bias; for example, this could cause the estimate to be too high if areas containing many samples of the plant were deliberately chosen.

2. In a belt transect, the quadrats are placed in a line; this is to investigate if the distribution of a species changes in a particular direction.

Page 69 Biodiversity

1. Answers may vary, e.g.
   - limiting how many fish can be caught in a given period of time (a quota)
   - returning the young fish to the sea so that they can reproduce.

2. Species maintain stable ecosystems by providing food and shelter for one another. If one species disappears, others could also be affected too, reducing biodiversity.

Page 70 Maintaining biodiversity

1. Answers may vary, e.g.
   - burn less fossil fuels and use alternative fuel sources instead
   - reduce energy use, e.g. reduce energy used in heating by having better building insulation.

2. Advantage: it increases the biodiversity and so strengthens the ecosystem.

   Disadvantage: it takes up valuable farm land that could be used to grow crops.

Page 71 Carbon cycle

1. The dead animal is decayed and broken down by microorganisms/detritus feeders/decomposers. When these respire, they release the carbon as carbon dioxide.

2. Plants use the carbon in carbon dioxide in photosynthesis to make glucose, which they then convert into many other substances as they grow. When other organisms, such as animals or microorganisms, feed on plants they take in these substances containing carbon and also use them to grow. There is only a fixed amount of carbon on Earth and without carbon being recycled, plants, animals and other organisms would not get the carbon they need to live and grow.

Page 72 Water cycle

1. It may be sea water. It may contain harmful microorganisms or toxins.

2. The water cycle allows water to move around the planet, providing a supply to sustain plants and animals. Although living things are constantly losing water, the water cycle ensures there is more available.

Page 73 Nitrogen cycle

Decomposers break down remains/protein to ammonium ions/ammonia. Nitrifying bacteria convert ammonium ions/ammonia to nitrates. Denitrifying bacteria convert nitrates to nitrogen gas.

Page 74 Atoms, elements and compounds

1. It cannot be chemically broken down into anything simpler.

2. Al

3. **(a)** Sodium

   (b) (i) Hydrogen, H

   (ii) hydrogen + chlorine → hydrogen chloride

Page 75 The model of the atom

1. protons, neutrons and electrons

2. Dalton thought that atoms were the smallest unit of matter and were solid, featureless spheres. This view changed when it was discovered that atoms are made of smaller particles with positive and negative charges (protons and electrons). Most of the atom is now thought to be empty space with electrons outside a nucleus of positive and neutral particles (neutrons).

Page 76 Subatomic particles

1. $1 \times 10^{-5} = 0.00001\,nm$

2. Positive

3. Protons and neutrons

4. **(a)** 2

   (b) There are the same number of positive protons as there are negative electrons.

   (c) A helium atom contains two protons and two neutrons in the nucleus, and two electrons in the first electron shell.

Page 77 Size and mass of atoms

(a) The atomic number is the number of protons.

The mass number is the number of protons plus the number of neutrons.

(b)

Subatomic particle	Relative mass	Relative charge
electron	$\frac{1}{1835}$	−1
neutron	1	0
proton	1	+1

(c) 10

Page 78 Isotopes and relative atomic mass

(a) R and S, because the isotopes have the same number of protons (same atomic number) but a different number of neutrons (different atomic mass).

(b) Lithium

Page 79 Developing the periodic table

(a) Any three from: carbon, silicon, titanium, zirconium.

(b) A – atomic mass

(c) He realised that some undiscovered elements must exist with properties like those of the rest of their groups.

(d) Atoms of an element do not always have the same number of neutrons/isotopes of an element may exist.

If there is a greater proportion of the heavier isotope, then the mass of the element may be higher than the next element. / If there is a greater proportion of the lighter isotope, then the mass of the element may be lower than the previous element.

Page 80 The periodic table

1. **(a)** Group 5

   (b) Period 3

   (c) Nitrogen or any other named Group 5 element

2. **(a)** Group 2   **(b)** Period 3

3. The elements are arranged in the periodic table in ascending order of the number of protons in the nucleus (atomic number).

Page 81 Electronic structure

(a) C   **(b)** B   **(c)** D   **(d)** C

Page 82 Metals and non-metals

1. **(a)** It is the division which separates the metals and the non-metals.

   (b) Carbon is a non-metal. It is positioned to the right of the zigzag line.

2. The higher the number of outer electrons the further to the right of the periodic table the element will be positioned.

   Element A only has two outer electrons (so is in Group 2), will be positioned to the left of the table and so is most likely to be the metal.

Element B has six outer electrons (so is in Group 6), will be positioned to the right of the table and so is most likely to be the non-metal.

Page 83 Chemical bonds

(a) Free to move (e.g. electrons).

(b) Metallic bonding

Page 84 Ionic bonding

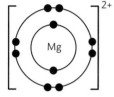 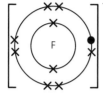 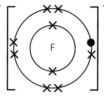

magnesium ion, Mg²⁺   fluoride ion, F⁻

Page 85 Ionic compounds

1. Sodium chloride forms a giant ionic lattice held together by strong electrostatic forces of attraction.

2. **(a)** Ionic

   (b) Limitation: the diagram incorrectly suggests there are gaps between the atoms/the ions are not to scale/ the ionic bonds are represented by straight lines when they are actually forces of attraction.

   Advantage: the diagram shows the positions of the ions in space/the layout of the bonds between the atoms.

Page 86 Properties of ionic compounds

1. **(a)** $2Na + Cl_2 \rightarrow 2NaCl$

   (b)

   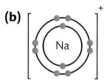

   sodium ion, **Na⁺**   chloride ion, **Cl⁻**

2. **(a)** Magnesium oxide is an ionic compound formed by the transfer of two electrons from a magnesium atom to an oxygen atom, forming Mg^{2+} and O^{2-}.

   (b) When molten, the ions are free to move, which allows electrical charge to flow.

   (c) Ionic bonds are very strong. There are many bonds in an ionic lattice and they must all be broken to melt magnesium oxide.

Page 87 Covalent bonding

1. A bond between non-metal atoms sharing a pair of electrons.

2. There are two (covalent) bonds between each oxygen and the carbon atom.

3.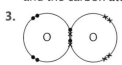

Page 88 Properties of simple molecular substances

1. They have low melting (and boiling points); gases or liquids at room temperature; do not conduct electricity.

2. Covalent

3. The substance must be heated to provide enough energy for intermolecular forces between molecules to be overcome.

Page 89 Giant covalent structures

1. Three

2. Four

3. Covalent

4. **(a)** Both graphite and diamond have huge lattice structures in which each carbon atom is bonded covalently to several others.

   (b) Graphite and diamond both have high melting and boiling points because all the bonds in their structures are covalent bonds. A lot of energy is required to break these strong bonds.

Page 90 Diamond

1. **(a)** The bonds between the carbon atoms are very strong, so it takes a lot of energy to break them.

   (b) It does not have any charged particles that are free to move. It has a giant structure (lattice).

2. Its atoms are bonded with strong covalent bonds. Each carbon atom is bonded to four other carbon atoms. A lot of energy is needed to break the bonds. This makes diamond a very hard substance, which means it is able to cut through other materials.

Page 91 Graphite

(a) It conducts electricity and it has a high melting point.

(b) Covalent

(c) A

(d) Pencil lead and lubricant

Page 92 Graphene and fullerenes

1. Carbon

2. Similarities:

   • In both, each carbon atom is bonded to three others.

   • They both conduct electricity.

   Difference:

   • Graphite is soft because it consists of layers, whereas carbon fullerenes are strong.

Page 93 Polymers

1.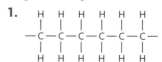

2. Polymers are very large molecules made from many smaller molecules joined together by strong covalent bonds in long chains.

3. Covalent bonds

Page 94 Metallic bonding

1. C
2. The metal particles have not got the negative charge from the delocalised electrons, so the remainder of the metal particle is positively charged.
3. The metal's outer electrons are delocalised, and these are attracted to the positive nuclei of the atoms.

Page 95 Properties of metals

1. Conductor
2. They have delocalised electrons that carry the thermal energy.
3. Many strong metallic bonds must be broken to melt/boil a metal.

Page 96 Relative formula mass

1. (a) C = 9; H = 8; O = 4
   (b) $9 \times 12 = 108$
       $4 \times 16 = 64$
       $8 \times 1 = 8$
       $108 + 64 + 8 = 180$
2. $2 \times 27 = 54$
   $3 \times 32 = 96$
   $12 \times 16 = 192$
   $54 + 96 + 192 = 342$

Page 97 Empirical formulae

(a) Mass of magnesium = 5.00 – 2.61 = 2.39 g
(b) Mass of oxygen = 6.39 – 5.00 = 1.39 g
(c) Empirical formula:

	Mg	O
mass (g)	2.39	1.39
Divide by A_r ...	/24	/16
... to find amount in mol	= 0.1	= 0.09
Divide by smaller to give atom ratio	1.1	1

Ratio is 1 : 1, suggesting the empirical formula is MgO.

Page 98 Balancing equations

1. $4Fe + 3O_2 \rightarrow 2Fe_2O_3$
2. Balanced equations give the formulas of substances. They show how many molecules of each substance are involved in the reaction.
3. Chemical equations always balance because mass cannot be created or destroyed in a chemical reaction.

Page 99 Conservation of mass

1. (a) zinc carbonate ➔ zinc oxide + carbon dioxide
   (b) Carbon dioxide gas produced in the reaction escaped.
   (c) The zinc carbonate could be heated with oxygen in a test tube and the gases collected, which would allow the products to be measured more accurately.

2. $C_2H_5OH(l) + 3O_2\,(g) \rightarrow 2CO_2\,(g) + 3H_2O(l)$

Page 100 Calculating masses in reactions

1. 50 g
2. (a) magnesium carbonate ➔ magnesium oxide + carbon dioxide
   (b) 84 g = 40 + ?
       84 – 40 = 44 g of carbon dioxide

Page 101 Concentrations of solutions

1. $40\,g\,dm^{-3}$
2. 50 g
3. The concentration will increase as the mass of solute used increases.

Page 102 Moles

1. $1\,mol\,O_2 = 2 \times mass\,of\,O = 2 \times 16 = 32\,g$
2. Mg = 1
   HCl = 2
3. $M_r = Ca + C + (3 \times O)$
   $40 + 12 + (3 \times 16) = 100$
   1 mole $CaCO_3$ is 100 g, so in 10 000 g there are $10\,000 \div 100 = 100\,mol$ of $CaCO_3$.

Page 103 Amounts of substances

1. 2.3 g
2. 106
3. Amount of Mg = $\dfrac{55\,g}{24}$ = 2.3 mol
   so 1 mol Mg produces 1 mol MgO, so 2.3 mol MgO produced
   2.3 mol × (24 + 16) = 92 g MgO

Page 104 Using mass to balance equations

1. $\dfrac{15.9}{79.5}$ $\dfrac{0.4}{2}$ $\dfrac{12.7}{63.5}$ $\dfrac{3.6}{18}$
   0.2   0.2   0.2   0.2
   $CuO + H_2 \rightarrow Cu + H_2O$
2. moles = mass ÷ M_r
   Or mass = moles × M_r
   Or M_r = mass ÷ moles
3. $\dfrac{13}{65}$ $\dfrac{14.6}{36.5}$ $\dfrac{27.2}{136}$ $\dfrac{0.4}{2}$
   0.2   0.4   0.2   0.2
   1 : 2 : 1 : 1
   $Zn + 2HCl \rightarrow ZnCl_2 + H_2$
4. The numbers represent how many molecules of that substance are involved in the reaction.

Page 105 States of matter

1. LiCl – solid

   $BeCl_2$ – solid

   CCl_4 – liquid

   NCl_3 – liquid

   OCl_2 – gas

2. Liquid

3. Liquid

Page 106 Pure substances

1. Compare the boiling point, melting point or density of the sample with the given data.

2. A, C and E are all pure; B and D are impure. Pure substances produce a sharp melting point, whereas impure substances produce a range over which they melt.

3. The sample is impure.

Page 107 Mixtures

1. ink and water – simple distillation

   sand and water – filtration

   sugar and water – evaporation

2. W – conical flask; X – filter paper; Y – filter funnel

Page 108 Chromatography

1. The brown food colourant contains yellow, red and purple pigment.

2. R_f values tell you the ratio of the distance moved by the dye and the distance moved by the solvent. They are used to identify substances by comparing their R_f values with known R_f values.

3. R_f values are not given units because they are a ratio.

Page 109 Practical: Investigating inks

1. (a) Any one from:
   - heating liquids could burn – wear eye protection
   - breaking glass could cut – alert teacher/use dust pan and brush
   - spilled liquids someone could slip over – wipe up immediately.

   (b) To check the temperature the mixture is being heated at/to control the temperature at 100 °C.

   So that it does not get too hot causing both liquids to evaporate.

2. $R_f = \dfrac{23}{74} = 0.31$

Page 110 Potable water

1. Distillation

2. Chlorine

3. It contains large amounts of dissolved solids/salt.

4. Rainwater

5. Any three from:
   - rainwater
   - groundwater
   - rivers
   - lakes
   - oceans.

6. Dissolved ions/salts

Page 111 The pH scale and neutralisation

1. hydrochloric acid + sodium hydroxide ➔ sodium chloride + water

2. (a) alkali/base

   (b) OH^-

3. A pH probe

Page 112 Strong and weak acids

1. A strong acid is one that completely dissociates (splits up) into ions in aqueous solution.

2. Any two from:
   - sulfuric acid
   - nitric acid
   - hydrochloric acid.

3. (a) $H^+ + OH^- \rightarrow H_2O$

   (b) H^+

   (c) The hydrogen ion concentration increases by a factor of ten for every pH unit decrease.

Page 113 Core practical: pH change

(a)

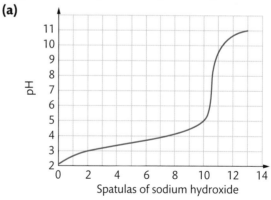

Spatulas of sodium hydroxide

1 mark for labelled axes

1 mark for plotted points

1 mark for smooth curve through all/most points

(b) pH 7/approximately the middle of the vertical line

(c) Approximately 10.5 spatulas of alkali

(Student should show markings to show how answer is derived.)

Page 114 Salt production

1. Potassium nitrate

2. Neutralisation

3. Hydrochloric acid

4. $Zn^{2+} + SO_4^{2-} \rightarrow ZnSO_4$
5. **(a)** Li_2SO_4
   (b) $MgCl_2$
   (c) $Ca(NO_3)_2$

Page 115 Reactions of acids with metals

1. $Mg(s) + 2HCl(aq) \rightarrow MgCl_2(aq) + H_2(g)$
2. Reduction is the addition of electrons and loss of oxygen.
3. Metals lose the electrons in their outer shell fairly easily.
4. Calcium nitrate

Page 116 Soluble salts

1. Filtration
2. C
3. copper nitrate
4. The substance will dissolve in a solvent, e.g. water.

Page 117 Practical: Making salts

1. Any five relevant stages:
   - Warm the dilute sulfuric acid and add copper oxide.
   - Stir to ensure the reaction is complete.
   - Filter the solution (retaining the filtrate).
   - Heat the solution (gently) until it begins to evaporate.
   - Stop heating when crystals begin to form (to the point of crystallisation).
   - Allow to cool so more crystals form.
   - Dry the crystals (between two pieces of filter paper).
2. Copper sulfate

Page 118 Titration

(a) $HCl(aq) + NaOH(aq) \rightarrow NaCl(s) + H_2O(l)$
(b) colourless in acid, pink in alkali

Page 119 Solubility rules

1. How much mass of a substance will dissolve in a fixed volume of solvent/water **or** how easily something dissolves.
2. **(a)**

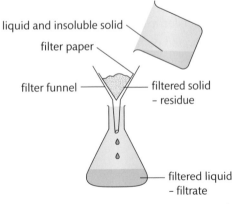

liquid and insoluble solid
filter paper
filter funnel
filtered solid – residue
filtered liquid – filtrate

(Filter paper and filter funnel must be labelled.)
(b) To remove soluble impurities.

Page 120 Oxidation and reduction

(a) $Mg + CuO \rightarrow MgO + Cu$
(b) $Mg \rightarrow Mg^{2+} + 2e^-$

Page 121 Electrolysis

1. electrolyte – liquid used for electrolysis
   electrode – solid, electrical conductor
   anode – electrode with a positive charge
   cathode – electrode with a negative charge
2. The cathode/negative electrode

Page 122 Electrolysis of molten ionic compounds

1. **(a)**

(b) $Pb^{2+} + 2e^- \rightarrow Pb$
   $2Br^- \rightarrow Br_2 + 2e^-$
(c) Bubbles (of bromine gas)
2. **(a)** Cathode: lead Anode: iodine
   (b) Cathode: zinc Anode: bromine
   (c) Cathode: magnesium Anode: oxygen
   (d) Cathode: lithium Anode: chlorine

Page 123 Electrolysis of aqueous solutions

(a) The solution conducts electricity.
   Bubbling is seen at the electrodes (as hydrogen and chlorine gas are produced).
   The ions move to oppositely charged electrodes.
   The negative ions lose electrons and the positive ions gain electrons.
(b) $2Cl^- + 2e^- \rightarrow Cl_2$

Page 124 Half equations

1. Anode: $2Cl^- \rightarrow Cl_2 + 2e^-$
   Cathode: $Cu^{2+} + 2e^- \rightarrow Cu$
2. So that the electrodes don't react with the electrolyte

Page 125 Practical: Electrolysis of copper sulfate

(a) Oxygen and copper
(b) Hydroxide ions are negative, so are attracted to the anode.
   Copper ions are positive, so are attracted to the cathode.

Page 126 The reactivity series

1. A – calcium
   B – iron
   C – copper
   D – magnesium

2. The more easily a metal forms a positive ion, the more reactive it will be.

3. Ca(s) + **2**H$_2$O(l) ➜ Ca(OH)$_2$(aq)+ H$_2$(g)

Page 127 Extraction of metals and reduction

1. (a) lead oxide + carbon ➜ lead + carbon dioxide

(b) Oxidation

(c) The lead in lead oxide has an oxidation state of +2. After reduction to lead the oxidation state is zero, so the lead has gained electrons.

2. Calcium is above carbon in the reactivity series. Metals can only be extracted by elements that are more reactive than them.

Page 128 Electrolysis to extract metals

1. Large amounts of energy are needed to melt the magnesium chloride. Energy is also needed to generate an electric current.

2. It is dissolved in cryolite.

3. Reduction requires a lot of energy to be provided in the form of high temperatures, which is expensive. It usually involves burning fossil fuels, which are a limited resource. Burning fossil fuels and reduction also produce carbon dioxide, which enhances the greenhouse effect. Additionally, reduction can only be used for metals lower on the reactivity series than carbon and metal products are impure and may need further processing.

Electrolysis is very expensive as it requires a lot of energy to melt the metal and to provide electricity for the electrolysis process. It also involves burning fossil fuels, which are limited and cause global warming. Electrodes often need replacing.

However, it can be used to extract any metal and metal products are pure.

Page 129 Alternative methods of extracting metals

1. Any two from:
- only small amounts of high-grade copper ores are left
- copper is in high demand
- copper is expensive
- it is now economical to extract copper from low-grade ores.

2. Plants that naturally absorb copper ions are grown. The plants are then burned and copper compounds are removed from the ash.

3. Bioleaching

4. Mining destroys habitats, which has a negative impact on plant and animal species. It also creates dust and noise pollution. Mining requires a lot of energy, making it expensive. It also involves burning fossil fuels which are a finite resource. Carbon dioxide is produced during the process, which leads to global warming. In addition, waste rock needs to be disposed of – usually as landfill. However, mining is likely to be cheaper and quicker than phytoextraction to extract copper ore from high percentage ores.

Phytoextraction improves habitats and the landscape as plants grow. Plants are carbon neutral so don't contribute to global warming. Phytoextraction saves valuable ores of copper and uses low percentage sources of copper. Phytoextraction can be used to extract metals from contaminated soils. However, growing plants is dependent on weather conditions so timescales for extraction could be longer and energy would still be needed to extract the copper from the plants. There is also the potential for pollution when burning the plants.

Page 130 Metal oxides

(a) iron + oxygen ➜ iron oxide

(b) redox

(c) oxygen

Page 131 Recycling and life-cycle assessment

1. It will produce less waste, less pollution and less carbon dioxide by reducing the amount of iron ore that has to be extracted.

2. To assess the environmental impact of a product. To compare environmental impact of products with the same use.

3. Recycling needs energy to melt the product down. Burning fossil fuels to power this process releases carbon dioxide into the atmosphere, leading to global warming.

Transporting the products to and from the recycling plant requires the burning of fuel to power the vehicle used to transport the products. This produces greenhouse gases and may also produce nitrogen oxides and sulfur dioxide, leading to global warming and acid rain.

Page 132 Reversible reactions

1. The products of the reaction can react to form the original reactants.

2. (a) By reversing the reaction (adding water) the original substance (hydrated copper sulfate) is formed.

(b) hydrated ⇌ anhydrous + water
copper sulfate   copper sulfate

Page 133 Dynamic equilibrium and the Haber process

1. A relatively low temperature is used as a higher temperature will move the position of equilibrium towards the reactants and so less product (ammonia) will be produced.

2. This is a compromise as the lower the temperature, the slower the rate of the reaction (production of ammonia will take longer at lower temperatures).

3. Removing the product, ammonia, would drive the reaction to the right-hand side, thus producing more ammonia.

Page 134 Temperature and equilibrium

(a) Heat energy is needed to drive the forward reaction to maximise the production of hydrogen gas.

(b) Endothermic

Page 135 Pressure and equilibrium

(a) B

(b) A, because it has more product molecules, so the system will move the equilibrium to reduce the number of molecules.

(c) The yield of methanol will decrease, because the system will move the equilibrium to increase the number of molecules.

Page 136 Concentration and equilibrium

(a) The yield of hydrogen would increase because the system would try to oppose the change and reduce the amount of methane present.

(b) An equilibrium is reached in a reversible reaction when the forward reaction occurs at exactly the same rate as the reverse reaction.

Page 137 Group 1

1. As you move down the group the elements become more reactive.

2. Lithium and water produce hydrogen gas (and lithium hydroxide). The bubbles are the gas being produced.

3. The rubidium will react explosively with the water and catch fire.

Page 138 Group 7

1. **(a)** 2.8.7

   (b) Chlorine has seven outer-shell electrons and readily accepts one electron to become an anion with a full outer shell. Thus it forms ionic compounds with positively-charged metal ions.

   (c) Fluorine is more reactive than chlorine so it will react more vigorously.

2. **(a)** The gas will dissolve.

   (b) The paper will turn red because the hydrogen bromide has dissolved to give hydrobromic acid.

Page 139 Group 7 reactivity

1. $2KI + Br_2 \rightarrow 2KBr + I_2$
   I^- (iodide) oxidised to I_2
   Br (bromine) reduced to Br^-

2. Chlorine is more reactive than iodine because it is higher in the group. This means that its outer shell is closer to its nucleus, which can therefore more easily attract and hold an extra electron than iodine can.

3. Chlorine or fluorine

Page 140 Group 0

1. All Group 0 atoms have a full outer shell.

2. **(a)** The atomic mass increases because there are more protons and neutrons in the atom.

   (b) Because their outer shells are full, noble gas atoms are unreactive.

3.

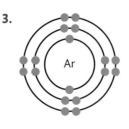

Page 141 Calculating rate of reaction

(a) $cm^3 \, s^{-1}$

(b) $120 \div 120 = 1 \, cm^3 \, s^{-1}$

(c) It has increased the rate of reaction. However, the same amount of product is formed.

Page 142 Factors affecting rate of reaction

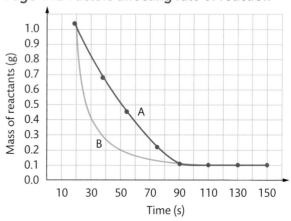

(a) Line A on graph. 1 mark for correct axes with units. 2 marks for correct plotting – lose one mark per incorrect plot. 1 mark for the line of best fit – smooth curve passing through or very close to each point.

(b) Line B on graph. A sketched curve with the same start and end points, but a steeper curve.

(c) Increase the concentration of hydrochloric acid. Increase the surface area of the marble chips.

Page 143 Practical: Monitoring rate of reaction – colour change

(a) The more concentrated the acid is, the faster the reaction will be and the quicker the cross will disappear. This is because a greater number of acid particles in the reaction mixture increases the chance of successful collisions (the same would apply if the concentration of sodium thiosulfate is increased).

(b) Independent variable – the concentration of the acid (or thiosulfate) Dependent variable – the time taken for the cross to disappear

Control variables – the volume of acid, the volume and concentration of thiosulfate (or acid) and the temperature of the reaction

Page 144 Practical: Monitoring rate of reaction – gas production

1. Smaller marble chips have a larger total surface area. Therefore, there are more particles of marble/calcium carbonate exposed to the acid, and more collisions

1. The rate of reaction will increase. This is because the particles have more energy and therefore will move quicker, increasing the chance of collisions.

2. The gas particles become more crowded, so there is more chance of successful collisions and a higher rate of reaction.

Page 146 Reaction profiles

1.

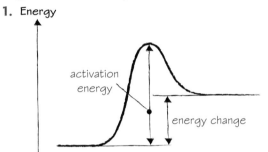

- 1 mark for correctly labelled axes

- 1 mark to show the position of the reactants and products - with the products having more energy than the reactants

- 1 mark for the labelling and arrow for activation energy

- 1 mark for labelling the energy change.

2. **(a)** Exothermic, because the products have less energy than the reactants (as heat is lost to the surroundings).

(b)

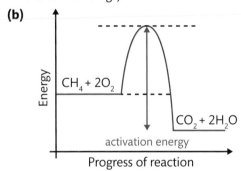

Page 147 Catalysts

1. Iron

2. Enzymes

Page 148 Exothermic and endothermic reactions

1. Exothermic

2. It will decrease.

Page 149 Temperature changes

$-6.3\,°C$

The reaction was endothermic because the temperature decreased.

Page 150 Energy change in reactions

(a) $-549\,kJ\,mol^{-1}$

(b) Exothermic

Page 151 Crude oil and hydrocarbons

1. A limited supply of something that is not being made any more, or which is being made extremely slowly.

2. A group of organic compounds that have the same general formula (differ only by the number of CH_2 units in the main carbon chain), have the same chemical properties and show a gradual variation in physical properties, such as their boiling points.

   Example: alkanes/alkenes/alcohols/halogenoalkanes.

3. For alkanes, general formula is C_nH_{2n+2}

   If C = 6

   H = (6 × 2) + 2 = 12 + 2 = 14

Page 152 Fractional distillation

1. The crude oil is heated to evaporate the hydrocarbons. The column is cooler at the top and hotter at the bottom. The gaseous fractions travel up the column until they reach their boiling point, where they condense and can be collected.

2. X – evaporation

   Z – condensation

Page 153 Properties of hydrocarbons

1. Water and carbon dioxide

2. propane + oxygen ➜ carbon monoxide + carbon + water

3. As molecular size increases, viscosity increases too.

4. Because in the combustion of a hydrocarbon both the carbon and the hydrogen atoms gain oxygen.

Page 154 Atmospheric pollutants

1. $S(s) + O_2(g) \rightarrow SO_2(g)$

2. A substance which may harm health or the environment.

3. Any three from: carbon monoxide, carbon/soot, sulfur dioxide/sulfuric acid/acid rain, oxides of nitrogen/nitrogen oxide/nitrogen dioxide.

Page 155 Comparing fuels

If hydrogen is produced from natural gas/crude oil derivatives and steam, it is still using non-renewable resources. If produced by electrolysis, electricity is required, which is usually generated using fossil fuels, which are non-renewable and release carbon dioxide into the atmosphere causing global warming.

Hydrogen is difficult to store safely in a small space in a vehicle.

Page 156 Cracking and alkenes

(a) Gases, petrol and diesel oil

(b) 12%

(c) Petrol, because there is a very large demand for it that cannot be satisfied from the supply of uncracked crude oil.

Page 157 Earth's early atmosphere

(a) 3.5%

(b) There are no plants to carry out photosynthesis and produce oxygen.

(c) Argon is inert/unreactive.

Page 158 Oxygen and carbon dioxide levels

1. Approximately 20%

2. Carbon from carbon dioxide is used by algae and plants to make glucose by photosynthesis. The oxygen atoms from the carbon dioxide are released in the form of oxygen gas. Over billions of years the process of photosynthesis has reduced levels of carbon dioxide and increased those of oxygen to their current levels.

Page 159 Gases in the atmosphere

1. 78–80%

2. The fraction of oxygen is about 20%, which is $\frac{20}{100}$.

   Divide both by a common factor to get the lowest values:

   $20 \div 20 = 1$

   $100 \div 20 = 5$

   So oxygen is $\frac{1}{5}$

Page 160 Greenhouse gases

1. Methane, carbon dioxide and water vapour

2. Infrared radiation emitted by the Earth's surface is absorbed and re-emitted by greenhouse gases. The reflected energy becomes trapped, maintaining the temperature of the planet.

3. By volcanoes

Page 161 Human contribution to greenhouse gases

1. Any two from:
   - increased combustion of fossil fuels
   - increased population
   - increased waste
   - deforestation.

2. They think it may lead to global climate change.

Page 162 Global climate change

1. Any two from:
   - rising sea levels
   - heatwaves
   - change in precipitation patterns
   - increasing storm intensity.

2. More rainfall could cause flooding, which would damage crops and homes.

   Less rainfall could lead to drought, which would cause crops to fail, leading to starvation.

3. An increase in greenhouse gases in the atmosphere contributing to increasing global temperatures.

Page 163 Reducing the use of resources

(a) A - livestock farming

(b) 32% of the methane generated by humans is produced from livestock.

(c) Methane (is a greenhouse gas which) contributes to global warming.

   Any two from:
   - reducing levels of methane by reducing our dependence on cattle for food/milk OR by eating more crops
   - using less fossil fuels/using renewable energy sources/ investing in hydrogen as a fuel
   - decomposing animal manure so that it does not release methane/convert to biogas for energy production. (Or any sensible alternative related to the data provided.)

(d) The oceans will become acidic/pH will decrease. This could harm/kill aquatic plants and animals.

Page 164 Key concepts in physics

1. **(a)** 1×10^{-10} m

   (b) 0.1 nm

2. $\frac{(5 \times 10^{-10})}{(8.2 \times 10^{-15})} = 61\,000$ times (to 2 s.f)

Page 165 Scalar and vector quantities

1. **(a)** 77 m/s due north

   (b) 53 m/s due south

2. 15 m/s at 37° east of north (or bearing 037°)

Page 166 Distance and speed

(a) Distance = 600 km
    Displacement = 200 km east

(b) Distance = 230 m
    Displacement = 187 m at 16° to the vertical
    (or 74° to the floor)

(c) Distance = 700 m
    Displacement = 0 m

(d) Distance = $2 \times \pi \times 5 = 31.42$ m
    Displacement = 0 m

Page 167 Speed and velocity

1. $22\,000 \div 3 = 7333$ s

   $7333 \div 60 = 122$ mins

2. A: $600 \div 24 = 25$ m/s
   B: $200\,000 \div (1.5 \times 60 \times 60) = 37$ m/s,
   C: $20 \div 0.5 = 40$ m/s,
   D: $3\,000\,000 \div (24 \times 60 \times 60)$ s = 35 m/s.
   C is fastest on average.

Page 168 Distance–time relationships

1. The gradient is increasing, which means the speed is increasing. Therefore, the cyclist is accelerating.

2.

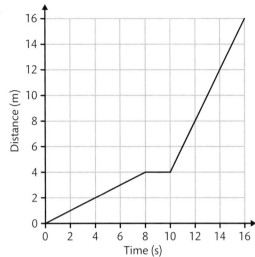

Page 169 Uniform acceleration

1. $1.5 \times 10 = 15\,\text{m/s}$
2. **(a)** $65\,\text{m/s} \div 5\,\text{m/s}^2 = 13\,\text{s}$
   (b) $-(65)^2 \div (-2 \times 5) = 422.5\,\text{m}$
3. $-2.5\,\text{m/s}^2$
4. **(a)** The object is getting faster.
   (b) The object is getting slower (decelerating).

Page 170 Velocity–time graphs

(a) The velocity is increasing, but the acceleration is decreasing because the gradient is becoming less steep.

(b) At 10 s the gradient is $0.5\,\text{m/s}^2$.
At 35 s the gradient is $0.16\,\text{m/s}^2$.

Page 171 Gravity

1. Using a calibrated spring-balance or force meter (like a newtonmeter)
2. Downwards, towards the centre of the planet
3. It is true that an astronaut might have difficulty walking on the Moon. However, this is not because of a lack of atmosphere. The Moon has less gravity than Earth because it has less mass. The astronaut would experience less downwards force on the Moon, which would make them feel lighter and more bouncy. This could make it more difficult to move.
4. 1920 N

Page 172 Newton's laws of motion

1. For a car to move at a constant speed, all forces need to be balanced. The car will experience backwards force from friction and air resistance, so an equal forwards force from the engine is needed. This balances the friction and air resistance, making the resultant force zero. Without the forwards force from the engine, the imbalance would cause the car to slow down.
2. **(a)** 30 N
   (b) The student applies a 30 N force to the desk. If the desk is in equilibrium, there is no resultant force. Something

must be balancing the force out, for example friction acting in the opposite direction to the 30 N force applied by the student.

Page 173 Newton's second law

(a) $m = F \div a = (300 - 50) \div 1.67 = 150\,\text{kg}$

(b) It would be half as much:
$1.67 \div 2 = 0.835\,\text{m/s}^2$

Page 174 Centripetal force

(a) Towards the centre of the corner

(b) $F = m \times a$
$F = 1000 \times 3 = 3000\,\text{N}$

Page 175 Practical: Investigating acceleration

1. The force accelerating the trolley is found by calculating the weight of the masses using the equation:
   weight = mass $\times$ gravitational field strength
2. In theory, the trolley's acceleration should be constant. As long as the light gate is placed where the trolley is still accelerating, its position should not matter. However, there could be a change in friction as the trolley increases in speed, which would affect the resultant force on the trolley and therefore change its acceleration. The light gate might give a different reading for acceleration if it is moved to a faster or slower part of the movement.
3. Mass is inversely proportional to acceleration. If the mass of the trolley doubled, the acceleration would halve (for the same force). Force and acceleration are proportional. If the force doubles, the acceleration would double too.

Page 176 Momentum

1. **(a)** $m = p \div v = 5400 \div 12 = 450\,\text{kg}$
   (b) $-5400\,\text{kg\,m/s}$
2. $1.5\,\text{mm/s} = 0.0015\,\text{m/s}$, $22\,\text{g} = 0.022\,\text{kg}$
   $p = mv = 0.022 \times 0.0015 = 0.000033$
   $\qquad\qquad\qquad\qquad\quad 3.3 \times 10^{-5}\,\text{kg\,m/s}$
3. Start momentum $= 0.85 \times 20 = 17\,\text{kg\,m/s}$
   New mass $= 850 - 300 = 550\,\text{g}$ or $0.55\,\text{kg}$
   End momentum $= 0.55 \times 35 = 19.25\,\text{kg\,m/s}$
   Change in momentum $= 19.25 - 17 = 2.25\,\text{kg\,m/s}$.

Page 177 Conservation of momentum

1. The cannonball is fired forwards with a large velocity and the cannon moves backwards with a smaller velocity. Before the cannon fires the momentum is zero. For the total momentum to still be zero, the cannon and ball must have equal momentums, but one will be negative (so they would add up to zero).

   Momentum = mass $\times$ velocity. The cannonball has a much smaller mass and therefore will have a higher velocity to give it the same momentum.

2. Momentum must be conserved so the two players after the tackle must have the same momentum as both the players running before the tackle. As the mass of the object moving has increased after the tackle (being two people it has roughly doubled) the velocity must decrease in order to have the same momentum (in fact it will roughly halve to 4 m/s).

Page 178 Stopping distance

1. distance = speed × time = 31 m/s × 0.6 = 18.6 m

2. Only method 1 actually measures reaction time, method 2 does not use a time, but a distance. Both methods can be used to compare reaction times. Method 1 is more useful because if the time doubled, we can say reaction time has doubled, however as the ruler is accelerating downwards, if the distance doubled, this does not mean the reaction time has doubled. The repeat readings in method 1 were more similar, suggesting this is a more reliable (repeatable) method. Method 2 repeat readings were more varied suggesting this is a less reliable method.

Page 179 Factors affecting braking distance

1. $F = \dfrac{mv^2}{2d}$

$\dfrac{1200 \times 25^5}{2 \times 40} = 9375$ N

2. Kinetic energy = $\dfrac{1}{2}$ × mass × velocity². Doubling the speed increases the kinetic energy by four times. The brakes have to do four times the work to stop the car, so the car has to travel four times further when braking. Therefore, the braking distance is four times larger. Doubling the speed doubles the distance the car travels while the driver reacts, so the thinking distance is doubled.

Page 180 Gravitational potential energy

1. 70 × 10 × 100 = 70 000 J

2. $h = E_p \div (m \times g) = 50\,000 \div (70 \times 10) = 71.4$ m

3. **(a)** As the ball falls its height decreases, which means its GPE decreases. The GPE is being transferred to kinetic energy, which increases. Therefore, its speed increases.

   (b) An object's GPE transfers to kinetic energy as it falls. An object dropped from a greater height begins with more GPE to transfer, so will have more kinetic energy when it reaches the ground. Therefore, it will hit the ground faster.

4. **(a)** Twice the change in height, so twice the increase in GPE: 1000 × 2 = 2000 J

   (b) The work done by the crane is equal to the GPE gained, so 1000 J and 2000 J respectively.

Page 181 Kinetic energy

1. **(a)** 0.5 × 1200 × 20² = 240 000 J
   (b) 240 000 J

2. The van has twice the mass of the car, so has twice the kinetic energy if they are travelling at the same speed.

However, the car has twice the speed of the van, so has four times the kinetic energy. Overall, the car has twice as much kinetic energy.

3. **(a)** $m = 12\,000 \div (0.5 \times 8^2) = 375$ kg

   (b) $v = \sqrt{\dfrac{17\,000}{0.5 \times 375}} = 9.5$ m/s

Page 182 Energy transfers in a system

1. **(a)** chemical → thermal + kinetic + sound

   (b) chemical → kinetic (dissipated as light + thermal + sound) → gravitational potential energy

   (c) chemical → kinetic + thermal + sound

2. Thermal energy is wasted when water is heated to make steam, in the wires and through friction between moving parts. This could be reduced by insulation or reusing the wasted energy for heating, lubricating the moving parts, and using thicker wires to reduce resistance.

3. The jumper is thick and the wool traps air. Air has poor thermal conductivity, so reduces the jumper's rate of heat loss.

Page 183 Efficiency

1. Useful energy = 400 − 150 = 250 J
   Efficiency = 250 ÷ 400 = 0.625

2. 85% of the energy produced is used to heat the house, and 15% is wasted.

3. Appliance A: 35 ÷ 100 = 0.35

   Appliance B: 35 ÷ 50 = 0.70

   Appliance B has the higher efficiency because it uses a greater proportion of the input power usefully.

4. Efficiency of 60%

   60 ÷ 100 = 0.6 as a decimal

   input energy = useful output energy ÷ efficiency

   2000 ÷ 0.6 = 3333 J.

5. Thermal energy is produced by friction in moving parts. Friction can be reduced by making sure any surfaces that touch are smooth, ensuring that moving parts can move freely and fit together perfectly, or by adding lubrication.

Page 184 Renewable energy resources

1. Food prices will increase as demand will increase.

2. Wind: only works when windy; can't be used in storms.

   Hydroelectricity: more reliable as doesn't depend on weather / nature to work.

3. Advantage: any one from: reliable; high power output.

   Disadvantage: any one from: fuel crops can drive up cost of food; environmental impact if spaces are cleared to make room for crops.

Page 185 Non-renewable energy resources

1. Nuclear and coal-fired power stations are equally as reliable and both have a high power output. Nuclear power stations are clean and do not produce any smoke

or greenhouse gases. However, they do produce nuclear waste that must be stored safely; if there is an accident, there is a risk of radiation getting into the environment. Coal-fired power stations do produce smoke, greenhouse gases and sulfur dioxide. This can cause respiratory diseases, increase global warming and cause acid rain. They also need a large amount of coal to be transported.

2. Any four from:

- non-renewables are running out so renewables need to be used to replace the demand for energy
- other than biofuel, renewables produce little chemical pollution
- no renewable resource adds to carbon emissions (biofuels do produce CO_2 when burned, but are carbon neutral overall) and so do not contribute to global warming, whereas fossil fuels do
- nuclear accidents can affect a large area for a long period of time, but renewable resources tend to be safer
- while the cost of building some renewable power sources is still high, the running costs or fuel costs are cheaper and in some cases virtually free, compared to the rising cost of non-renewable resources, especially as they become rarer
- people are more interested in saving the environment so it has become popular for individuals to use renewable resources to generate electricity in their own home or use biofuels in cars
- governments are under pressure to reduce the carbon emissions produced by their countries, which has caused a shift towards more renewable resources like wind farms and solar cells
- farms are using spare land to generate electricity by creating wind or solar farms to generate additional income.

3. Any four from:

- the cost of replacing all the current power stations would be high, it makes more sense to replace them gradually over time
- public opinion may be against renewable resources, for example protesting about building wind turbines because they spoil a landscape. They can also be a danger to wildlife and cannot be built where there are endangered birds
- in countries like the UK, poor weather makes solar resources less reliable so relying only on renewables might not produce enough electricity at peak times. Some biofuels use food crops or land which would otherwise be used for food. This can drive up the cost of food
- people have not shifted to using renewable resources (like biofuels or fuel cells) for cars because the technology is new and still more expensive than diesel or petrol-powered cars
- some people dislike change and are wary of relying on alternative methods of energy production too suddenly.

Page 186 Types of wave

1. Using speed = distance/time the student can use distance = 4100 m (distance to the wall and back) and time = the time recorded divided by 10 (as they timed for ten claps). Inputting these into the equation will give the speed of sound.

2. The main source of error is the reaction time involved in starting and stopping the stop clock. A further source of error is being sure that the stop clock is stopped at the same point in the clap/echo each time. To improve the experiment, microphones and data loggers could be used instead.

3. There are no particles for sound to transfer through.

Page 187 Properties of waves

1. $speed = \dfrac{distance}{time}$

$\dfrac{174}{0.03} = 5800$ m/s

2. $time = \dfrac{distance}{speed}$

$\dfrac{2000}{1500} = 1.33$ s

3. $\dfrac{20 \text{ waves}}{5} = 4$ waves per second or 4 Hz

period $= \dfrac{1}{f} = \dfrac{1}{4} = 0.25$ s

wavelength: 20 waves are 15 cm long, so one wave is $\dfrac{15 \text{ cm}}{20 \text{ waves}} = 0.75$ cm (0.0075 m)

wave speed = frequency × wavelength

4 Hz × 0.0075 m = 0.03 m/s (or 3 cm/s)

Page 188 Practical: Investigating waves

A data logger is more precise and a data logger would give more accurate results as it is not dependent on human reaction time.

Page 189 Types of electromagnetic waves

1. Microwaves: cause a heating effect in water
Infrared: can burn skin

2. Any two from:

- premature ageing of the skin
- skin cancer (caused by UV light)
- sunburn.

3. Patients are exposed to very small doses of radiation, so the risk of cell damage only increases slightly. This is considered less of a risk than being unable to diagnose and treat conditions.

4. **(a)** $\dfrac{50}{0.1} = 500$ X-rays per year

(b) This number is not considered safe, because greater exposure to X-rays means greater risk. X-rays are kept to a minimum to keep the risk as low as possible.

Page 190 Properties of electromagnetic waves

1. Thermal energy
2. **(a)** Only the green light is transmitted, because the other colours are absorbed.

   (b) All the colours are absorbed.

   (c) All the colours are reflected, so the car appears white.
3. The prism shows refraction. The light slows down when it enters glass, causing it to change direction. When it exits the prism it speeds up and changes direction again. The spectrum caused by a prism shows that the different colours in white light slow down by different rates when they enter the glass. Red light bends the least, so must slow down the least, and therefore travels fastest inside glass.
4. They are not correct. Light still slows down as it enters glass, but it only bends when the light hits the surface at an angle, because only then is one part of the wavefront affected before the rest.

Page 191 Practical: Investigating refraction

(a) Angle of incidence

(b) Thinner ray of light to reduce difficulty in judging where the centre of the ray is

(c) The speed of light in glass is slower than in air. As light passes through the air–glass boundary it will slow down, causing the wavefronts to become closer together and the light to bend towards the normal.

Page 192 Applications of EM waves

1. Radio: TV, radio, two-way radio

   Microwaves: mobile phones, satellites, satellite TV

   Infrared: remote controls, wireless links between computers

   Visible light: car indicators, warning lights, flashing torches, optical fibres
2. Radio waves are produced by vibrating electrons in electrical circuits. The flow of current in an electrical device can produce radio waves that might be picked up by the radio aerial receiver, causing interference.

Page 193 The structure of an atom

1. It will have 12 electrons. As an atom, it has neutral charge and so must have equal numbers of electrons and protons.
2. No this is not true. If a magnesium atom was broken in half, there would be 6 protons on each side. The atom needs to have 12 protons to be magnesium. The atom with 6 protons is carbon.
3. Differences: electrons are negative and have a very small mass; protons are positive and have a larger mass. They are also found in different places in the atom.
4. Similarities: protons and neutrons have similar masses and are both found in the nucleus.

Page 194 Mass number, atomic number and isotopes

1. **(a)** 4 protons, 4 electrons, 5 neutrons

   (b) 3 protons, 3 electrons, 4 neutrons

   (c) 26 protons, 26 electrons, 30 neutrons
2. **(a)** 2 electrons

   (b) 2 electrons

   (c) 23 electrons
3. The number of neutrons can be different if it is an isotope of carbon. The number of electrons can change if it is an ion.

Page 195 Development of the atomic model

1. The atom is a positively-charged sphere with tiny negatively-charged electrons embedded in it.
2. Unlike the plum pudding model, the nuclear model puts the majority of the mass and the positive charge at the centre, the outside carries the negative charge and the rest is empty space.
3. **(a)** The alpha particles would all have bounced back. None, or very few, would have passed straight through.

   (b) Alpha particles would still have mostly passed through, some would be diverted when they passed close to the nucleus. The ones that hit would be attracted rather than repelled and so would not have bounced back, showing the nucleus is negative.
4. No model is considered correct, just the best idea based on the evidence. As more evidence is found the models will change, including the nuclear model.

Page 196 Ionising radiation

1. Alpha particles are larger and have a greater charge, meaning they have a higher ionising power.
2. Alpha – stopped by paper, so would not be transmitted through to the monitor

   Gamma – passes through paper easily and would not be stopped by even a ream of paper
3. Beta or gamma as they would readily pass out of the body.

Page 197 Background radiation

1. $50 - 2 = 48\,Bq$
2. Gamma radiation passes easily into the body and may cause damage to cells.

Page 198 Detecting and measuring radioactivity

1. **(a)** decreases by one

   (b) stays the same
2. $^{11}_{6}C \rightarrow {}^{11}_{5}B + {}^{0}_{+1}e$

Page 199 Nuclear decay

1. **(a)** $^{235}_{92}U + {}^{4}_{2}\alpha$

   (b) $^{15}_{5}B + n$
2. $^{238}_{92}U \rightarrow {}^{234}_{90}Th + {}^{4}_{2}\alpha$

3. $^{212}_{82}Pb \rightarrow ^{212}_{83}Bi + ^{0}_{-1}e$

4. $^{222}_{86}Rn \rightarrow ^{218}_{84}Po + ^{4}_{2}\alpha$

$^{218}_{84}Po \rightarrow ^{214}_{82}PB + ^{4}_{2}\alpha$

$^{214}_{82}Pb \rightarrow ^{214}_{83}Bi + ^{0}_{-1}e$

Page 200 Half-lives

1. 1 half-life ➔ 1/2, 2 half-lives ➔ 1/4,
   3 half-lives ➔ 1/8, 4 half-lives ➔ 1/16

2. $\dfrac{1440}{2} = 720\,Bq$

   $\dfrac{720}{2} = 360\,Bq$

   $\dfrac{360}{2} = 180\,Bq$

   $\dfrac{180}{2} = 90\,Bq$

   $\dfrac{90}{2} = 45\,Bq$

   5 half-lives

   $5 \times 10 = 50\,mins$

3. $\dfrac{640}{2} = 320\,Bq$

   $\dfrac{320}{2} = 160\,Bq$

   2 half-lives

   $\dfrac{12}{2} = 6\,years$

4. 2 half-lives. $2 \times 3 = 6\,hours$

Page 201 Dangers of radioactivity

(a) Medical benefits of using radioisotopes outweigh the risks.

(b) Wearing of lead aprons to minimise exposure; wearing of dosiometers/badges to record levels.

Page 202 Radioactive contamination and irradiation

1. They are at risk of irradiation because they are quite close to the rocks. They are at risk of contamination because the rocks may produce dust particles that would stick to their skin if they came into contact. They should not touch the rocks and should keep them in a sealed container to avoid contamination. To reduce their dose they should keep their distance from the sources, use them at arm's length by using long tongs or tweezers and only be near them when actually using them.

2. (a) The person may be exposed to radiation for longer periods of time, may work closer to sources of radiation or be exposed to radiation that has a higher activity. It is possible that person A has a higher level of protective equipment, making their dose lower.

   (b) It is never true to say that any amount of radiation exposure is completely safe. However, person A has been exposed to a dose much lower than that considered low risk.

Page 203 Revising energy transfers

1. (a)

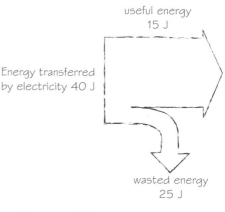

useful energy
15 J

Energy transferred by electricity 40 J

wasted energy
25 J

(b) total energy − light energy = heat energy
(40 − 15 = 25)

2. (a) electrical to light, sound and heat

   (b)

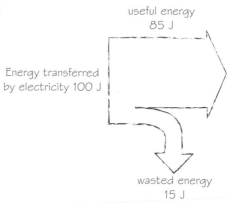

useful energy
85 J

Energy transferred by electricity 100 J

wasted energy
15 J

Page 204 Work done and energy transfer

1. (a) 0 J, the force and distance are in different directions so no work is done.

   (b) $500 \times 35 = 17\,500\,J$

   (c) $20 \times 1.5 = 30\,J$

   (d) 0 J, the force and distance are in different directions so no work is done.

2. (a) Work has been done as friction will have caused them to stop which would have acted in the opposite direction to the way they were moving. Kinetic energy has been transferred to thermal energy.

   (b) 400 J of work would be needed to stop them.
   $s = W \div F$
   $400 \div 80 = 5\,m$.

Page 205 Power

1. (a) $P = \dfrac{E}{t} = \dfrac{4800}{60} = 80\,W$

   (b) $P = \dfrac{E}{t} = \dfrac{2160}{60} = 36\,W$

2. (a) Total work done = $40 \times 30 = 1200\,J$

   $P = \dfrac{E}{t} = \dfrac{1200}{90} = 13.3\,W$

   (b) $(10\,mins \times 60 = 600\,s)$ $E = P \times t = 13.3 \times 600 = 7980\,J$ (or 8000 J)

3. If the rate of energy loss decreases as it cools, the power of the heat loss is decreasing as temperature decreases.

Page 206 Forces

1.

The weight arrow must be longer than the magnetic force arrow.

2. Electrostatic force

3. Air resistance is caused by air particles hitting a moving object. The particles have to touch the object to apply the force, so it is a contact force.

Page 207 Resultant forces

1. The resultant force is zero. Resultant forces make an object accelerate, so to travel at a constant speed, all the forces must be balanced.

2. $F = ma = 1200 \times 1.4 = 1680\,N$

The force from the engine must be $1680 + 800 = 2480\,N$ in order to cancel out the drag and provide enough force to accelerate the car.

Page 208 Circuit diagrams

1. Bulb A would not light. There is no complete circuit from the positive to negative of the cell through the lamp.

Bulbs B and C and the LED (D) would not light. The LED would allow current to flow anticlockwise around the loop, but the current from the cell would flow clockwise.

2. (a)

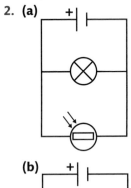

(b)

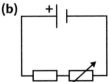

3. (a) Devices: Variable resistor: dimmer switch

(b) LDR: security lights

(c) Thermistor: thermostats

Page 209 Current, resistance and potential difference

1. $R = \dfrac{V}{I} = \dfrac{6}{0.1} = 60\,\Omega$

2. It would have no effect on the potential difference of the battery. The potential difference would be shared between the two bulbs, so they would get 3 V each.

3. (a) $I = \dfrac{V}{R} = \dfrac{6}{80} = 0.075\,A$

(b) Doubling the potential difference of the battery to 12 V would double the current ($0.075 \times 2 = 0.15\,A$).

Page 210 Charge, current and energy

1. $t = \dfrac{Q}{I} = \dfrac{30}{60} = 0.5\,s$

2. (a) 0.6 A

(b) $Q = It = 0.5 \times 15 = 9\,C$

Page 211 Series and parallel circuits

1. $12 + 4 = 16\,\Omega$

2. (a) As more bulbs are added in series, they become less bright. As each bulb is added, the overall resistance increases and the current through each bulb decreases. The potential difference is shared out between more bulbs, so each receives less volts.

(b) If more bulbs are added in parallel, they all have same potential difference, so are equally bright. This means that each bulb receives the same current, so the total current increases as bulbs are added.

3. If one of the heating elements breaks, there are fewer routes for the current to take. This means the current would decrease, because the resistance has increased.

Page 212 Practical: Resistance

For the LDR:

Replace the test wire in the circuit with an LDR.

Shine a light source on the LDR from different distances, measuring the distance, voltage and current.

Calculate the resistance using voltage ÷ current.

Plot a graph with distance to light source on the *x*-axis and resistance of LDR on the *y*-axis. The resistance of the LDR should decrease as the light source gets closer.

For the thermistor:

Replace the test wire in the circuit with a thermistor.

Place the thermistor in hot water, being careful not to get water near the electrical equipment.

At regular time intervals, measure the temperature of the water using a thermometer and record the potential difference and current.

Calculate the resistance at difference temperatures using voltage ÷ current.

Plot a graph with temperature on the *x*-axis and resistance on the *y*-axis.

The resistance should decrease as the temperature increases.

Page 213 Resistors

1.

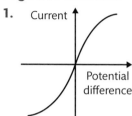

2. The lines on the *I–V* graph for a resistor are straight and pass through the origin. This shows that if you double *V* you double *I*, and therefore *I* is proportional to *V*. For a filament bulb the line is not straight so *V* is not proportional to *I* and the resistance is changing.

Page 214 Practical: *I–V* characteristics

1. The graph's decreasing gradient shows that the resistance is increasing at higher potential differences, or currents. This is probably caused by the wire heating up when larger currents pass through it.

   To improve the experiment, the student could:

   - use smaller potential differences to keep the current low
   - make sure the circuit is switched off and allowed to cool between each measurement
   - use longer lengths of wire to keep the resistance high and stop the current getting too large
   - place a resistor in the series with the wire to reduce the potential difference across the wire.

2. They could reduce random error by taking repeat readings, letting the component cool down between tests.

Page 215 Energy transfer in circuits

1. $E = 230 \times 4.5 \times 300 = 310.5$ kJ

2. $I = \dfrac{7750000}{(2700 \times 230)} = 12.5$ A

Page 216 Electrical power

1. power rating $= 230 \times 0.5 = 115$ W

2. Current $= 3.96$ A

3. **(a)** Power $= 0.6$ W

   (b) Time $= \dfrac{21\,666 \text{ seconds}}{6 \text{ hours}}$

Page 217 Mains electricity

1. If the appliance has a case made of plastic (or another insulating material), it cannot conduct electric current. If there is a fault inside, the casing cannot become live and shock a person who touches it, so there is no need for an earth wire.

2. The potential difference goes up and down. However, it is always positive, so always flows the same direction and is therefore d.c.

Page 218 Energy transfers in appliances

1. *Wasted energy is underlined.*

   (a) electrical ➜ sound + thermal

   (b) electrical ➜ kinetic + thermal + sound

   (c) chemical ➜ electrical ➜ kinetic + sound + thermal

   (d) chemical ➜ thermal (light and heat) + sound

2. Not all of the heat it produces will go into warming up the room. Some is used to warm up parts of the heater first and some of the heat might escape from the room.

3. 200 J must have been transferred and wasted as heat energy.

Page 219 Magnetic fields

1. Place a compass near one of the poles. If the north arrow on the compass points towards the pole, it is the south. If it points away, it is the north.

   Or:

   Place the north pole of another bar magnet near one pole. It will be attracted to the south pole and repelled by the north.

2. Use a magnet to repel or attract another without touching it.

   Or:

   Show how a magnet moves a compass arrow without touching it.

3. A permanent magnet always has a magnetic field. An induced magnet only has one when placed near another magnet.

   A bar magnet is a permanent magnet. An induced magnet is an object made of cobalt, iron, nickel or steel that is being attracted to a magnet, for example, a fridge door with a magnet stuck to it.

Page 220 Electromagnetism

1. It can be switched off to put objects down, and its strength can be increased to pick up heavier objects.

2.

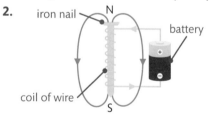

   North is at the top.

3. Change the direction of the electric current.

Page 221 The motor effect

1. To the left

2. The force would change direction when the current changed, but then change direction again when the poles were swapped, so it would still be acting downwards.

3. $F = BII$

$0.1 \times 3 \times 0.05 = 0.015\,N$

4. Any three from:

- increase the strength of the magnets/increase the flux density
- increase the current in the wire
- use longer or wider magnets so there can be a longer length of wire in the field
- wrap the wire into a coil so there can be a longer length of wire in the field.

Page 222 Transformers

1. A transformer is formed when 2 coils of wire are placed onto a soft iron core. To increase the potential difference, the secondary coil must have more turns on the coil than the primary coil. To decrease the potential difference, the secondary coil has fewer turns than the primary coil.

2. (a) $V_s = \dfrac{(30\,000 \times 1500)}{150} = 300\,000\,V$

(b) It is a step-up transformer as the secondary voltage is greater than the primary voltage

Page 223 Transformers and the National Grid

1. Reduce the resistance by using wires with a wider diameter, or multiple wires in parallel. The wires could also be made from metals that are better conductors.

2. The potential difference is being decreased, so it is a step-down transformer.

Page 224 Changes of state

1. At its boiling point, the water will start to evaporate. The energy is used to break the weak bonds in water to make steam, rather than going into kinetic energy of the particles that would increase the temperature.

2. Solid – stuck in place, so they will vibrate.

Liquid – loosely bonded together and allowed to move around randomly. They will collide with each other.

Gas – very well spaced out and fast moving, free to move around with no bonds between particles. They will collide with each other.

3. The energy will flow from the water (higher temperature) to the ice (lower temperature). The particles in the water will collide with the particles in the ice and lose kinetic energy. The water particles will slow down as the temperature decreases. The particles in the ice will gain kinetic energy and vibrate more quickly. When the ice reaches melting point (0°C), the energy lost from the kinetic energy in the water particles is passed to the ice by collision. This will be used to break bonds between particles in the ice and cause it to melt and therefore change state.

Page 225 Density

1. The density stays the same as it is a property of water. The volume of the water in the bucket is greater as there is a higher capacity than in the bottle. The mass of water in the bucket will also be greater.

2. (a) Densities:

- apple: $\dfrac{0.074}{1.04 \times 10^{-4}} = 712\,kg/m^3$ – floats
- steel box: $\dfrac{1.3}{2 \times 10^{-3}} = 650\,kg/m^3$ – floats
- plastic: $\dfrac{0.5}{4.1 \times 10^{-4}} = 1220\,kg/m^3$ – sinks
- human: $\dfrac{70}{0.071} = 986\,kg/m^3$ – floats

(b) $m = \rho \times V = 712 \times 1.5 \times 10^{-4} = 0.107\,kg$

Page 226 Practical: Density of materials

(a) The density can be calculated from mass divided by volume. The masses of the rock and metal cubes could be found using an electronic balance. The mass of the oil could be found by measuring the mass of a container then pouring in the oil and measuring the mass again; the difference would be the mass of the oil. The volume of the metal cube can be found using vernier calipers to get the length, depth and width. Volume = width × depth × length. The volume of the rock can be found by placing it in a displacement can filled with water and measure the amount of water it displaces in a measuring cylinder. The volume of the oil can be measured in a measuring cylinder.

(b) Some of the things you could mention are:

- stand the measuring cylinder on a flat surface when measuring liquid volumes
- ignore the meniscus when measuring water volume in a measuring cylinder
- use vernier calipers to measure the metal cube to a high precision
- make sure all the water droplets have fallen out of the spout when using the displacement can.

Page 227 Specific heat capacity

1. (a) Temperature change $= \dfrac{\text{energy}}{(\text{mass} \times \text{specific heat capacity})}$

$= \dfrac{84\,000}{(2 \times 4200)} = 10\,°C$

Temperature $= 20 + 10 = 30\,°C$

(b) Temperature $= 80 + 10 = 90\,°C$

2. Liquid A has a melting point of 15°C, which means it would be solid at freezer temperatures (0°C and below). It also has a very low specific heat capacity, which means it would heat up very quickly without removing much energy (or would not be able to carry much energy out of the freezer).

Page 228 Specific latent heat

1. **(a)** It takes 200 J to melt 1 kg of copper, it takes a lot less energy to melt 1 kg of gold (64 J).

   (b) Mass of copper $= \dfrac{Q}{l} = \dfrac{2500}{200} = 12.5 \, \text{kg}$

   Mass of gold $= \dfrac{Q}{l} = \dfrac{2500}{64} = 39 \, \text{kg}$

2. $Q = ml = 0.05 \times 336\,000 = 16\,800 \, \text{J}$

Page 229 Practical: Properties of water

1. There is still energy in the heater that needs to conduct into the metal or water and be detected by the thermometer. It may take some time for the thermal energy to conduct to the thermometer.

2. Measure the temperature of water in the middle, as hot water rises to the top. Take the mass of the water before and after heating and calculate an average.

   Reduce the initial temperature of the water to allow for a greater increase in temperature.

Page 230 Particle motion in gases

1. When it is heated but not sealed, the gas will expand, increasing the pressure more than the pressure outside. The gas will then escape, reducing the mass of gas in the container. After it is sealed and cooled, the pressure of the gas will drop again, but air from outside cannot get into the container to even up the pressure. As the pressure pushing down on the lid from outside is greater than the pressure pushing out, the lid will take more force to remove.

2. When heated, the particles gain kinetic energy and collide with the side of syringe with more force, more frequently. This means they exert more pressure, which forces the syringe out. The gas takes up more volume, but it is the same mass of gas inside.

Page 231 Forces and elasticity

(a) About 18 N

(b) The graph is not a straight line: part of the graph shows a non-linear extension; the spring has been distorted inelastically.

(c) Energy stored $= 0.5 \times 44.7 \times 0.3^2$

$= 2.01 \, \text{J}$

(d) Extension at 10 N = 22.5 cm

22.5 + 9 cm = 31.5 cm

Page 232 Practical: Force and extension

(a) gradient = 19.4 N/m

(b) Measure the extension for forces above 7 N and plot them on the graph to see whether they follow a straight line of best fit or continue to curve.

(c) The scatter is caused by random error, such as variations in the masses. This could be reduced by measuring them using a mass balance. Another source of random error could be the masses bouncing on the spring after each one is added. Reduce this error by ensuring the masses are still before measuring the extension.

Page 233 Equations

1. **(a)** $m = \rho V, V = \dfrac{m}{\rho}$

   (b) $k = E_p \div \left(\dfrac{1}{2}e^2\right), e = \sqrt{\dfrac{V}{\frac{1}{2}k}}$

   (c) $m = \dfrac{E}{c\Delta\theta}, c = \dfrac{E}{m\Delta\theta}, \Delta\theta = \dfrac{E}{mc}$

   (d) $\Delta v = at, t = \dfrac{\Delta v}{a}$

2. m – mass kg, ρ – density kg/m³, V – volume m³, E – Energy J, k – spring constant N/m, e – extension m, $\Delta\theta$ – change of temperature °C, a – acceleration m/s², t – time s, $\Delta\theta$ – change in velocity m/s.

Page 234 Converting units

1. **(a)** $200 \, \mu\text{g} \div 10^6 = 2 \times 10^{-4} \, \text{g}$

   (b) $10 \div 1000 = 0.01 \, \text{N/g}$

   (c) $330 \div 60 = 5.5 \, \text{J/s}$

2. 1 kg is 1000 so 10^3 or three orders of magnitude larger. So 10 kg is 4 orders of magnitude larger than 1 g.

Page 235 Making estimations

All these numbers are approximate and any similar number would be acceptable.

1. 1–6 mm/s

2. 80–100 kg

Page 236 Interpreting data

1. Mean:

   (1.1 kg + 1.2 kg + 1.2 kg + 1.3 kg + 2.3 kg) ÷ 5 = 1.62 kg. As there is one larger puppy, the mean is much larger than most of the puppies.

   The mode and median are both 1.2 kg, which is in the middle of and close to most of the puppies' weights, so it represents the majority of puppies well.

2. The distance at a speed of 40 m/s will be double the distance at a speed of 20 m/s. 4 × 64 m = 256 m

Page 237 Using charts and graphs

1. **(a)** Bar chart – different cars are a discrete variable.

   (b) Line graph (or scatter graph with line of best fit) – they best show the relationship between two quantities.

   (c) Pie chart – they are best for showing the proportions of something that can be compared.

2. $y = mx + c$ becomes force = 120 × extension. As it goes through the origin, the y intercept, $c = 0$. This is like the equation force = spring constant × extension so the gradient tells us that the spring constant is 120 (N/m).

Page 238 Using diagrams

1.

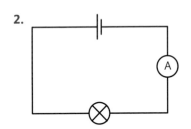

air resistance = 300 N

side wind
200 N

weight = 600 N

2.

Page 239 Planning practicals

1. (a) Change the material, either thin paper, a few mm of aluminium or several cm of lead. You would measure the activity of the source (through the material). You should keep the amount of air between the source and detector the same and leave the detector counting the activity rate for the same time in each test.

(b) A ruler will be needed to maintain the air distance and measure the thickness of materials (or a vernier caliper or micrometer). A Geiger-Muller (GM) tube and counter will detect the radiation.

(c) Not handle the source directly and use tongs or tweezers. Handle them at arms length and limit their exposure to as short a time as possible by putting the source in a radioactive container when not in use.

2. (a) The temperature of the metal (placing it in warm water perhaps) and the resistance which is found by measuring the current and potential difference. $R = V \div I$. You should use the same piece of wire, keeping the length and diameter constant for each test. The current should be kept the same each time. The current should also be kept low as possible to avoid internal heating.

(b) Potential difference by a voltmeter, current by an ammeter, a thermometer to monitor the temperature of the water, or if the wire is heated in some other way an infrared thermometer would measure its temperature directly.

Page 240 Improving results

(a)

Normal

angle of incidence

transparent block

angle of refraction

(b)

1. Draw around a rectangular block of glass using a pencil.

2. Draw the normal line perpendicular to the side of the glass block.

3. Shine a ray of light into the block at the point at which the normal line meets the glass block.

4. Trace over this ray and label it as the incident ray.

5. Measure the angle between the normal line and the incident ray and record this in a table.

6. Trace over the ray as it leaves the glass block.

7. Remove the block and draw a line joining the point where the ray enters the block and the point where it leaves the block.

8. Measure the angle of refraction as the angle between this line and the normal line and record this in the table.

9. Repeat this with different angles of refraction.

(c) Use a thinner ray to get a more precise measurement for the angles.

Page 241 Comparing data

1. (a) For both sets of tyres, as speed increases, stopping distance increases. At lower speeds, stopping distance is proportional to speed. At higher speeds the gradients of both lines increases, meaning that the stopping distance increases more for the same increase in speed. This happens at around 70 km/h for tyre B and 80 km/h for tyre A. At all speeds, the stopping distance of tyre A is greater than tyre B. The difference in stopping distance increases and is greatest around 70 km/h, but they become more similar as the speed increases above this.

(b) We would expect that the wet road would make the stopping distances much longer. Water on the road means there is less friction and therefore a lower braking force, meaning the car has to travel further to stop.

2. They are all ionizing forms of radiation and so are all able to destroy cancerous cells. Alpha is the most ionizing and would be destroy cells most easily, though this makes it more likely to destroy healthy cells as well. Beta is less ionizing, and gamma is the least ionizing, so they would do less damage to both cancerous and healthy cells. Alpha cannot penetrate paper and so will be unable to penetrate the skin. Beta is stopped by a few mm of aluminum and so would not be able to penetrate deeply into the skin, whereas gamma can pass through the body so could be used to target cells anywhere in the body. Overall, gamma would be the best suited. Although it is least ionizing, it will still destroy cancerous cells, be able to reach them anywhere in the body and do the least damage to healthy cells.

Page 242 Working scientifically

1. The independent variable (the one you change) would be the type of metal. To measure the resistance, you would need to measure the potential difference and current through the sample of metal and calculate resistance = potential difference ÷ current. This requires wires and crocodile clips to connect the metal, a power source like a cell, an ammeter and a voltmeter. The variables that could affect the resistance and need to be controlled are: temperature of the metal (an infra-red thermometer could be used to monitor this); the length of the sample of wire (metre rule); and the diameter or cross sectional area of a sample (vernier calipers or micrometer). The current/potential difference should be the same and kept quite low to avoid heating. The resistance of each metal could be presented in a table or as a bar chart.

2. Understanding how alpha, beta and gamma radiation can be stopped and what damage they do to living cells makes working with radiation safer and also tells us which uses are unsafe. Knowledge of the properties have led to uses in industry, such as beta being used to produce paper of uniform thickness, which has developed the paper industry and therefore created jobs. Alpha can be used in smoke detectors, which can save lives by detecting and warning people of smoke and fires that could otherwise be fatal. Gamma radiation is used to diagnose and treat cancer and so also saves lives. It is also used to sterilise medical equipment, reducing deaths through infection in surgery, and to sterilise food. This means fresh food lasts longer and increases the opportunity for the food industry to export fresh food over longer distances, expanding the food industry and creating jobs.

There is no right or wrong answer here, if you can justify the link to the effect then it is worth marks.

Page 243 Extended response questions

The circulatory system is an organ system made up of several organs, including the heart and blood vessels, working together. The organs consist of different types of tissues, epithelial, muscle, nervous or connective tissues. The tissues are made up of cells, such as red blood cells.

Published by BBC Active, an imprint of Educational Publishers LLP, part of the Pearson Education Group, 80 Strand, London, WC2R 0RL.

www.pearsonschools.co.uk/BBCBitesize

© Educational Publishers LLP 2019

BBC logo © BBC 1996. BBC and BBC Active are trademarks of the British Broadcasting Corporation.

Typeset by Newgen KnowledgeWorks Pvt. Ltd., Chennai, India

Produced and illustrated by Newgen Publishing UK

Cover design by Andrew Magee & Pearson Education Limited 2019

Cover illustration by Darren Lingard / Oxford Designers & Illustrators

The rights of Karen Bailey, Jen Randall and Mike Smith to be identified as authors of this work has been asserted by them in accordance with the Copyright, Designs and Patents Act 1988.

First published 2019

22 21 20 19

10 9 8 7 6 5 4 3 2 1

British Library Cataloguing in Publication Data

A catalogue record for this book is available from the British Library

ISBN 978 1 406 68576 3

Copyright notice

Printed and bound in Slovakia by Neografia.

The Publisher's policy is to use paper manufactured from sustainable forests.

Acknowledgements

Content written by Byron Dawson is included.

Text credits:

BBC: P 1-232, IV: © **2019.**

Photographs:

(Key: T-top; B-bottom; C-centre; L-left; R-right)

123RF: Jarun Ontakrai 59tr, **Alamy Stock Photo:** Peter Hermes Furian 3, The Natural History Museum 27, Geogphotos 35, Pr Bouree/BSIP 36, Chronicle 39, Wayne Lynch/All Canada Photos 66, AfriPics.com 67tr, Peter Parks/Image Quest Marine 67cr, Xue Yubin/Xinhua 70, Nigel Cattlin 73, David J. Green 90, Studio/PhotoCuisine RM 94, Charles Stirling 174tr, Andrew Findlay 176, **Shutterstock:** D. Kucharski K. Kucharska 6, Matej Hudovernik 28, NatUlrich 33cr, GraphicsRF 33br, Cliparea/ Custom media 43, Luis Santos 44, Number-One 59bl, SvenButstraen 69, Josep Curto 93, Vladimir Nenezic 129, AP 174tl, Dario Lo Presti 197, Smallcreative 201.

Note from the publisher

Pearson has robust editorial processes, including answer and fact checks, to ensure the accuracy of the content in this publication, and every effort is made to ensure this publication is free of errors. We are, however, only human, and occasionally errors do occur. Pearson is not liable for any misunderstandings that arise as a result of errors in this publication, but it is our priority to ensure that the content is accurate. If you spot an error, please do contact us at resourcescorrections@pearson.com so we can make sure it is corrected.

Websites

Pearson Education Limited is not responsible for the content of third-party websites.